Elite Discourse
and Racism

SAGE SERIES ON RACE AND ETHNIC RELATIONS

Series Editor:
JOHN H. STANFIELD II
College of William and Mary

This series is designed for scholars working in creative theoretical areas related to race and ethnic relations. The series will publish books and collections of original articles that critically assess and expand upon race and ethnic relations issues from American and comparative points of view.

SERIES EDITORIAL BOARD

Volumes in this series include

1. Roger Waldinger, Howard Aldrich, Robin Ward, and Associates, ETHNIC ENTREPRENEURS: Immigrant Business in Industrial Societies
2. Philomena Essed, UNDERSTANDING EVERYDAY RACISM: An Interdisciplinary Theory
3. Samuel V. Duh, BLACKS AND AIDS: Causes and Origins
4. Steven J. Gold, REFUGEE COMMUNITIES: A Comparative Field Study
5. Mary E. Andereck, ETHNIC AWARENESS AND THE SCHOOL: An Ethnographic Study
6. Teun A. van Dijk, ELITE DISCOURSE AND RACISM
7. Rebecca Morales and Frank Bonilla, LATINOS IN A CHANGING U.S. ECONOMY: Comparative Perspectives on Growing Inequality

Title page to come from design

Elite Discourse and Racism

Teun A. van Dijk

**Sage Series on Race
and Ethnic Relations**

v o l u m e   6

SAGE Publications
International Educational and Professional Publisher
Newbury Park   London   New Delhi

For information address:

SAGE Publications, Inc.
2455 Teller Road
Newbury Park, California 91320

SAGE Publications Ltd.
6 Bonhill Street
London EC2A 4PU
United Kingdom

SAGE Publications India Pvt. Ltd.
M-32 Market
Greater Kailash I
New Delhi 110 048 India

Printed in the United States of America

Library of Congress Cataloging-in-Publication Data

Dijk, Teun Adrianus van, 1943-
    Elite discourse and racism / Teun A. van Dijk.
       p.   cm.—(Sage series on race and ethnic relations ; v. 6)
    Includes bibliographical references and index.
    ISBN 0-8039-5070-5.—ISBN 0-8039-5071-3 (pbk.)
    1. Racism.   2. Elite (Social sciences).   3. Communication.
   4. Racism in language.   5. Race relations.   6. Ethnic relations.
   I. Title.   II. Series.
   HM291.D4962   1993
   305.8—dc20
                                 92-39455
                                    CIP

93 94 95 96 10 9 8 7 6 5 4 3 2

Sage Production Editor: Judith L. Hunter

Contents

Foreword

Usually class-based analyses of race and racism focus on European-descent working and middle classes. In this path-breaking book, Teun van Dijk offers a fascinating analysis of elite racist discourse. The power of his analysis lies in its serendipity. What he has to say about the mundane ways in which Dutch elites structure and reproduce their whiteness and the inferior status of non-whites certainly can be applied with some modification to the elite origins of racism in other European-descent-dominated multiracial societies.

Van Dijk's provocative analysis reminds us of the top-to-bottom origins of racism that often get ignored due to the ways in which elites are able to deflect cause and effect throught their privileged status and resources. His observations have much to offer not only scholars who have yet to explore how elites created and reproduce racial inequality but also raises a number of unexplored questions regarding how the racial inclinations of elites provide the paradigms of the racialism of the less powerful classes as well as for major institutional forms. In sum, Van Dijk's examination of elite racism reminds us, as in the case of his earlier *Communicating Racism,* of the need to understand how racialist discourse produces racialist class structures that deeply mark the stratification and social organizational character of race-centered industrial states.

John H. Stanfield II
Series Editor

Preface

This book provisionally concludes more than a decade of research into the relationship between discourse and racism. My earlier projects in this research program focused on the reproduction of racism through informal everyday conversations, textbooks, and the press. Some of these previous research results are analyzed here from a different perspective, namely, that of the role of the elites in the reproduction of ethnic dominance. My earlier book in Dutch on high school textbooks is here summarized in English for the first time. The present study extends this range of genres and issues by also paying attention to such other types of elite discourse as those of politicians, scholars, and corporate managers. It looks at how some Western parliaments debate on ethnic affairs and immigration, what academic sociology textbooks say about ethnic relations, and how personnel managers of large corporations talk about minority hiring and Affirmative Action.

As was the case for the earlier studies on discourse and racism, the approach of this study is multidisciplinary. Various areas of discourse analysis are combined with ideas, theories, and concepts from social psychology and, especially in this book, from sociology, anthropology, and political science. To avoid superficial eclecticism, however, the unifying theoretical framework is a discourse analytical approach to the reproduction of racism. Such an approach is particularly well matched with the present focus on elite racism, because such racism is often enacted or legitimated by text and talk. Further, the definition of elites will be largely based on the assumption that contemporary elite power and influence are often discursive and are implemented by preferential access to and control over public discourse and its consequences for the manufacture of consensus. This is particularly the case for the symbolic elites, those who control the means of communication and who are engaged in the manufacturing of public opinion.

Although our overall perspective, our multidisciplinary discourse approach, and our data are new, elite racism is as old as racism itself. Much earlier research has amply documented the role of white politicians, philosophers, historians, social scientists, psychologists, journalists, writers, the military, the clergy, managers, and other elites in the enactment, legitimation, and reproduction of racism through the ages. The appearance of this book 500 years after the "discovery" of the Americas by Columbus and his crew is a useful reminder of the historical background and continuity of a worldwide system of military, economic, and cultural power of the white West over the Rest. This global dominance is not only firmly in place even today, but is also replicated in the local ethnic and racial dominance of white majorities over mostly non-European immigrants and other minorities within white-dominated countries. This study shows not only that ethnic dominance and racism are still a major problem of contemporary Western societies but also that elites continue to play a primary role in their reproduction. Unlike most other work on racism, it especially focuses on the more subtle discursive dimensions of modern elite racism. In that respect, the study may also serve as a source book of ideas, theories, and methods for the practical critique of various types of elite racism.

This book addresses advanced students and scholars in most of the disciplines of the humanities and social sciences, as well as all others interested in the problem of elites, discourse, and racism. Such a broad audience requires that I occasionally need to explain notions or principles that are already familiar to some of the readers. The discourse analyses in this book are intentionally very informal. Unlike some other, sometimes rather fashionable, contemporary studies on discourse in the humanities and social sciences, my work shuns the esoteric. I believe that especially for the study of an important social issue like racism, accessibility is a crucial criterion for adequate scholarly communication.

The writing of this book has been an arduous enterprise if not, at times, an impossible task. The complexity of the theoretical framework, the vast historical literature on the many forms of elite racism in the past, the many elite domains involved, the large amounts of empirical data, and the difficulty in obtaining data either from or about the elites presented more than the usual challenge of scholarly research. A more or less complete and satisfactory account of contemporary elite racism in Western countries would have required a whole series of mono-graphs. Therefore, in order to keep this study within reasonable propor-tions and to avoid overlap with other work on elite racism, I was obliged to focus on only a few types of elite racism in a few countries, and to do so mainly from a discourse analytical perspective, thereby neglect-ing numerous economic, social, political, and cultural aspects of mod-ern racism. Thus, the vast debate on pseudo-scientific racism, for instance in biology and psychology, had to be briefly summarized in favor of an analysis of the much more subtle and moderate features of academic discourse about ethnic affairs. In general, I am interested in these subtle and seemingly respectable forms of elite racism and in the building of the dominant ethnic consensus, that is, in what most of the elites refuse to call racism in the first place, rather than in the more overt and blatant manifestations of what they see as the real racism.

Facing the steady rise of racism, anti-Semitism, and xenophobia, especially in contemporary Europe, and the often cynical and hypocrit-ical reactions, if not the more or less subtle contributions to this development by the elites, it is sometimes difficult to maintain the usual academic style of detachment and distance. Therefore, I shall not apologize for the occasional sharpness of my critical comments, nor further argue for the need to mobilize academic research in combating contemporary elite racism.

Call to the Readers

Since there is still little systematic work on discourse and racism, I am particularly interested in personal feedback from readers and users of this book: scholars as well as undergraduate and graduate students or others involved in the analysis of or the struggle against racism. I welcome suggestions, comments, criticism, as well as results of re-search in this field. Please write to me at the following address: Uni-versity of Amsterdam, Program of Discourse Studies, 210 Spuistraat, 1012 VT Amsterdam (E-mail address: teun@alf.let.uva.nl).

Acknowledgments

During my decade-long research on discourse and racism, I have become indebted to numerous people, unfortunately too many to ac-knowledge individually here. Nevertheless, I should mention my stu-dents, who have helped me collect and analyze many of the data on which this study is based, as well as students and colleagues at several universities in Europe and the Americas for their comments on lectures about the topics of this book. For the new research reported in this book, I am indebted to Bob Boynton for sending me the relevant U.S. Congressional Records; to Gabe Kaimowitz for sending U.S. press clippings about the Civil Rights Bill of 1990; to parliamentary librarians in France and the Netherlands; to Jessika Ter Wal for sending me material on Italian parliamentary debates; to various (anonymous) officials of the Dutch Association of Employers (VNO), the Dutch Labor Foundation, and the Federation of Dutch Trade Unions (FNV); to Sandra Servais of FNV for transcribing several interviews; and to various publishers for making available introductory sociology textbooks in Great Britain and the United States.

I am particularly grateful to Ruth Wodak for her critical reading of the first draft of this study. Unfortunately, a painful lack of space did not allow me to follow all her suggestions to elaborate on this or that point that had received insufficient attention.

As was also the case for my earlier research on discourse and racism, I am most profoundly indebted to Philomena Essed, who not only critically commented on this book, but whose innovative insights into the nature of what she called "everyday racism" are a permanent source of inspiration for my own work, and whose personal experiences with the elite racism of the Dutch press and academia continue to confirm her own theories as well as those discussed in this book.

Teun A. van Dijk
Amsterdam, Winter 1991–Summer 1992

1

Introduction

THE REALITY OF RACISM

In late 1991 and early 1992, as the last versions of this book were being written, ethnic minorities, immigrants, and refugees in North America and especially in Europe continued to be confronted with increasing racism, ethnicism, and xenophobia. In view of the unification of the European Community (EC) in 1993, minority policies and restrictions on immigration become harsher each day. The ideological legitimation of these policies and practices leaves little doubt about the ways people with a different color or culture are being viewed by white politicians in power, and about the position of minorities in the future united fortress of Europe.

Affirmative Action and Equal Opportunity policies, if any, are subject to constant pressure, despite widespread discrimination in hiring and promotion, and despite the alarmingly high unemployment rates among minorities. Much of the press is hardly less cynical. If not overtly xenophobic, as is the case for most right-wing tabloids, the mainstream media are less interested in majority problems such as xenophobia and discrimination than in alleged minority crime, deviance, or cultural differences interpreted as a threat to white, Western norms and values. Rather, sharing their denial of racism with other elites, they tend to direct their wrath toward anti-racist "busybodies," and especially against those who have the temerity to conclude, on the basis of solid research facts and figures, that the white media themselves are part of the problem of racism.

Encouraged by this general rise of chauvinism, the growth of explicitly racist parties and other extremist organizations is frightening, and so are their increasingly blatant acts and attitudes. But the percentage

of active supporters of such parties would be less ominous if it were not
dwarfed by the percentage, locally in excess of 70%, of those among the
population at large who share their more or less virulent anti-immigrant
attitudes. Similarly, the political implications of this situation would be
less serious if the respectable parties in Europe did not increasingly
adopt moderate versions of the racist ideologies of the extreme right in
order to capture the votes representing this widespread xenophobic
resentment, thereby legitimizing and reinforcing the racism that feeds
such resentment in the first place.

Racism at the Top

Racism, thus, is not just in the streets nor the exclusive reaction of
ordinary white folks in a social or economic impasse. Much of the
development sketched above is, sometimes subtly and indirectly, enacted or preformulated by various elite groups and their discourses. The
racism of the political elites, for instance, has a long tradition and,
despite routine disclaimers and official appeals to tolerance, continues
even today, and at the very top.

Examples abound. Thus, in the United States, President Bush played
the effective "quota" card when he vetoed the 1990 Civil Rights Bill,
after earlier playing the equally successful "fear of black crime" card
during his election campaign. Similarly, despite international laws on
political asylum, his administration keeps returning black Haitians to a
precarious situation in their country, while letting in refugees from
communist Cuba. In the 1992 presidential primaries one of the candidates, Patrick Buchanan, was able to get the support of a sizable chunk
of the conservative vote despite his widely published anti-Semitic and
racist remarks.

On the other side of the ocean, at the end of the 1970s, Margaret Thatcher
came to power in Great Britain after expressing her fear that the country
would be "rather swamped" by immigrants with a different culture, a
statement that now seems to have been promoted to national policy.

In France, President Mitterand's usual calls for interethnic tolerance
appear to be limited by what he and others see as a *seuil de tolérance*,
that is, a tolerance threshold of the white dominant group. In 1991
former government leader and Mayor of Paris Chirac empathized with
the popular feeling that minority neighbors might be "smelling." Shortly
thereafter, former president Giscard d'Estaing tried to win right-wing
votes for his party by denouncing the invasion of immigrants and by

requiring blood ties for acquiring citizenship. Such opinions predictably delighted the leaders of the racist National Front in France, who are now moving even further to the right with a rabid racist policy that openly advocates a grisly French version of apartheid.

At the same time, Chancellor Kohl and other conservative German politicians helped create an atmosphere of public panic by their continuous and vocal references to the threat of a massive immigration of refugees. Similarly, other European leaders and their administrations are involved in preparing or implementing treaties, such as the half-secret Schengen Treaty, which are mainly designed to keep refugees and especially non-Europeans, that is, people of color, out of their unified fortress. Even if only to counterbalance the ideological spirit of this exclusion, none of them, nor other political leaders for that matter, have taken the lead in firmly combating the increasing forms of xenophobia and racism within the confines of the EC itself. This should not surprise us when we realize that they have themselves helped to conjure up these age-old European specters, if only by acquiescing to the reality that permissive immigration policies, Affirmative Action, or an energetic stand against racism may cost white votes.

This is, literally, the most visible tip of the cold racist iceberg in Europe and other Europeanized countries. Seemingly rather innocent (an "unfortunate" phrase here or there), at least for many white people, these ethnic attitudes of world or national leaders merely show how broad and powerful the underlying ethnic consensus among the white group in general must be. It is easy to infer the ethnic attitudes of the less visible political establishment and of the administrations these leaders are managing or whose public voice they represent.

Such cynical and opportunistic attitudes and practices are also represented among other elite groups, for instance in business corporations, in academia, and especially in the press. We have seen that mainstream news media largely support the prevailing political attitudes on ethnic affairs and immigration. At the same time they contribute to the public reproduction of the ideologies of the political and other elites by publishing scare stories or so-called in-depth reports about "floods" or "massive invasions" of refugees, "illegal" immigration, "crime-riddled" ghettos, drug abuse or mugging by blacks, violence of street gangs, threats of Muslim fundamentalists, "strange" customs, immigrants' lacking motivation to work, welfare scroungers, black racism, the political correctness of multiculturalism, the foibles of Affirmative Action, and similar stories that do not fail to either instill or confirm top-down, xenophobic, or anti-minority resentment among the white population at large.

Top-Down Effects

The more gruesome top-down effects of such elite racism hardly need to be detailed here. In Great Britain, Asian families have been the victims of racial harassment, attacks, and arson for years. North Africans in France are often shot at and sometimes killed, while Jewish graves continue to be desecrated in various countries. In Germany in 1991 and 1992, skinheads massively and repeatedly attacked minorities and refugees and set fire to their homes and shelters. Recent Third World immigrants in Italy, fleeing poverty or oppression at home, now face exploitation, assault, and insult in a country that was surprised at its own potential of *razzismo*. Even in the seemingly tolerant Scandinavian countries, refugees are not safe from aggression and intimidation. In the United States names such as Howard Beach, Bensonhurst, and Los Angeles need only be mentioned to call to mind what can still happen to African-Americans today. There have been similar events in Belgium, Canada, Australia, New Zealand, and of course, South Africa. The fledgling democracies of Eastern Europe have shown how quickly they learn from the West—or are able to lapse into their old traditions—when it comes to discriminating and assaulting Jews, Roma and Sinti (Gypsies), Third World workers, as well as their "own" minorities.

The authorities and the police are much less effective in combating these crimes than when they are confronted with other forms of terrorism. The general move to the Right that accompanied the fall of communism typically involves warnings against rising crime, but racism is not categorized as a crime and hence not targeted. Again, this should not surprise us when we observe that young Africans, Caribbeans, and other immigrant, aboriginal, or minority youths of color continue to be harassed, if not sometimes assaulted, by the police in virtually all Western countries. To wit, a video camera in Los Angeles in the spring of 1991 recorded by chance what is usually hidden from public view and forcefully denied, despite black accusations, namely, how a group of white police officers took pleasure in bludgeoning a black driver stopped for speeding. Despite the incontrovertible evidence of the video camera, the police officers were acquitted by a white jury in April 1992, a decision that sparked the ensuing revolt that left large parts of central Los Angeles in ashes.

Everyday Racism

Although these violent forms of blatant street racism are shocking and although some of them occur quite frequently, not all of them define the everyday lives of all members of minority groups in Western countries. Possibly even more serious and insidious is the cumulative and structural effect of less violent forms of everyday racism that all minority group members may encounter in politics, on the job, in school, in academic research, in government agencies, in shops, in the media, in public places, or in any other interactional situation with whites.

Before we analyze the notion of racism in more theoretical terms in the next chapter (which also provides the references to the scholarly literature that underlies the informal presentation of the problem in this chapter), it should be emphasized that this concept of everyday racism is compatible with the approach of this book. That is, racism does not consist of only white supremacist ideologies of race, or only of aggressive overt or blatant discriminatory acts, the forms of racism as it is currently understood in informal conversations, in the media, or in much of the social sciences. Racism also involves the everyday, mundane, negative opinions, attitudes, and ideologies and the seemingly subtle acts and conditions of discrimination against minorities, namely, those social cognitions and social acts, processes, structures, or institutions that directly or indirectly contribute to the dominance of the white group and the subordinate position of minorities.

It should be emphasized from the outset that our conception of racism also includes *ethnicism*, that is, a system of ethnic group dominance based on cultural criteria of categorization, differentiation, and exclusion, such as those of language, religion, customs, or worldviews. Often racial and ethnic criteria are inextricably linked in these systems of group dominance, as is the case in anti-Semitism. Following general academic and political usage we therefore will generally use the term *racism* rather than *ethnicism* in this book.

Our analyses of racism focus on contemporary white or European racism as it is directed against people in/from the South, and in particular against various ethnic minorities, native peoples, or people of color in Europe, North America, South Africa, Australia, and New Zealand. This historically specific type of racism might be termed *euracism*, a handy neologism but one we shall not further use in this book. We do not discuss other forms of ethnic dominance or conflict in the past, in Eastern Europe, or on other continents. As we shall see in more detail later, the crucial criteria for the identification of euracism are white group power (dominance) and the ensuing inequality of the minority position. Such racism also embodies supporting attitudes and ideologies, as they developed against a historical background of slavery, segregation, and colonization, and in the present context of South-North labor and refugee migration.

Many of both the subtly and the blatantly racist events that define the system of everyday racism are enacted, controlled, or condoned by white elites, that is, by leading politicians, professors, editors, judges, officials, bureaucrats, and managers. If whites are not themselves actively involved in these modern forms of segregation, exclusion, aggression, inferiorization, or marginalization, then their involvement in the problem of racism consists in their passivity, their acquiescence, their ignorance, and their indifference regarding ethnic or racial inequality.

This broad systemic approach to elite racism implies that much of the discourse we shall study in this book does not appear to be racist at all. On the contrary, much elite text and talk about minorities may occasionally seem to express tolerance, understanding, acceptance, or humanitarian worldviews, although such discourse is contradicted by a situation of structured inequality largely caused or condoned by these elites. Since we are primarily interested in general properties of dominant discourses and practices, we shall avoid making distinctions between racist and non-racist white people. The involvement of dominant group members in the reproduction of—or the resistance to—the system of ethnic dominance is too complex to allow for such simplistic categorizations. The same is true for the evaluation of individual discourses as racist or not, although we may sometimes informally do so when such text and talk is blatantly and explicitly derogatory about minorities.

Rather, we focus on the social and cultural system of racism as a whole, and will study individual discourses and acts of discrimination only as the locally variable, micro-level manifestation of such a system. At the same time, we are not merely interested in the system of racism and its discursive reproduction, but more generally in the ways whites speak and write about Others, for instance, in anthropological or political discourse about other peoples and other nations, especially those of the South. In this book, however, we shall mainly focus on discourse about ethnic minorities in Europe and North America.

Continuity and Change

While many of the manifestations of racism discussed above are well known, and its more extreme forms sometimes shamefully but more often reluctantly admitted, it would be a fundamental error to assume that such racism is a thing of the past. This assumption gained wide acceptance in the United States as part of the conservative backlash in the 1980s associated with the Reagan administration. True, the slave trade and slavery were both banned and abolished more than a century ago. One generation ago, most peoples in Asia and Africa wrested independence from their colonial masters and thus made global empires crumble. As a result, international relations are now—in principle—based on laws and treaties that affirm equality of all peoples. Mainstream scholarship and media no longer openly advocate or legitimize white supremacy. The Civil Rights Movement, antidiscrimination laws, policies of equal opportunities, and modest forms of Affirmative Action have today curtailed the more blatant and overt manifestations of racism against minorities.

However, both internationally and nationally, this undeniable progress has only softened the style of dominance of white Western nations and their majority populations. Far from abolished are the deeply entrenched economic, social, and cultural remnants of past oppression and inequality; the modern prejudices about minorities; the economic and military power or the cultural hegemony of white over black, North over South, majorities over minorities.

Thus, the changes in race and ethnic relations during the twentieth century did not mean steady progress. On the contrary, it took centuries to build up and fully harvest the spoils of conquest, slavery, colonialism, imperialism, and their supporting ideologies. By the time these systems slowly started to collapse, approximately between 1850 and 1950, ideological racism, anti-Semitism, and colonialist exploitation reached their most widespread and extreme expressions, for instance, in the vicious colonization of Africa, in Jim Crow and segregation in the United States, in the Holocaust of the Jews by the Nazis and their supporters in Europe, and in apartheid in South Africa, among many other examples.

Compared to these moral cataclysms of Western civilization, and despite the continued manifestations of rabid right-wing racism, the subtleties of most contemporary everyday racism seem almost benign. This suggests a fundamental and comparatively sudden change of the system of ethnic and racial dominance, both ideologically and practically, during the past decades.

We have seen, however, that despite these changes, there is also continuity in the system of white group dominance. Social and political events during the 1980s and early 1990s have shown that ethnicism and racism continue to be a major problem of white-dominated societies in Europe, North America, and other Europeanized countries. Increasing

aggression, as well as enduring prejudice and discrimination against Third
World refugees, immigrants, and minority groups have shattered the illusion that increased tolerance and elementary civil rights gains in some
countries were the first steps on the way to full equality and acceptance.
De facto segregation, high unemployment rates, bad schooling, inferior
housing, and cultural marginalization remain the structural features,
among many others, of minority group position. At the micro-level of daily
interaction and experience, these macro-level characteristics correspond
to many subtle forms of everyday racism. And we already pointed out that
these prevailing forms of "normal" racism are exacerbated, especially in
Europe, by less subtle forms of racial attacks, outside the present consensus, such as assaults, arson, and murder of women, men, and children who
happen to have a different color or culture.

THE ROLE OF THE ELITES

Against this structural and historical background, this book sketches
an approach to the study of racism that focuses on the role of the elites
in the reproduction of contemporary ethnic and racial inequality. It
shows how the political, media, educational, academic, and corporate
elites contribute to this reproduction process by persuasively preformulating the dominant ethnic consensus on ethnic affairs. Through
their influential text and talk, they manufacture the consent needed for
the legitimation of their own power in general, and for their leadership
in maintaining the dominance of the white group in particular. Characteristic properties of such elite racism are its denial and mitigation, as
well its attribution to ordinary white people.

To avoid misunderstanding, it should be stressed again that this study
does not primarily examine the explicitly, intentionally, or blatantly
racist ideologies and practices of the extreme right. It is this kind of
overt racism that most elites reject and see as the only form of racism.
That is, their denial of racism presupposes a definition of racism that
conveniently excludes them as part of the problem. In critical opposition against this prevailing ideology, we are interested in those groups
who define the moderate mainstream, that is, the politicians of respectable parties, the journalists of our daily newspapers, the writers of the
textbooks our children use at school, the well-known scholars who write
introductory sociology texts, the personnel managers of leading business
companies, and all those who thus manage public opinion, dominant

ideologies, and consensual everyday practices. It is our claim that white group dominance in general, and racism in particular, including overt and blatant right-wing racism, presuppose a creative process in which these moderate elites play a crucial role.

For most members of elite groups, this thesis is hard to swallow, being fundamentally inconsistent with their normative self-concept. After all, elites often see themselves as moral leaders and will therefore generally dissociate themselves from anything that has to do with racism as they define it. As a consequence, and as we shall see in our study of the press (Chapter 7), conclusions of research on racism and accusations of minority groups are often denied, marginalized, or even violently attacked by the elites, who thereby precisely confirm the plausibility of the thesis. As a rule, we may assume that as soon as elite interests are challenged, as in the domain of ethnic affairs, such elites will quickly forget the norms of tolerance and the values of equality that they supposedly espoused. This is not only true for politicians or corporate managers, but also for the cultural or symbolic elites, for example, in education, scholarship, the arts, and the media. The vicious conservative attack on "political correctness" when there are modest changes in the curricula of schools and colleges (mostly in the United States, but also elsewhere), in view of a more adequate reflection of the multicultural nature of society, show how deeply Eurocentrism is rooted as a force of ethnic and cultural dominance.

Elite Racism and Discourse

It is the major goal of this book to unravel some of the subtle forms this racism of the elites may take. In particular, we examine how elite racism enables the very reproduction of racism throughout society, namely, by what we call the preformulation of popular forms of racism. Since the public actions of the elites are predominantly discursive, such an analysis will focus on the generation of racism through the many types of text and talk that define both their own everyday racism and the modalities of the management of the ethnic consensus within white society at large.

Little argument is needed to make such a discourse perspective on elite racism a useful starting point of research. By far the largest part of the population only has active access to everyday conversations with family members, friends, neighbors, or colleagues on the job. Ordinary people are more or less passive participants in the many discourse types and communicative events controlled by the elites, such as those of the mass media, politics, education, scholarship, business corporations, the churches, the unions, and the welfare offices, among many other domains and organizations of society.

We assume that since the elites dominate these means of symbolic reproduction, they also control the communicative conditions in the formation of the popular mind and hence, the ethnic consensus. Although the social and cognitive mechanisms involved in this communicative process are exceedingly complex, if not at times replete with real or apparent contradictions, it is this fundamental hypothesis that will guide the theoretical and empirical research reported in this book.

Elite Racism and Popular Racism

Without disregarding the role of everyday interethnic or interracial experiences and conversations among all white in-group members, in the formation of ethnic group attitudes and ideologies that form the socio-cognitive dimension of structural racism, our hypothesis claims that the elites have a leading role in shaping the production and interpretation framework underlying such conversations.

However, it should be repeated that this special focus on the influence of elite discourse and racism does not imply that there is no popular racism, nor that popular discourse and racism may not influence, bottom-up, the social cognitions and actions of the elites. Research has repeatedly documented white popular resentment against either new immigrants or resident minorities, especially under conditions of competition for scarce resources or in political crises. At the same time, it is also well known that the elites may again take advantage of such popular reactions in order to develop and legitimate their own ethnic and racial policies.

The specific point of view this book *does* imply, however, is that not all racism is based on spontaneous popular resentment, and that much of the motivation and many prejudiced arguments that seem to inspire popular racism are "prepared" by elites. Thus, our perspective is intended as a correction against the common view, not least among the elites themselves, and also in the social sciences, that if there is racism in society, it should not primarily be sought within their own group. In sum, although the relations between elites and non-elite groups are dialectical, we focus on the top-down direction of these relationships.

The sociopolitical implications of our claim are obvious: If racism is also a major problem among different elite groups, the *consequences* for minorities are even more serious than those of popular racism. After all, the elites largely define and constrain the major life chances of minority groups, especially in or through education, employment, economic affairs, social affairs, the media, and culture. Spontaneous popular racism can be effective only when it is spread throughout the population at large by the mass media and similar forms of public discourse controlled by the elites.

Whereas socialization discourse in the family, as well as early peer group talk, may provide the elementary formats for the interpretation framework that defines the ethnic consensus about intergroup conflict, the developing child is soon confronted by more sophisticated forms of discourse about Other people, for instance in children's stories, television programs, lessons, and textbooks. Indeed, most children will learn about other ethnic groups or Third World peoples first, or perhaps only, through such forms of elite-controlled discourse and communication.

The same is true for adults in their acquisition of knowledge and beliefs from the media, advanced educational texts, scholarship, and the (mass mediated) discourse of politics. In sum, if the social mind is essentially formed by public discourse, and if public discourse is largely controlled by various elite groups, it warrants searching for at least some of the roots of racism among these elite groups themselves. We suggest that the same is probably also the cause for the role of oppositional elites in the creation of anti-racism, but a separate study would be needed to examine the details of such dissident discourse.

AN INTERDISCIPLINARY DISCOURSE ANALYTICAL FRAMEWORK

Discourse as Data

The empirical data on which this book is based have been gathered and analyzed in several research projects, carried out at the University of Amsterdam during the 1980s and early 1990s, within the framework of a larger project on discourse and racism. Whereas earlier books and articles primarily reported on these individual projects, for example, on conversations and the press, this book is intended as an integration and theoretical elaboration of this earlier research in a more specific and more coherent conceptual framework. More than in the earlier studies, for instance, this book emphasizes the role of the institutions and the elites—and their discourses—in the reproduction of racism. Therefore, besides reporting new research results, we pay more attention here to the sociopolitical dimension of racism than in the earlier studies. For instance, Chapter 3 extensively examines and compares the ways parliamentary or congressional representatives debate about minorities, refugees, ethnic affairs, Affirmative Action, and civil rights in the United States, Great Britain, Germany, France, and the Netherlands. Other chapters then focus on the discourses of education, scholarship, business corporations, and the press.

The analyses and conclusions of this study are based on a vast corpus of various types of text and talk: many thousands of pages of interview transcript, news reports, textbooks, parliamentary records, scholarly publications, letters and informal everyday communication, originating from several countries in North America and Europe. However, although such a massive database allows some modest generalizations, we still lack data and analyses about other discourse genres, and about other elite groups, in most European or Europeanized countries. Most of our data are from the 1980s, precluding a more historically oriented analysis that can only be supplied by other studies of racism, which are, however, seldom discourse-oriented. In other words, those generalizations formulated in the rest of this book should be understood to be limited to the context, time, countries, and type of discourse discussed.

The Multidisciplinary Analysis of Text and Context

Before we give a more theoretical account of the multidisciplinary framework informing this study (see Chapter 2), we will informally summarize here the main features of this discourse analytical approach. Thus, when speaking about the *structures* or *strategies* of text and talk, we refer for instance to graphic layout, intonation, stylistic variations of word selection or syntax, semantic implications and coherence, overall discourse topics, schematic forms and strategies of argumentation or news reports, rhetorical figures such as metaphors and hyperbole, speech acts, and dialogical strategies of face-keeping and persuasion, among others. Note that these structures are not racist as such: They may have a racist function only within specific contexts; in other contexts the same structures may well have different and even anti-racist functions.

These structures and strategies are typically studied in sentence and discourse grammars, stylistics, rhetoric, semiotics, pragmatics, conversational analysis, and argumentation theory. To facilitate readability of this study, however, we shall make only very limited use of the concepts and other theoretical instruments of these sub-domains and sister disciplines of discourse analysis; most of our analyses of text and talk will be highly informal. Another important restriction, due to space limitations, is that the vast amount of texts analyzed for this study did not allow us to present detailed analyses of complete discourses or large discourse fragments, such as a parliamentary debate, an interview, a textbook lesson, or a news report. Such analyses would also be relevant in capturing the properties of dialogical interaction.

As we shall see in somewhat more detail below and more extensively in the next chapter, these structural properties of text and talk are assumed to be monitored (and explained) by underlying *cognitions* of language users, that is, by memory processes and representations such as mental models of specific events, knowledge, attitudes, norms, values, and ideologies. At the same time these discourses, interpreted as situated forms of action, as well as their underlying social cognitions, are acquired and used in *sociocultural contexts*, such as those of politics, education, scholarship, the media, and corporate business.

Since we interpret racism essentially as a social system of group dominance, it should be stressed that we are only interested in the discourses and cognitions of individual persons as members of groups or institutions. This also implies that individuals and their discourses may not always appear racist at all. Indeed, we shall see that they may occasionally also exhibit tolerant or humanitarian values. Similarly, depending on the speaker and other elements of the context, the same statement may have different functions in the overall system of racism.

A discourse analytical approach does not imply that we reduce the problem of racism to a language or communication problem. Obviously, racism also manifests itself in many non-discursive practices and structures, such as discrimination in employment, housing, health care, and social services, or in physical aggression. Our major claim and interest, then, are twofold: (1) Racism also manifests itself in discourse and communication, often in relation with other social practices of oppression and exclusion, and (2) the social cognitions that underlie these practices are largely shaped through discursive communication within the dominant white group. In other words, although discourse is not the only form of racist practice, it nevertheless plays a crucial role in the societal reproduction of the basic mechanisms of most other racist practices.

Social Cognition

We suggested that an interdisciplinary account of the role of elite discourse in the reproduction of racism also has an important cognitive dimension: Text and talk are produced and interpreted on the basis of mental models of ethnic events, and such models are in turn shaped by shared social representations in memory (knowledge, attitudes, ideologies) about one's own group, about minority groups, and about ethnic relations. The same social representations control other, nonverbal actions of group members, for instance, acts of discrimination.

Since processes of reproduction involve both social representations and discriminatory acts, and social representations are formed and changed through discourse and communication, we need to know exactly how structures of text and talk affect the structures of social cognition. Conversely, we need to know by what mental strategies ethnic attitudes and ideologies influence the production of discourse.

In the same way as a discourse analytical approach does not imply that we reduce racism to a study of text and talk, a cognitive analysis does not suggest that racism and its reproduction are reduced to a problem of individual psychology, for instance, to a study of personal bigotry. On the contrary, social representations are properties of the social mind and are shared by members of *groups*. As we shall see below, they are acquired, changed, and used in social situations. Thus, they are *both* cognitive and social. It is this two-sided property that allows us to relate the societal and structural nature of racism as a system of social inequality, including shared ethnic prejudices or racist ideologies of white groups, on the one hand, with individual group members and their opinions and discourses as well as their contextual and personal variations, on the other hand.

Social Action and Social Structure

We also indicated that both social discourse and social cognition are of course embedded in social situations that in turn feature elements of more complex social structures and relations, such as groups, institutions, or relations of inequality and dominance. The very notion of elites needs to be defined in a broader societal framework. Although enacted at the micro levels of discourse, action, and thought, the proliferation of racism obviously also needs analysis at this structural macro level. Thus, it is not merely the individual journalist or a specific news report that plays a role in this process, but also the socially situated discourses and other social interactions of newsgathering and editorial meetings of groups of newsmakers, at the micro level. Similarly, the latter needs to be analyzed within the broader context of the social, economic, and cultural structures of the press as an institution, of the newspaper as an organization, and of journalists as a professional group, at the macro level. The same is true for the reproduction of racism in politics, education, research, and corporate business. It is within these broader frameworks that discourse and social representations about ethnic affairs take their specific contextual functions.

In sum, our multidisciplinary approach links discourse and other actions not only with social cognitions but also with the various micro and macro levels of society. Although discourse and cognition seem to be typical micro-level phenomena, they are unique in that they may be *about* macro-level phenomena: People can talk and think about groups, inequality, or racism. In other words, discourse and cognition are able to relate the micro and macro structures of racism and its reproduction. A multidisciplinary account describes and explains the multiple relations involved here, and discourse analysis provides us with the special tools to study these relationships.

Culture

Racism and its reproduction are not usually accounted for in terms of "culture," as it is understood in modern sociology and anthropology. However, even in the rather informal account, given above, of the role of elite discourse in the reproduction of racism, we have encountered many cultural dimensions of inequality. We have stressed, for instance, that modern racism is no longer primarily racial, but also culturally based and legitimated. This presupposes that members of dominant groups also operate with cultural hierarchies between groups, and that racism also involves cultural dominance. This is particularly the case for the group we focus on: the elites. The complex set of elite discourses that define, for example, the Rushdie affair and the conservative campaign against multiculturalism in teaching and research, are prominent examples.

Similarly, prevailing ethnic attitudes and ideologies, as well as the typical ways to express or to legitimate them in text and talk, are also characteristic properties of this dominant white or European culture. Literature, movies, news in the press, political talk in parliament, scholarly reports, and everyday stories, among other genres, as well as their narrative, argumentative, stylistic, or rhetorical structures and strategies, are all cultural phenomena, especially when they pertain to ethnic groups and ethnic affairs.

There are many interesting relationships between the ways lay people, including elites, talk and write about Others and the more or less professional ways anthropologists and ethnographers have done so for many years. In line with some critical directions of modern anthropology, this study is not interested in "exotic" people, here or there, but focuses on Our own ways of thinking and writing about Them. And unlike many contemporary studies of popular culture, our critical approach focuses on elite culture. That is, a study of the reproduction of racism is also a study of the reproduction of dominant elite culture.

Theoretical Integration

This informal sketch of some major elements of the theoretical framework needed to account for a complex problem such as the reproduction of racism in society stresses that our approach needs to be multidisciplinary: Notions from linguistics, sociolinguistics, discourse analysis, interpersonal and mass communication studies, cognitive and social psychology, macro- and micro-sociology, ethnography, political science, history, and other disciplines appear to be involved.

Such an approach has its own characteristic problems. The theories and methodologies in which such notions have been developed are not always directly compatible. For instance, a study of discourse structures provides a rather different view on communication than a cognitive or a social analysis of text or talk, which may be primarily interested in actual processes, ongoing interactions, or societal functions of discourse. Despite this disparity, we have good reasons to assume that multidisciplinary integration is not only possible but also both theoretically and empirically crucial to seriously account for such a complex phenomenon as racism and its processes of reproduction.

We suggested that one approach toward such an integration is the multidimensional account of discourse, cognition, and interaction as having both a mental as well as a sociocultural dimension, and that the cognitive, the social, and the cultural need analysis both at a micro level and at a structural, macro level, thus forming a square of relevant relationships that are all involved in racism and its reproduction. Discourse analysis is ideally placed to account for these relationships. That is, we may account for discourse in structural (e.g., grammatical, stylistic, rhetorical) terms when describing elite discourse itself, and also in the micro-sociological terms of ongoing interactions and socio-cultural practices of elites, as a mental event (of interpretation, memorization, and so on), or as an expression of overall group cognitions such as attitudes and ideologies. Thus, the theoretical complexity of our conceptual analysis necessarily mirrors the empirical complexity of racism in society.

SUMMARY

This introductory chapter has argued for the need to study the role of the elites in the reproduction of contemporary racism in Europe, North America, and other Europeanized countries. The leading elites in politics, the media, scholarship, education, corporate business, and many other social domains control the access to valued social resources and privileges, and thus are mainly responsible for inequality between majority and minority groups. Among many other actions, elite discourse is one of the important means that establishes, enacts, maintains, expresses, and legitimates such dominance. Indeed, the power of elites is also defined by their privileged access to various forms of public discourse, and hence by their control of the ethnic consensus that sustains white, European dominance over ethnic minorities. A critical and multidisciplinary discourse analysis thus enables us to reveal not only the discursive patterns of white elite text and talk about ethnic affairs, but also the socio-cognitive and the sociocultural structures and strategies of their role in the reproduction of racism.

This critical approach to racism and elite power hardly needs to be justified. It is inscribed in a research paradigm that aims at providing insight and expertise that may be used in the development of oppositional, anti-racist practices and ideologies. This book shows that, despite their carefully managed self-image as tolerant citizens and leaders, white elites are fundamentally part of the problem of racism. Besides necessary political action, scholarly work is needed to unravel and expose the prevailing myths about the role of the elites in ethnic affairs. Our study is merely one contribution, among others, to this form of academic dissent, in which scholars join forces with minority groups and others who oppose racism in view of fundamental changes toward a truly multicultural society.

2

Theoretical Framework

THE CRITICAL ANALYSIS OF RACISM

The critical theory of racism that informs the analyses of elite racism in this book is the result of a complex interplay of scholarly, social, cultural, and political insights. Such a critical theory is problem-oriented and not discipline-oriented. That is, we primarily focus on racism as a social and political problem of white, Western societies, and theoretical and methodological tools from different disciplines are chosen, or where necessary crafted, only as a function of their relevance to the description and explanation of the various manifestations of elite racism. We do not operate within the narrow boundaries of a pre-established paradigm or "school" to describe and explain racism. Rather, as we suggested in the previous chapter, we make use of discourse analysis, linguistics, cognitive and social psychology, sociology, anthropology, political science, and history in our effort to describe the multiple dimensions of such a complex problem as the role of the elites and their discourses in the reproduction of racism. However, instead of eclectically borrowing and combining incompatible notions, we propose to reconstruct this problem within a coherent theoretical framework in which a multidisciplinary concept of discourse plays a central and organizing role.

This analysis of racism acknowledges the relevance of a perspective that is consistent with that of those who *experience* racism as such, that is, the competent or "conscious" members of minority groups. This competence consists of the fundamental knowledge as well as the evaluative and decision-making strategies needed to interpret the opinions, attitudes, discourses, or other practices of whites in relation to the system of ethnic dominance. In other words, in principle we adopt the "definition of the ethnic situation" as it is given by knowledgeable minority group members (Essed, 1991). Obviously, this knowledge is evolving historically and hence is variable for different individuals, for different subgroups of minorities, and for different times and sociocultural and political circumstances. Thus, among African-Americans, insight into the mechanisms of racism is more sophisticated, partially as a result of the Civil Rights Movement, than it was 40 or 100 years ago (Marable, 1985; Marx, 1967; Morris, 1984; Sigelman & Welch, 1991). In our interpretation of sometimes subtle forms of discursive racism, we combine this minority competence with relevant contextual data and knowledge about relevant consequences, as they are accounted for in a multidisciplinary framework.

For many white scholars of ethnic relations, the acknowledgment of a minority perspective is controversial. If they do not simply ignore them, they see minority evaluations of white practices as being biased and self-serving, if not oversensitive, vindictive, or even as examples of reverse racism (for critical analysis, see, e.g., Essed, 1987; Ladner, 1973). This very position and the general tendency to see minority evidence as less reliable, is a typical example of academic elite racism. This is especially true if the same white scholars self-servingly deny or mitigate racism, and assume that they themselves are in a better position to determine or define what racism is. Hence, academic approaches to ethnic relations are an object of critical analysis in this book. This does not mean that white scholars are unable to study racism. On the contrary, anybody who has acquired the perspective, the practical knowledge, the sensibilities, and the necessary theoretical framework accounting for white dominance is of course, in principle, able to understand the many manifestations of racism.

Both in our earlier work on the reproduction of racism, as well as in this book, we occasionally identify this critical position as anti-racist. This term is not without problems, and we use it with some reluctance. After all, it is more positive and rewarding to be *for* something, such as multiculturalism or ethnic democracy, than to define one's approach as being *against* something. Second, as we shall often find in this study, most elites claim to be against racism, so that our position would not appear to be very distinctive. We hope to show, however, that there is a rather crucial difference between strategically saying that one "is of course against racism," on the one hand, and consistently supporting anti-racist positions and policies, on the other hand. Third, in the same way as it makes little theoretical or political sense to categorize people as racist or not, it also does not make sense to distinguish between those who are anti-racists and those who are not; egalitarian and anti-egalitarian norms, attitudes, and practices may be mixed in complex ways. Despite these serious objections, we have at present no terminological alternative, whether political or academic, to denote theories, analyses, and actions that critically oppose all manifestations of racism, including subtle elite racism, in favor of true ethnic-racial equality and justice.

Within this overall framework of critical, anti-racist problem orientation, multidisciplinarity, and the acknowledgment of a minority perspective, this chapter discusses some major theoretical notions needed in the account of the role of elite discourse in the reproduction of racism in the next chapters. For the sometimes complex details of these notions, we refer to the scholarly literature cited, although such references are kept to a minimum for reasons of space.

Groups

A first important dimension of racism is its intergroup nature. Categorization, stereotyping, prejudice, and discrimination affect Other People primarily because they are thought to belong to another group, that is, as group members and not as individuals. Negative properties attributed to the group as a whole are thus applied to its members, who therefore are seen as essentially alike and interchangeable. And vice versa, negative characteristics attributed to a group member in a particular situation may be generalized to those holding for the group as a whole. Similarly, whites who have ethnic prejudices or engage in discrimination also do so as group members. This means that in our theoretical framework, prejudice and discrimination are not tied to individual personality structures, but to the social and cultural norms, values, or ideologies of dominant groups. Viewed from the perspective of minority group members, they may in principle be expected of *any* member or the entire group. Thus, when we analyze the reproduction of racism, we are concerned with the reproduction processes of groups, that is, with the reproduction of the norms, values, attitudes, and ideologies that govern their group practices, as well as with the properties of conflict and dominance between groups (Billig, 1976; Brewer & Kramer, 1985; Tajfel, 1978; 1981; Turner & Giles, 1981).

Power and Dominance

Racism is not characteristic of any intergroup relation, although many properties of intergroup relations are also typical for racism.

Essential for racism is a relation of group power or dominance (Giles & Evans, 1986). It follows from our definition of racism as a property of intergroup relations that such power is not personal or individual, but social, cultural, political, or economic (for details on various approaches to social power, see, e.g. Cartwright, 1959; Clegg, 1989; Galbraith, 1985; Lukes, 1974; 1986; Wrong, 1979). Such a definition allows for the possibility that in specific situations or positions, individual minority group members, for instance a black professor or mayor, may be more powerful than certain majority group members, that is, when they are exercising their function.

Group power is basically a form of control: The range and nature of the actions of dominated group members are limited by the actions, the influence, or the perceived wishes of dominant group members. In other words, the exercise of social control over other groups limits the social freedom of these other groups. Given the definition of racism as a form of dominance, reverse racism or black racism in white-dominated societies are theoretically excluded in our framework. Indeed, as we shall see quite often in this study, such reversals are, in their own right, a prominent device of racist discourse.

The resources on which this white group power is based are multiple and may be socioeconomic as well as cultural and ideological (French & Raven, 1959; Wrong, 1979). The very membership of the dominant group may be considered by its members as sufficient entitlement for the exercise of control over Others. Usually, however, the power base is also defined in terms of status, privileges, income, and access to better jobs, better housing, or better education. Morally or legally unwarranted control over and preferential access to such resources define the very notion of dominance and are at the heart of all forms of social inequality, and hence, of racism. In other words, group dominance is a form of power abuse. This is also true for the power relationships within the dominant group itself, and hence for the definition of elites (see below). This means that the relative power of majority and minority elites plays an important role in the nature of ethnic relationships.

As we shall see in more detail below, dominance defined as social control has both a cognitive and a social dimension. Besides their control over the access to valued social resources, dominant groups may indirectly control the minds of others. They may do so through persuasive discourse and by other means (biased news reporting, bad education) that limit the acquisition and the use of relevant knowledge and beliefs necessary to act freely and in one's own interests. This book pays special attention to this discourse dimension of dominance, namely, as a means to shape the ethnic consensus about the legitimacy of white group dominance within the dominant group itself.

The reproduction of racism is essentially geared toward the maintenance of white group control: The dominant group wants to stay in power and does so by securing privileged access to its relevant socioeconomic or cultural power resources, if only by preventing minority groups from acquiring such access. However, in ethnic relations, control is seldom total and is usually met with resistance, that is, with practices geared toward the acquisition of counterpower, at least in some social domains. If patterns of access are changed, as is the case in Affirmative Action, housing, or welfare programs, the real or imaginary increase in counterpower of minorities may be opposed by whites and seen as unfair favoritism. We shall see later that this is one of the major manifestations of modern racism (Dovidio & Gaertner, 1986).

Difference: Race and Ethnicity

Whereas the forms of group power introduced above are general in character, and also apply to define class and gender dominance, among others, racism presupposes the social construction of ethnic or racial difference. Traditionally, the notion of racism was applied to those forms of group dominance in which specific differences of physical appearance (mostly color) were used to construe primary in-group and out-group membership (Miles, 1989). Although such differences between in- and out-group may be minimal, sometimes even nonexistent, their social construction is based on various cognitive operations to define racial difference, such as the use of prototypes, exaggeration of intergroup differences, and minimization of in-group variation (Hamilton, 1981; Jones, 1972; Miller, 1982; Tajfel, 1981). These sociocognitive constructions may vary considerably for different cultures or countries: Whereas in the United States and Europe, one fundamental difference may be construed between black and white or between African and European (Caucasian) groups, the differentiation in the Caribbean or Brazil may be much more detailed and, for example, distinguish between many different groups of blacks.

Group differentiation and categorization based on appearance seldom come alone. They are often associated with differences of origin of the group (or its ancestors), and especially with sets of attributed cultural characteristics, such as language, religion, customs, habits, norms, values, or even character traits and their associated social practices.

Although appearance and origin often remain major criteria, it may well be that other criteria of group differentiation, for example, a set of cultural characteristics, become more dominant in the process of categorization and differentiation (M. Barker, 1981). Group dominance based on these forms of group differentiation may be called *ethnicism* (Mullard, 1985). In the course of this book, however, we shall continue to use the term *racism* to denote these other forms of ethnicism, even when racial differences are minimal or play a subordinate role in the categorization process. Thus, in Europe it may also be applied to describe the ethnicism directed against Turkish or other Mediterranean peoples, and in the United States to characterize the relations with Mexicans or other Latin Americans.

We see that this dimension of racism involves many different conceptual aspects, including geographical, physiological, cultural, social, and cognitive elements. It is the socio-cognitive interface that is crucial: the categorization of other people as belonging to the Other group on the basis of sometimes rather arbitrary but socially construed and attributed distinctions of origin, appearance, or various aspects of culture. Typical for the system of racism is that properties attributed to the out-group, for example, those of character, intelligence, morals, or characteristic actions, are assumed to be inherently related to the racial or ethnic identity of the group. As we shall see in more detail below, the process of reproducing racism precisely involves the social reproduction of these constructions, although the criteria underlying these constructions may undergo historical changes.

White Racism

Although this analysis of racism as group dominance based on socio-cognitively construed ethnic or racial differences may theoretically apply to other forms of inequality, we focus on white or European racism. This does not mean that white people are inherently racist, but that historically Europeans have acquired or appropriated the power that has been reproduced in racial terms, namely, as various forms of racial superiority felt with respect to non-Europeans, and as a system of discrimination implemented as practices of exclusion, marginalization, or other forms of oppression or control (Bowser & Hunt, 1981; Katz, 1976b; Katz & Taylor, 1988; Miles, 1989; Wellman, 1977). Whereas in current, more sophisticated forms of racism the "difference" with other groups is especially emphasized, traditional racism presupposed the inherent superiority of the "white race" (M. Barker, 1981).

In other words, racism, as it is analyzed here, is European group dominance exercised especially with respect to non-European (nonwhite) groups or peoples identified in terms of a complex set of attributed physical, cultural, and socioeconomic differences. This special kind of white racism developed in close relationship with Western colonialism and imperialism, but remains relevant in the present relations between North and South, and between European majorities and non-European minorities (Lauren, 1988; Robinson, 1983)

Social Practices and Social Cognitions

We have argued above that ethnic group dominance has two complementary dimensions: those of social action and those of social cognition. Thus, control is enacted through social practices of oppression, suppression, exclusion, or marginalization of out-group members by in-group members. However, such practices are specifically racist—or perpetuate the system of racist power—only if they are also cognitively informed, for instance by prejudiced attitudes or ideologies (Allport, 1954; Apostle, Glock, Piazza, & Suelze, 1983; Jones, 1972). This does not mean that such practices are always consciously or intentionally racist, but only that they are informed by beliefs that lead to actions with negative consequences for others as minority group members.

This also means that the problem of discrimination-without-prejudice or unintentional discrimination is spurious in our approach. First, this is so because in our minority-perspective definition of racism, discriminatory acts are experienced and evaluated as such by their consequences for minorities. Second, at the level of groups and group dominance, discriminatory practices of a group presuppose prejudiced social cognitions shared by many or most members of the dominant group. Individuals without ethnic prejudices (if any), who discriminate against minorities only because of group norms or social pressure, still discriminate precisely because of the shared prejudiced consensus, and thus contribute to the growth of racism. That is, in an analysis of racism as group power, prejudice defined as only an individual attitude is irrelevant.

It should be noted here that our approach to racism (including ethnicism) as a system of group dominance, manifesting itself both in social cognitions (attitudes, ideologies) as well as in systematic social practices of exclusion, inferiorization, or marginalization, differs from common sociological conceptions of racism as racist ideology (Miles, 1989; see also Chapter 5). We have argued that racism also involves discriminatory practices, and that their underlying social cognitions need not feature an ideology about white racial superiority.

At the local level of interaction and experiences, the overall societal system of racism is implemented as everyday racism, namely, as a breach of the rules, norms, and values underlying appropriate behavior in social interaction (Essed, 1984, 1991). These everyday practices may or may not be institutionalized, for instance, in terms of laws and regulations; they may be subtle or blatant, overt or covert, intentional or unintentional. They are interpreted as racist practices when minority group members, on the basis of their generalized knowledge about racism, interpret them as such, and when no other reasonable explanation or excuse can be given for such negative actions: for instance, when a professor underestimates the academic abilities of a student only because she is black, and not because of a specific critical mood or because of the academic performance of the student (for further theory, analysis, and examples of such evaluation procedures, see especially Essed, 1991).

As a first approximation, we now have some main elements of racism, namely, as a societal system of white group dominance over non-European groups or peoples, implemented by generalized everyday negative practices and informed by shared social cognitions about socially construed and usually negatively valued racial or ethnic differences of the out-group. We have also seen that the concepts involved in such an analysis need to be made explicit in terms that involve both cognitive and social theories, at the local as well as the global level of societal organization. We shall see below what theoretical languages are necessary to provide such an advanced explication.

REPRODUCTION

One of the central concepts of this book is the notion of *reproduction*. Unfortunately, it is one of those concepts that are often used in the social sciences but seldom precisely defined or analyzed (see, however, Bourdieu & Passeron, 1977). Both its biological and its technological meanings suggest the continuity or duplication of existing objects, organisms, species, or images. Social reproduction also involves the continuity of the same structures, namely as a result of active processes, as is the case of a culture or class or, indeed, of the whole social system itself. Essential in this case is that social members themselves are actively engaged in the process of continuity: With their compliance they continuously contribute to the perpetuation of a social structure or cultural norms and values.

The same is true for the reproduction of the system of racism, which also continues to exist as long as there are white group members or institutions that implement the system, that is, share ethnic prejudices and regularly engage in discriminatory practices. Besides this bottom-up (or micro-macro) aspect of reproduction, there is also a top-down (macro-micro) aspect: White group members acquire prejudices and learn to discriminate because of their knowledge of a social system of ethnic or racial inequality. In other words, this system of inequality is being reproduced by all arrangements, structures, social cognitions, and actions that contribute to its historical continuity.

The same is true for processes of change, that is, for the reproduction of a system of ethnic and racial equality: Only when a system of multicultural norms, rules, laws, and ideologies prevails and is actively implemented and shared in social cognitions and interactions throughout the group, will the system of racism cease to exist. This logic of reproduction implies that under a system of racism, collusion, passivity, inaction, or failure to combat prejudice and discrimination contribute to the continuity of the system. Instead of speaking about racist or anti-racist actors and actions, we therefore evaluate actions as more or less contributing to, or opposing, the reproduction of racism.

Specifically for this book this assumption also implies that those who have more power, and hence more control over the actions of more people in more situations, also have a broader range of opportunities to contribute to, or to oppose, the reproduction of racism. This also supports our hypothesis that the elites have a special responsibility in the reproduction of racism: They have most resources not only to actively propagate it but also to actively oppose it. From a conceptual analysis of the mechanisms of social reproduction, we thus arrive at the elements of an applied ethics: Who is most responsible for the reproduction of racism?

Cognitive and Ideological Reproduction

The process of reproduction is not limited to the overall social processes of dominance at the macro level, or to social interaction at the micro level of everyday situations. We have repeatedly argued that the system of racism also has an important socio-cognitive dimension.

These social cognitions, such as shared group norms, values, attitudes, and ideologies, enable discriminatory acts in the first place, because all human action presupposes cognition. To implement and reproduce the system of racism, white group members must implicitly know the system, much like the users of English must know the grammar and the rules of syntax of English.

Social cognitions have a crucial double function in the reproduction process. On the one hand, at the micro level of situated interaction, they underlie the actual planning, execution, and understanding of actions that may have discriminatory effects. On the other hand, along the micro-macro dimension, social cognitions link these individual cognitions, actions, or events of particular participants in specific situations to the overall system defining the relationships between ethnic groups. For instance, a white manager who opposes Affirmative Action in his or her organization does so on the basis of knowledge and beliefs about Affirmative Action policies in general, about relations between majorities and minorities, and other general beliefs about ethnic affairs, social equality, and the ideology of the freedom of corporate enterprise, as we shall see in more detail in Chapter 4.

It is at this crucial point where social cognition establishes the important missing link between individual and society, between individual opinions and social group attitudes, and hence between discourse and racism. Thus, the reproduction of the system of racism presupposes the reproduction of its social cognitions, for instance, through processes of inference, learning, and sharing within the group. In our theoretical framework these socio-cognitive reproduction processes are essentially implemented by public discourse and communication.

The second major assumption is that since the elites have the most control over such public discourse and communication, they also are most responsible for the cognitive or ideological reproduction of racism. Recall that this special responsibility also holds by default, for instance, when elites either condone or refrain from taking action against the discursive reproduction of racism—perhaps by allowing the use of racist media discourse, textbooks, or political propaganda. Here we touch upon complex ethical and political problems, such as the tensions arising between the freedom of speech and the freedom from racism. We shall see later that the white elites in Western countries usually self-servingly opt for freedom of speech, that is, for the rights of in-group members, and against the right of out-group members to be free from racism.

DISCOURSE

Since this study focuses on the discursive reproduction of racism, we need to pay special attention to the role of text and talk in this process: What communicative events, types of discourse, speech participants, modes of communication, and discursive structures and strategies are involved? The answer to these questions requires a systematic discourse analysis of the genres or communicative events that play a role in the reproduction of racism, such as everyday conversations, institutional dialogues, news reports, editorials, advertisements, novels, films, textbooks, lessons, laws, political propaganda, parliamentary debates, corporate discourse, or any other discourse genre that may be about ethnic groups and ethnic relations.

Such a systematic discourse analysis provides an interdisciplinary description of the respective levels and dimensions of discourse and its social, cultural, and cognitive contexts, such as:

- graphic and phonetic expression or realization (writing and speech)
- phonological features of talk, for example, intonation
- syntactic structures of (sequences of) sentences, for example, word order
- lexicalization (selection of words)
- semantic (micro)structures (meanings) of sentences and sentence pairs
- semantic (macro)structures of sentence sequences and whole texts (topics or themes)
- illocutionary functions (speech acts such as assertions, commands, and requests) and other pragmatic properties (e.g., strategies of politeness)
- stylistic variations of expression structures, for example, of lexicon and syntax
- rhetorical operations (figures of speech, such as metaphors or hyperbole)
- overall conventional text forms, schemata, or superstructures (e.g., of narrative, argumentation, news discourse, conversation, or institutional dialogues)
- interactional structures of talk, for example, turns, moves, strategies
- other properties of communicative events and situations, for example, properties of and relations between participants, communicative goals and interests, setting, circumstances, relations with other actions, institutional context, and so on
- cognitive processes, strategies, and knowledge and belief structures of production, comprehension, memorization, learning, and so on

Each of these levels or dimensions, which will be further explained in the chapters that follow, is itself vastly complex and accounted for by linguistic (discourse) grammars and by theories of style, rhetoric, narrative, argumentation and conversation, pragmatics, ethnography, semiotics, interaction analysis, the cognitive and social psychology of text and talk, the sociolinguistics of language use, among other more or less independent sister- or daughter-disciplines of an interdisciplinary discourse analysis (for details, see the contributions in van Dijk, 1985c). More specifically, in order to analyze the role of the many structures involved in the reproduction of discourse, we need a functional description. Such a functional description makes explicit how each structural feature of text and talk, or a combination of features, may contribute to the social and cognitive processes that define the reproduction of white group dominance.

As the list of levels or dimensions of discourse analysis suggests, there are many ways to approach the discourses involved in the reproduction of racism. We also argue that the vast field of discourse analysis and related disciplines provides many theoretical and analytical proposals for detailed, and at time highly sophisticated, description of text and talk. Although the various chapters of this book address many of the levels mentioned above, our aim is not primarily to contribute to these theories of discourse, but only to use and apply some of their relevant notions. Moreover, we do so in a highly informal way, for reasons of space, to guarantee accessibility for readers from other disciplines, and in order to be able to study several perspectives or dimensions at the same time. Another problem is that the large amounts of text data studied for this book do not readily allow a detailed discourse analysis, except of some small fragments. Once a general framework of research has been sketched, as we do in this study, future work may go into the more technical details of the respective discourse features involved.

It should be emphasized again that formal structures of discourse are seldom specific for racist talk and text: Syntactic forms, lexical style, rhetorical operations, text schemata, and conversational strategies may have many functions in communication and interaction and are of course not exclusively used in the reproduction of racism. If we observe typical forms or strategies in prejudiced discourse, such as the semantic moves of positive self-presentation ("I am not a racist, but . . ."), they derive their special role or function only in combination with the semantics of meaning and reference, that is, with what the discourse is about, and in a particular context (that is, specific participants and their goals).

There are two basic modes of the role of discourse in the reproduction of racism, namely, as discourse between majority and minority group members, and as discourse among majority group members about minorities or ethnic relations. The first mode, discourse with minorities, may be prejudiced or racist like any other form of discrimination, and may involve a complex set of strategies that either willingly or unwittingly aim at the direct or indirect exercise of dominance. This is the case for speech acts such as inappropriate commands or accusations, for the unfounded assertion or implication of negative characteristics of minority listeners, or conversely, an exclusive focus on positive in-group properties, and so on. The overall social strategies governing such discourse may be attack, marginalization, problematization, or inferiorization. It is not likely that white informants will spontaneously provide data about these forms of verbal abuse in their interviews. Therefore, only accounts of minorities themselves about their experiences should be seen as crucial indicators of this form of racism (Essed, 1984, 1991).

Discourse About Minorities

Our research, however, does not focus on these direct forms of discursive interaction and their role in the reproduction of racism, but on the ways whites write and talk about minority groups or about ethnic relations. Such discourse is largely addressed to other whites, although minorities may indirectly be addressed, or may overhear it, as is the case in all public discourse. In this way, ethnic power relations are not so much implemented as such, but rather presupposed, commented upon, and communicated. The major functions of such discourse about minorities are persuasive, that is, speakers aim to influence the minds of their listeners or readers in such a way that the opinions or attitudes of the audience either become or remain close(r) to those of the speaker or writer. In this way, speakers or writers may justify or legitimate specific cognitions or actions of themselves or other in-group members, or derogate those of out-group members.

We are primarily interested here in the socio-cognitive or ideological functions of discourse about ethnic affairs: How do in-group members acquire, share, modify, or confirm their beliefs about other ethnic groups? Once we understand these processes of ideological reproduction, we also have insight into the underlying mechanisms that monitor more direct forms of discrimination or racist action, including text and talk directed against minority group members. Note that the expressive and persuasive functions of talk about minorities also have a number of indirect sociocultural functions: White group members may thus change personal experiences into group experiences, suggest what can be done in situations of ethnic conflict, signal their own ethnic group membership and allegiance, emphasize shared interests and values, enact group dominance, and finally help reproduce racism.

Semantics and Beliefs

One important theoretical and methodological question that should be addressed is the relationship between discourse and underlying ethnic beliefs. Granted, discourse analysis can provide insight into the ways people write or talk about ethnic affairs, but how is it able to establish a link between such discourse and the underlying social cognitions of white group members? The same question also applies to the analysis of the processes of comprehension and influence: How are discourse structures understood, and especially, how do they either influence the formation or change mental models of ethnic events, or of opinions and attitudes about ethnic minorities or ethnic affairs more generally?

The most straightforward expression of underlying social beliefs about ethnic affairs seems to be their direct insertion into the semantic structures constructed during cognitive planning of text or talk (for details about these processes, see Levelt, 1989; van Dijk & Kintsch, 1983). If a speaker believes that "refugees come here to live off our pockets," then such a proposition may in principle be inserted into the semantic representation of a conversation. It is this fundamental communicative principle of expressibility that allows commonsense inferences about what people believe from what they say. Thus, semantic analysis of discourse provides at least partial access to underlying social cognitions.

However, there are other strategies and constraints involved in the expression of social beliefs as meanings of discourse. First, people have vast belief structures, and only fragments of these will usually be expressed in discourse. That is, expression is usually partial, if only because readers or listeners are themselves able to infer other relevant beliefs from the beliefs expressed in discourse, or simply because most other beliefs are irrelevant in the present communicative context. Indeed, from the belief about refugees mentioned above, the hearer may infer such speaker beliefs as "refugees are coming to our country," "I don't like it when people live off our pockets," and "I do not like refugees coming to our country," and many other related presumed and implied propositions.

Second, partial expression not only results from cognitive and communicative economy, but may also be a functional move in a strategy of impression formation, in which speakers want to avoid negative inferences about their social beliefs (Arkin, 1981). That is, expression strategies are directly related to interactional strategies of "face-keeping" or positive self-presentation of white group members, which we shall encounter very often in our analyses.

Thus, expression strategies may involve different kinds of transformation. People may believe proposition p but actually express a related but different proposition q, a proposition that is more credible, less offensive, less biased, or less face-threatening, for instance: "Many refugees come here for economic reasons," or "Economic refugees should be received in their own region of the world." In other words, there are many communicative and other interactional reasons why people do not exactly say what they mean or believe. Such transformations are well known to speech participants, and may even result in the expression of inconsistent or opposite beliefs, as is the case in irony or lying. Language users, after many years of conversational or textual practice, have become experts in detecting real speaker beliefs, for example, by interpreting various textual or contextual signals, such as intonation, specific syntactic structures, meanings of other words and sentences in the text, gestures, or facial expressions.

Hence, although a semantic discourse analysis reveals underlying meanings, such an analysis does not always allow a straightforward inference about actual beliefs, especially in texts and talk that are about beliefs that are sensitive or otherwise socially risky. It is the joint task of the various theories and methodologies of the analysis of discourse, cognition, and social context to establish the nature and the conditions of such transformations between beliefs and their discursive expression. We may also need methods of research that provide a less obtrusive access to what people actually believe, including the analysis of communicative events that have less social self-control, for instance talk among family members or close friends.

Discursive and Mental Structures

Whereas subtle text and context analyses often provide more or less direct access to what people believe, that is, to the contents of mental representations about ethnic affairs, discourse analysis may also reveal how such beliefs are organized in memory. The discourse structures involved may be of various types. Whereas the semantics of sentences reveal (some of) the contents of mental representations, an analysis of coherence relations between these sentences may show how people relate propositions in their minds, such as, by the relationship of causes or reasons that play such an important role in the explanation of ethnic events. Similarly, a study of the semantic macrostructures (topics, themes) of a text may show how propositions are ordered in hierarchical networks of importance, relevance, or conceptual dominance. Thus, in the mind and the discourse of white speakers, the arrival of new groups of refugees or other immigrants may be related as a cause to real or imagined social problems, such as unemployment or bad housing, and may be subsumed under higher-level semantic (macro)propositions about the problems immigrants are believed to create for the in-group.

In the same way, the narrative structures of stories may be analyzed relative to the structures of models in memory, that is, representations of the events, actions and participants of the episode told about (see below). For instance, those meanings that are typically organized in the Complication category of the conventional narrative schema that organizes the stories in most Western cultures may be understood as representing a problem for the narrator, or at least as an event or action that is unexpected, remarkable, or interesting relative to the normal course of events in everyday life. Similarly, the Evaluation category of stories expresses the opinions or emotions of the storyteller about this extraordinary event (e.g., "I hated that!" or "I was so afraid!"). Finally, the Coda or Conclusion formulates those conclusions that are relevant for the overall evaluation of the participants or the consequences of the events for future actions (e.g., "I won't do that ever again!"). Narrative structures reveal not only the organization of mental models, that is, how an event is experienced, interpreted, and evaluated, but also, implicitly or explicitly, the norms, values, and expectations of the storyteller about social episodes.

The same is true for other schematic structures of discourse. Argumentative structures, for instance, show how the social beliefs of the speaker are related, for example, by various types of inference. And, as we shall see in more detail in Chapter 7, the structures of news reports show the importance or relevance hierarchies in the mental models and attitudes of journalists.

Besides these more abstract or deeper semantic and schematic structures of discourse, we may find correlation between text and mind at the more local and superficial levels of description. Thus, an analysis of word order and other syntactic structures may reveal what concepts or propositions are more important or prominent in the mind of the speaker, who is seen to be responsible for actions and events, or what general point of view or perspective the speaker has on an episode. If it is known that immigrants come to our country to find work, then this episode may be described from either *their* or *our* perspective, and we have seen that *our* perspective may be associated with positive or negative evaluations, such as: "Immigrants contribute to the Dutch economy," or "Immigrants take away our jobs," respectively. Such differences may also be signaled by the actual syntactic structures of the sentences expressing these propositions, as in "Immigrants take away our jobs," "Our jobs are taken away by immigrants," or "Our jobs are being taken away." Such syntactic differences may be related to various constraints on the structure of sequences of sentences in text and talk, but also to the subjective distinction of the immigrants as being responsible for increasing unemployment, as well as to the social strategies of persuasion or face-keeping. Similarly, in written communication such as news reports, position, layout, size, typeface, and other graphic or visual elements may signal importance or relevance. Thus, many properties of the expression level of discourse may be interpreted as signals of underlying meaning, perspective, interaction strategies, persuasion tactics, and opinions or attitudes. This is exactly what language users do themselves: Aside from their enormous repertoire of knowledge and beliefs, both personal and social, about the present situation, context, or topic, they have only these expression or surface characteristics as "data" for the process of interpretation.

Although certain aspects of meaning may be expressed or signaled by such things as intonation, layout, or word order, meanings are usually expressed by lexical items, that is, by the words of a natural language. However, we may use different words to refer to the same event, action, object, or person. These *stylistic* variations signal various elements of the social context, such as the relationship between the participants, or the membership of social groups. They also express the opinions about such referents (Sandell, 1977; Scherer & Giles, 1979). This is most typically the case for the words used to describe minority groups and their actions (as in racist abuse and in the uses of *Coloreds, Negroes, Blacks, Afro-Americans, African-Americans* accordingly). Hence, lexical style also has multiple links with underlying mental structures, including our knowledge of what the appropriate words are in each sociocultural situation. The same is also true for the variations in the graphical and phonological structures used to express words and sentences, as it is for intonation patterns, which may signal various emotions and opinions about the episodes referred to, such as hate, dislike, sympathy, approval, or pity.

Strategies: Discursive, Cognitive, and Social

Finally, in interdisciplinary analyses of discourse, we may also establish links between various strategies of text and talk, the mental strategies of belief manipulation, and the social strategies of communicative interaction. Thus, in everyday conversations, people use different strategies of topic introduction, maintenance, and change (Button & Casey, 1984; Sigman, 1983). They may try to introduce new topics in a discourse about another topic if they believe it is relevant to express one's beliefs about that other topic, or conversely, they may also want to change an ongoing topic because it is somehow socially risky for the speaker (Grice, 1975). Talk about a delicate topic such as ethnic affairs is particularly sensitive to such strategies of topicalization.

At the global level of overall discourse organization, we find strategies of argumentation, for instance when speakers are defending their own position (belief) by credible, supportive arguments, or by attacking the position of the interlocutor by undermining his or her arguments (Bell, 1990; Hirschberg, 1990). Stories may be made more effective or more credible by emphasizing the remarkable, unexpected, or otherwise interesting nature of their Complication, for example, by establishing a marked contrast with what would be the normal course of events in such a situation (Polanyi, 1985). Again, such strategies also tell us something about the mental strategies used by the speakers in the establishment of relationships between underlying beliefs, or in the representation of an episode in a mental model.

At the same time, such discursive strategies are functional within the communicative context itself. That is, they may be interactional, social strategies and play a role in providing information, in persuasion, or in impression formation. Thus, argumentative and rhetorical strategies will typically play a role as part of an overall strategy of persuasion, whereas semantic moves of apparent denial or concession may be used in a combined strategy of positive self-presentation and negative presentation of the Other ("I have nothing against foreigners, but . . . ").

In sum, the contents, structures, and strategies of discourse are multiply connected to underlying cognitive representations and processes, and at the same time they implement various properties of social interaction in communicative situations. In this way, discourse is indeed the interface between the individual and the social, between cognition and communication, between social beliefs and the ways they are expressed and reproduced by group members. It is one major task of this book to further explore these relationships between discourse, cognition, and society that define the process of white group dominance and its reproduction.

SOCIAL COGNITION

In the theoretical approach to discourse and racism outlined above, we have repeatedly stressed that social cognition plays a crucial role in reproduction. Sociological accounts of reproduction often ignore or minimize this cognitive aspect of social processes, if only out of the quite respectable fear of psychological reductionism. Nevertheless, no analysis of social structures and processes, even those at the macro level, is complete without an explicit analysis of the role of social beliefs, including knowledge, opinions, attitudes, norms, and values of groups. The same is true for social understanding or interpretation at the micro level, that is, for the processes involved in making sense of the social world by social members (Cicourel, 1973). While the importance of such processes has been recognized, especially by phenomenologically oriented micro-sociologists dealing with routine interactions in everyday life, it was seldom made explicit in terms of a cognitive theory of understanding (however, see, e.g., Cicourel, 1983, 1987). Conversely, most psychologists have shown little interest in the broader societal conditions and functions of social cognitions (but see the contributions in Himmelweit & Gaskell, 1990; Resnick, Levine, & Teasley, 1991).

These limitations of earlier research also apply to the more specific field of race relations, which focused either on the social psychology of prejudice and intergroup theory or on the sociology of ethnic and racial groups and institutions, and on such phenomena as discrimination and racism in politics, the economy, education, and culture. In our view racism and its reproduction have both cognitive and sociocultural dimensions, and these should be explicitly related in order to understand the mechanisms of the reproduction process.

Fortunately, social psychology has seen the development of theoretical frameworks during the past 15 years that are particularly suited to establishing such a connection, namely, in the study of *social cognitions*, mostly in U.S. research (Fiske & Taylor, 1984; Wyer & Srull, 1984), or *social representations*, predominantly in French and other European social psychology (Farr & Moscovici, 1984). One major advantage of these developments is that the mental processes and structures involved in social cognition are taken seriously. This does not mean that we already have detailed theories on the precise nature of these processes and structures. On the contrary, although we do have some insight into the structures and functions of social knowledge, we still lack detailed theories of the "hot" social cognitions traditionally known as the opinions, attitudes, norms, values, and ideologies of groups.

In our own theoretical framework, then, social cognition is understood as the interplay of specific mental structures and processes: not only the cognitive representations shared by members of a group or culture about social affairs but also the strategies that enable the effective uses of such representations in various social tasks, such as interpretations, inferences, categorization, comparisons, and evaluations, and even more fundamental processes such as those of storage and retrieval. In a broad sense, social representations embody all that people must know or believe in order to function as competent members of a group or culture. Thus social cognitions underlie all processes of making sense, both of the details of social situations and interactions, and of broader social relations, structures, and institutions. Similarly, in active production, social cognition monitors social interaction itself, for instance, ethnic interaction, discourse, and communication.

Besides the fundamental knowledge dimension of interpretation, social cognitions also involve the processes of social evaluation, that is, group-based, shared opinions about social events, situations, and structures. Social members need to know not only what is going on, but also whether they like or dislike, agree or disagree with other people, social events, or social structures. Indeed, many of their actions are premised on such opinions, while geared toward the realization of desired (preferred, wanted, and so on) goals. Although many such opinions and the correlated action goals are purely personal, other opinions are shared with other members of the group or culture. Only the latter will here be called social representations, even if personal opinions and actions are actually related to shared social and cultural cognitions.

When dealing with the problem of racism, the analysis of social representations and strategies consists in spelling out the uses of knowledge and opinions white people have about their own group, about minority groups, and about majority-minority relations. The dynamic strategies operating on such representations show how people make sense of ethnic events, how prejudiced opinions may bias their understanding and memory representation of such events, how ethnic beliefs inform action and discourse, and more generally how social cognitions about ethnic affairs are reproduced.

Personal Models Versus Social Representations

To understand the role of cognition in the reproduction of racism, we make a distinction between *individual* knowledge, opinions, and representations of personal experiences, including those about ethnic groups and events, on the one hand, and shared *social* beliefs of group members, on the other hand. The first are stored in the area of Long-Term Memory usually called Episodic Memory (which might also be called Personal Memory). This personal knowledge is represented in *models*, that is, as unique mental representations of specific situations, events, actions, and persons (Johnson-Laird, 1983; van Dijk & Kintsch, 1983). Each particular action, interaction, and discourse we are personally involved in is planned and executed—together with our personal evaluations of each—in the form of such a model, and the same is true for each event we witness, read about, understand, memorize, or evaluate. Models are personal because individuals bring to bear a large number of personal experiences, associations, knowledge, and opinions that emerge from their own mental "biography" (van Dijk, 1985a, 1987b).

As we shall see in more detail below, these models play an important role in a theory of reproduction because they link personal experiences with shared group experiences, individual opinions with social attitudes, and individual text and talk with social, political, or cultural discourse of a group or institution. Models also explain why members of a social group sharing more or less the same knowledge and attitudes may nevertheless have variable, individual opinions and therefore engage in unique personal actions and discourse. These unique personal models also explain a crucial condition of social change, namely, deviance from prevailing norms, rules, attitudes, and ideologies; that is, the very possibility of social change.

Despite this important role of models in the description of unique cases, and hence in the analysis of particular instances of text and talk, social cognition theory is of course more specifically interested in *social* representations shared by the members of a *group*, such as social knowledge, attitudes, norms, values, and ideologies. We assume that these social representations are stored in the vast area of Long-Term Memory usually called Semantic Memory, which we however prefer to call Social Memory in order to distinguish it from the memory area in which personal experiences are stored as models. Through processes of decontextualization, generalization, and abstraction, group members may derive social representations from their own personal models about particular social events. However, social representations may also be acquired more directly, for example, by thinking (inferences from existing social representations), and through discourse and communication with other group members (Roloff & Berger, 1982; Turner, 1991; Zanna, Olson, & Herman, 1987).

One type of social representation is the knowledge and belief schemata people build about their own group as well as about other groups (Bar-Tal, 1990). Others embody the rules and principles of appropriate social interaction in stereotypical social episodes, such as the "going to school" or "going to the movies" scripts (Schank & Abelson, 1977). If belief schemata involve general evaluative beliefs (opinions), they explain the traditional notion of social attitudes. These schemata, such as group prejudices or stereotypes, may be represented as hierarchical structures of high-level opinions at the top (e.g., "We don't like blacks") and more detailed opinions toward the bottom (e.g., "Blacks are over-sensitive about discrimination").

Group schemata may be further organized by one or more socially relevant mental categories, such as those of Origin (Where are they from?), Appearance (What do they look like?), Socioeconomic Goals (What do they want here?), Sociocultural Properties (What language, religion, and so on, do they have?) and Personality (What kind of people are they?). These are typically associated with ethnic minority groups but are also relevant for the analysis of gender or other social group representations. Hence ethnic prejudices, assumed to be shared and group-based, should be described in terms of such general group attitudes or social representations, *not* as the individual opinions about specific ethnic events or experiences as they are stored in personal models. In this book we only use the terms *attitude* and *prejudice* in this way, as mental representations in social memory consisting of structured schemata of general opinions shared by a group, and not as specific personal opinions, as is often the case in everyday usage and much traditional social psychology (see also the discussion in, e.g., Allport, 1954; Bar-Tal, Graumann, Kruglanski, & Stroebe, 1989; Dovidio & Gaertner, 1986; Hamilton, 1981; Jones, 1972).

General ethnic attitudes influence the formation of specific models, such as specific action plans or event interpretations. Thus, white group members interpret and evaluate a concrete discourse or event featuring ethnic minorities as a function of their more general opinions about these ethnic minorities, a process traditionally called *bias* if the general attitude is negative. And they may use negative models of ethnic events, including stories about such events heard from other white group members, in order to infer a more general attitude about ethnic minorities, a process of overgeneralization that characterizes the formation of ethnic prejudices (Allport, 1954). In our framework personal models and social representations, and the mental strategies that relate them, are the basic notions that allow us to account for the structures and processes of ethnic bias and prejudice, as well as for the basic socio-cognitive processes involved in the reproduction of racism.

Ideology

Finally, social attitudes are themselves further organized by more fundamental social representations, namely, *ideologies* (for more or less different approaches to the notion of ideology, see, e.g., Billig, 1982, 1988; Kinloch, 1981; Larrain, 1979). According to this rather specific use of the notion, ideologies feature the fundamental social principles and building blocks, such as norms and values, underlying the structures and formation of attitudes. That is, they represent the mental embodiment of the fundamental social, economic, and/or cultural goals and interests of a group. If we may use a computer metaphor, we might say that together these ideologies form the basic social operating system of a group or culture, whereas the respective attitudes are the specific programs running under this system in order to perform specific socio-cognitive tasks.

Thus, ideologies assign coherence to the system and development of attitudes. For instance, given a specific anti-foreigner ideology, it may be expected that negative attitudes about Turks, Moroccans, and Caribbeans will show remarkable resemblances. At a more abstract level of ideological control, such a racist ideology may again show similarities with sexist ideologies of men, a type of coherence that is commonly known and often associated with reactionary anti-egalitarianism. This is a level that is even more general and fundamental, and comes closer to what are usually called ideologies.

It should be emphasized that there is considerable mental distance between such ideological systems and concrete discourses. Between the basic, culturally variable, ideological building blocks, such as general norms and values (e.g., about tolerance or hospitality), and actual discourses, we find specific ideologies (e.g. about immigration), social knowledge, attitudes (e.g., about Turks, or refugees), and personal models (e.g., about my encounter this morning with a Turkish refugee). It is eventually this model, including its personal—but socially dependent—opinions, that directly informs the production of the text, for example, a story about my encounter with a Turkish refugee this morning.

To avoid confusion it should be emphasized that unlike much work in the social sciences on ideology, we neither simply define an ideology as a "system of beliefs" (in which case ideologies would coincide with other cognitive representations) nor vaguely see it as a form of "consciousness" (whatever that may be exactly). In our view, ideologies do not encompass the social practices, including discourse, that control them, as is sometimes assumed in present work on ideology in philosophy and the social sciences (Althusser, 1971a; Barrett, Corrigan, Kuhn, & Wolff, 1979; Donald & Hall, 1986; Therborn, 1980). In sum: Ideologies in our theoretical framework are merely the most fundamental social representations shared by a group, namely, those representations that embody its overall interests and goals.

Although we carefully distinguish between discourse and ideology, ideology and other social cognitions are of course involved in the production and understanding of discourse (van Dijk, 1990). Indeed, people routinely express fragments of their social representations in text and talk, namely, as general statements, and use them to understand the events and opinions expressed in the discourse of others. The general and relatively abstract nature of social representations even requires symbolic communication; probably only through discourse can people come to know directly what the general opinions are of other group members, although interpretation of the actions of others allows people to infer such attitudes in an indirect, more empirical way. Consequently, discourse is the most effective way to both acquire and share general attitudes, and hence ethnic prejudices. Therefore, a combined analysis of discourse and social cognition is a crucial component of a theory of the reproduction of racism.

SOCIAL INTERACTION
AND SOCIAL STRUCTURE

The social nature of social cognitions is not merely due to the fact that they are about social objects, like groups, or to the fact that they are shared by members of a group or culture. What is usually overlooked in social cognition research is that they are actually acquired, used, and changed in social situations, social interactions, and within the context of broader social structures, such as groups, institutions, or social domains. Thus, in different social situations, group members acquire information and opinions about other social groups, including minorities, from everyday conversations, from newspaper and television, from textbooks, and from a host of other discourse genres.

Opinions and attitudes are not acquired, structured, or used arbitrarily. As social and cultural beliefs they must be functional, that is, they must in principle serve the goals or interests of the group or institution. It is therefore likely that their contents and cognitive organization are optimally tailored to such social uses and functions. In other words, social cognitions are themselves a function of their social context. Note however that this functionality may itself be biased because the social context is not an objective outside factor, but is itself cognitively represented. That is, cognitions about other groups develop as a function of what group members *believe* to be relevant for them. We see that in order to relate cognition and society, we cannot escape the cognitive framework. At this level of analysis, even social structure is relevant to us only as a mental construct (Himmelweit & Gaskell, 1990). However, the reverse also holds true: The only cognitions that will be relevant for interaction, communication, and discourse are those that are shared, and hence social. Here we again see how closely cognitive and social dimensions of reproduction are related.

Yet, within a related but theoretically different sociocultural framework of analysis, we may well devise an autonomous theory that specifically accounts for the role of social interaction, social structure or culture in the reproduction process. Here we may detail what conversational structures and strategies are involved in the interpersonal communication of social cognitions about ethnic events and groups, or what role is played by institutions such as the State, the mass media, or the schools in the reproduction of racism. Thus, we have seen that in conversations social members not only express their personal opinions or fragments of their group-based attitudes, but also are involved in strategies of face-keeping and persuasion, which in turn presuppose social knowledge and norms for the adequate social actions of competent citizens or in-group members.

Similarly, if we want to understand the role of news and textbooks in the reproduction of racism, we must go beyond a theory of the discursive or cognitive structures and strategies involved in their production, understanding, or social uses. In the case of news production, we need to specify which social routines are involved in newsmaking, which rules and roles organize such activities, and in which institutional relations and structures (e.g., of power) these activities are embedded (Tuchman, 1978). Thus, if we find that minority group members are comparatively little quoted in news, we may partly explain this fact in terms of a mental schema in which minority groups are represented as less credible sources. However, in such a case we should also account for the fact that smaller minority groups may be less organized and may lack their own press or public relations department, press officers, or other social or economic conditions of prestructured media access, which could make it more difficult for journalists to obtain minority comments, even if they are desired.

Similarly, for textbooks, the contents may be studied as expressions of prevalent stereotypes about Third World peoples or immigrant minorities, but true understanding also requires analysis of the whole curriculum, the school system, the participation of minority children, the presence of educational organizations that oppose racism in educational material, and many other factors that influence the contents of textbooks (see, e.g., Apple, 1979). The same is true for legal discourse and its role in the legal system, for political discourse and its functions in the polity, or for medical discourse and the position of doctors and clients, among other forms of elite discourse.

In our analysis of racism given above, we have found that power relations between groups are involved. These power relations are also relevant in the analysis of the reproduction process itself. That is, we have seen that white elite groups and institutions control and/or have preferential access to the mass media and other means of ideological reproduction (van Dijk, 1993). Hence, we may expect that their social cognitions will tend to prevail in the definitions of the ethnic situation as it is routinely reproduced in elite discourse.

Racism, Institutions, and the Elites

It is this social group power in the control of discourse that also inspires our hypothesis about the role of the elites in the reproduction of racism. Let us therefore finally elaborate this hypothesis in somewhat more detail. For instance, what elites are we referring to and how exactly are they involved in the reproduction of racism?

Although the notion of elites is not without problems (see, e.g., Domhoff & Ballard, 1968), we initially use the concept as an informal, heuristic notion to denote groups in society that have special power resources. Depending on the societal domain or field in which they wield power, we may speak of, for example, political, state, corporate, scientific, military, or social elites, although some elites may operate across domain boundaries as well, for instance when corporate or military elites are able to influence the process of political decision making. The power resources of elites may be multiple and include property, income, decision control, knowledge, expertise, position, rank, as well as social and ideological resources such as status, prestige, fame, influence, respect, and similar resources ascribed to them by groups, institutions, or society at large (Bottomore, 1964; Domhoff, 1978; Mills, 1956; Stanworth & Giddens, 1974).

Elite power can be defined in terms of the type or amount of control elites have over the actions and minds of other people. Although this control may also be implicit, it is usually explicitly implemented by decision making, use of special speech acts and discourse genres (e.g., commands, orders, advice, analyses, and all forms of public discourse), and other forms of action that directly or indirectly influence the actions of others. This control is usually in the interest of the elites themselves, or at least in a way that is consistent with the preferences of the elites. Examples of such elites in Western societies are, leading politicians in government, parliament, and political parties; owners, directors, and top-level managers of business corporations; directors or other high officers of state institutions (including the police); judges of higher courts; union leaders; high church officials; the military upper echelons; publishers and editors of major news media; professors and leaders of large research institutions, and so on. Although elites usually represent the top levels of institutions or organizations, some elites, such as famous writers or film stars, may also be influential due to such power resources as prestige, respect, and admiration. In classical sociological terms, elites do not form a class. Indeed, different elite groups may be in conflict if they have inconsistent goals and interests.

Essential for our discussion is that power elites also have special symbolic resources, such as preferential access to systems of sociocultural discourse (van Dijk, 1993). Not only do they make decisions that may affect the lives of many people, they also have significant control over the means of production of public opinion. That is, they have special access to a range of discourse genres and communicative events that go beyond the meetings or other institutional dialogues of their immediate everyday context of decision making. Thus, they control PR departments, press offices, press releases, advertisements, reports, and other publications that describe, explain, or legitimate what they do and say, and thus also have broad access to public discourse, primarily that of the mass media (Tuchman, 1978). Their major activities are usually newsworthy for the news media; they are known to a large public or to specific gatekeepers of mass media and other institutions; and their opinions, even when not always agreed with, are taken seriously. That is, they are both subjects and objects of public text and talk, and their power is, so to speak, symbiotic with that of the media themselves (Altschull, 1984; Bagdikian, 1983; Lichter, Rothman, & Lichter, 1990; Paletz & Entman, 1981; Tuchman, 1978).

Through this special active and passive access to public discourse, elites also have special access to the public mind, according to the complex processes of social cognition formation and change outlined above. That is, they produce self-evaluations, definitions of the situation, selections of problems, and agendas that may have significant public impact. In other words, elites have the means to manufacture consent (Herman & Chomsky, 1988). This does not mean that all opinions of the elites are always adopted by the public at large, but only that their opinions are well known, that they have the most effective means of public persuasion and the best resources for suppressing or marginalizing alternative opinions.

In an analysis of the reproduction of racism, we are especially interested in the elites involved in the control of ethnic affairs and ethnic relations. Since ethnic affairs are relevant in virtually all sectors of society, elites generally also play a role in the management of such affairs. This is primarily the case for politicians who control the public budget and make the major policy decisions regarding ethnic affairs. Within more specific social domains, corporate managers are involved in ethnic affairs through their control of hiring and firing ethnic minorities; leading police officers and judges in the effective control of public order and hence in the definition of "minority crime"; and the directors of state or city agencies in the control of employment and welfare programs for minority groups. These elite decisions and actions not only affect minority groups and their members directly, but often also require legitimation by the white population at large and hence, discursive strategies in forming the ethnic consensus.

Symbolic Elites

Despite the preferential access of most elites to public discourse and despite their large potential to influence public opinion, we pay special attention to those elites who have close control over public discourse about race and ethnic affairs. The traditional term *opinion leader* already suggests that specific elites have a more prominent role in public debate, also on issues of race, immigration, or minorities. Indeed, although generals in a democratic state may control some sector of ethnic affairs (e.g., ethnic relations in the army), their opinions about ethnic affairs are seldom known and discussed by the public at large. And although corporate managers play a crucial role in ethnic affairs, namely, by controlling employment (and unemployment) among minorities, their views on minorities are also seldom publicly expressed and debated, even when directly related to issues of employment, such as discrimination and Affirmative Action. Instead, their trade organizations or political lobbyists speak for them on such topics, as was the case during the U.S. congressional debate, to be analyzed in Chapter 3, on the Civil Rights Bills of 1990 and 1991. Similar remarks hold for leading police officers, judges, union leaders, church officials, and directors of state agencies.

More relevant, then, are the decisions, actions, and opinions of the symbolic elites, those groups that are directly involved in making and legitimating general policy decisions about minorities, namely, leading politicians, and those who directly address public opinion and debate, such as leading editors, TV program directors, columnists, writers, textbook authors, and scholars in the fields of the humanities and social sciences (see, e.g., Bourdieu, 1984, 1988). A good education and control of public knowledge, beliefs, and discourse are the major power resources of such symbolic elites. In the modern state, discourses and opinions of these elites are primarily channeled through the media of mass communication, which provides special control to leading directors or editors of newspapers and television programs. This means that media elites not only have direct power and influence as managers of large media corporations, but they also wield considerable indirect power—by significantly contributing to the power of other elites. Besides the mass media, the other major symbolic domain is that of education and scholarly research. Here teachers, textbook writers, and scholars have control over curricula, lessons, and research projects involving knowledge and opinions about ethnic affairs and social affairs in general. Their influence is also both direct (e.g., as advisers of policymakers) and indirect, namely, through the education and the social cognitions of the elites of the future (Bourdieu, 1984).

With the exception of leading politicians, most symbolic elites have little direct power in terms of wealth or decision making that affects large groups of people. Indeed, their control is limited to the domain of words and ideas, even when, indirectly, these may have a significant effect on the minds of other elites (e.g., those of the politicians) and hence on public policy. That is, such elites have a power base consisting of "symbolic capital" (Bourdieu, 1984, 1988). Journalists, writers, professors, and other symbolic elites thus have a primary role in setting the agenda, and hence have considerable influence in defining the terms and the margins of consent and dissent for public debate, in formulating the problems people speak and think about, and especially in controlling the changing systems of norms and values by which ethnic events are evaluated. We assume, therefore, that this group of elites plays a crucial role in both the reproduction of and the resistance against racism. It will be the task of this book to examine the detailed mechanisms of this ideological power of the symbolic elites. We do this by analyzing the structures of their discourses, their access to public discourse and communicative events, and how these affect public discussion and opinion about ethnic affairs.

CONCLUSIONS

The theoretical framework that forms the background of the analyses of different genres of elite discourse in the next chapter is complex and multidisciplinary. Within a critical perspective that focuses on racism as a major social problem of Western societies rather than on specific disciplinary paradigms, and that specifically acknowledges the experiences and the expertise of minorities, reproduction processes are examined as an interplay of discourse, social cognition, and social structures. Racism is here defined as a property of ethnic group dominance and is identified as the historically rooted dominance of whites (Europeans) over Others. It involves both shared social cognitions (prejudice), as well as social practices (discrimination), at both the macro level of societal structures and the micro level of specific interactions or communicative events. In this study the term *racism* is also intended to include *ethnicism*, that is, group dominance based on perceived or constructed cultural differences. Contrary to much usage, especially by the elites, racism is not restricted to overt, blatant, or violent forms of racial racism, but also involves more subtle, indirect forms of everyday racism. For the current situation in the United States, some of the properties of this kind of modern elite racism, especially among the younger generation, have been summarized as "yuppie racism" (Lowy, 1991).

Given their dominant role, various elites have the special means to enact, express, legitimate, or conceal their role in the reproduction of racism, especially in various forms of public discourse. Specifically focusing on symbolic elites, this study examines in detail how such elites speak and write about ethnic minorities, and thereby persuasively contribute to the manufacture of the ethnic consensus among the white group at large. Such an analysis has three major components. First, such discourses are systematically studied in their own right, at various levels or dimensions of structure, although this study does so largely in rather informal terms. Second, these discourse structures are related to the social cognitions, including ethnic attitudes, of the authors, namely, the elites themselves, as well as to those of the recipients. Third, such discourses and the social cognitions they presuppose or control are embedded in a broader social, cultural, and political framework, in which the role of elites and their institutions, and relations between different social or ethnic groups, are studied as elements in the reproduction of racism.

This complex framework also aims to provide, in the next chapters, the basis for an integrated account of the various modes and modalities of elite racism. This means that properties of discourse are related with underlying beliefs, and discourse plus beliefs with social structures or functions, or conversely. This link between discourse, social cognition, and society is still highly fragmentary, because psychology, even social psychology, and sociology are hardly on speaking terms. In some respects, we hope, discourse and discourse analysis may give clues about these complex relationships, if only because discourse is a form of social action and a cultural product, on the one hand, and a rather explicit manifestation of and source of social knowledge and beliefs, on the other hand. In other words, discourse reflects much of the contents and structures of the social cognitions, including prejudices and racist ideologies, which are otherwise difficult to access. Given both the close association between elites, elite power, and elite influence, and not only the privileged access to but also the structures and functions of public discourse, such a discourse orientation at the same time provides us with a unique tool to study elite racism and its reproduction.

3

Political Discourse

INTRODUCTION

As predicted by W.E.B. Du Bois in 1903, race and ethnic affairs have been and continue to be a major political issue throughout the twentieth century (Du Bois, 1969). Therefore, a closer analysis of the discourse of political elites on these issues may contribute not only to our insight into the discursive reproduction of racism, but also to an understanding of the more general political context of these reproduction processes in other domains, for instance, in the media, academic research, education, or in corporate business and employment, analyzed in the next chapters. It is with this general aim that this chapter makes a comparative study of political text and talk on ethnic affairs in the United States, Great Britain, France, Germany, and the Netherlands. To limit the vast field of political discourse, this chapter primarily focuses on some recent parliamentary debates on immigration, discrimination, Affirmative Action, and other ethnic issues in these respective countries.

Governments, parliaments, political parties, the bureaucracies, as well as other political organizations are regularly deeply involved in the discursive practices of policy debates, decision making, and legislation about what they define as pressing ethnic issues, such as increasing illegal immigration, waves of refugees, housing, ghettos, black crime, minority unemployment, Affirmative Action, multicultural education, poverty and disadvantaged minority groups, as well as discrimination and racial hate directed against minorities by white majority groups. Thus, in the United States, such political discourse and cognition focused on the many events that mark U.S. race and ethnic relations from the Civil Rights Movement in the 1960s until the Senate Hearings of Supreme Court Justice nominee Clarence Thomas in 1991; in Britain on the urban riots, the Honeyford case, and the Rushdie affair in the 1980s (see also Chapter 7); in France on the rise of Le Pen's Front National, the desecration of Jewish graves in Carpentras, and the affair of the veils of Muslim schoolgirls in 1990; in Germany, on the attacks by white skinheads of families of refugees and other minorities; and in North America and Europe alike on the continuous immigration of poor people and refugees from the South.

Within the framework of a study of elite discourse on ethnic affairs, such political discourse both reflects and influences popular as well as other elite concerns. It will be one of the aims of this chapter to examine these mutual influences in more detail. Thus, first of all, white politicians are citizens like others of their group, and share their social representations about minorities with other white middle-class people. They get feedback from their constituencies, for instance, during party conferences and election campaigns. Second, at a more sophisticated level of knowledge and expertise, politicians are influenced by academics and other experts, state agencies and bureaucracies, and other specialized organizations. Reports, bills, and many other forms of institutional discourse form the basis of everyday legislation and political debate about ethnic affairs. Third, the influence of the media on knowledge and opinion formation of politicians is very powerful, regardless of whether this influence is in agreement with public opinion.

Conversely, political discourse and decision making, especially on ethnic affairs, also affect other elites, organizations, and both the majority and minority populations at large. That is, political definitions of ethnic events and issues may in turn influence public debate and opinion formation, which—again, through the news media—in turn influence and legitimate policies and legislation, thereby closing the full circle of mutual influence. Following the main argument of this book, however, we shall assume that the thrust of the process of influence is predominantly top-down: In ethnic affairs, it is primarily the administration and the politicians who define the ethnic situation and set the terms and boundaries of public debate and opinion formation.

A comparison between parliamentary debates in several Western countries allows us to unravel not only national differences, but also especially the more fundamental international similarities in political discourse, cognition, and action relative to minorities and immigrants. These similarities may then be explained in terms of the more general political, social, or cultural response of white-dominated Western democ-racies to the presence or arrival of racially or ethnically different Others.

Parliamentary debates are recorded in literal transcripts, and hence produce a massive corpus of discourse. Even the study of a few debates in each country means collecting, reading, and analyzing many thousands of pages of parliamentary or congressional records. A detailed local analysis of so many text data is virtually impossible and must be highly selective. Therefore, apart from an analysis of topics, style, and rhetoric of specific fragments, we focused on a number of characteristic argumentative moves in the discussions of policies about immigration, employment, and Affirmative Action. As is assumed for other forms of elite discourse studied in this book, this analysis may also reveal the underlying ideologies and other social representations of the political elites, as well as their social, cultural, and political role in the reproduction of racism.

HISTORICAL BACKGROUND

Contemporary political discourse on race and ethnic affairs has a long tradition both in Europe and in North America: First contacts with and conquest of other peoples in Asia, Africa, and the Americas; slavery and abolition, colonialism, imperialism, and decolonization; social Darwinism and eugenics; Nazism and the Holocaust; apartheid, segregation, desegre-gation, and the Civil Rights Movement; labor immigration and refugees; Affirmative Action and equal opportunities; and the continuing debate on Eurocentrism and racism, were among the major issues that have been debated by political and other elites during the past 500 years. In an even broader historical perspective, some of the issues, such as slavery and subjugation of non-European peoples, go back to Greek and Roman antiquity. As may be expected, this tradition is characterized by both continuity and change in the ways European leaders and their representa-tives and descendants on other continents perceived and treated the Others.

This long history of political discourse and cognition about other peoples and cultures cannot even be summarized here (see, e.g., Lauren, 1988). However, it should be recalled that for centuries the predominant practice of the political and other elites in Europe has been the deroga-tion, inferiorization, exploitation, subjugation, and occasional genocide of non-Europeans. These Others were variously seen and treated as barbarians, savages, infidels, semi-animals, monsters, slaves, subordi-nates, "niggers" (and related racist words), wetbacks, guest workers, insurgents, terrorists, economic refugees, or many other categories combining the concepts of threat, inferiority, and alien origin, appearance, and culture.

More recently, slow recognition of the universal application of democratic principles and civil rights, humanitarian values, and ethnic and racial tolerance and acceptance, on the one hand, and significantly increasing resistance by enslaved, colonized, or discriminated peoples and their liberal supporters, on the other hand (Grant, 1968; Marable, 1984; Robinson, 1983), produced an ideological and political countermovement that today seems to prevail in Europe and North America. The analyses of this chapter should show whether this liberal challenge of the long history of political racism has indeed resulted in fundamentally different political ideologies, discourses, and practices.

The very formulation of this research aim suggests implausibility. As we shall see in their discourses analyzed in this chapter, most contemporary Western politicians, including most conservative ones, define themselves as heirs to the values of the Enlightenment, as proponents of racial and ethnic tolerance, as champions of equal rights, and as opponents of colonialism and racism.

These emphatic claims suggest a powerful moral consensus, and there is evidence suggesting that not only their text and talk but also their decisions and actions regarding immigrants and minorities at least partly reflect this prevailing ideology. Thus, there can be little doubt that dominant political discourse and action of today have significantly changed from those prevalent in 1950, 1850, or 1750. On the other hand, political advances do not preclude reaction, and ideological change does not exclude continuity. To highlight this change and continuity, let us summarize some of the properties of past political discourse. Part of our summary is based on the detailed history of political racism provided by Lauren (1988).

From Antiquity to Modern Times

It is appropriate to start a historical survey with a brief mention of the powerful sociocultural and political influence of European antiquity. We recalled above the well-known fact that Ancient Greece and Rome were slave societies. Obviously, they could be such only with the consent and active participation of their legislatures and political leaders (Finley, 1980). A lively slave trade, as well as warfare, conquest, and imperialism extending toward the Middle East and North Africa, often led to the enslavement of both European and non-European "barbarians." Slaves (and women) had few rights in these early democracies. Slaves were property, although property "with a soul" (Aristotle, quoted in Finley, 1980, p. 73). The very notions of slave, slavery, and enslavement are part and parcel of the origins of Western culture.

On the other hand, there has been some controversy about whether Greek and Roman slavery, and more general political, social, and cultural responses to the encounters with Asian and African peoples, should be categorized as racist. Through a study of art objects representing Africans, and on the basis of an analysis of historical, literary, and other texts, Snowden (1983), among others, concludes that such is not the case. Whereas ethnocentrism is seldom absent, even in antiquity, and although occasional derogatory or bizarre remarks about the "strange" appearance of Africans may be found in many texts of ancient writers, there seems to be little color-based prejudice against African and Asian peoples. Note though that early forms of anti-Semitism appeared already in the work of classical writers such as Seneca and Tacitus (Poliakov, 1977).

Between the fall of the Roman empire and the European Middle Ages, the overall picture of Asians and Africans largely remained framed in the terms already set by Greek and especially Roman philosophers and historians. Crucial for European perceptions during this period were the centuries of Arab-Muslim occupation of Spain, generally experienced as an alien threat to Europe and Christianity. The influence of this experience can also be traced in the long tradition of Orientalism in literature and academia (Said, 1979). Its modern versions appear in contemporary European and U.S. reactions and attitudes following, if not working up to, the Oil Crisis in 1973, the Middle East conflict, and the Gulf War in 1991 (Chomsky, 1987, 1992). Similar observations may be made about the continuous military, political, economic, religious, and cultural confrontation with the Turks and the Ottoman Empire after the Middle Ages.

Five Hundred Years of Western "Civilization"

Despite these continuities, both in the cultural and political realms, of a long tradition of European conflict with and portrayal of its Asian and African neighbors, the major historical watershed of present-day Western dominance, ideology, and political decision making is, of course, 1492. This year not only marked the "discovery" of the Americas, but also the beginning of large-scale European conquest, slavery, imperialism, and colonialism. These forms of dominance were supported and legitimated by military, political, religious, commercial, and cultural attitudes and ideologies in which the assumed inferiority of the Others played an increasingly explicit and systematic role until the mid-twentieth century (A. J. Barker, 1978; Jordan, 1968; Lauren, 1988; Todorov, 1988). Although we have little direct evidence of the ethnic or racial attitudes and discourse of the leading political elites of the time, their power or influence was generally such that their own attitudes and practices regarding non-Europeans must have helped to shape both ideological as well as military and economic European dominance.

Although such was the consensus, early resistance against European oppression and exploitation was not uncommon. Protests against military, commercial, and religious conquest and exploitation of the Americas had been heard in early sixteenth-century Spain, for example, by the jurist Francisco de Vitoria and the well-known priest Bartholomé de Las Casas (Lauren, 1988). Note though that this form of dissent was rather an exception in the Church of the time, whose attitudes about the Other were primarily defined in terms of the oppositions between Christians and heathens (see also Wood, 1990). Similarly, toward the end of the eighteenth century, political and religious opposition against slavery and the slave trade made itself increasingly felt, although for a variety of reasons that vacillated between libertarian and humanitarian values and political and commercial opportunism. Also, resistance against the slave trade did not always imply more general opposition against racial supremacist attitudes and practices. More generally, then, the period between 1492 and 1792, when seen and judged from our present perspective, showed a mixture of curiosity, ignorance, Eurocentrism, prejudice, and attitudes about sociocultural African inferiority developed to legitimate the slave trade and slavery (A. J. Barker, 1978).

Despite ideological transformations associated with the changing forms of slavery, colonialism, and imperialism, and despite the new (but not always positive) attitudes about other peoples emerging from the Enlightenment and the French Revolution, inherent attitudes about the Others did not fundamentally change between the fifteenth and nineteenth centuries. White, European supremacy became the moral and political consensus of the time in Spain, Portugal, France, Britain, and the Netherlands, as well as in their overseas colonies (Lauren, 1988, p. 19). These attitudes were often supported by scholarly views of the differences of the races, for example, by such philosophers as Hume and Diderot, among others (M. Barker, 1981; Lauren, 1988, pp. 22-23; Poliakov, 1974; Todorov, 1988; see also Chapter 5).

The resistance against the slave trade only gained enough political momentum in the early nineteenth century, for example, when at the Vienna Congress in 1815 the colonial powers at least promised to "soon" stop it, although the United States, itself increasingly involved in this trade, consistently refused to sign any such treaty (Lauren, 1988, p. 29). Decades were to go by before slavery was effectively abolished in the Americas, usually after revolutions, struggles for independence waged against European colonial powers, or other conflicts or economic pressures that made slavery less attractive. However, the abolition of slavery neither ended colonialism nor did it coincide with a fundamentally different ideology about non-European peoples. On the contrary, the second half of the nineteenth century saw increased ideological elaboration of white supremacist attitudes, supported by pseudoscientific arguments associated with social Darwinism and related ideologies (Barkan, 1992; M. Barker, 1981; Chase, 1975; Geiss, 1988).

Whereas the European countries already had earlier laws of racial exclusion and segregation, such as the *Code Noir* in France, the United States continued its effective subjection of blacks as well as other immigrant minority groups. White union resistance against immigration and alleged competition fostered political reactions, like that of President Rutherford Hayes, who was neither the first nor the last president to view peoples of color in this way, nor the last politician to see immigration as a threat and an invasion:

1. I am satisfied that the present Chinese labor invasion . . . is pernicious and should be discouraged. Our experience with the weaker races—the Negroes and Indians, for example—is not encouraging. (Lauren, 1988, p. 38)

The other white-dominated former colonies, such as Canada and Australia, followed the United States in restricting nonwhite immigration, in a period when the European powers further extended their empires in Asia and especially in Africa. The political statements expressing the prevailing ideology between 1850 and 1950, as well as the practices implementing them, could fill an encyclopedia and provide the foundation for many of the racial and colonial policies of the early twentieth century. Earl Grey, still known for giving his name to a special blend of Indian tea, formulated the gist of this prevailing political ideology of his time as follows:

2. The colored people are generally looked upon by the Whites as an inferior race, whose interest ought to be systematically regarded when they

come into competition with our own, and who ought to be governed mainly with a view to the advantages of the superior race. (Lauren, 1988, p. 40)

Thus, well into the twentieth century, the growing popularity of explicit racist ideologies, usually supported by scholars in biology, anthropology, and other disciplines (see Chapter 5), contributed to a dominant consensus about the "racial struggle," especially directed against Jews in Europe, as well as against Asian, African, and Native American peoples. Such views were commonly shared by those in power, such as President Theodore Roosevelt, who favored a racial war against

3. [S]cattered savage tribes, whose life was but a few degrees less meaningless, squalid, and ferocious than that of the wild beasts. [such a war would be] for the benefit of civilization and the interests of mankind. (Lauren, 1988, p. 48)

Obviously, the prevailing political attitudes about non-Europeans had hardly become more tolerant, egalitarian, and respectful since the end of the Middle Ages. On the contrary, slavery, continuing segregation, colonialism, and imperialism only made them more detailed, more explicit, and more radical as race awareness grew among white Europeans and North Americans.

Racial exclusion and racist attitudes were no less extreme in South Africa, Australia, and New Zealand, which officially and explicitly opted to remain "white" and blocked any immigration from the "colored races," while treating their nonwhite native populations with similar forms of supremacist ideologies and practices. The British High Commissioner in South Africa formulated these attitudes, as follows:

4. A political equality of white and black is impossible. The white man must rule, because he is elevated by many, many steps above the black man; steps which it will take the latter centuries to climb, and which it is quite possible that the vast bulk if the black population may never climb at all. (Lauren, 1988, p. 59)

It is apparent that if high officials could make such statements, they must have reflected both a moral consensus as well as political consent among the leading political and other elites, as the similarly racist statements and policies of President Theodore Roosevelt continued to show during his "racial wars" and his "big stick" imperialism in Central

America and the Pacific. To assuage the few feelings of guilt there were, such attitudes and practices were at best excused or legitimated with the philosophy of the "white man's burden" and with the conviction that a mission of "civilization" was called for.

It took a world war to shatter at least some of these white attitudes. Thus, after the First World War in 1919, and despite much administrative and political harassment by the governments of most Western nations of the non-European participants from all around the globe, the first Pan African Congress was held in Paris. Racial equality increasingly became a worldwide political issue, which only Japan had the political power to insist on when the nearly all-white League of Nations was formed. Virtually all white Western nations, however, stonewalled any claim about the equality of the races.

In more or less blatant terms, political leaders such as President Wilson, British Foreign Secretary Balfour (see also Said, 1979, p. 31 ff.), and especially Prime Minister William Hughes of Australia, among others, explicitly emphasized their belief in white supremacy (Lauren, 1988, p. 84), beliefs that were consistent with those formulated in much modern scholarship in the inter-war period (Barkan, 1992). One U.S. senator said he could not imagine sitting around the same table and making decisions with a couple of "niggers" from India, Liberia, and other nations of the League. It was not surprising, therefore, that most Western nations were adamantly opposed to human rights and equality of all members of the League of Nations; nonetheless, there was strong public opinion, as well as opposition by the Japanese and other non-Western nations, that kept insisting on these principles after the war.

However, these counterforces did not prevail, and racial equality and self-determination of the many colonized peoples remained on the agenda until after the next world war, when universal loathing of the Nazi Holocaust of the Jews made resistance against racial oppression and genocide no longer a morally and politically viable position. Before that, however, political, Christian, and "scientific" racism and anti-Semitism reached its culmination in legitimating ethnic and racial inequality and oppression, directed both against the Jews and against the colonized peoples and immigrants of other continents.

After World War II

Although the Second World War shook the foundations of empire and colonialism, and the foundation of the United Nations required declarations of human rights and equality, the political leaders of the West were hardly prepared to change their fundamental attitudes. Churchill, for instance, noted for his racist feelings, simply declared that there was little reason to be "apologetic about Anglo-Saxon superiority. We are superior" (Lauren, 1988, p. 139). Similar attitudes continued to be voiced by whites elsewhere in the commonwealth, while blacks and their white supporters in the United States, among whom Eleanor Roosevelt played a prominent role, vainly called for desegregation and a ban on discrimination. Finally, when human rights principles could no longer be excluded from international treaties and charters, the Western nations did all they could to prevent them from being applied to their subjects in the colonies or their citizens of color at home, for instance in South Africa and the United States. Thus, from the inception of the United Nations, the most powerful Western nations effectively sabotaged the human rights and freedom from discrimination and racism that were being demanded by the majority of the world.

Decades of increasing resistance, such as international decolonization and the Civil Rights Movement in the United States, were necessary to further weaken this bastion of white Western attitudes and practices of supremacy. Ironically, in this historical perspective, and borrowing their own common qualification of other young nations, most Western nations appear to be no more than "fledgling" democracies, whose tradition of equal rights for all can be measured in only a few decades. They had to be shown the way by those women and men of color who not too long ago had been subjected to vicious forms of discrimination, derogation, and other forms of Western ethnocentrism and racism (Carmichael & Hamilton, 1967; Marable, 1984, 1985; Morris, 1984; Weisbrot, 1991).

Therefore, it is not surprising, as this chapter will show for political discourse about racial and ethnic affairs in the 1980s, that not only contemporary attitudes of white political elites may have changed under the pressure of worldwide moral and political opposition against white supremacist attitudes and policies, but also that such changes could hardly be fundamental in a situation in which both Western nations and their white populations still withheld power in virtually all political, social, economic, and cultural domains.

The issue of racism and colonialism posed in international debate became a primary issue at home, especially when an increasing number of people in the South of the world began to return the favor of the earlier white invasion of their nations—and migrated to the territories of the old imperial and colonial powers. It is in this perspective, then, and against this background of a long history of white racist ideologies and practices, that we shall examine the present situation in Europe and the United States. We shall focus in particular on the contemporary political consensus on ethnic affairs, as it is formulated by leading politicians in the respective parliaments of these states.

CONTEMPORARY POLITICS
AND RACISM IN EUROPE

We have witnessed, since World War II and especially since the decade of international decolonization and the Civil Rights Movement in the United States, a slow development toward more tolerant and even multicultural attitudes, discourses, and practices in politics. However, racism is still a fact of life in contemporary Europe and North America, and politicians are undeniably part of that problem (Miles, 1989; Omi & Winant, 1986). This does *not* mean that the majority of the mainstream political elites still advocate explicitly racist positions, as is the case for some extremist right-wing parties in most European countries (Ford, 1990), such as National Front in Great Britain (Billig, 1978; Fielding, 1981), the Front National (FN) in France (Tristan, 1987; Wieviorka, 1992), or the *Republikaner* in Germany (Butterwegge & Isola, 1991; Jaschke, 1990). On the contrary, most governments and most mainstream parties emphasize their distance toward explicit racist attitudes and practices, if only because these are generally against the law.

This book does not, however, focus on explicit right-wing racism, but on the much more subtle and indirect forms of ethnic and racial dominance as they are reproduced by elites operating within the framework of the consensus. This implies that the political elites must be involved in the reproduction of this system of ethnic or racial dominance. They do so in many apparently innocent and impeccable ways. Thus, they may legislate against further immigration because of unemployment, serious housing shortage, or other "good" socioeconomic reasons. However, such legislation may particularly affect, directly or indirectly, immigrants from non-European countries more than other immigrants, which effectively means that people of color are discriminated against. The same may be true for residence rights, social welfare, employment, education, political organization, and so on. Politicians may also be involved in the reproduction of racism by default, for instance, by

failing to legislate against the many forms of either subtle or more
blatant discrimination.

Before we examine some of these more subtle forms of political
participation, including those of opposition and resistance, in the com-
plimentary systems of racism and anti-racism, we may briefly summarize some findings of the second *Report of the Committee of Inquiry
into Racism and Xenophobia* of the European parliament (Ford, 1990).
This report is based on more or less official documents and declarations,
sometimes even by representatives of the administration of the respective EC countries. We may therefore assume that it deals with the tip of
the racist iceberg in Europe, while also mitigating the nature and the
extent of racism. Moreover, given the prevalent political as well as
commonsense definition of racism in terms of explicit, supremacist
racist attitudes, intentional discrimination, and overt aggression, the
report virtually disregards the many forms of everyday racism (Essed,
1991). Our summary of this report specifically focuses on activities and
reactions of politicians and political organizations.

The political situation in Europe at the end of the 1980s was characterized by the presence of extremist right-wing parties that are commonly
considered (except by themselves) as being racist. These parties formulate
blatantly derogatory opinions about minorities and immigrants, especially
those of a different color or culture; promulgate involuntary repatriation;
want to abolish many of their elementary civil rights, and so on. These
parties have a rather uneven constituency. In most countries they may get
only a small percentage of the vote in national parliamentary elections, but
in some cities or regions they may occasionally get more than 50% or 60%
of the vote. A recent poll in France showed that one-third of the population
announced they would vote for Le Pen's Front National; however, more
than half of the people agreed with the ideas of this party. The same is true
for the Flemish Block in Belgium and the "Liberal" party of Haider in
Austria, among others. That is, the actual support for such parties may even
be larger, since many people who agree with their anti-foreigner slogans
may nevertheless continue to vote for a mainstream party for various
reasons. On the other hand, many people may only vote for such parties
out of protest against mainstream parties and/or out of frustration about
unemployment or other socioeconomic problems. The racist parties' attributing virtually all socioeconomic problems to minorities or immigrants is
the illusionary solution voters may be attracted to.

Whereas the presence and influence of such racist parties is an
increasingly serious problem in Europe, this problem would be much

less consequential if such parties did not affect the political positions of other parties. Whether out of competition for voters or for other political reasons, especially—but not exclusively—the more conservative parties may tend to adopt some of the anti-minority attitudes of the extreme right, as has been the case most notably for the conservative parties in Great Britain, France, and Germany. We saw in Chapter 1 what such leaders as Bush, Thatcher, Chirac, Giscard d'Estaing, and others have to say about minorities and immigrants. It comes as no surprise that the Front National's leader, Le Pen, could triumphantly declare in 1992 that the Front's ideas were now generally shared, and that some of the other parties now overtook the FN on the right. Reinforced by this success, his party reacted to this political development by formulating a new program in the fall of 1991 that proposed a blatantly racist system of apartheid, forced repatriation, and unequal rights for minorities and immigrants.

Another problem is that whereas radical left-wing parties have always been either prohibited or harassed by the authorities, such is not, or is seldom the case for extremist right-wing parties. Party freedom, extant laws, and other reasons of state and opportunism militate against their prohibition. Indeed, for the other mainstream parties, the extreme right has many uses. First, as long as there are extremist right-wing parties, the conservative parties may declare opposition to them and imply that they are therefore not racist. In actual practice, they may favor more or less the same policies, though packaged in more palatable language. Second, as is especially the case for large-scale immigration of refugees, as in Germany since 1990, the slogans and violent activities of such right-wing parties or their street gangs may be an effective unofficial means to reduce such immigration. Third, such parties or their ideas may be used as a threat against the liberals or the Left: If you are too liberal in your legislation, especially in matters of immigration or Affirmative Action, the people may move en masse to such racist parties. And finally, leftist parties themselves often do not favor the prohibition of racist parties, because they may—not entirely without grounds—fear that, given the present power relations, their own parties might well be the second, if not the first target of prohibition. The common official reason for failing to prohibit racist parties is the argument that prohibition would force them to go underground. It takes little argument to see that if that were an effective means to combat racist organizations, we might as well make the Mafia legitimate.

It is against this background that the EP Report (Ford, 1990) finds that for instance in Belgium mayors of several cities actively oppose the settlement, housing, or education of legal immigrant families and their children. These mayors may even describe immigrants as barbarians, or have so-called information brochures distributed in schools in which non-European immigrants, especially Muslims, are characterized as terrorists, fundamentalists, or drug addicts. Most of these policies and practices are simply condoned by national politicians, parties or state organizations, and the courts. As is the case for police harassment of minorities, these and related racist practices are virtually never prosecuted or otherwise officially combated. Indeed, as elsewhere in Europe, tolerance is nowhere as clear as in the tolerance of racism. The political results of this lax attitude toward racism appeared in the 1991 elections: The racist party *Vlaams Blok* (Flemish Block) dramatically increased its constituency, becoming the largest party in the city of Antwerp. Similar stories about local politicians are reported from other countries, for instance from France and Denmark. One Danish mayor limited entry of foreigners to his city in order to promote integration of resident minorities and to prevent further racism. We shall examine such familiar argumentative moves of Apparent Empathy in more detail in our study of parliamentary discourse. Finally, in Sweden a local referendum was organized in which two-thirds of the population voted against the settlement of further refugees.

Several countries, such as Denmark, Italy, and Germany, do not have special antidiscrimination legislation, and are not inclined to introduce such legal means to combat discrimination, despite the binding obligations under the U.N. Charter and agreements. Their leading politicians declare that present criminal law is sufficient, as the German representative declared at the hearing organized by the EP committee:

> The Federal Government considers that the legal instruments in force are sufficient to counter undesirable developments effectively. It did not therefore take any special legislative measures in connection with the adoption of the declaration against racism and xenophobia.

France originally resisted further legislation after its 1972 law, but the events in 1990, such as repeated attacks against citizens of North African descent, as well as the scandal of the desecration of Jewish graves in Carpentras, led to a law against racism that in many respects is the most explicit in Europe. For instance, people convicted on the basis of this law may lose their political rights and are not allowed to become civil servants. The Netherlands has no special antidiscrimination law focusing on minorities either, apart from antidiscrimination paragraphs in criminal law, but there is an equal opportunity bill that is intended to cover some of the issues. Not being a member, Switzerland has not even ratified the U.N. Convention against racism.

Perhaps with the exception of Ireland, whose poverty has not attracted many immigrants, virtually all European countries and their politicians are part of the problem of European racism. The major conclusions of these and related findings are: (a) There are substantial and growing extremist right-wing parties, whose uninhibited and unprohibited racist propaganda, as well as media coverage, reach millions and influence many. (b) There is a general reluctance, if not a more or less opportunistic policy, of the mainstream parties not to prohibit or otherwise combat such right-wing organizations and their actions. If they do, they do not do so energetically. Incidentally, not only politics but also the courts in most countries are generally lenient toward racist harassment and discrimination, sometimes even open racial attacks. (c) More generally, the struggle against ethnic prejudice, discrimination, and racism seldom has political priority in Europe. Indeed, there is little funding for anti-racist organizations, institutions, or research. (d) The conservative mainstream parties particularly adopt several of the tenets of racist parties. (e) As we shall see in more detail below, political debate about several controversial ethnic issues, especially immigration, cultural differences, and Affirmative Action programs, is such that extant stereotypes and prejudices are confirmed rather than combated. (f) EC policies and practices regarding immigration more generally define non-European immigrants as unwelcome citizens, if not as illegal aliens (for further details, see also "Europe," 1991).

PARLIAMENTARY DEBATES

To further examine the discourse dimensions of the politics of race and ethnicity, we analyzed a number of parliamentary debates in the United States, Great Britain, France, Germany, and the Netherlands. First we established which prominent debates about immigration, refugees, or various ethnic issues had taken place during the 1980s, and a selection of congressional or parliamentary records was collected from the U.S. House of Representatives and Senate, the British House of Commons, the French Assemblée Nationale, the German Bundestag, and the Dutch Tweede Kamer (Second Chamber of Parliament). For further background information, we also used records of parliamentary debates in Italy, but these are not analyzed in this chapter. For the United States, news items in the press about the congressional debate on the Civil Rights Bills of 1990 and 1991 were also collected and analyzed. To complete our insight into political decision making, we also collected, in the Netherlands, policy documents, public speeches of the Prime Minister and other Cabinet members, as well as other political documents about ethnic affairs.

As we have indicated earlier, it is impossible to carry out a detailed discourse analysis of the thousands of pages of this corpus of political text and talk about ethnic affairs. Therefore, we selected those passages that more or less explicitly deal with attributed properties of immigrants or resident minorities, as well as those about discrimination, racism, and general policies and principles of political action regarding immigration and minority affairs. For those passages, we focused primarily on the persuasive dimension of text and talk, that is, on argumentative strategies, style, and rhetoric.

Unfortunately, there is no straightforward method to prove that either such a selection or our analyses are representative. Our qualitative approach, however, does not aim at such quantitative proof. We are interested in what Members of Parliament (Congress) say, and how they do so, but not how often. As we may expect, based on our analysis of other forms of elite discourse, most politicians, most of the time, will not engage in explicitly derogatory remarks about minorities or immigrants. However, occasionally, more or less implicitly or indirectly, some remarks will show what politicians actually think of minority groups, or which statements they think are politically warranted or opportune in their persuasive rhetoric.

As for our other inferences from text and talk, there may be a theoretical and methodological problem here. That is, when politicians claim they are not racist, say they have nothing against minorities, or make positive remarks about minorities, we may well not take such expressions at face value, but might analyze them primarily as rhetorical strategies, such as disclaimers or positive self-presentation, and not as transparent expressions of true underlying attitudes. On the other hand, when they *do* say negative things about immigrants or minorities, we *do* tend to believe what they say and make much more direct inferences about underlying social representations. This may seem a biased procedure, which seeks to establish that politicians are really racists, maybe deep down, whatever they say.

However, this is not the case. In this book, and in our other work on the reproduction of racism, we are not interested in showing or proving whether individuals are racist. We are generally interested in the properties of text and talk about other ethnic or racial groups or peoples. Second, we are more generally interested in the social system, processes, activities, and cognitions involved in the reproduction (and the challenge) of racism. Thus, some remark by some politician may be interpreted, *in its specific context*, as characteristic of a style, topos, rhetorical figure, or argument that generally may be interpreted as a contribution to the reproduction (or challenge) of racism. That is, interpretations depend on context, whereas generalizations require comparisons—for instance, with other statements, with other politicians, or with other elite groups.

Also, there are more specific reasons and methods underlying our interpretations and evaluations. For instance, if a politician says something negative about minorities or immigrants, we assume that there is no valid psychological or social reason why such an overt statement would *not* express underlying opinions or attitudes. Although an expression of xenophobic or racist attitudes may appeal to some voters, it will be assumed that this very political strategy is racist, and that there is no point in assuming that such politicians may not mean what they say. In other words, even if politicians would only derogate minorities or immigrants because of election campaign tactics, we assume that they can do so only if their underlying attitudes are consistent with such a strategy. This is not the case for positive statements or denials because they may be well-known moves in strategies of face-keeping or positive self-presentation, given prevailing norms and values of official tolerance.

Our criterion for distinguishing true from apparent statements against racism, then, is first of all that true anti-racism is consistent, across contexts, and backed up with arguments; whereas face-keeping moves are typically introductions to otherwise negative statements, backed up with further negative arguments, about minorities or ethnic relations or, indeed, about anti-racism. In sum, both contextual and textual structures, possibly including style and rhetoric, tell seemingly similar expressions apart. However, this does not mean that there is always a clear-cut division between the two: There are gradual transitions, as is the case for all sociopolitical positions and their discursive expression. We shall discuss other methodological implications and complications during our analysis.

Finally, our analysis should reflect the properties of the specific discursive genre of parliamentary debates. Contributions to such debates, although spoken in parliament, generally do not have the properties of spontaneous ongoing talk, such as hesitations, false starts, repairs, repetition, ungrammatical sentences, simplified syntax, lack of local coherence, and so on. Often, if not mostly, such contributions are read, possibly with spontaneous deviations, from a prepared written text. That is, parliamentary discourse is generally planned, fixed, and actually formulated in advance. Only in some cases, do we witness more spontaneous, ad hoc, "on line" dialogues in parliament.

Parliamentarians also know, that their talk is "for the record," and they act accordingly. They do not speak merely to argue for or against a policy, a bill, or other political activities, they also make official statements that reflect party positions, which are to be inserted into the records and which may be quoted in the news media. That is, their contributions, which occasionally are even changed in the final version of the records, are those for which they may be held politically and morally responsible. This is especially crucial in the domain of ethnic affairs since the controversiality and sensitive nature of most ethnic topics require that the politicians be aware of what they can say, and what should not be said. In other words, control and monitoring of self and others are crucial in parliamentary texts and talk about ethnic and immigration affairs, and this will particularly affect the ways opinions are formulated. Hence, there is generally no question of spontaneous "errors" when delegates talk about ethnic affairs, although there are examples where such is not the case (see also Wodak, Nowak, Pelikan, Gruber, De Cillia, & Mitten, 1990).

One of the ways to validate our findings is by comparison to previous analyses of parliamentary debates about ethnic affairs. Unfortunately, there is virtually no scholarly research on this topic. One of the few detailed studies of political discourse on race is the one by Reeves (1983), who studied the "racialization" and "deracialization" of British political discourse on ethnic affairs. In this study he also pays attention to earlier debates on immigration that were held in the British House of Commons through the 1960s. Interestingly, several of the rhetorical and argumentative forms he found in those earlier debates appear to have changed little during the past 20 to 30 years, regardless of whether they are used by Tories or Labour. Here is a summary of the argument forms and rhetorical modes he encountered (Reeves, 1983, p. 210):

1. *Personalized, dispositional, and agential:* Blacks are inferior or different from Whites; they are a threat, they are privileged in comparison to Whites.

2. *Abstracted social process:* Black focused, white focused, government focused.
3. *Populist.*
4. *Economic.*
5. *Pro bono publico:* to the advantage of all, Whites or Blacks.
6. *Reciprocity:* They do it, why not us; they are affected, we are affected; debit balanced against credit.
7. *Means-oriented:* Descriptive of means; procedural—correct procedure; effective—has intended effect; consistency—is internally consistent.
8. *Rhetorical modes:* Techniques of quantification, analogical transformation, ambiguity, attribution.

As we shall see in more detail in our own analysis, most of these arguments play a role in the legitimation of immigration restrictions today, and in several other countries as well, namely, by emphasizing alleged privileges or negative characteristics of immigrants, by focusing on wide popular support or on the economic necessity of the measures, or by reversal: Negative measures have positive social impact for all involved.

The Debates

To understand the debates, of which we shall examine some fragments below, we need to provide some context for each country. For our comparative and discourse analytical perspective, we do not discuss the debates individually, nor by country, but each fragment according to its structural properties, such as topic or argumentative strategy. This procedure requires a brief preliminary discussion of the debates in each country.

The Netherlands

For the Netherlands we examined not only fragments of several parliamentary discussions, but also statements made in a radio interview by Prime Minister Ruud Lubbers on new minority policy, as well as official reports on minority policy and various other documents, such as talks or declarations of Cabinet members on various occasions, as well as press interviews. The parliamentary debates focused on Refugee Policy (apart from smaller interventions, notably the larger debates on April 9 and October 15, 1987), proposed changes—stricter border security; judicial competence—in the Aliens Acts (December 15, 1988; February 16, 1989; January 30, 1990); the threat to Salman Rushdie (February 21, 1989); the proposed treaty of Schengen, agreed upon by

several Western European countries and aiming to coordinate actions
against crime and against illegal immigration and refugees (June 28,
1989); and finally, changes in the General Welfare Act (May 22, 1990),
and the general Minority Policy Action Program (February 19, 1990).

Apart from an occasional debate on minority policies, especially in
the field of education, employment, social affairs, and justice, we see
that most of the recent debates have focused on immigration, and
especially on refugees (see also Okojie, 1992). These debates are
generally rather technical, in the sense that they discuss which are the
precise rules and regulations, police tasks and competencies, and other
measures that, essentially, limit the number of refugees and other
immigrants, while also streamlining the procedures for those who are
actually admitted to the country. The political controversies on the
various minority issues are rather moderate, regardless of whether the
government is Center-Right (a coalition of Christian Democrats and
Liberal Conservatives) during the last years of the 1980s, or whether
the Christian Democrats are joined by the Social Democrats, as from
1989. Apart from some critical parliamentary quibbles on individual
harsh cases (e.g., specific refugee categories), the overall agreement on
basic principles shows a broad consensus. In fact, only the small
Green-Left Party is usually more critical of what it sees as the miserly
attitudes, the inhospitality, and the growing strictness and intolerance
of the administration and of the bureaucracy, if not of the population at
large. That is the only political group that rather consistently takes an
anti-racist position in these debates, although individual members of
other parties, such as the social democratic Labour Party, may similarly
take an decisively critical stance against more explicit forms of discrimination and racism.

Great Britain

According to a computer search on immigration, ethnic affairs, and
related issues, the British House of Commons does not discuss such
topics very often. Thus, between 1983 and 1990 we examined the
Hansard records of only a handful of general debates and a few smaller
discussions. For instance, on April 16, 1985, there was a special debate
on the national affair around Ray Honeyford, Headmaster of a Bradford
school, who was suspended, then reinstated, but finally let go because
of his controversial, if not racist writing on multi-ethnic education. We
shall come back to this situation in the chapter on the media, because
the media paid much attention to this affair in 1985. Also in Great

Britain, most debates are about immigration (February 4, 1985; July 23, 1985; March 26, 1986; March 26, 1987; February 16, 1988; June 20, 1989; May 15, 1990); about asylum seekers or refugees (March 3, 1987; May 26, 1989); and about DNA testing of immigrants (July 5, 1989). One debate dealt with the education of minority children (March 14, 1985).

As is the case for the Netherlands, Germany, and other European countries, we see that the debates in Great Britain during the 1980s increasingly focus on the various measures for the control of refugees and other immigrants. DNA testing is a prominent example. Few debates either pay attention to the principles and foundations of minority policy or deal with the many issues and problems with which minority groups in Britain are confronted. As elsewhere, with the exception of France, there is virtually no discussion of discrimination and racism. The overall tone, style, and argumentative strategy in the House of Commons are considerably more forceful than those in the Netherlands, where truly harsh words are quite uncommon.

Germany

For Germany we selected a few significant debates in the Bundestag about related issues, such as the associated discussions about the New Regulations of Alien Rights, a Bill for an Amendment to the Aliens Act, another amendment to the Asylum-Procedure Act, and so on (February, 9, 1990; April 26, 1990). In these debates minority policies, immigration policies, and refugee policies are increasingly mingled, but here the primary focus is one of control: how to limit influx, or who can or will be sent back under what conditions. Whereas the coalition government maintains that the new proposals improve the situation of minorities and immigrants, the opposition—with the support of virtually all major social organizations (churches, unions, minority organizations, and so on)—insists that the amendments are weakening their position.

The overall style of these debates is somewhat similar to that in the British House of Commons, with much open aggression, constant interruption, cat calls, derision, ridicule, and protests against the respective parties, namely, the governing coalition of Christian Democrats (CDU-CSU) and liberal conservatives (FDP), on the one hand, and the social-democrat SPD and the Grüne (Greens) opposition parties, on the other hand. As we shall see below, especially the critical remarks of the Greens Party usually lead to furious reactions from the more conservative Right.

France

Although there are many similarities with other parliamentary debates in Europe, French debates are nevertheless quite unique as far as the topics are concerned. During the presidency of Mitterand in the 1980s, there were several immigration bills of different (socialist or centrist-conservative) governments, where the socialists consistently took a somewhat more lenient position, and the conservatives a much stricter stand on immigration control. In particular, the presence in the Assemblée of the racist and very vocal Front National dramatically changed the nature, the style, and the general tone of the debate on ethnic affairs and immigration. Thus, for the centrist and conservative parties it is difficult to either attack the socialists or defend their own policies while distancing themselves from the explicitly racist Right.

Most debates are headed by the recurring name *Conditions d'entrée et de séjour des étrangers en France* (Entry and residence conditions for aliens in France), and are occasioned by bills that keep changing the terms of immigration. (July 9-11, 15-16, 1986 [the Loi "Pascua"]; August 8, May 29, 30, June 2, 1989). Most remarkable is the unique Bill of July 13, 1990, called the *Loi tendant à reprimer tout acte raciste, antisémite ou xenophobe* (Bill aiming to repress any racist, anti-Semitic or xenophobic act) (debated on May 2 and June 28, 1990), the only explicitly anti-racist bill in Western Europe. This bill not only prohibits, in a detailed way, all forms of discrimination and racism, including revisionist denials of the Holocaust (also prohibited in Germany), but also has clear sanctions against violations, such as restrictions of political rights of politicians. As might be expected, this bill is violently opposed not only by the Front National, but also by the conservative parties, which specifically oppose what they see as censorship of the press. The bill was occasioned by the continuous attacks against and assassinations of citizens of North African origin, as well as the desecration of Jewish graves in the spring of 1990.

The United States

From the United States, we analyzed the debates in the House of Representative on the Civil Rights Bills of 1990 (August 2 and 3) and 1991, the first being vetoed by President George Bush (a veto that could not be overridden by a two-thirds majority). The latter bill focused not only on discrimination in employment of minorities, but also on employment of women, especially in regard to compensation regulations in discrimination cases. Both bills were occasioned by a number of recent decisions of the Supreme Court that effectively turned back the clock on earlier, more liberal antidiscrimination law (such as *Griggs,* 1971). Although the 1991 bill was adopted by Congress, it was also threatened with a presidential veto, but a compromise bill was worked out and adopted in the fall of 1991. Republican opposition, as well as President Bush's objections, focused entirely on the question of whether these bills were or were not quota bills, in the sense that stricter legislation on discrimination would force employers to "hire by the numbers" to avoid costly litigation. Since quotas were also clearly rejected by the Democratic backers of the bills, it was relatively easy for them to meet the opposition by introducing special articles that explicitly prohibit quotas.

The Analysis

Parliamentary debates as well as other political discourse about ethnic affairs generally have persuasive functions: Speakers try to convince their audience within or outside of parliament that their position on some issue is well founded, reasonable, or otherwise acceptable, or, conversely, they try to show why opposed positions are not. To do so, they have recourse to various argumentative moves and strategies, they select specific lexical items or make use of rhetorical figures that emphasize the points they make. Interestingly, despite a wide variety of possible topics, issues, or positions that may be involved in such cases, the range of persuasive strategies is rather stereotypical. In the same way as ethnic affairs tend to be discussed within the confines of stereotypical topics, the arguments and persuasive strategies may also be rather stereotypical, even across national boundaries.

Our analysis focuses on the major argumentative and semantic moves and rhetorical ploys within an overall persuasive framework. More specifically we analyze those moves that seem to be typical of parliamentary debates on ethnic affairs anywhere in the Western world. Occasionally, however, we shall also focus on other discursive properties, such as lexical style or speech acts. Since most texts are read, and offer few examples of spontaneous dialogical interaction, we shall pay little attention to the interactional or conversational aspects of parliamentary debates.

Examples from Dutch, French, and German parliaments have been translated into English, usually as literally as possible in order to maintain their stylistic and rhetorical flavor. Unfortunately, however,

some of the more subtle details of formulation are lost in these translations, and we therefore focus on meaning and argumentative strategy,
rather than on form. Examples that occur in running text are marked by
double quotes; all others appear in separate paragraphs. Each example
is followed by the following information: country, speaker, date, and
page number in the parliamentary record, and where relevant, by information about the party affiliation of the speaker. Unless otherwise
indicated, the sources are always the following:

Netherlands: Handelingen, Tweede Kamer der Staten-Generaal

France: Journal Officiel. Débats de l'Assemblée Nationale, Compte Rendu
    Intégral

Germany: Deutscher Bundestag, Stenographischer Bericht

Great Britain: House of Commons, Weekly Hansard

United States: Congressional Record, House of Representatives; Senate.

Positive Self-Presentation: Nationalist Rhetoric

Parliaments are the prime setting for nationalist rhetoric. Pride, self-
glorification, positive comparisons with other countries, and related
forms of positive self-presentation are common features in the political
discourse of representatives. Especially in debates about immigration
and ethnic affairs in general, it is important to show that Our party, Our
country, Our people, are humane, benevolent, hospitable, tolerant, and
modern. Such affirmations would be a natural self-defense tactic if there
were attacks on or explicit doubts about these civic virtues; however,
we also find them when no such attacks or doubts have been voiced.
That is, they may function as a defense against potential doubts or
possible objections, or—as we shall see later—they may be used to
block negative inferences about negative things said about immigrants
or minorities. Following are typical examples from all five countries.
    Let us begin with a stylistically rather confused statement made by
Dutch Prime Minister, Mr. Ruud Lubbers, during a notorious radio
interview that would occasion a later parliamentary debate. Lubbers
addresses a new minority policy, and also speaks rather marginally
about "expressions" of discrimination:

5. [E]xpressions that aren't good, and that do not suit us Dutch, with our
fundamentally democratic feeling, which after all we have. (The Netherlands,
Mr. Lubbers, IKON Radio, March 25, 1990, Transcript from the PM's office)

In this highly controversial interview, to which we shall return several times, Mr. Lubbers argues for a "less soft" minority policy, which should stimulate minorities to take more "responsibility" in finding jobs and which might also prevent the growing resentment among white majority group members against minorities, an argument which we also shall examine shortly. He then goes on to say that there are "boundaries" of discrimination that should not be crossed. In this fragment, then, he does not merely condemn such forms of discrimination and prejudice, though in rather moderate terms (they are "not good"), he also claims that discrimination is incompatible with the "fundamentally democratic feelings" he supposes the Dutch to have. This claim of incompatibility may have several implications, such as: (a) The Dutch are generally tolerant, so that discrimination, where it occurs, is an incidental aberration of Our basic norms. (b) Most Dutch people are tolerant, but some of them are not. (c) Most Dutch condemn such expressions of discrimination. (d) We should not discriminate, because it is against our basic democratic attitudes. The basic message, however, is clear: The Dutch are basically tolerant people, and discrimination is incidental.

Compared to that of the generally less nationalist Dutch, national self-praise in other countries is often more pronounced rhetorically, as is the case in this excerpt from a speech about immigration of a Conservative MP in the British House of Commons:

> 6. I believe that we are a wonderfully fair country. We stick to the rules unlike some foreign Governments. (Great Britain, Sir John Stokes, May 15, 1990, columns 842-844)

Self-praise for British immigration policies and practices is formulated in the familiar terms of good sportsmanship ("fair," "sticking to the rules"). Negative comparison with other countries ("unlike some foreign Governments") not only lightly implies that other countries do not stick to the rules (of the so-called immigration game), but also enhances the alleged special merits of Britain. We shall later comment on the stereotypical use of "fair" in such debates, in Great Britain as well as in other countries.

In another debate on immigration, another conservative MP enacts a dialogue with someone "in the street," whom he believes would answer the following to the question of whether Great Britain is overly strict in its rules of entry: "No, over the past 25 years this country has been extraordinarily generous in letting in many people into the country"

(Great Britain, June 20, 1990, c. 390). There is no argument that this would not be the answer of most immigrants, let alone the many thousands, for instance in South Asia, who were denied entry to Great Britain. The populist use of the "voice of the man or woman in the street" will receive more analysis below.

Whereas Dutch and British self-praise may be understated, nationalist self-glorification in France is part of routine rhetoric when a new bill is being presented:

> 7. Our country has for a long time been open to foreigners, a tradition of hospitality going back, beyond the Revolution, to the *Ancien Régime*. (France, Mr. Mazeaud, July 9, 1990, p. 3049)

As is the case in the other examples, such beautiful words seem to be especially provoked by debates about immigration and ethnic minority affairs, as if implicitly—or maybe in Freudian terms, rather unconsciously—accusations or guilt have to be challenged: in this case, of being closed to foreigners and being inhospitable to refugees. Says another representative: "What characterizes a great nation, is its openness to the world and its international radiation, but it is also its capacity to welcome foreigners" (ibid., p. 3051). Obviously, such a statement is not a meaningless generalization, but specifically applied to France, in terms ("great nation") that also can be heard, as we shall see shortly, in the United States, both in Congress and generally in political discourse. In France, we would normally expect to hear about the *gloire* of France.

Grand claims like these may need historical warrants, such as "we have a long history of tolerance," an argumentative move also found in much other elite discourse about tolerance and intolerance. Indeed, hospitality and tolerance, according to this view, are not merely ad hoc, opportunistic policies, but rather the inherent national virtues of a long tradition. Interestingly, this historical sense of the French MP does not, as would be the normal case, claim to continue the just heritage of the Revolution, but also that of the *Ancien Régime*. Obviously, if such were the case, the many political opponents of this *Ancien Régime* would not have had to flee the country to, for example, the Netherlands. We see that political discourse is not effective because of the historical facts, but because of the selective, rhetorical uses that are made of such facts.

For whatever social, political, or historical reasons, contemporary political discourse in Germany, and especially the rather self-conscious debates in the Bundestag, do not seem to be exuberantly self-glorifying, despite the undoubtedly strong undercurrents of nationalism, especially on the Right. However, during the many debates about immigration and refugees during the last few years, it has often been claimed by German politicians that they see their immigration and refugee laws as the most liberal in the world, as for instance the new *Ausländergesetz* discussed in 1990:

> 8. I know no other country on this earth that gives more prominence to the rights of resident foreigners as does this bill in our country. (Germany, Mr. Hirsch, February 9, 1990, p. 16279)

True, in Western Europe, no other country has as many refugees as Germany, both because of the obvious economic attraction of Germany, occasioned by German unification and the demise of communism in Eastern Europe, as well as because of the explicit and succinct constitutional article saying that political refugees are accorded asylum. However, as far as the rights of residing minorities are concerned, there may be more doubts about this claim, especially since the bill does not exactly make the rules, regulations, and conditions for immigrants much more liberal in Germany. The leftist (Green) opposition, as we shall see shortly, simply speaks of a racist bill, whereas the social-democratic SPD, as well as numerous social organizations, also resolutely reject it. Note that the positive comparison here is not merely with other countries, but universal: "no other country on this earth," which again is not exactly the product of an international contest or of thorough independent research, but rather a ploy of political rhetoric.

Although it would be a pointless exercise to establish a rank order of degrees of nationalism or nationalist rhetoric, the following passage suggests that the United States would score quite high:

> 9. This is a nation whose values and traditions now excite the world, as we all know. I think we all have a deep pride in American views, American ideals, American government, American principle, which excite hundreds of millions of people around the world who struggle for freedom. (United States, Mr. Foley, August 2, 1990, H6768)

Again, there is a long tradition both to these claims as well as to such rhetoric, which goes back to the American Revolution, the Declaration of Independence, and similar legacies of national and nationalist pride of virtually any young nation state. In the case of the United States, however, such rhetoric and its underlying ideologies are vastly more consequential, given the economic and especially the military hegemony of the United States after the collapse of the Soviet Union. The Representative whose words we quote here is Mr. Foley, Speaker of the House; and despite his being a Democrat, he reflects some basic tenets of President's Bush ideology of a New World Order under U.S. leadership. Rather distinctive as compared to other countries, the rhetoric here stresses the key notions of "values," so dear to Reagan and Bush, as well as the main topos of U.S. rhetoric: "freedom." Whereas the claim of universality might be simple rhetorical exaggeration in the German case, here it is very serious: The U.S. administration actually and explicitly sees itself not only as the military or economic leader of the world but also, if not primarily, as its moral leader. It comes as no surprise that this statement was made on August 2, 1990—on the day Saddam Hussein's army invaded Kuwait—and other speakers aptly use the comparison with the tyranny of that despot to emphasize the freedom of U.S. institutions.

Recall that whereas virtually all European debates deal with immigration and its consequences, the U.S. debate is about the Civil Rights Bill of 1990, supported by most Democrats and opposed by most Republicans. That is, we may expect Democrats to use this and related nationalist rhetoric to emphasize the values and principles also underlying civil rights and the struggle against discrimination in employment. On the other hand, as we shall examine in more detail below, the Republicans may use the same words in order to emphasize their adherence to American "ideals," but in their case to argue against the bill and to make sure that their opposition should not be construed as a breach of the same principles. Indeed, despite claims to the contrary, their main concern is not the freedom of minorities from discrimination by employers, but rather the so-called freedom of corporate enterprise.

Disclaimers and the Denial of Racism

Why do politicians feel compelled to glorify their country or their party? Why would each debate about immigration, minorities, and civil rights be replete with exalted claims of freedom, democracy, tolerance, hospitality, and other lofty ideals of a "long tradition"? Is this mere political rhetoric as would befit a National Assembly? Is it a comprehensible expression of national pride, that is, normal posturing in international affairs or in competitive relations with other countries?

Although all this may be part of the answer, there is more at stake in this case. To understand the broader ideological, sociopolitical, and local argumentative function of such passages, we need to examine the context in which they are uttered. We already suggested that such statements seem to be responses to other, opposed claims, that is, denials of implicit or explicit accusations: You do not respect your/our values, you are not tolerant, not hospitable, and so on. Sometimes, such counter-claims are effectively made, typically by the opposition, as is often the case in the debates we analyzed.

Sometimes, however, no such accusations are made, and in that case positive self-presentation seems to express underlying norms and values of a consensus, or rather a felt inconsistency between present opinions (about policies regarding migrants, minorities) and such general norms and values, a feeling that both common sense and psychoanalytically oriented observers may describe as guilt. That is, in such cases, the grand claims of virtue and superiority are the classical introductions of disclaimers such as, "We are very tolerant toward minorities, but . . ." stereotypically followed by a negative statement about such minorities, or a defense of actions or policies that have negative consequences for minorities. As we shall see repeatedly in this study, such disclaimers are often a clear symptom of underlying prejudices or antagonistic attitudes, if not a sure sign of subtle or not so subtle racism. Let us examine such disclaimers and other moves of racism denial, in more detail.

We have earlier noted that for Dutch Prime Minister Mr. Lubbers, the new minority policy of his cabinet means that the State should stop pampering minorities, and that minorities should assume their own "responsibility." He argues that if the State, and his government in particular, have failed, it is by excessive kindness, by being too "soft" for minorities. He advocates a dual system of rights and duties:

10. Minority policy begins by taking each other totally seriously in rights, and those who live here have the right to the same rights, but those who live here also have the same obligation to fulfill their duties. (The Netherlands, Mr. Lubbers, IKON, Radio Interview, March 25, 1990)

The general structure of disclaimers in discourse about ethnic affairs usually is We do/are positive, but They do/are negative, as in We are very tolerant, but They abuse our tolerance. Or, it may start with a denial of a negative property of the own group followed by a negative property attributed to others, or followed by a negative decision, as in, We have nothing against immigrants, but we can't let everybody in. Below, we shall examine examples of these standard disclaimers, such as these Apparent Denials.

Lubbers's example, however, is somewhat more complicated. It also has the overall format of a positive property associated with Us, followed by a clause, starting with *but* and then saying or implying something negative about the Others. The positive self-description here, however, is indirect. It does not say that we are tolerant or democratic, but only that "they have rights," paternalistically implying that we have given them these rights. At the same time, this statement presupposes that They are not fulfilling their duties, although We, the State, guarantee their rights.

The way Lubbers formulates the rules of the game of dual responsibilities seems reasonable and fair: Who would deny that equal rights also means equal duties? And who would disagree that "taking each other totally seriously" is a sound policy, if not an affirmation of equality between two partners? However, this passage is not problematic because of its moral implications or policy goals, but rather because of its carefully concealed presuppositions, namely, that equal rights have been realized and that minorities are being taken seriously. In other words, the rhetoric defending this new policy effectively says something like this: We have done our best, we have done everything for you we could, but now it is your turn. And politically more relevant, it also implies: If our minority policy has failed, it is your fault because you did not fulfill your duties and you have not taken us seriously.

We see that these and similar innocent passages, which seem to express only reasonable arguments or social universality, actually are the tip of an iceberg of underlying, concealed ideological and political presuppositions. That is, these propositions could never be actually expressed, but must nevertheless be true (for the speaker) for such a passage to make political sense in the first place. Other fragments of this radio interview support such assumptions about these inferred propositions.

The classical case of this combination of positive self-presentation and negative other-presentation may regularly be read in debates about immigrants and refugees, where the conflicting ideologies of humanitarianism and political pragmatism find their typical expression in passages like the following from a Christian Democrat MP in the Second Chamber of Dutch Parliament:

11. National and international responsibility for people in emergency situations, combined with obligations that follow from agreements, are our policy principles. This should remain as it is. But of course we need to take measures, especially when it is clear that many improper, not bonafide, apparently unfounded applications for asylum are being made, and that in some cases also the problems people experience are being exploited for commercial ends. (Netherlands, Mr. Krajenbrink, April 9, 1987, p. 3622)

The first sentences express the humanitarian ideals: care and sympathy for the oppressed, as they are legally required according to international agreements, such as the Geneva refugee treaty. The *but* initiating the third sentence, however, is predictable, and the following arguments and proposals are not exactly an example of how the Netherlands should enact its "national and international responsibility" or carry out its "obligations." On the contrary, the logic of such discourses predicts restrictions, constraints, and other "measures" that effectively impair the chances of refugees or other immigrants. The use of "of course" (instead of, say, "unfortunately") implies that such a realistic policy is only natural: We are forced to be less generous because of special circumstances.

The usual argument involved might simply and straightforwardly run like this: "There are too many of them and therefore we can't handle (house, employ, etc.) them." However, this MP goes on to find additional, more serious ("especially") reasons, namely, in the realm of negative if not criminal properties and behavior attributed to asylum seekers. Such a negative portrayal is intended to warrant a tough reaction against further immigration: "It is easier, if not natural or imperative, to withhold hospitality to people who break the law."

The way this is done is by invoking what might be called the Fake Refugee Schema, an attitude consisting of largely negative opinions about what is usually called the economic refugee, a buzzword in Dutch and European political and media language for fake, while not really political, refugees. This schema features evaluative propositions about illegal entry, fake passports, lying, making several refugee/welfare applications in different countries or cities, and the activities of traffickers, seen as the merchants of human misery. Some of these elements are also expressed in this passage. The latter one, about refugees "being exploited" is especially powerful because it suggests empathy with the predicament of refugees, while at the same time associating their flight with crime and (other) foreign criminals. That is, this argument again combines positive self-presentation and negative other-presentation.

Note the use of the phrase "apparently unfounded" in the last sentence. This phrase has become the official standard phrase in political decision making and discourse about refugees in Europe. The ideology and especially the political logic and expedience of this term are compelling: Both the political and the legal bureaucracies cannot process tens of thousands (in Germany: hundreds of thousands) of refugee applications each year, and regardless of whether a refugee is economic or real, there must be another, more practical criterion of fast selection. This criterion is the intuition of the immigration officers first confronted with the refugee. If they believe that the refugee story (to which we turn below) is too flimsy, they categorize the case as an "apparently unfounded" application. Since 1990 this practical criterion, which has not (yet) been codified in law, has been used increasingly to keep most refugees and other immigrants out because it can be applied at the total discretion of the authorities. It is not an objective property of the refugee, nor even of his or her story about personal background or experiences, but merely a personal but institutionalized judgment of a representative of the state.

Denials and disclaimers need not always be that explicit. A conservative British MP formulates the following We are good, *but* They are bad comparison, this time, however, with an implied *but*:

12. The rules are reasonable and necessary. British citizenship should be a most valuable prize for anyone and it should not be granted lightly to all and sundry. (Great Britain, Sir John Stokes, May 15, 1990, columns 842-844)

That we are "reasonable and rational" is of course a standard ideological proposition of Eurocentrism. Here such a statement follows a long plea of the speaker to toughen immigration law. Again, note the British preference to describe immigration as a game, in which We play by the rules, and we award the "prize" to the winner. At the same time, there is the well-known opposition between "reasonable" and "necessary," as we also shall see in our analysis below of the ubiquitous pair, "tough, but fair." Necessity, interpreted here as political and social obligation, entails limited responsibility: We have to restrict immigration. Citizenship is the prize, which not only presupposes the metaphorical domain of games, fairness, and let-the-best-win, but also that British citizenship is not a right, and that such citizenship is something very special, which of course is a standard component of nationalist ideology. Those scrambling for the prize, and especially those who do not get it, are simply categorized and derogated as "all and sundry": That arbitrary poor people from Third World countries would dare to aspire to becoming British citizens is preposterous, and that is not the way We play the immigration game.

Positive self-presentation, face-keeping, keeping up appearances, and related strategies of impression formation in ethnic affairs discourse not only emphasize our positive properties but also, and even more emphatically, deny conceal, play down, excuse, or otherwise mitigate our negative ones, according to the standard formula: "We are not racist, *but* . . ." Tough immigration policies and other measures that have negative effects on the situation of minorities or immigrants may be seen as expressions of anti-foreigner feelings, and it is imperative that such inferences be blocked, as is the case in the following example from the British House of Commons:

> 13. I hope that people outside, whether they are black or white and wherever they come from, will recognize that these are not major changes resulting from prejudice. (Great Britain, Mr. Hanley, May 15, 1990, c. 849)

Changes in the law are minimized in order to mitigate our responsibility and to keep the others, such as the opposition as well as the people "outside," from seriously objecting to them. They are merely practically and politically necessary, not inspired by xenophobia. The standard color-blindness move ("whether they are black or white") further emphasizes the claim that there is no bias involved.

Denials of racism are the stock in trade of racist discourse. Such denials may take many forms. In the following passage, the French Interior Minister first denies racism for "the French" as a whole, but then seems to be forced to admit concern about less positive developments, namely, xenophobia.

> 14. The French are not racist. But, facing this continuous increase of the foreign population in France, one has witnessed the development, in certain cities and neighborhoods, of reactions that come close to xenophobia. (France, Mr. Pascua, July 9, 1986, p. 3053)

The denial of racism may also be more direct:

> 15. Well, France today, according to what those creatures of the whole world tell us who often have come to take refuge in our country . . . France

is the least racist country that exists in the world. We can't tolerate to hear
said that France is a racist country. (France, Mr. de Villiers, May 2, 1990,
p. 907)

As is the case elsewhere, for instance in the Netherlands and Germany, the very accusation of racism is firmly rejected. At most, incidental xenophobia or discrimination may be admitted. In this case, the
admission is properly hedged in many ways: Xenophobia occurs only
in "certain cities and neighborhoods," and the reactions are not really
xenophobic, but come "close to" it. Whereas the denial of racism may
be strategically more persuasive by admitting at least a mitigated form
of it, note that such an admission is applied again to another group, in
this case the people of "certain cities and neighborhoods"—the poor
whites in the inner cities, not to the elites, or Us. At the same time, the
admission also has a built-in excuse: Xenophobia is the result of a
"continuous increase of the foreign population in France," which implies that at least part of the blame is again transferred to the immigrants
themselves. Self-presentation here is associated with the discursive as
well as the sociopolitical moves of denial, excuses, mitigation, and
transfer, all moves that keep Us as clean as possible.

Example 15 further shows that the denial of racism may also need
further argumentative support. The presence of so many people who
took refuge in "our" country is seen as contrary evidence, and the very
accusation of racism is declared off-limits in such nationalist rhetoric.
As we see elsewhere in this study, accusations of racism are generally
rejected by the elites.

The force of the official norm is such that even the most blatant racists
will deny racism, as is the case for Le Pen, the leader of the Front National:

16. We are neither racist nor xenophobic. Our aim is only that, quite
naturally, there be a hierarchy, because we are dealing with France, and
France is the country of the French. (France, Le Pen, July 7, 1986, p. 3064)

The denial of racism by the leader of a racist party, as well as by white
people in general, implies not only the denial of having committed a
social crime or an immoral act but also a different definition of racism
in the first place. In everyday situations such denials usually pertain to
intentions ("I did not mean in that way") or to a different concept of
racism ("I don't call that racist"). We have seen before that racism in
Europe is commonly interpreted as classical racism, that is, as a feeling

of racial superiority or as intentional discrimination of people of other races. Even Le Pen claims that he does not feel racially superior. He would only admit to categorizing French versus non-French—by nationality, irrespective of race. In other situations, he categorizes by culture (language, religion, and so on) and the degree of integration into France. The *but* (here "only") following his denial explains this different nationalistic conception of racism, namely, the one also expressed in the FN slogan: *Les français d'abord!* Note though that such nationalist priority for him is nevertheless a "hierarchy," and moreover a "natural" one, which associates his concept with a form of white, French supremacism. Such explicit formulations of nationalism are quite rare in other parliaments. However, it should be noted that underlying most immigration debates in Europe, there is the same ideological assumption: that We (whites, Westerners, Europeans, and so on) have priority over Them (non-Europeans) when it comes to immigration and citizenship. In past immigration debates, neither Le Pen nor other European parties have rallied against the immigration of (white) Americans, Swedes, Dutch, or Germans.

Finally, another familiar denial of racism may be found in explicit defense or counter-accusation moves. Here are two examples from the U.S. House of Representatives:

17. Well, now can we also agree this afternoon that you can have different philosophies about how to achieve through law civil rights and equal opportunities for everybody without somehow being anti-civil-rights or being a racist or something like that. (United States, Mr. Gunderson, August 2, 1990, H6781)

18. I am saddened that when we discuss legislation such as this that intolerance seems to be the No 1 word of the No 1 effort in this House. It appears that if you are not 100 percent behind the legislation which we have before us, the Kennedy-Hawkins bill, you are somehow not as pro-civil rights as someone else. It seems to me tolerance should be the name of the game when we are discussing civil rights. (United States, Mr. Goodling, August 2, 1990, H6748)

Note that nobody explicitly accuses the Republicans of racism. However, opposition against civil rights may be construed as racist. Hence, the feeling of guilt and the need to defend oneself, at least against implicit or possible accusations. Although most Republican speakers, as well as President Bush himself, are not against civil rights in general, they oppose this bill because it would, in their opinion, give minorities too many rights, namely, in effective litigation against discrimination, at the expense of employers.

Thus, although the first speaker explicitly affirms to be in favor of civil rights, he wants to realize them in a different way. This is a powerful argumentative move because it presupposes that the ultimate goal is the same and there is only a difference of means. The second speaker uses another familiar ploy, that of reversal: Accuse those of intolerance who implicitly accuse you of intolerance. We shall find other examples of this widespread reversal move in much of the other anti-anti-racist text and talk.

Negative Other-Presentation

The derogation of other ethnic or racial groups forms the core of racist attitudes, ideologies, and practices. However, there is a significant difference between the explicit verbal defamation in much elite discourse of several decades ago, and the more subtle or indirect ways others may be disparaged, as is typically the case for modern or symbolic racism (Dovidio & Gaertner, 1986). As in most other forms of public elite discourse, then, we generally should not expect explicit racial slurs in Western parliaments.

This does not mean that ethnic attitudes have fundamentally changed. Instead of categorizing the members of another group as less intelligent, as lazy, or as criminal, white elites may represented them as oversensitive, underachieving, or too demanding. Blatant derogatory labels are being replaced by seemingly innocent buzzwords and complicated "buzz tactics," which need little decoding to be understood: After all, attributing oversensitiveness to others is tantamount to denying one's own racism, and "less motivated" is simply a less harsh synonym for "lazy."

The very use of indirect derogation and buzzwords confirms the growing prevalence of egalitarian norms and increased sensibility regarding at least the overt manifestations of ethnic bias. We have seen above that such changes are partly due to international moral pressure by Third World countries, as well as by minority resistance. Where such minority groups are smaller or politically less influential, as is the case in Europe, we may expect less verbal sensibility. The presence of extremist racist parties may also contribute to more explicit derogation, also by mainstream parties, in order to appeal to white voters. One well-known discursive move in that case is to oppose the taboo and tell the truth about minorities.

That is, even if the norms and attitudes have changed, in order to reproduce the system of ethnic inequality, immigrants and minorities need to be represented in negative terms. Thus, if politicians want to stop the invasion of refugees, they will hardly emphasize their positive properties. On the contrary, they focus on illegal practices or unacceptable cultural differences. Or they detail the allegedly negative consequences of their stay: overpopulation, unemployment, and strains on housing and social services. Within a broader populist framework, such negative portrayals highlight those negative consequences that provoke strong popular resentment and scapegoating. This in turn creates legitimation for policies that otherwise may be opposed from a more humanitarian point of view.

Let us examine some passages in Western parliamentary discourse that display such strategies. Returning to Dutch Prime Minister Lubbers's radio interview, note the following statement about immigrants:

19. They said: you work to gain your bread, and if you can get bread from somebody else, then you need not work. That is obviously the meaning of Dutch society. (The Netherlands, Lubbers, IKON Radio, March 25, 1990)

So Lubbers here reflects—and thereby confirms with his authority as Prime Minister—the widespread prejudice that immigrants and minorities are welfare cheats, too lazy to work and too ignorant to understand what Dutch society is all about. He may then concede, as he does, that the administration may have given "the wrong signals" by having been "too soft," but that is hardly a serious self-accusation. Who can be blamed for having been too nice? Obviously, this is a persuasive political ploy to present the alternative, namely, being tough, as both palatable and unremarkable. If not, minorities won't accept their "responsibilities" and won't realize that besides rights, they also have "duties," as we saw earlier.

Note also the style of this passage. Whereas the rest of his statements in this interview are stylistically complex as well as confused, and exhibit what is famous in the Netherlands as "Lubberish" (Lubberiaans), a style of evasive, elusive, and vague political talk, this passage mimics a quotation ("they said") of simplistic style and reasoning. In other words, besides being cheats, lazy, and ignorant, minorities are also simple-minded.

The rather acrimonious debate in parliament occasioned by this interview shows that Lubbers violently denies such implications and inferences. True, *as such*—that is, once made explicit—these implications are energetically rejected by Lubbers. However, this only shows that politicians often are not aware of the presuppositions and other implications of their talk and text about minorities. Methodologically, this also shows the limitations of simplistic survey techniques of ethnic attitudes in present-day Western societies. The example also suggests that interviews may be able to tap underlying attitudes by addressing issues that seem to be ideologically less sensitive, such as the causes of unemployment, the climate of success at work, and the imminent economic collapse of the welfare state.

The rhetoric of negative associations need not always be that indirect and subtle. A British conservative has this to say about minorities and immigrants during a debate on immigration restrictions:

> 20. [O]ne in three children born in London today is of ethnic origin. . . . That is a frightening concept for the country to come to terms with. We have already seen the problems of massive Moslem immigration . . . unless we want to create major problems in the decades or the century ahead, we must not only stop immigration but must move to voluntary resettlement to reduce the immigrant population. (Great Britain, Mr. Janman, June 20, 1990, c. 293-294)

This echo of the apocalyptic visions of the former Tory MP Enoch Powell, well known for his racist diatribes against immigrants, provokes vigorous protests from the opposition, and even a moderate rebuke from other Tories. Such reactions suggest that this MP has crossed the boundaries of the official consensus, or at least those of what may be called the *discourse consensus*: One might feel or think this way, but not say it. The "frightening concept" of one-third of all London children being "of ethnic origin" suggests fear, but obviously more is at stake than panic, namely, open resistance of a dominant group member against the multicultural society, as is also signaled by his call to proceed to "voluntary resettlement." Only the notion of "voluntary" distinguishes him from the explicitly racist parties of the extreme right. The internal contradiction of the passage, which shows bleak awareness of the fact that many "immigrants" are actually born in Great Britain, and the call for "resettlement," goes unnoticed by this MP.

Whereas the previous fragment expresses "fear" of racial differences, negative other-presentation of minorities by contemporary elites often focuses on what is seen as a cultural threat:

21. What is the future of our country to be in another 25 years, even if all immigration is stopped tomorrow? What the effect on our religion, morals, customs, habits and so on? Already there have been some dangerous eruptions from parts of the Moslem community. (Great Britain, Sir John Stokes, July 5, 1989, c. 390)

The real or alleged fears of the Muslim threat are as old as Europe's conflict with the Muslim world. Today, they are skillfully manipulated by Western politicians in their opposition to immigration and humane minority policies. After the Rushdie affair, to which this passage obviously alludes, Muslims may again be openly described as violent or dangerous. For elites, the major threat is a cultural one to Western norms and values.

Cultural "threat rhetoric" may also be heard at the other side of the Channel, in the French Assemblée:

22. [I]nserting (*sic*) immigrants into a regularized situation will not make them French, but means that we make place for those who want to conserve their own identity, their culture and their customs. Mister Secretary, inserting immigrants is creating a multicultural society. . . . We don't want anything to do with such a multicultural society, for that would be the end of the unity of France, that would be the end of civil peace. (France, Mr. Mégret, July 11, 1986, p. 3359)

Again, this is the voice of the extreme Right, which openly disavows what is slowly becoming official policy and consensus, namely, that European countries are becoming "multicultural" societies. That the resistance against multiculturalism is hardly based on real competition or fear, but on racist attitudes, may also be concluded from the fact that in most Western European countries, minorities add up to less than 10%. Moreover, the fact that even immigrants who are fully integrated culturally can never become "really French" for FN speakers, also shows that such racist attitudes are not really about culture, but about race.

Unfortunately, the rhetoric of cultural differences and threat is compelling to a broad audience. It allows drawing upon age-old prejudices, especially about the threat of Islam, while at the same time denying racism. This is how a representative of the Front National speaks for the people:

23. No, the French[man] is neither racist, nor anti-Semitic, nor xenophobic nor revisionist. He is worried in face of an immigration out of control, in

face of an Islam pure and hard that might cross the Mediterranean. But the French[man] stays tolerant. (France, Mr. de Broissia, June 28, 1990, p. 3124)

The well-known denial of racism has been analyzed before. It shows again that denials are actually Apparent Denials, because the assertion is not supported but belied by the vicious attack on Africans that follows. At the same time, the denial takes the form of a mitigation, namely, when French people are said not to be racist but "worried." The positive, tolerant attitudes of the French are even further emphasized because they stay tolerant *despite* the threats of a "pure and hard" Islam: a classic example of a combination of positive self-presentation and negative other-presentation.

Such chauvinistic statements against Muslims and Arabs, especially since the Oil Crisis and during and after the Gulf War, may also be heard in the United States. However, politicians are generally more cautious in Congress when resident minorities (voters!) are concerned. Yet, in order to effectively oppose the Civil Rights Bill, Republicans somehow need to discredit its proponents or beneficiaries. We have seen that the major scare tactic used to discredit the Democratic supporters of this bill is summarized by the compelling buzzword *quota*. Even when succeeding versions of the bill explicitly prohibited quota, its opponents still claimed that expensive discrimination litigation would force employers to hire by the numbers. Another tactic was to call the bill a lawyer's bonanza, because of the benefits to be allegedly reaped by lawyers in the numerous discrimination cases that would result from this bill.

The presumption of these tactics, sometimes expressed during the congressional debate, is that minorities often level unfounded accusations of discrimination against employers. This presumption is part of a broader configuration of contemporary white prejudices, according to which minorities, and especially African-Americans, have a chip on their shoulder: They are oversensitive and tend to blame their own shortcomings on discrimination by white employers. Research has shown that this prejudice is widespread in corporate life (Fernandez, 1981; see also Chapter 4) as well as among the white population at large, despite the fact that blacks are typically reticent to voice such accusations, precisely because they know they will not be believed, or will face allegations of seeing discrimination where there is none (Essed, 1991).

Against the background of this complex framework of modern elite racism, we should understand the following intervention:

24. [G]iven the huge litigation expenses that an employer would have to incur in order to vindicate his name, there is an encouragement to settle these cases, whether they have merit or not. And then we have turned this issue not into a civil rights bill but to a bill that legalizes extortion against employers who are subjected to claims of unlawful discrimination that are without merit. (United States, Sensenbrenner, August 2, 1990, H6773)

Note that this passage, and in particular "vindicate," presupposes that accused employers are usually innocent, and that minorities often level unfounded accusations of discrimination. The use of "extort" further implies that such accusations are not just unfounded accusations, but rather are acts of a serious criminal nature. This argumentative rhetoric disparages minorities and denies own racism as well as the long history of corporate discrimination. It even reverses the roles in the sociopolitical drama of racism, following the well-known Blaming the Victim move: Those who engage in criminal discrimination become victims, whereas the victims are turned into vindictive avengers. Much of the Republican side of this debate paints employers as innocent, hard-working people who are ruined by the self-serving lies of their black employees.

These conservative opponents of the Civil Rights Bill are aware that in a social system of ethnic group dominance, increasing rights—and hence power—for the dominated group usually entail less power for dominant groups. In that case the traditional ploy of conservative rhetoric is to claim that freedom is at stake. Let us quote in full one prominent example of this and several other strategic moves of the conservative attack on the Civil Rights Bill of 1990:

25. Freedom is at stake, the freedom to work at your life as you see fit. The world our liberal friends on the Democratic side seek to bring to us with this bill was described by Frederick Lynch of California State University at Los Angeles. Describing his attempts to find a university teaching position, Lynch, a white male, observed:

Once, for example, I was informed by a plainly discomfited chairman that I had lost a position at Sweet Briar College strictly because I was male. On another occasion the department chairman at Pomona College told me that the only sociologists he could hire was (*sic*) black. On yet a third occasion, Occidental College abruptly canceled an interview, later notifying me—and several other candidates—that it had hired a female "native of Jamaica."

This nonsense about quotas has to stop because when we begin to hire and promote people on the basis of their race, we are going to bring to our society feelings of distress, feelings of unhappiness, and these emotions will accumulate and ultimately explode and destroy us.

This nonsense that there is a benevolent state out there that is going to decide we are all going to be equal at the finish line is a tragedy, and the sooner we divest ourselves of this nonsense, the better off we are all going to be. (United States, Mr. Dannemeyer, August 2, 1990, p. H6332-6333).

This passage is replete with ideological meanings and implications. First, "freedom" is such a well-known ideological concept, arguably the most often abused concept of conservative rhetoric, in which it is associated with the "freedom" of corporate enterprise, or the "freedom" of the market, and not with the freedom from want or discrimination. The second ploy of this passage is to present a white victim of Affirmative Action, a well-known reversal move: Blacks are not the victims of discrimination, We are. Note also that this passage implies, but does not provide evidence for the fact that the white applicant was indeed better than the black ones. Moreover, that the chairman of Sweet Briar College reportedly was "clearly discomfited"—instead of "elated"—that he had to hire a black woman (a "native from Jamaica," so not only black but also a foreigner), also suggests that Affirmative Action is also met by serious white resistance to hire minorities in universities.

Third, the conservative Representative not only discredits Affirmative Action by categorizing such a hiring decision as the application of quotas, and not just by categorically rejecting quotas as "nonsense," but also sketches, first through a rhetorical understatement ("distress" and "unhappiness") then in more apocalyptic hyperbole ("explosion and destruction"), the disastrous consequences of quotas. More generally, we have found in conservative elite discourse that the consequences of immigration and civil rights are portrayed in terms of social, economic, and cultural catastrophe, and hence as a fundamental threat to white society.

Finally, formulating the political presuppositions of his conservative ideology, this Representative associates Affirmative Action with the over-zealous meddling of the "benevolent" state, with the obviously ridiculous objective of manufacturing equality "at the finish line." These words presuppose and invoke a complex ideology on civil rights, in which conservatives reluctantly claim to accept equal opportunities at the starting line, but categorically reject equality of outcomes. This rejection should be understood in the perspective of a long history of racism, which hardly allowed minorities to arrive at the starting line with equal chances in the first place. At the same time, the reference to the "benevolent" state presupposes the conservative ideology of individual responsibility and merit. This reference also implies that minorities apparently cannot make it on their own, which is one of the ways of disparaging blacks in conservative elite discourse.

We see that although minorities are not explicitly derogated in such interventions, it is clearly implied that they, and their liberal supporters in the House, are considered to be against freedom, against equal opportunities for everybody (also white males), as establishing quotas, as falsely accusing employers of discrimination, as fomenting racial strife, as leading the nation to destruction, and as expecting unfair competition.

Another ploy in U.S. ethnic affairs debates is to display one's civil rights credits. Having marched with Martin Luther King or having actively participated in the Civil Rights Movement of the 1960s are standard moves of positive self-presentation, a move extensively used in the following example, which we shall quote in full:

> 26. Mr. Speaker, I rise today in strong opposition to the misnamed Civil Rights Act of 1990. It should really be called the Trial Lawyers Act. This bill does nothing to advance civil rights. In fact, it is diametrically opposed to the original intent of the civil rights movement, of which I am proud to have participated as a young Air Force captain in my off-duty hours. Those of us who marched with Dr. Martin Luther King in Washington in 1963, were not marching for hiring quotas or other racial preferences. We were marching for a colorblind society in which all Americans would be judged by the "content of their character" in King's words, not the color of their skin. Instead of building on that dream, we are being asked today to embrace a bill that reinforces one of America's oldest and ugliest racial myths, that Whites are superior to Blacks. In that respect it can truly be said that passing this legislation will be turning the clock back. How ironic.
> (United States, Mr. Dornan, August 2, 1990, H6334)

The argumentative moves in this passage are well known and transparent, and may be summarized as follows: (a) Associate your opponent's position with clearly unintended consequences (lawyers will get rich); (b) point at contradictions in your opponents strategy (the present bill is opposed to the original meaning of civil rights); (c) present yourself as a supporter of civil rights; and (d) confront your opponents with the different views of their heroes (Martin Luther King). Apart from the latter—Authority—move, this sequence of moves suggests that the present bill is in fact a perversion of the old, revered "dream" of the Civil Rights Movement, and that those who oppose this bill should be

seen as the true heirs to the civil rights legacy. This paradox is followed
by another: Tough antidiscrimination legislation allegedly confirms the
racist prejudice that blacks are inferior.

Without making explicit a complex network of presuppositions, such
a paradoxical conclusion would be virtually incomprehensible. This
network may be spelled out as follows: By facilitating legal action
against discrimination, this bill will force employers to hire by the
numbers to avoid costly litigation; and to hire by the numbers, instead
of on the basis of quality and merit, entails that minorities would be
unable to compete without quota, which presupposes that whites are
superior. Thus, not only are conservatives the true heirs to the civil
rights legacy, they are also the self-styled opponents of racist myths of
white superiority. We see that the paradox also features the familiar
move of a reversal: We are not racist, They are the real racists!

Here is how the speaker spells out the paradoxes and the reversal:

> 27. Any honest liberal would have to admit that affirmative action has been
> a dismal failure. . . . Instead of advancing the cause of Blacks, affirmative
> action has hurt the cause of Blacks. Why? Because racial preference
> implies inferiority. And this implied inferiority actually aggravates the
> white racism affirmative action was designed to eradicate. That is why
> there has been an increase in racial incidents, for instance on college
> campuses, around the country. (United States, Mr. Dornan, August 2, 1990,
> p. H6334)

Again, the argumentative moves of this passage are common fare in text
and talk of those elites who oppose anti-racist actions and policies. In
the same way as victims are often blamed for their own oppression, the
causes of oppression may also be attributed to the actions of those who
claim to fight oppression and inequality. Along this line of reasoning,
anti-racists aggravate racism, for example, because Affirmative Action
only leads to ethnic or racial resentment of whites. Hence, the Republican opponents of the bill are the real opponents of racism.

This self-congratulatory conclusion not only implements the familiar
moves of transfer, reversal, and positive self-presentation, but at the same
time derogates the opponents. We see that negative other-presentation in
racial affairs discourse does not target only minority groups. On the
contrary, such attacks might be too obviously racist, and hence their
negative portrayals may sometimes focus primarily on those whites who
are seen as staunch supporters of the minority cause. They can be attacked

without moral or political restraint because the counter-accusation of racism would be void in that case. Moreover, white liberals are the only social group that share white elite power and therefore need to be taken seriously.

Firm, but Fair

The complex and continuous interplay between positive self-description and negative other-description in ethnic affairs discourse not only produces the familiar disclaimers and other semantic moves, such as "We have nothing against minorities, but . . . " or "There are also very intelligent blacks, but . . ." There is also an inverse form to this disclaimer, in which first a negative property of Us is affirmed or even conceded, followed however by a contrast or paradoxical conclusion. Thus Apparent Concessions may be a strong argumentative method of placating opponents, for example, by admitting to one of their points, but then reaching a different conclusion: "There are racist parties and there is some discrimination in the Netherlands, *but* on the whole it is a tolerant country." Such concessions are called apparent because of the discursive support for the argument following *but* in the main clause. There is usually little evidence supplied to make the first argument more credible.

One other way to combine quasi-negative and positive self-descriptions is to invoke the routine rhetorical pair *firm, but fair* (or *tough, but fair*). This phrase is mostly used to legitimate immigration restrictions or other limitations of (or refusals to extend) the rights of refugees, immigrants, or resident minorities. Self-description as being "firm" or "tough" or admissions that one has been "too soft" may hardly seem positive, but the combination with the positive qualification "fair" does make the pair positive. Firmness in that case is like that of the stern father, or the wise doctor, whose firmness only benefits his children or her clients. The addition of "fair" also suggests that there is no question of being too firm: Fairness prevails in all decisions.

This paternalistic strategy is apparent in many parliamentary debates, for example, in the defense of their bills by Hurd and Schäuble, Interior Secretaries of Great Britain and Germany, respectively.

> If we are to work seriously for harmony, non-discrimination and equality of opportunity in our cities, that has to be accompanied by firm and fair immigration control. (Great Britain, Mr. Hurd, July 5, 1989, c. 380)

My hon. Friend and I will continue to apply a strict but fair system of control. (Great Britain, Mr. Hurd, July 5, 1989, c. 386)

It belongs to this fair balance of interests that the further immigration of foreigners must be limited, because for each society there are limits to the ability and the readiness to integrate. (Germany, Mr. Schäuble, April 26, 1990, p. 16281)

Mr. Chairman, this substitute offers the House of Representatives an opportunity to enact a landmark civil rights bill that is both fair and pragmatic. (United States, Mr. Moorhead, August 2, 1990, H6786)

These passages show that combining fairness with firmness, or with pragmatism in the U.S. example, is qualified as a positive political strategy in several Houses of Representatives. Those who are fair without firmness are unrealistic, bleeding heart liberals, who would ruin the country by letting everyone in, or who create resentment among the white population. That is, firmness in this view is also a condition of harmony "in our cities," as the British MP suggests. Putting firmness in the balance with positively valued conditions of ethnic relations, such as "non-discrimination and equality of opportunity," strategically aims at putting the Left in a predicament: They will have to take the political consequences of popular white resentment.

The German Secretary gives a different turn to his argument: Immigration must be restricted because there are limits to the ability of society to integrate. This argument recalls the frequent references, also made years earlier by President Mitterand of France, to a threshold of tolerance, a seemingly natural limit that can only be crossed at the peril of racial unrest. It needs no further argument that this mythical threshold, which is belied by many peaceful multicultural societies in the world, is usually set quite low, namely, in one-digit percentages in Europe.

The political expedience of the "firm, but fair" move in such argumentations is defined by the constituencies being addressed by such parliamentary discourse. By acknowledging the need for fairness, and by thus expressing humanitarian values regarding immigrants and minorities, the more liberal and tolerant voters are persuasively addressed. On the other hand, firmness should appeal to those who advocate law and order, and especially a tough stance toward minorities.

In the more direct political context, however, there is also little doubt that "firm, but fair" is a disclaimer that functions as part of a strategy of positive self-presentation. The fairness is often primarily humanitarian window dressing and intended to avoid accusations of xenophobia or racism. All strict rules and regulations that control immigration and ethnic affairs show that firmness and not fairness is the actual aim being pursued and implemented.

For Their Own Good

The paternalistic view of immigration and race relations that we encountered in our analysis of the "firm, but fair" move is even more pronounced in arguments that suggest that the speaker is doing all these firm things "for their own good." This Apparent Empathy or Apparent Altruism move is again a functional part of the overall strategy of positive self-presentation: We are doing something good for Them. A standard argument, heard in everyday conversations as well as in racist propaganda about immigrants, is that they should go back to their own (poor) country, and help to build it up. That is, limiting immigration would not be better for *us*, but for *them*, because that would be good for their country. The same is true for Affirmative Action or welfare programs, such as in the United States, where less legal or political intervention is defended with the previously encountered argument that this would only create dependency, confirm victim-role thinking, or imply racist inferiorization of minorities.

Fragments in the radio interview of Prime Minister Lubbers of the Netherlands are typical examples of this Apparent Empathy:

28. But minority policy as care-policy, minority policy as prevention of discrimination, as only offering things, is insufficient . . . Well-meaning policies in favor of minorities will have reverse effects, therefore we should have a mature approach. . . . Moreover, such a measure is hard to implement. It leads to demotivation. (Netherlands, Mr. Lubbers, IKON Radio, March 25, 1990)

So tough policies are advocated, and care and welfare policies or anti-discrimination measures will get less priority (than they have ever had). Doing good is declared out of fashion by offering the argument that welfare policies have reverse effects: They are bad for minorities. This implies that our new "mature" approach will be good for them, and that policies that care for minorities are "immature," if not "childish." Thus, firmness and toughness are associated with the realism and pragmatism of the adult parents who really care for their children, even when it seems to "hurt a little." Other approaches only lead to "de-motivation," the well-known buzzword for "they don't want to work."

Note that such passages are largely configurations of positive and negative associations. They do not report or presuppose facts, but merely persuasively define ethnic relations in terms of parent-child relations, or associate minorities with children who have been pampered if not spoiled. The fact that many members of minority groups, especially in the Netherlands, are unemployed and living on welfare is presented, in the well-known conservative Reaganomic framework of blaming the victim, as a proof of their lack of "motivation."

It hardly needs to be added that such "firm, but fair" and "for their own good" decisions in ethnic affairs are *not* addressed to employers who have been shown to discriminate against minorities, and who therefore contributed to high minority unemployment—and hence to costly welfare—in the Netherlands in the first place, or to educators who fail to provide minorities with a competitive education. On the contrary, even more so than in the United States, corporate employers in Europe are handled with kid gloves, at least in such "moral" matters as minority employment. Thus, one of the implications of the "for their own good" move is not only to blame the victims, but also to punish them for being victims in the first place. At the same time, the sociopolitical and economic implication of this policy is that the true responsibilities for social problems are being concealed.

Whereas such a conservative approach characterizes the growing no-nonsense policies towards resident minorities, it also defines one of the major arguments to stop or limit immigration, as may be frequently heard in the British House of Commons:

29. It is fair to establish visa controls as long as there is mutual agreement about them between the countries involved. They are the best way to control immigration fairly, so that those who properly qualify to come here or to leave this country to visit other countries can do so. Such controls make sure that people have the right qualifications for travel. (Great Britain, Mr. Hanley, May 15, 1990, c. 849)

The repeated self-categorization in terms of fairness in this passage has already been discussed above. In this case, such qualifications are buttressed by all the good things for *them* that may follow, such as free travel to other countries, or having the "right qualifications" for such travel. However, to become beneficiaries of these rights, handed out as if they were extraordinary privileges, applicants must of course first obtain a visa for Great Britain, a privilege not to be awarded to "all and sundry." However, even those who are disappointed and do not get such a visa are better off, and should probably be grateful for being turned down:

> 30. Those who do not qualify avoid the disappointment, expense and inconvenience of being refused entry after their journey here. . . . I am glad to say that the new arrangements have been successful. The difficulties at our ports have been resolved, which has enables us to provide a better service for bona fide travelers. (Great Britain, Waddington, May 15, 1990, c. 854)

The generosity of the British administration is truly overwhelming in this passage, which details all the troubles that potential immigrants may be spared by such a sympathetic refusal of entry. Indeed, the new immigration policies work so well that virtually no one is admitted any more, which again results in providing "better service" for "bona fide" travelers. The familiar presupposition here is that everybody who is not admitted is by definition a "mala fide" traveler. The overall style of such interventions recalls that of the publicity campaign for a new product or service.

It was already observed before that "firm and fair" immigration controls are defended as being better for the inner cities, that is, for our own white population:

> 31. If we are to work seriously for harmony, non-discrimination and equality of opportunity in our cities, that has to be accompanied by firm and fair immigration control. (Great Britain, Mr. Hurd, July 5, 1989, c. 380)

However, the immigrants will also benefit because, according to this argument, the presence of fewer foreigners means less discrimination and more opportunities, a commonsense logic on which everyday stereotypes and prejudices of "unfair competition" are also premised. "Harmony" is the key word, presupposing chaos and civil strife, which constantly lurk between the lines of such interventions, namely, as a threat to all those, notably among the liberal opposition, who are so foolish as to advocate anything else. Here and elsewhere in such statements, we find the simplistic biosocial presumption, present in much contemporary racist discourse, that numbers and mixtures of cultures and peoples automatically lead to such chaos.

How much such assumptions are part of an ideology may be shown by the self-evident claims made to "common sense":

> 32. Surely common sense says that there must be strict immigration controls, in the interests not only of the indigenous population but of immigrants. (Great Britain, Sir John Stokes, July 5, 1989, c. 390-391)

This right-wing speaker admits that immigration restrictions are not advantageous only for the immigrants. Hence, the liberals, supposed to have only the well-being of minorities in mind, are seduced by such arguments. And the white majority (that is, the bulk of the voters) will obviously also reap the fruit of the new policies.

The debate in U.S. Congress has a different orientation. Although sometimes an object of heated debate, such as when poor Caribbeans (most recently the Haitians) or Latin Americans are presenting themselves at the borders, immigration is a less controversial topic in a country that is almost wholly populated with old and new immigrants. We have found above that the new conservative approach to ethnic affairs seldom derogates blacks openly, but has other ways to associate African-Americans and other minorities with negative values of the dominant white group. Affirmative Action in general and quotas in particular are merely the labels of such attitudes on ethnic affairs and minorities, featuring such negative opinions as lack of motivation, oversensitivity, pushiness, and ungratefulness.

Yet, being tough on Affirmative Action is also for their own good. To oppose threatening policies of state intervention in the private affairs of citizens and companies has positive consequences for blacks because:

> 33. Affirmative action also produces self-doubts in the minds of black people. (United States, Mr. Dornan, August 2, 1990, H6334)

True, not all blacks are in favor of Affirmative Action, and probably all of them would welcome not having to enter the work force burdened with the racist reaction of doubt about their qualifications, if only they could be sure that discrimination would be totally absent in business, services, and public employment. Hence, what this speaker is in fact doing is what a psychoanalytical approach probably would call projection: White doubts about qualifications are projected as alleged self-doubts upon blacks. In this way, virtually any measure that favors whites can be explained as one that favors blacks.

Vox Populi or White Racism as Threat

Sympathy with the oppressed is a noble sentiment. There are, however, even more forceful argumentative moves to persuade both liberal white elites and minorities, namely, the threat of intolerance, discrimination, and racism. Who would be in favor of racism; who would condone popular resentment? Thus, to persuasively argue against immigration or against favoritism or other alleged privileges for minorities, one only needs to conjure up the specter of racist reactions among the white population at large. Obviously, this is a specific elite strategy, because it exclusively attributes potential racism to the white lower class, and in particular to those in the inner cities. The argument is: Stop immigration or stop Affirmative Action because otherwise, *we* will get even more racist.

However, as such, this move might be counter-productive because it may alienate white voters. Therefore, it is often combined with the populist claim that the politicians speak for the people, or at least acknowledge hearing their voice. Especially on the Right, politicians may attack their liberal colleagues by emphasizing that they at least listen to ordinary people. Preferential hiring "may also give rise to feelings of jealousy of the other involved in such a business enterprise," says Dutch Prime Minister Lubbers in his radio interview, thus declaring serious Affirmative Action as unworkable.

British Tories especially like to play this game of the people's voice, thereby sneering at Labour while at the same time inviting popular support and legitimation for their own restrictive policies, as right-wing speaker Sir John Stokes formulates them:

34. In debates of this kind, I have always been struck forcibly by how much Labour and Liberal Members have distanced themselves from the feelings of ordinary people. . . . In so far as the small changes in the rules reduce the flow of immigration to this country, they will be welcomed wholeheartedly by the British public. We must be careful to respect the views of the people who elected us to this place. (Great Britain, Sir John Stokes, May 15, 1990, columns 842-844)

There are probably few issues on which Conservatives would be expecting support from "ordinary people," but ethnic affairs is certainly one of them. This strategic use of assumed popular resentment, euphemistically described as "feelings" against further immigration or favoritism is a powerful move. Not only do they invite popular support by implying "We are listening to you," but they also attack the opposition by suggesting that they are less democratic, having "distanced" themselves from ordinary (white) British people. At the same time, however, the pretense of listening to the voice of the people conceals the fact that much of the resentment against immigrants is not primarily, or even not at all, formulated at the grass-roots level, but rather by conservative elites themselves.

Such examples provide strong support for the major thesis of this book, namely, that discourse of the political elites, especially of the Right, may claim popular support while at the same time preformulating the terms that help create the state of mind that gives rise to such support in the first place. We have argued several times that although elite racism and popular racism mutually influence and reinforce each other, "the people" does not have a public voice itself, simply because it hardly has access to the media or other means of mass communication. They are "made heard," namely, by politicians, journalists, or other elites who either let them speak or speak for them. Not all elites can speak for the people, however:

> 35. The burden of receiving and coping with these newcomers in our midst has fallen not on the intellectuals, Labour Members of Parliament and others of that ilk but on the ordinary English working-class people. Surely they are entitled to have a voice here. (Great Britain, Sir John Stokes, July 5, 1989, c. 390-391)

This example not only makes a distinction between middle-class elites and the "ordinary English working class," but also between Us and Them ("ilk") within the elites, where the liberal "intellectuals" associated with Labour are branded as being especially estranged from the people. This anti-intellectualism move is not only characteristic of the political Right, but is also familiar in the British press, especially in the tabloids, when they attack the "sociologists" who allegedly excuse minority crime and violence (van Dijk, 1991).

Alleged popular resentment suggests that it is especially the lower class that objects to immigration or multiculturalism. However, the broad support for extremist racist parties among the lower middle class, and in neighborhoods where either no or few minorities could be "unfair competitors," shows that the elite assumptions about popular racism may well be a self-serving transfer and denial of own racism. To see such thinking and talking at work, consider another fragment of a speech by Interior Minister Mr. Douglas Hurd in the British House of Commons:

> 36. I do not think that the right hon. Gentleman wants the National Front to triumph in his Constituency. The National Front had no candidates at all in the last election. I do not think that the right hon. Gentleman wants to see in Britain the changes in public opinion which sent six German MEP's representing anti-foreigner parties far Right, to the European Parliament, and a similar number from France. I do not think that the right hon. Gentleman wants that, but his attitude towards immigration control would bring that about if it were realized. It would cause suspicion and resentment, and plenty of people are ready to jump on that bandwagon. My hon. Friend and I will continue to apply a strict but fair system of control, not because we are prejudiced or inhumane, but because we believe that control is needed if all the people who live in our cities are to live together in tolerance and decent harmony. (Great Britain, Mr. Hurd, July 5, 1989, c. 386)

The populist argument in such examples turns into a threat frequently heard in European parliaments: If we are too lenient toward immigrants or minorities, this will only favor the racist Right. Such an argument is typical of Conservatives who want to distance themselves from the extreme Right, while at the same time blaming Labour for the rise of racism. Transfer of blame becomes a complete reversal of possible accusations leveled against the Conservatives for sharing many anti-minority attitudes with the extreme Right and for contributing to the rise of racism.

The negative and ironic rhetorical questions addressed to the Left in Example 36 precisely feed on this assumption that being "soft" on immigration and related issues is the real cause of popular resentment and hence, of racism. The strength of this strategy lies in the common-sense reaction of popular protests against immigration, namely, that politicians don't do anything against it. The Right, in this perspective, may hope to pick up votes by continuously showing that it is doing something about "it." However, "it" is selectively defined here as the problems allegedly caused by immigration or a multicultural society, not the major socioeconomic problems the Right is scarcely motivated to solve (such as unemployment, bad housing, and failing social services, among many others).

To conceal the results of such Conservative policies, Mr. Hurd virtually accuses the Left of sending racists to the European parliament and of causing popular resentment and massive support of the National Front. At the same time, thus legitimated by the people's voice, the speaker feels entitled to defend "strict but fair" controls on immigration. Note the familiar disclaimer of the Apparent Denial ("We are not prejudiced, *but* . . . "), which suggests that strict immigration controls are not inconsistent with a humanitarian system of values. This argument is closed by the move of Apparent Altruism we have met before: It is good for all of Us and all of Them. Tough restrictions lead to harmony. Marginalization is tolerance. Oppression is Peace. These indeed are some of the fragments of the Ethnospeak and the Ethnologic of the Right.

Such talk is no accident. On the contrary, it is the stock in trade of the policies and persuasive arguments of conservative MPs, repeated and repeated again and then picked up, or sometimes even first formulated, by the popular press. These newspapers then make sure that the very people, for whom this text and talk have been spoken, read the message, which is difficult to resist:

> 37. Anyone listening to speeches by Opposition Members would imagine that we are being unduly restrictive in our rules of entry. If one were to go outside this place and ask someone in the street, "Is that true?" they would say, "No, over the past 25 years this country has been extraordinarily generous in letting in many people into the country, some of whom have done very well, and how glad we are about it." (Great Britain, Sir John Stokes, July 5, 1989, c. 390-391)

The alleged voice of the imaginary "WoMan in the Street" is supposedly quoted here, but the very elite style of the quote betrays the conservative MP-ventriloquist boasting the "generosity" of his country, that is, of his own policies and ideologies: Indeed some have done very well, according to the ideology of Thatcherist popular capitalism. The problem is that *most* minorities or immigrants have not. There is little evidence that the Conservative speaker is *not* glad about that, or indeed, could be bothered at all. Note also in this example that immigrants are not "coming in" or "arriving" but are passively "let in," that is, by an act of grace and tolerance of the conservative gatekeepers. Conservatives thus play a political game with the Left by trying to beat them on their own turf of assumed popular support, and by defending their own precarious argumentative position by shoving the accusation of racism back to the Left.

Similar populist appeals may be expected from the racist Right. Here is what a colleague of Jean-Marie Le Pen, of the Front National in the French Assemblée has to say:

38. Addressing myself to the people of the left, I repeat again that we are against nobody, against no color, against no race, and against no religion. The only reason we are sitting in this national Assembly is that we have been elected representatives by French people who think like us. . . . In the Front National we are invested by a mission, and we shall accomplish it. That mission is to defend the French . . . all the French, whatever their color. (France, Mr. Holeindre, July 11, 1986, p. 3349)

Starting with the now familiar disclaimer of the Apparent Denial of racism, the "but" is not followed, at least not in this passage, by derogating the immigrants, but by a more positive ploy of claiming democratic respectability, if not a legitimate mission: to say what "the most lucid citizens of this country" think. There is no need to quote the many other FN speeches to show how often they fulminate against the alleged threat of other religions, most notably Islam, and how often they imply that French citizens of another color, namely, those from North Africa or the Caribbean, are not really French. The point here is the populist claim that one speaks for the people and thus says what "everybody" thinks, which is the routine pretense of all racists.

As is the case in Britain, the French conservatives, caught between the Left and the Front National, also go through the usual moves of distancing themselves from both, for example, by accusing the Socialists of being the real cause of the rise of racism in France, a now familiar move of reversal:

39. But it is you, with Mr. Mitterand and with Mr. Rocard, who have created Mr. Le Pen, with all means. After having made of it a party that counts among the voters of our country, you want to make a martyr of him, and weave him a crown. Beware, my dear colleagues, of this criminal maneuver. (France, Mr. Broissia, May 2, 1990, p. 928)

The opposition here is directed against the only explicitly anti-racist bill proposed in France, occasioned by the desecration of Jewish graves in Carpentras in the spring of 1990. The conservative view is that energetic measures against racist discourse and action, such as curtailing the rights of racist politicians who incite to racial hatred, would only be counterproductive, while making a martyr of Le Pen. Although Le Pen was quite influential during the time he was not a martyr, and could freely speak out, this argument seems to be quite persuasive. As we have seen earlier, similar arguments are brought forward when, occasionally, it is suggested that racist parties should be prohibited, but not when *real* criminal organizations are forbidden. This merely shows that the expression of racist prejudice, incitement to racial hatred, and systematic discrimination are seen not as crimes but as a belonging to a *moral* order, in which criteria such as the freedom of speech or the freedom of assembly are deemed to be more important than the freedom from prejudice, discrimination, and racism. It is apparently crucial *whose* freedoms are being curtailed.

Le Pen's vociferous colleague in the Assemblée, Ms. Stirbois, attacks the present anti-racist law by addressing the right of free speech:

40. A project that attacks the Declaration rights of man and citizen: by the brutality of the sanctions foreseen for simple remarks, by the imprecision of the definitions of racism and incitement to hatred or to violence, this bill attacks article 10 of the Declaration of the rights of man and citizen . . . "The free communication of thoughts and opinions is one of the most precious rights of Man." (France, Ms. Stirbois, May 2, 1990, p. 909)

The now familiar strategic moves of reversal and counterattack also characterize this passage. The racists claim precisely the freedom they deny to others, and refer to a Constitution that prohibits what they practice. The same lofty ideals of the *Déclaration des droits de l'homme et du citoyen* are thus used and abused to defend the freedom to discriminate.

Incidentally, this analysis does not conceal the sociopolitical problems involved in the contradictory consequences of granting, protecting, or limiting democratic rights. The problem is that the racist abuse of the freedom of expression is not just a question of "mere words" that cannot hurt other people. Discourse analysts are familiar with the elementary insight from the philosophy of language, speech act theory, and sociolinguistics, namely, that discourse is also a form of social action. More or less subtly or blatantly racist discourse is an action that not only may hurt large groups of people, but also has a powerful influence on the very restriction of equal rights. Besides sociopolitical and philosophical issues about the foundations of the democratic state, we here touch upon the fundamental ethics of ethnic affairs, in which discriminatory text and talk are seen as serious social transgressions, limiting the elementary rights of minorities. In fact, despite such formal or moral prohibitions, the range of negatively oriented discourses about minorities or immigrants is still very large, as these parliamentary contributions show.

The extreme Right in France thus plays on the democratic conscience as well as on the doubtful allegiances of the other parties as soon as "free speech" about minorities and migrants is concerned:

41. In the world there are two great political regimes, democratic regimes and totalitarian regimes. In democratic regimes, it is the people which, by its votes, is the arbiter between those in power and the opposition. In totalitarian regimes, it is the judiciary which, on demand of those in power, persecutes the opposition. This is exactly what you ask us to do today by providing a punishment that consists in depriving somebody of his civil rights not on account of his acts but on account of simple words. How can the people freely choose its representatives when these cannot freely express themselves? (France, Ms. Stirbois, June 28, 1990, p. 3108)

Thus lecturing parliament about democracy, the Front National banks on the support of the people, while at the same time attacking legal sanctions that would be incurred by saying what the people say. As in the other reversals we encounter in this study, the extreme Right may paradoxically accuse its opponents of being totalitarian.

Similar arguments (restrict immigration to avoid more *Ausländerfeindlichkeit*) may be heard from conservatives in Germany. This does not mean, as we shall see in more detail later, that they are not being attacked by the Left, when it opposes the new Foreigner Bill:

42. The bill is dominated by the spirit of barriers [*Abschottung*] and defense. You are offering us a complex, bureaucratic instrument. . . . Suspicion and mistrust characterize your bill, where tolerance and indulgence would have been required. [Addressing the Minister of the Interior, Mr. Schäuble]. As long as you do as if the rights of foreigners should be cut down to prevent xenophobia, you accomplish the opposite; for those who designate foreigners as a threat, foment xenophobia. (Germany, Ms. Sonntag-Wohlgast, April 26, 1990, p. 16273)

Unfortunately, as the recent events in Germany have shown, there is a lot of truth in *this* accusation: The continued and overt political fights about the limitation of refugees did indeed increase xenophobia in Germany and should be seen as one of the legitimating causes of the violence against refugees and other minorities since the fall of 1991.

Similar remarks may be made about the general debate about civil rights in the United States, where white popular resentment against what is seen as favoritism, especially of blacks, is also widespread.

Therefore, it may be routinely addressed, although in the indirect and subtle ways analyzed above, namely, by warning or threatening that business will no longer be competitive and that tougher antidiscrimination legislation will only make lawyers richer. In the United States the appeal to common sense is one of the well-known elements of populist rhetoric, whose effectiveness may be further enhanced by humor:

43. I try to use what they call, where I come from, west Texas tractor seat common sense. Under Kennedy-Hawkins, I believe employment decisions based on tractor seat common sense probably will be an unlawful practice. (United States, Mr. Stenholm, August 2, 1990, H6807)

Even more persuasive is the example of Lebanon, that is, the symbol of chaos, destruction, and civil war, as right-wing Senator Helms sees it in the Senate debate on the Civil Rights Bill later that year:

44. Do we want a nation where privilege and employment are handed out on the basis of group identity rather than on individual merit? Do we want quota justice? There already exists a model for this type of stratified and proportionalized society: it is called Lebanon. (United States, Mr. Helms, October 24, 1990, S16584)

Such rhetoric, in which general fears are addressed, is also based on the preferred denial of such questions: "No, we do not hand out jobs and privilege on the basis of group identity," because that would mean discrimination. And "Yes, we do recognize that merit should be the only criterion," as competitive capitalism requires. Apart from addressing his colleagues, this Senator also addresses the people, and preformulates its verdict: no quotas and hence, no strict Civil Rights Bill. The presupposition of the first rhetorical question of this passage is that privilege and employment were not and are not "handed out" on the basis of group membership. It needs no further demonstration that this presupposition is of course rather inconsistent with prevailing white power and privilege in the United States, which are indirectly denied by this rhetoric.

Populist rhetoric is not limited to the Right. As soon as the rights and interests of workers are concerned, liberals also may explicitly address—or claim to speak for—the people, as does Senator Metzenbaum after President's Bush veto of the Civil Rights Bill of 1990:

45. The public should learn a great lesson from this veto. When push comes to shove, the real George Bush reverts to his roots and his instincts. He

supports the interests of the wealthy employers over the legitimate concerns of women and minority workers. (United States, Mr. Metzenbaum, October 24, 1990, S16573)

Thus, besides slick lawyers for whom this bill is seen as a bonanza by the Republican opposition, wealthy employers may also be conjured up, by the Democratic backers of this bill, as a powerful prototype of greed, of which women and minorities are the victims. Although such populist rhetoric also indulges in unwarranted generalizations about employers, there is enough evidence showing that the rights and concerns of women and minorities are not generally respected by all employers. (Fernandez, 1981; see also Chapter 4).

The Numbers Game

Another well-known move in the negative presentation of immigration is the numbers game, which is also familiar in the press. This rhetorical use of quasi-objective figures, convincingly suggesting how many "come in" every day, week, month, or year, is one of the most compelling scare tactics in the formation of public opinion. Figures need not be lied about or exaggerated. It is the way they are presented or extrapolated that makes them impressive. For instance, they are always given in absolute numbers, so that thousands or even hundreds of thousands of refugees or immigrants arriving each year appear to be quite impressive. In percentages of the total population, even all minorities and immigrants counted together amount to only a small percentage, at least in Europe. This percentage is increasing very slowly, a numerical fact, however, that is *not* routinely presented to the public, nor is the absolute numbers of people who *leave* the country. Similarly, reference may be made to only one city or one specific period, as we saw above, when one MP finds it a "frightening concept" that one in three children born in London is of ethnic origin.

With a disclaimer referring to immigration restrictions, this is how British Conservatives continue to focus on numbers:

46. Despite all the legislation and the rules, large numbers of people are still entering this country for settlement every year. It is true that there is some attempt to stop primary immigration, but thousands are still entering this country as relatives or for other reasons. (Great Britain, Sir John Stokes, May 15, 1990, c. 844)

47. We have allowed many people into this densely populated island, with all the pressures that that caused, and about 40,000 or 50,000 people are still allowed to come here every year. . . . In the past 25 years, we have allowed hundreds of thousands of immigrants into this small island so that we now have ethnic minorities or several million people and in some cases, as we all know, their birth rate far exceeds that of the indigenous population. (Great Britain, Sir John Stokes, May 15, 1990, c. 390-391)

We see that this numbers rhetoric operates in several ways. First, as in Example 46, "thousands" may be mentioned, but it doesn't say whether this is per week, month, or year. Example 47 is more specific about this time frame, but the use of absolute numbers, if they are correct, instead of percentages is more impressive in this case. Second, the process is presented as being *out of control*: It is argued that our rules and laws don't seem to help, which is an effective way to create a panic both among the administration and the other elites, as well as among the public. Third, family reunification and of course the birthrate are used as arguments to suggest that it is not merely large numbers, but also the explosion of a demographic time bomb that must be feared. Again, it is not stated that after several years, or at least after one generation, birthrates in immigrant communities generally approach the average of the native population. Note finally that references to high birthrates are a familiar disparaging qualification of "backward" peoples: Modern people have birth control.

The numbers game is well known and duly attacked by the opposition, which also emphasizes that it is not numbers per se, but rather the numbers of non-Europeans, that is, people of color, that are kept down, says Mr. Hattersley, speaker for Labour:

48. The Government's policy towards those visitors and to immigrants is based on the simple principle of keeping the numbers down to an absolute minimum—at least keeping numbers down to an absolute minimum when those visitors come from Africa, the Caribbean or the Indian sub-continent. (Great Britain, Mr. Hattersley, July 5, 1989, c. 371, 373)

In the debates we analyzed, the numbers game is less pronounced in other countries. However, the element of lack of control of total numbers is also apparent elsewhere, as is the case in the following remark by Interior Secretary Mr. Schäuble, defending his Immigration Bill in the German Bundestag:

49. An uncontrolled increase of foreigners from non-European cultural backgrounds would further exacerbate the integration of non-European citizens, which is already difficult enough. (Germany, Mr. Schäuble, February 9, 1990, p. 15035)

Later debates in reunified Germany will focus on the hundreds of thousands of "Asylanten" that arrive in Germany each year. That numbers game in political rhetoric is magnified daily by the right-wing press, especially by tabloids like *Bild Zeitung*, providing a message that comes over loud and clear among the population at large (Jäger, 1992). In this passage, lack of control is due not only to numbers but also to what is explicitly called "non-European cultural backgrounds," which are, a priori, assumed to clash with those of native Germans. This is also emphasized in statements featuring the tolerance thresholds we encountered before: "It belongs to this fair balance of interests that the further immigration of foreigners must be limited, because for each society there are limits to the ability and the readiness to integrate" (p. 16281). Note the crucial code phrase "non-European," which obviously does not apply to white Americans, Swedes, or Russians, but to people of color from the South. That is, it is not so much cultural difference per se, but also origin and appearance that remain crucial criteria in Western immigration policies. In other words, ethnic differences are often merely a somewhat more respectable criterion for exclusion than racial differences.

Anti-Racism and Resistance

We have seen above that conservative and right-wing parliamentary discourse on ethnic affairs may be opposed by liberals. Note though that such opposition is primarily also political: That is, it is formulated as party-political opposition, and not just, or not primarily, as moral or ideological opposition against everyday political racism of the Right. Indeed, many of the more negative statements on minorities, immigrants, and refugees may be heard when the Left happens to be in power. That is, statements against racism may also have opportunistic overtones sometimes, and need not always be expressions of fundamental anti-racist ideologies. Nevertheless, when expressed publicly in political debates, such statements may very well function as a support of opposition against ethnic inequality. Here are a few examples among many:

50. The history of immigration rules is almost the history of allowing people to drown within the sight of shore. Indeed, they should no longer

be called "immigration" rules; "exclusion" rules would describe their purpose much more accurately. (Great Britain, Mr. Fraser, May 15, 1990, c. 845)

51. Men and women who are entitled to enter this country, even under the present oppressive rules, are often kept out because of the harsh way in which these rules are implemented. The best that can be said about the implementation of the rules, the way they are used at ports of entry and the frequent attitude of officers towards them, is that the Government are so anxious to keep one illegal immigrant out of Britain that they exclude a dozen legitimate applicants just to make sure. (Great Britain, Mr. Hattersley, July 5, 1989, c. 371, 373)

Such examples first show that rhetorical figures are also part of anti-racist discourse: Repetition ("history of"), metaphor ("to drown"), contrasts ("immigration" versus "exclusion," "illegal" versus "legitimate"), and numbers ("one" versus "dozen") also appear in such discourse. Note also the irony in the last sentence of example 51. Similarly, where discourse that opposes immigration or rights of minorities tends to describe Them with distancing pronouns or demonstratives ("those people"), or with overall, sometimes negative reference to their group status or evaluative qualification ("immigrants," "illegal"), these anti-racist passages try to humanize such references by referring to "people" and even more concretely to "men and women." Finally, and most important, the critical evaluation of government policies makes explicit what official discourse would leave implicit or conceal, such as the de facto "exclusion" of most immigrants, and especially the discriminatory practices, moderately referred to as "attitudes" here, of immigration officers.

The reactions of the coalition parties are truly furious when critical opposition turns into forms of action, as when a Representative of the Greens in the Bundestag, himself from an immigrant family, gives a minute of his time to observe silence:

52. I give you a minute of silence from the time I am allowed to speak here, so that you can contemplate whether you want to support this bill, a bill that refuses help when foreign children seek in this republic their last possibility to survive, a bill that fundamentally barricades this republic against people who seek refuge, a bill that invites German citizens to spy on foreign citizens . . . a bill that characterizes as foreigners and discourages young people who are born here and have grown up here and who know no other country and no other language as well as Germany and the

German language, a bill that contradicts the democratic claims of this country. This minute of silence also intends to commemorate the future victims of this bill, the refugees who are expelled to face a certain death, the destroyed families that will never come together, the foreign youth whose future will be shattered by this bill. (Germany, Mr. Messeses Vogl, April 26, 1990, p. 16277)

The effective rhetoric of repetition, enumeration, and hyperbole combines with a bleak picture of the consequences for minorities and immigrants, for example, by representing these as victims who may face death, whose future may be shattered, and so on. Victimization is one of the elements of the discourse of humanitarian values because it presupposes which norms and values have not been observed. Appeal to such values ("democratic claims") is therefore an important strategic reminder of these shared values and principles. Notice again the more concrete and personalized reference to children, young people, youths, and families.

Anti-racist discourse is itself permanently controversial. Opposing a bill is one thing, but categorizing those who back it as intolerant, and especially as racist, is an accusation that is always ferociously rejected, as we have seen before. However, whereas the use of racism in French, British, and U.S. parliaments is not uncommon, although generally denied, it may be taboo in the Netherlands and Germany. In Germany, at most the word *Ausländerfeindlich* may be used. Thus, when a representative of the Green Party in Germany calls the new bill racist, there is instant disapproval by a member of the liberal-conservative FDP:

53. A chill ran down my back when our colleague Mrs. Trenz said that this bill was a form of institutionalized racism. Whereas the older ones among us had to live twelve years under institutionalized racism, Ladies and Gentlemen, I beg you, and in particular our younger colleagues, to show respect for these terrible experiences, and not to introduce such concepts into our everyday political business. (Germany, Ms. Hamm-Brücher, April 26, 1990, p. 16295)

The denial of racism is rather specific in this case. One overall means of denying racism is by distancing oneself from those who are engaged in what is generally called racist, for instance the extreme Right. Another one is transfer to the working class (the inner cities) or to another country: racism in the United States or South Africa in European political, media, or educational discourse. In this example, distancing is temporal and political: Racism is only what happened during the Third Reich and as perpetrated by the Nazis. In this view, the more subtle contemporary treatment of minorities and immigrants can never be racist; even the word itself may not be used. Similar reactions are routine in everyday German debates, where sometimes *Rassismus* now replaces *Ausländerfeindlichkeit* in much anti-racist discourse (see also Jäger, 1992). The same is true in the Netherlands, where racism is not only generally denied, but even the very use of the term is often treated as highly exaggerated and as blemishing the tolerant image of the country. It is experienced as a moral accusation, never as a factual description of the situation. Ms. Trenz in the German Bundestag responds along similar lines:

54. [I have been criticized for having used the word "racism".] Let me explain. Racism is a word that always provokes outrage here in the German Bundestag. Racism need not be homicidal. Racism is a word that, for instance, in France is normally used. In the Federal Republic of Germany, I am not allowed to mention it, or at least I am severely criticized for it. According to its definition, racism merely means that people are being evaluated, devalued and discredited only because of their different nature, different nationality, etc. That is exactly what happens in this bill. That is why I said it. (Germany, Ms. Trenz, April 26, 1990, p. 16297)

There are furious reactions from the coalition benches, and even the Vice President of the Bundestag, chairing this session, intervenes:

55. Ladies and Gentlemen, the president is not allowed to intervene in the debate. As someone who belongs to a slightly older generation, however, I would like to say this: Racism embodies the notion of ideology, if only because of the expression itself. We have experienced something that has characterized it, and that was of great concern to us. That is why we are not people who are able to use that word in a way, as possibly our French neighbors do so. (Germany, Mr. Westphal, April 26, 1990, p. 16298)

By using his age as an argument, and claiming to have witnessed "real" institutional racism, this highly irregular intervention of the Chair shows how much the very notion of racism may be a taboo, even when properly defined, as by Ms. Trenz. Again we see that "true" racism is associated with an explicit ideology of racial supremacy, as prevailed during the Nazi period. The consensus now ("we are not people who . . . ") agrees that this is no longer the case. These interventions also show that the freedom of speech, so often strategically claimed by the Right, is curtailed as soon as critical opponents of racism take the floor.

Although this and similar debates point at the real issue of differences of degree or type of racism, their function is different, namely, to mitigate or deny contemporary racism. We have seen before that defining racism away, for example, by exclusively reserving the term for the ideology of racial supremacy, or politically by attributing it only to the far Right or the working class, is a familiar move in elite discourse.

CONCLUSION

This last section on anti-racist discourse shows that the reproduction of racism is a complex process. It should not simply be analyzed as the imposition by the white political elites of a dominant ideology of white ethnic difference or priorities. On the contrary, in the realm of politics, contemporary ethnic-racial attitudes and practices that maintain or legitimate an overall system of inequality are usually much more sophisticated and even contradictory. They may incorporate general egalitarian and humanitarian norms and values, they may be subtle and indirect, and they may focus on negatively construed properties of other groups that presuppose apparently well-founded in-group norms. Especially in the domain of culture, different norm and value systems may conflict. The unity of the state may be at variance with fundamental differences between ethnic identities. Some humanitarian or democratic values may be inconsistent with others, as we have seen with the conflict between the freedom of the press or the freedom of assembly, and hence the freedom of racist propaganda and racist parties, on the one hand, and the freedom from racial, ethnic, or religious prejudice and discrimination, on the other hand.

Moreover, ethnic or racial dominance is not absolute. Different groups, also different elite groups and subgroups, may be variously involved in the reproduction, as well as in the challenge of dominance. Subtle ethnicism and racism may be countered by equally moderate anti-racism. Tolerance and intolerance, either way, may be combined with indifference. Also, political discourse, cognition, and decision making are not independent or autonomous, but multiply interact with those of other elites, as well as with broader, popular forms of xenophobia. Minority groups themselves may more or less accept, become resigned to, or even internalize a system of inequality, or they may more or less radically oppose and resist it.

The debates in Western parliaments we have analyzed show some of these contradictions and complexities, both in their discursive structures and strategies and in the underlying social cognitions and the ensuing decision making of (white) politicians. However, despite these complexities and despite the various degrees and types of resistance, there is no question about the overall nature of the system of racism, as it is also, sometimes subtly, sometimes more blatantly, reproduced by prevailing political forces in Europe and Northern America. Despite the obvious national and regional differences, we have been particularly struck by the surprising similarities across national boundaries: The prevailing political discourse of race is remarkably homogeneous, both as to topical content and as to rhetorical and argumentative strategies of persuasion, rationalization, and legitimation. And despite the differences between, for example, the United States and most European countries, as far as Affirmative Action and legislation against discrimination are concerned, true ethnic-racial equality, justice, and multiculturalism have still not been realized anywhere in the West. Unfortunately, we have not found evidence that the dominant political elites in the West have such fundamental goals on their agenda.

4

Corporate Discourse

INTRODUCTION

In studies of elites, business corporations play a prominent role (Domhoff, 1978; Mills, 1956). Whether as owners or as top managers, corporate elites have been shown to wield increasing power, not only economically or financially, but also in political, social, and cultural affairs (Mattelart, 1979; Schiller, 1989). The virtual world hegemony of market ideologies, emphasized by the crumbling of communism around 1990, and the increasing size and transnationalization of companies further contribute to this unparalleled growth of corporate control.

Against this background it is more than relevant to examine the role of corporate elites in the reproduction of racism. Since racism has been defined in this book as an overall system of structures and ideologies of inequality between dominant and dominated ethnic or racial groups, it may be expected that racism also has economic and financial dimensions. Social inequality is often rooted in economic inequality, and the same is true for the position of minority groups. Discrimination in employment and unemployment, in the business of buying and selling, in recruitment and promotion practices, as well as in ethnic relations within the work force, involves structures, procedures, and attitudes that directly involve the corporate elites in this overall system of racism. The same is true for the reactions of the corporate community against state intervention and legislation in the domain of equal opportunities and Affirmative Action (Blanchard & Crosby, 1989; Combs & Gruhl, 1986; Wyzan, 1990).

Relevant for our discourse analytical approach to elite racism is the fact that business managers are involved daily in many forms of text, talk, and communication, such as meetings, decision making, giving orders, informal conversations, and reports (Mumby, 1988). And many issues of ethnic affairs, such as the need for a multicultural work force, Affirmative Action policies, and criteria for the hiring and promotion of minorities, are routine topics of managerial discourse. Such discourse may have many interest-bound forms and functions, ranging from legitimation of hiring practices, to managing ethnic conflicts in the company, to producing self-serving PR for the public at large. Such discourses are the object of study in this chapter.

Our data are provided by semistructured interviews with personnel managers of Dutch multinational companies. As in the other chapters of this study, the analysis of this type of elite discourse aims at finding out the *what, how*, and *why* of such text and talk, that is, its topics, its argumentative strategies, and its underlying cognitive attitudes and social functions. Similarly, we are not interested in the discourse of blatantly racist employers, but rather in the modern, seemingly liberal text and talk of highly educated personnel professionals of large companies, a form of policy discourse that is often reminiscent of the political discourse in the previous chapter.

RACISM IN CORPORATE LIFE

To furnish an understanding of corporate discourse about ethnic affairs, we first briefly summarize some research results in a number of Western countries about the role of business corporations in the reproduction of racism. Much research, as well as daily experiences by minority workers, have shown that ethnic and racial discrimination in both the work force and the corporate domain is still widespread, despite advances in attitudes and practices that have come about because of the Civil Rights Movement (Burstein, 1985). Such discrimination takes many forms, including differential hiring and promotion, higher demands, underestimation, lower pay, and racist slurs against minority workers (Braham, Rhodes, & Pearn, 1981; Marshall, Knapp, Ligget, & Glover, 1978; J. Williams, 1987; see also below). As is true for the other elites studied in this book, corporate managers also generally tend to deny or mitigate such discrimination, or blame the victim.

Racial and ethnic prejudice and discrimination in corporate life have a history that stretches back as long as corporations and businesses have existed. This history is too lengthy to be discussed here, but it should be recalled in passing that the early development of Western capitalism depended on forced labor, slavery, colonialism, imperialism, and exploitation of non-European workers, and of white European workers, for that matter (Jordan, 1968; Mintz, 1974; Robinson, 1983; Ross, 1982; E. Williams, 1964). This situation barely improved after the abolition of the slave trade and slavery more than a century ago, but continued through the long period of Jim Crow laws and segregation in the United States, in all European colonies, and within the European countries themselves, until well after the Second World War.

The more recent history of labor immigration, especially from the South, in both North America and Europe, of Mexican and Mediterranean workers, respectively, is similarly marked by many forms of exploitation, inequality, and injustice (Castles, 1984; Castles & Kosack, 1985; Cohen, 1987; Miles, 1982; Phizacklea, 1983, 1990; Phizacklea & Miles, 1980). Details of the blatant forms of discrimination in hiring and promotion, or of the generally abominable work conditions of minorities, need not be spelled out here. These have been documented in much earlier research (Braham, Rhodes, & Pearn, 1981; Wallace, 1980). Such experiences are also, often more tellingly and more truthfully, recorded in the many accounts and stories written and told by former slaves, immigrants, and minority workers themselves (Essed, 1984, 1991; Gates, 1991; Gwaltney, 1980; Jones, 1985). Instead of detailing this history, we summarize more recent research, from several countries, on various forms of corporate racism and discourse on ethnic affairs.

The United States

In *A Common Destiny*, the report of The Committee on the Status of Black Americans (Jaynes & Williams, 1989), the role of African-Americans in the U.S. economy is reviewed. Overall, the conclusions of this study point to mixed results since the Civil Rights Movement, such as:

1. Despite clear progress in many respects, there has been stagnation during the 1980s, such as in white-collar jobs.
2. In 1985, 31% of blacks lived below the poverty line, nearly three times as much as the percentage of whites, and the average income of blacks was only 57% of that of whites, percentages that either had not progressed much since the early 1970s or were even lower than a decade earlier.
3. Blacks are disproportionally represented in low-wage groups, more often have part-time jobs, and have higher (usually double) percentages of

unemployment, especially in times of recession, illustrating their relative marginality in the work force.

4. Despite progress due to the enforcement of antidiscrimination laws and the activities of the Equal Employment Opportunity Commission (EEOC), discrimination remains widespread in both the private and the public sectors. Although white attitudes usually show support, in general terms, for equality on the job, federal intervention and implementation of equal rights were supported by only 34% of whites in 1974. Blacks generally conclude, much more than whites, that discrimination continues to be a fact of everyday life. Research shows that as much as 12% to 24% of the differences between whites and blacks in employment are due to factors of discrimination in 1978 (Farley, 1984).

A study of racism in U.S. corporate life by Fernandez (1981), based on interviews with white and black managers, examines the various modes, conditions, attitudes, and discursive legitimation of discrimination of various minority groups. This study also shows that whereas Asian-Americans have virtually closed the gap with Anglo-Americans, Mexican- and African-Americans continue to be confronted with many forms of ethnic inequality in employment.

Apart from other forms of differential treatment, to which we return in a moment, such differences may at least partly be due to stereotypes and prejudices about Mexican- and African-Americans. For instance, only 9% of interviewed managers did not support statements such as the following (Fernandez, 1981, p. 45):

Most minority managers use race as an alibi for many difficulties they have on the job.

Many minority managers come from different cultural backgrounds that are not conducive to their success in management.

These are among the standard opinions of the attitude schemata usually associated with symbolic racism (see also Dovidio & Gaertner, 1986). That the perception of the prevalence of racism in the corporation is usually drastically different for whites and blacks may also be concluded from the fact that whereas 27% of whites maintained that there was no issue of negative racial attitudes at work, only 10% of black managers said so. We shall encounter such forms of denial and ignorance about the position of minorities and the prevalence of racism more often in this chapter and other chapters of this study.

Another finding of Fernandez that is directly relevant for our argument about elite racism is that upper-level white management (men and women) tend to support such stereotyped statements more often (69%) than lower-level management (54%). These figures contrast with the common claim of higher-level managers that they fully support equal opportunities, but that their policies are often sabotaged at lower levels. Fernandez rightly concludes that these results are disturbing because equal opportunity policies need the support of the top. If higher-level management does not provide a good example, it is not likely that equal opportunities will be realized in the company. As soon as minority claims are viewed as threatening to white interests, similar attitudes may be found among younger and better educated whites (Caditz, 1976, pp. 53-87). The disparity between black and white views is particularly obvious when more than two-thirds of black managers but less than one-third of white managers negatively evaluate the possibilities of access to higher positions or informal networks. Because of their own experiences with discrimination, white female managers generally tend to agree more often with black managers. A familiar stereotype shared by many white managers is that blacks get their positions because of quotas, not ability, and that companies lower their standards because of equal opportunity policies. By contrast, most blacks agree that they have to perform better than whites to reach the same levels of achievement and remuneration (less than 1% of white males agree with this opinion). Statistics show they are right: Three times as many black men (39%) have a college degree than white males at the same managerial level.

Concluding his survey of some of the ways white managers see the position of minority managers, Fernandez (1981, p. 64) concludes that the denial of racism is pervasive in U.S. corporations:

> Americans in general, and white men in particular, do not like to think of themselves as unfair. Deep cultural and psychological conflicts occur among Americans because they have ideals of equality, freedom, God-given dignity of the individual, and inalienable rights on the one hand, yet they engage in practices of discrimination, humiliation, insult, and denial of opportunities to minorities on the other hand.

This conclusion points to the inherent ambiguity and contradiction between norms and values, or the American Creed, on the one hand, and the realities of ethnic relationships in the United States, on the other. Impelled by the strong Civil Rights Movement in the 1960s, significant changes characterize the position of minorities in the United States, but findings show that many changes tend to be superficial, that is, related to overtly expressed opinions about *general* principles of equal rights and opportunities. As soon as the everyday reality of work and personal interests is at stake, even these overtly, though anonymously, expressed opinions tend to contain much less understanding of the continuing effects of racism in corporate life (see also Dovidio & Gaertner, 1986; Wellman, 1977).

Europe

For some North Americans, the ethnic or racial grass may seem somewhat greener on the European side of the Atlantic. Lacking a history of segregation and local slavery, though heavily involved in slavery elsewhere, and without large non-European immigrant groups until the 1960s, European race relations have had a rather different starting point (for a recent comparison of the United States and Great Britain, see Small, 1991).

Although there are domains in which ethnic and race relations in at least some European countries are still somewhat less polarized than in the United States, the political and legal struggle in Europe against discrimination, as in the labor market, has so far been less successful than the Civil Rights Movement in the United States. Minorities in Europe, whether Mediterranean guest-workers or immigrants from former colonies, continue to face inequality in virtually all social domains when compared to original Europeans (Castles, 1984; Hoffmann & Even, 1984; Wieviorka, 1992).

In the areas of hiring, wages, work conditions, promotion, and ethnic relations on the job, ethnic equality and justice are legally guaranteed, but far from realized in practice: Minorities generally have the worst and lowest paid jobs, if they get work at all. Indeed, minority unemployment figures in the 1980s reached 40% or more (against about 10% for white Europeans), much of this due to prejudice and discrimination by employers. Affirmative Action and equal opportunity policies are few and far between and are generally seen, among the elites, as illegitimate favorable treatment of minorities. To further illustrate these points, let us consider the situations in Great Britain and the Netherlands in somewhat more detail. (Unfortunately, space limitations prevent us from examining corporate racism in other European countries.)

Great Britain

Unlike the other EC countries, Great Britain had little labor migration from the Mediterranean countries. Many of its post-colonial immigrants came to Great Britain to work and have an economically less miserable life than in East Africa, South Asia, or the Caribbean. Following the more highly educated, smaller groups of immigrants of earlier decades, who basically came to Great Britain for advanced academic degrees or specialized work, subsequent groups of immigrants were less prepared to face the hardships of economic life, discrimination, and marginalization in a country whose colonial and imperial history and practices were not redeemed by an excellent record of tolerance and acceptance of its new citizens. On the contrary, everyday racism, as well as racial attacks against minorities, are rampant, despite both the comparatively strong (for Europe) political opposition and organization of minorities and the presence of institutions to combat discrimination, such as the CRE, which often remain rather powerless because of the obstruction of conservative courts and politicians (Lustgarten, 1987; Solomos, 1987). Of some 1,000 complaints that reached the CRE in 1982, only 200 made it to court, and a mere 30, that is, 3%, were successful (Solomos, 1987).

In Great Britain, as elsewhere, discrimination is largely enacted, sustained, and legitimated by the elites, not least by those related to a Conservative Party whose race relations policies have always been abysmal, even before the Thatcherist onslaught on equal rights. This is, a fortiori, the case for most employers who have generally opposed any form of Affirmative Action and equal opportunity policies, which are usually seen as an attack against the freedom of enterprise. On the other hand, such Affirmative Action policies were generally supported by the largely white unions, although reluctantly and belatedly (Wrench, 1987).

Several employment schemes in favor of minorities, especially for black youths, have helped counter some of the otherwise massive unemployment figures in the dilapidated inner cities, such as the training programs of the Manpower Services Commission (whose name hardly encourages women to participate), which however focused more on minority "deficiencies" than on job creation (Cross, 1987). In line with Thatcher's popular capitalism, many of these underfunded schemes appealed to the personal "responsibilities" of the young, while urging them to "set up their own businesses," probably from scratch, in economic circumstances that hardly needed such businesses. And if minorities find work at all, they will tend to be tracked toward precisely those jobs white Britons don't favor anyway, so that the familiar labor split between decent jobs for whites and miserable jobs for blacks becomes firmly established (Jenkins, 1987; Rhodes & Braham, 1987). Sociocultural, economic, and historical factors also have divided Asian and West Indian immigrants in the labor market. The former, like East Asians in the United States, have been more successful in commerce and retail businesses, a difference that is sometimes used by conservative politicians and media to blame the black West Indians for the distinct racism and other factors that cause their predicament.

For a comparison of managerial discourse on ethnic affairs in Great Britain and the Netherlands, the study of racism and recruitment in Great Britain by Jenkins (1986) is especially useful, and his results are briefly summarized here by way of introduction to our own analyses. His interviews with (often more than reluctant) managers focused particularly on their discourses and cognitions on Affirmative Action. His theoretical approach is compatible to ours, and also tries to relate the level of macro inequality of racism with the micro level of everyday discriminatory practices and prejudices. He also uses the concept of a mental model, though in a sense where we would use the terms *script*, *group schema,* or *attitude*. Thus, recruiters have models of more or less desirable workers, as well as models of procedures of hiring and promotion, and they use such models in their everyday interactions in the company.

Managerial models feature various criteria for hiring and promotion, such as appearance, attitude, maturity, age, speech, and experience, some of which are quite subjective and of course open to ethnic bias. Jenkins therefore distinguishes between criteria of normative job *suitability* and actual *acceptability* of workers. As might be expected, certain minority applicants may very well be suitable for a job, but are not always acceptable, for example, because they do not match the preferred model of a normal, that is, manageable, worker. Jenkins found, however, that such judgments may differ among managers: Personnel specialists (who are sometimes committed to Affirmative Action schemes) generally have fewer stereotypical attitudes than line managers. The latter sometimes express themselves in racist terms that are generally more blatant than in the Netherlands and the United States, and seem to have changed very little over the past decades. Besides these attitudes or models, the recruitment procedures, such as word of mouth and advertising, also systematically favor white applicants.

Many of the argumentative moves used by British managers also appear in our own data. For instance, refusals to hire minorities are often impelled by the transfer move: I would hire them, but the other workers or the clients don't want them. Such decisions are often legitimated by blaming the victim, namely, by attributing language or education deficiencies or strange cultural behavior to applicants. Jenkins concludes his study with a play on words: It is both the acceptability of racism, and the racism of acceptability that closely intermingle in recruitment and selection procedures in British organizations.

We have reason to assume that the situation is hardly better in most other European countries. We have seen that the same is true for politically prepared public opinion about Affirmative Action and equal rights on the labor market. Consequently, European managers hardly feel pushed, except by economic reasons, to hire more minority personnel, and most of them are therefore ill prepared to manage the multicultural work force of the future.

The Netherlands

The position of ethnic minorities in the Netherlands, and in particular in Dutch corporations, is hardly better, and in many respects even worse, than in other Western countries. In the late 1980s ethnic policies followed the general no-nonsense trend, in which taboos in ethnic affairs—namely, to openly say racist things—should no longer be observed. "Pampered" minorities should be put to work, as the somewhat more moderate Dutch versions of Reaganomic and Thatcherist ideologies proposed. Although unemployment among ethnic minorities is among the highest in the Western world (in excess of 40%, although recently declining), Dutch tolerance, that is, tolerance of discrimination, also allowed corporations to successfully oppose legislation on Affirmative Action. In the Netherlands the preferred explanation for minority unemployment tends to blame the victims by emphasizing their true or alleged cultural differences and language and education "deficiencies," and either ignore or mitigate discrimination by employers.

True, overall, education levels of minority applicants, and especially of minority women, are generally lower than those of white Dutch, and the sociocultural background of many immigrant families may also limit access and success of applicants (Roeland & Veenman, 1990). However, these factors cannot fully account for the differences in employment since well-educated immigrants or those who speak Dutch fluently, for example, from Surinam and the Dutch Antilles, have less chances to be hired or promoted than the native Dutch. It may be concluded, therefore, that besides socioeconomic and cultural back-grounds, it is recruitment and employment procedures that effectively exclude minorities from both state institutions and private business corporations. Another major factor is what two influential Dutch re-searchers in this area cautiously call the "selective preferences of employers for autochthonous employees" (Roeland & Veenman, 1990, p. 87), that is, what we call ethnic prejudice and discrimination.

This is also clear from other empirical research on everyday racism in general, and biased recruitment practices, discrimination, and ethnic intoler-ance on the job in particular (Den Uyl, Choenni, & Bovenkerk, 1986; Essed, 1984, 1991; Niesing & Veenman, 1990; Pattipawae & Van der Burght, 1988; Sikking & Brassé, 1987). Indeed, earlier research shows that one-third of employers overtly admit preferring white Dutch employees, another third would accept only some minority groups, and only one-third said they would not make any distinction between white and minority (Veenman, 1984). When confronted with high unemployment among minorities, such as Moluccans, managers may respond as follows: "Maybe they have the ability, but not the ambition. They don't make an effort. They lack the necessary ambition, that's it" (Veenman, 1990, p. 142).

Characteristic of much white research about minorities in the Neth-erlands is that, despite such findings, the researcher adds a disclaimer like the following, thus discrediting the experiences and the knowledge of Moluccans, stated in many accounts: "It has of course not been demonstrated that each time Moluccan respondents thought to have observed discrimination, there had actually been a case of (intentional) discrimination" (Veenman, 1990, p. 142).

Thus, minority knowledge about discrimination is typically dealt with as a subjective opinion, whereas other, objective factors of unem-ployment are studied in much statistical detail. The very notion of racism is conspicuously absent in such scholarly accounts of minority unemployment in the Netherlands, because racism is still seen merely as an ideology of racial superiority (see also the critical study of Dutch academic racism by Essed, 1987). Similarly, many forms of unintended discrimination, or "good business reasons" for unequal treatment, may fall outside the scholarly definitions of discrimination in the Nether-lands. No wonder that white scholars are sometimes shocked when they encounter events like the following:

> There was the story of this Moluccan girl who after the job interview was
> invited to walk through the company. When she returned to the selector,

she was asked whether she hadn't noticed anything special. After the applicant had stated that it seemed a nice firm to her, she was told that was not the point. The selector explained: "Haven't you noticed that only white people work here? Well, that is how we would like to keep it." Then the girl was allowed to leave. (Veenman, 1990, p. 257)

It is the aim of this chapter to further examine such stories, especially the argumentative moves and style of the managerial discourses about ethnic employment practices and attitudes: Why is "involuntary" discrimination always mentioned last, if at all, in the explanations of minority unemployment, and why is it generally argued, also in politics, that the necessary changes of corporate mentality cannot be enforced by laws or regulations?

POLITICAL AND CORPORATE DISCOURSE: MUTUAL INFLUENCES

Corporate discourse on ethnic affairs is multiply related to other forms of elite discourse on this topic, but such a relationship would require a complex yet interesting study of inter-elite influences that cannot be provided here. A few words may suffice about the obvious links between corporate and political ideologies and discourse in the domain of race and ethnic relations, some of which have been briefly discussed in the previous chapter. Ideologies of free market liberalism, nonintervention by the state, the primacy of profits, and the laws of competition, among others, are clearly shared by business managers and currently prevailing neoliberal politicians alike. No-nonsense policies against social or ethnic outcasts, lowering minimum wages and cutting social welfare programs (if there are any), and other attacks against the welfare state are part of a new political credo, also found in Europe, about which corporate managers could not agree more. It need hardly be brought up that most politicians, some of whom are business people themselves, have in mind the attitudes and interests of their mostly white voters—and workers—while at the same time they are scarcely inclined to antagonize Big Business.

This also affects ethnic and race relations policies and the ways minority unemployment, Affirmative Action, and equal opportunity policies are being approached by most politicians and most managers. We have seen in the previous chapter how Republicans and the Bush administration consistently tried to hold back Democrat-supported anti-discrimination legislation by hammering on the "Quotas!" buzzword. Europe has not even come halfway, and serious Affirmative Action programs are barely discussed, let alone implemented in most European countries, despite growing minority unemployment and corporate discrimination, as pointed out above. In the Netherlands, as we shall see in somewhat more detail below, minority unemployment in excess of 40% is serious enough to keep the political and media discussion going, but so far no more than half-hearted attempts have been made to persuade employers to go the extra mile in hiring more minorities, and so far there are few tangible results. Most employment schemes are government sponsored, and it may be the case that the millions spent on them are largely being paid to white bureaucrats or social workers who monitor or implement such programs.

Slightly tougher measures, such as ethnic monitoring and contract compliance, seem to become somewhat more attractive for at least some politicians, but as yet, in 1992, these have not gone beyond initial political debate. Consequently, European employers have not yet felt the heat of strict legislation, and many of them continue to either ignore the issue or defend their turf with the well-known slogans of corporate freedom. If they are slowly changing toward a more ethnically diverse work force, employers are usually only accommodating economic constraints, such as a tight labor market or a growing number of minority consumers. As is the case in politics, explicitly anti-racist or emphatically multicultural employers exist, but they are the exceptions that prove the rule.

Without further analysis of these complex relations between politics and business in the domain of majority-minority relations, our point here is that political discourse on ethnic issues may borrow from corporate discourse, and vice versa. More specifically, conservative politicians in particular will tend to resort to legitimations and support of business practices and ideologies in order to block any attempt to introduce tougher antidiscrimination or Affirmative Action legislation. The communication lines are hardly obscure here: Most information and discourse will reach corporate managers through the mass media, through trade publications, and through negotiations with the unions and the state, apart from meetings and informal talk with other managers. In the Netherlands, where ethnic issues have become a major media topic, minority unemployment is hardly a secret. Yet, after the employers' organizations had pledged in 1990 to hire 60,000 minorities in 5 years, an evaluation in 1992 showed that more than 95% percent of employers pretended they had not heard about a deal that had been front-page news for days. Although such so-called ignorance may be a well-known example of strategic reluctance to implement the message, it does tell us something about a consensus of ignorance-cum-indifference among a large part of the corporate community.

How close corporate and political discourse may intermingle can be shown in the use of We in the following fragment of a speech by Republican Representative Dannemeyer in the United States:

> This nonsense about quotas has to stop because when we begin to hire and promote people on the basis of their race, we are going to bring to our society feelings of distress, feelings of unhappiness, and these emotions will accumulate and ultimately destroy us. (H6332, August 2, 1990)

Although the use of We could be interpreted as generic ("we, in America"), it certainly also suggests a close identification between political and corporate concerns ("we, who hire people"), and not primarily those of the workers, even if the rest of this fragment talks about the "feelings of distress" for society as a whole. Of the LaFalce-Goodling substitute bill, the same speaker says the following: "It also has the support of the business community, such as the chamber of commerce, National Federation of Independent Business, the National Retail Federation, and so on" (H6333).

It would indeed hardly support his argument if this speaker would recall that the substitute bill is opposed by hundreds of national organizations, including the major unions, the churches, minority organizations, the ACLU, the National Organization for Women, the American Bar Association, and many more. Similarly, many other Republican interventions in this debate appear to speak directly for the employers among the people they represent, and thus energetically reject what they see as the "presumption of employer's guilt" (Mr. Dornan) embodied by this bill. If discrimination is recognized at all, it is apparently a taboo to speak of those who actually do it: "The assumption is that the people who create the jobs is that they are wrong, they are bad, they will not do things on their own. Words such as 'bigoted,' 'mean-spirited,' 'discrimination,' 'unfairness,' have wafted through this debate, and I think that is wrong" (Houghton, H6797).

If we now go to the other side of the Atlantic and listen to the former Secretary of Social Affairs and Employment of the Netherlands, Mr. De Koning, giving a speech during a symposium on the occasion of the

10th anniversary of the Association of Moroccan Workers, we hear not only a condemnation of discrimination, but also a rejection of what in the Netherlands is still called "positive discrimination":

> [P]ositive discrimination also has a number of disadvantages, however. First, I may mention the risk of exacerbating the conflicts between foreign and Dutch employees. If we would improve integration of workers in the labor market by incidentally lowering the usual quality standards in business, then the danger exists that business firms would be forced to hire minorities who actually do not meet the requirements set for a specific function. . . . This again may lead to stigmatization. Finally, such a measure would be inconsistent with this administration's policy not to impose measures on the social partners. (Ministry of Social Affairs, Press Release, November 27, 1986)

Although Affirmative Action policies in the United States are far ahead of the Dutch ones, we still notice that there are similarities in the "discourse of caution" accompanying official talk on minority employment policies: Transfer by attributing resentment to the white workers, the presupposition that minority hiring may lead to lowering of standards, the false empathy with the Others ("We do it for Them, otherwise They would be stigmatized"), and the more honest recognition of prevailing policy: "We don't want to force employers." We will encounter more of such argumentative moves below in the discourses of business managers themselves. The point here is that the similarities between political and corporate discourses on ethnic affairs and Affirmative Action, even across national boundaries, suggests a well-established white elite consensus.

MANAGERIAL DISCOURSE

What do corporate managers themselves have to say about minorities? To answer that question, we need their text and talk, and this is where the first research problems present themselves. Despite their position of control, and hence their preferential access to public discourse, corporate managers generally are reluctant to express themselves in public. The corporate voice is primarily one of Public Relations, which focuses on optimal services or products, rather than on corporate personnel policies. Only in times of conflict, for instance during a strike, do we find public declarations on such policies. The same is true with the annual reports of corporations, specifically those speaking about hiring and promotion policies and practices. Apart from general figures, these too do not detail the experiences of personnel or applicants, but take the form of glossy positive self-presentation. Problems and conflicts are discussed only when they are either already public knowledge or too serious to conceal.

Access

This reluctance of corporate managers to talk for the record about social and personnel policies is even more pronounced when the position of minorities and women is concerned. Managers are acutely aware that these are very sensitive topics, and accusations of discrimination are seen as bad publicity. In an effort to get more insight into the discourse and opinions of managers, we interviewed personnel managers of a dozen major firms in the Netherlands. Some of these firms are well-known multinational companies, with thousands of employees in the Netherlands alone.

Access, especially to the larger companies, proved to be far from easy. In our case, therefore, we did not say that we were specifically interested in minority policies, Affirmative Action, discrimination, or related issues, but asked to talk about more general "social" policies of the organization. When the issue of Affirmative Action was discussed, this mostly meant that managers would talk about the position of women, which for most firms is a much more familiar issue than the position of minorities. However, we shall focus on what they have to say about minorities.

Method

All interviews were held in the offices of the managers, that is, within the immediate context of the organization, so interviews are occasionally interrupted by phone calls, colleagues, or secretaries. All interviews were audiotaped. As was the case with our earlier research on racism and discourse, the interviews were as informal as possible (for methodological detail, see van Dijk, 1987a). Although a number of possible questions and issues were previously programmed, the interviewees could speak at length about any other personnel issue, for example, recruitment, promotion, difficulties of getting or keeping personnel, and so on. Apart from simulating a normal conversation, this freedom of talk was also vital to creating a relaxed situation, in which managers would not feel "investigated" by academic researchers (in this case, students). The topics of diversity of employees, special policies for women and minorities, and Affirmative Action were brought up casually, sometimes by the interviewees themselves.

The interviews were typed out literally, though not in as much detail as we would do for a conversational analysis; however, hesitations, false starts, repetitions, or other properties of spontaneous talk were transcribed. Our examples will bear witness to this natural property of unplanned talk: Many sentences appear to be highly disorganized, even ungrammatical, a property further exacerbated in our quotes because translations from the Dutch are sometimes only approximate. Particularly because of the stringent monitoring of such sensitive talk, there is much self-correction, and it is often difficult to understand what exactly the managers are intending to convey.

Although our interviews were meant to resemble informal talks with these personnel managers, it should be stressed that such talk is institutionally grounded. They speak *as* personnel managers, and *as* representatives of their organizations, and they know it. At the same time, they realize that the interview is conducted as part of an academic research project. Hence, in such interviews, they see as their main tasks to (a) give information about the personnel policies and practices of the organization, and (b) persuasively present these as following good business norms, and to defend them in more general moral terms. As with their other products, managers see their personnel policies as something that should be sold as effectively as possible. Not only should their own personnel buy such policies, but outsiders, such as journalists or scholarly investigators, are assumed to need special PR talk that enhances a good impression (or avoids a bad impression) about the organization. However, when policies are not yet fully developed, as is the case for Affirmative Action and minority policies, especially in the smaller organizations in the Netherlands, managers will often improvise and present what they clearly mark as their personal opinions on such issues.

Our analysis of the relevant passages in these interviews focuses on overall topics, argumentation, and local moves, as we have done for political elite discourse. Particularly for the analysis of talk about what they see as delicate or controversial issues, such as Affirmative Action, it will be necessary to examine the argumentative structures and strategies involved. Underlying knowledge, relevant scripts, models of previous experiences, overall attitudes, and fundamental ideologies are presupposed in such discourse, and especially in argumentation.

Main topics

The overall structure of the interviews was approximately the following: The purpose of the interview was briefly (and vaguely) explained to the interviewee as a means of getting some information about the social policies of the organization. The more astute interviewees, most of whom have a university degree, wondered why students of discourse analysis would be interested in such an issue, a question answered by the true reply that we were especially interested in the way such policies were being formulated. After this preliminary presentation, there were usually lengthy sections about the nature, goals, products, or services of the company, and the position and tasks of the interviewee. Next, social and personnel policies were discussed, during which the issue of Affirmative Action was brought up. Most of the rest of the interview would be about that and related issues. As we already indicated above, much of this is about the position of women, a topic with which the managers are much more familiar. Indeed, 3 of 12 the managers are themselves women.

Topic Openings

The transition from relatively safe topics, such as the products or services of the company or the tasks of the manager, to more sensitive topics, such as Affirmative Action (AA), needs some analysis. Consider for instance the following fragment of an interview with a personnel manager of an international bank (I: interviewer; M: Manager interviewed):

1. (MM-1, 3, Bank)

I: I think I know enough about the company. We already talked about the percentage of women and about the percentage of aliens. Could you tell me a bit more about that? Do you do anything about positive action?

M: No.

I: Is there a special policy?

M: No, no, no, there isn't. Which, which, that doesn't mean that that women or foreign employees are being excluded.

This brief exchange presupposes and implies several things. First, the interviewer recalls the earlier topic of percentages for special personnel categories. This not only establishes topic coherence with the earlier part of the interview, but also makes the topic acceptable within the framework of possible topics, while prompting the interviewee for more specific information about such personnel categories. Against this topical background, the question about Affirmative Action follows naturally. The question of the interviewer about positive action also presupposes several things. First, he presupposes that the interviewer knows what positive action is, but on the other hand does not assume that positive action is a normal policy of the company, otherwise he would have asked something like, "What are your experiences with positive action in this bank?"

The flat "No" of the bank manager confirms that the question is to the point, a real question and not merely a rhetorical question, or a way of initiating a topic. Such a brief reply prompts a more detailed question about, for example, policies about Affirmative Action, a question that is also replied to negatively. However, in this case, both conversationally and socially, simple negation would seem unacceptable, because if the manager knows what Affirmative Action is, as is presupposed by his negative answers, then he also knows that, in principle, there is at least a moral requirement to do "something about positive action," and a flat denial may be heard as a lack of social responsibility, if not a form of discrimination. It is this possible inference that needs to be prevented, and so the manager denies that women and minorities are being excluded. This in turn implies that, according to him, lacking AA policies does not mean that the bank discriminates against women and minorities. As we have found in the previous chapter, this form of denial is classical in much talk about minorities or race relations, which we shall see in more detail below.

Ignorance and Evasion Tactics

If not brought up by the interviewees themselves, the topic of minorities is initiated by a direct question like, "Are there minorities in your company?" It is interesting to note that whereas the managers often have an idea of the percentages of women in the company, they often claim they do not know such percentages for minorities. One reason is that the registration of personnel may not include such information, as is required in "monitoring" policies, which have not yet been adopted in the Netherlands. Another reason for this ignorance, however, may be more strategic, and suggests that there are either no employees or few employees from minority groups. Consider the following responses to such a question about the presence of minorities. (Note that what has here been translated as *alien* is expressed in Dutch by the technical term *allochthone*, which has recently become current in official discourse in the Netherlands, and which is now often used instead of *minorities, guest workers*, or more generally, *foreigners*.)

2. (MM-2, 3-4, Oil Company)

M: We take all kinds of nationalities. The focus is on Dutch and English. Yes, we are in those two countries. But [name of oil company] is of course active in many countries, and it is important to be represented internationally.

I: And within . . . within the Netherlands, do you employ any aliens? You can't mention the precise number, but do you have any . . .

M: It is difficult to give a precise answer to that. I don't have a grasp of that. No, I don't think that until now we were aware of what an alien was.

3. (PW-1, 3, Chemical Company)

I: Do you have any idea regarding the relation between the Dutch and aliens?

M: No, I don't even know that. Because we have a lot of nationalities here, uhh, first because we are the international headquarters here.

In both cases the rather unambiguous question about minorities in the Netherlands is, at first, answered by the managers of two multinational companies in terms of "nationalities." Both use the same argument why they have an "international" staff: They are international companies. However, minorities in the Netherlands are not seen (or counted) as part of such an "international" work force—nor, for that matter, as employees to be proud of, it seems. Worse, the evasion tactic of the manager of the oil company in Example 2 shows that there are even conceptual problems: Despite the widely known minority policy of the government, and despite the frequent coverage in the press about minority unemployment, the speaker argues that he doesn't even know exactly which groups may be called minority groups. Only a few companies, especially those who are (or were, before privatization) public utility companies, have precise numbers and targets, and are correspondingly proud when they have a relatively large number of minority employees. There seems to be a correlation between various tactics of what may be called ignorance, evasion, or conceptual unclarity, on the one hand, and the lack of explicit minority employment policies, and low participation of minorities in the company, on the other hand. Positive self-presentation ("We are very international") is used as a move to cover for such ignorance or evasion tactics.

Concession and Self-Criticism

Some managers are not happy with the ethnic situation in the company and would have liked to have more minority personnel. The bank manager, who used to work in a hotel, favorably compares the hotel with his somewhat stuffy bank, and does so as follows, when asked whether the reason for this difference may be the educational level of possible employees:

4. (MM-1, 4, Bank)

M: Culture, education, uhhm, I rather think it is the supply, the broad range of job categories you have in a five-star hotel, and the specific, culturally determined, sometimes perhaps the somewhat stuffy uhh atmosphere that you have within a bank. The hotel business is much more informal. The bank has a culture which uhh has been going on, proceeding for centuries, before you get any changes. Also, you don't have trendy customers, with a trendy public.

Note that although this speaker obviously prefers the more relaxed ambiance of the big hotel, his reserves about the stuffy culture of the bank are hedged ("sometimes," "somewhat," and the like). Also, he does not speak about his own bank, but about the banking business in general, which is characterized as conservative, and thus contrasted with the "trendy" nature of hotel life. Such forms of strategic concession and self-criticism, even when hedged, are fairly rare in elite talk about minorities. Indeed, this speaker only briefly acknowledged the possible reason formulated by the interviewer. Instead of focusing on properties of the foreign workers, as most managers, and indeed most white speakers, would do, he blames the bank for its lack of change and openness. These are the typical discourse signals of moderate forms of multiculturalism.

Top-Down Policies

Although companies may have few minority employees, they may be aware of minority unemployment and the sociopolitical necessity to employ more minorities:

5. (MM-2, Oil Company)

M: Suddenly, this is now being emphasized. Like you have to hire aliens. . . . And now we are being asked to do that. [Organizing training] The same trend exists, the same trend now forces us to emphasize aliens. In that regard we are considering the training we may provide.

Note that this "trend" is not interpreted as a moral or business obligation, but as a top-down, political decision: Minorities are "forced" on companies. It needs little argument that such an attitude is not exactly favorable for the recruitment of minority workers. We shall come back to this corporate resentment against political pressure.

Targets

In 1990 the Dutch social "partners," as they are commonly and somewhat misleadingly called, namely, the business community, the government, and the unions (workers), finally agreed, after long and difficult negotiations, to set a target of 60,000 minority personnel to be hired by Dutch companies within 5 years. This would, in principle, lower minority unemployment from about 40% to the national level of about 11%. Employment agencies, special liaison officers, and other officials would be involved in this effort. Companies themselves would be asked to make special efforts to hire and train minority personnel. Although a precise target is set in this agreement, there is no sanction on noncompliance; the measure is largely voluntary. However, if there was no such agreement, and if the target was not realized, the business community would be confronted with a stricter (though still far from compulsory) policy of employment equity, as in Canada, or similar schemes for minority employment.

Let us examine how managers react to this national agreement between government, the unions, and their own business community, as represented by several organizations of employers.

6. (MM-2, Oil Company)

M: Well, exactly, yes uhm, we are working on it. We haven't got our
policies ready yet. Part of the policy is of course the awareness in the
organizations that there is a problem. I think we are now working on that.
A small publication about a policy for aliens, that we are thinking about
that in the first place. Uhh discussions with the central company council,
discussions with the company councils, and then such policies are gradually
taking shape. And usually you don't have it fixed at once. But okay, change
is taking place. But often the rest is slowly following. It isn't that we have
a ready-made policy for the coming 5 years. We are now gradually warming
up the organization.

The strategy of this answer is one that combines moves of positive
self-presentation ("we are working on that," "we are doing our best")
with moves of caution and reluctance ("change is slow"). Note that
there is also a trace of the move of transfer: Although "we" (management) have no full-fledged policies yet, it is suggested that first the
employees need to be persuaded, as if they would be the major obstacle
to minority hiring. Finally, the bureaucracy of corporate decision making, for example, the company councils (in which employees are also
represented), is used as an argument that betrays an underlying lack of
enthusiasm for change. Other examples emphasize skepticism about the
feasibility of the national agreement: They are seen as mere political
"statements" that may bring about "good intentions," but hardly concrete decisions. Such examples are replete with hedges ("I don't know"),
hesitations, and other stylistic forms that suggest reluctance about the
possibility of implementing such official policies. Only some employers explicitly support the agreement and see it as a collective responsibility of the business community, as is the case for the manager of a big
steel plant that has many immigrant workers.
   At the other end of the ideological spectrum, there are those who are
cynical at best and see it as a "hobby" of the personnel department:

7. (MM-3, Computer Company)

M: [The 60,000 jobs agreement. Did you hear about that?] Yes, I suppose
the information should be around here uhhh probably in the garbage. If a
personnel manager begins to bug us about that, then it depends on uhh . . .
the order we have scored, whether we listen to that. I am giving a caricature
of course, we have an asocial policy, but I think it works like that.
Uhh . . . only if there is an economic trigger for us.

This blatant reply is consistent with other statements of this employer about minorities and women (to him, women don't belong in computer companies). Throughout the interview, he emphasizes the need for economic criteria; he might be prepared to hire more minorities if he could make extra money. Usually underlying free market ideologies are more cautiously expressed than this when the topic of minority employment comes up. Thus, a representative of an employers' organization does support the national policy and also believes the target can be realized, but at the same time has doubts about the mentality of employers, thus attributing to others, in a well-known transfer move, his own ideological opinions about the profit-oriented nature of business, to be discussed in more detail below:

8. (SG-1, Employer Organization)

But what I do hear in the business community, from our members, they say "We do want to cooperate, but it has to come from both sides, business is not a welfare agency, production is essential, profits have to be made, and we do expect from people who get a wage that they perform well, and we also understand that those people should get a real training, and we are willing to pay for that." (p. 10)

This quote also introduces the assumption that hiring minorities is not seen as a business necessity, but as form of welfare. At the same time, the familiar presupposition about the lack of quality minority personnel is subtly voiced, as we shall see in more detail later.

Positive action

We have seen before that the issue of Affirmative Action is not exactly popular among business managers in the Netherlands, where it is usually called positive action or, more negatively, positive discrimination. Such policies are usually associated with the employment of women. As is the case in other countries, Affirmative Action policies tend to be linked with obligatory quota, with "imposing" women and minorities on a company. Let us examine some of the arguments managers use to reject, or to sometimes reluctantly accept, the very principles underlying Affirmative Action policies (passages between parentheses are summaries of actual talk):

9. (MM-2, Oil)

M: But . . . uhh . . . not making sacrifices, as a company. Not the person who is not competent. (We are already doing something like positive action). But, indeed, I am not in favor of uhh hiring aliens preferentially. We should rather give them a better education. Rather doing more about that than to make concessions in order to get them into the company.

10. (MM-3, Software)

M: Positive action, yes, that, uhhh . . . positive discrimination. Yes, as I already said before, I don't believe in that. I only believe in economic stimuli. Uhhh . . . I don't think you should formulate a policy if there is no rationale behind it. If you do that, that is irrational behavior. We should combat that with the intuition of business interest. Uhh . . . or you may want to do that because of PR considerations, and then it is rational again.

11. (PW-1, Chemicals)

[What is positive action?] (Silent and then cautiously) I find that a very difficult question. It seems very negative if I say there won't be any positive action, but in fact it is the ultimate form of discrimination. You fundamentally interfere in equal opportunities, in equal people. In our company black, or yellow, or red or white people must meet the same demands for function requirements, and if they do not meet these . . .

These reactions range from reluctance and skepticism to overt hostility. One strategic move is the "We are already doing that" reaction: Since we hire both men and women, since anybody may apply, since nobody is discriminated against, and we even provide special training if necessary, we are already engaging in positive action. Such answers, as well as the other, more directly negative reactions, are invariably followed by *but*, and therefore function as a disclaimer: It should not mean that we have to hire incompetent people. Apart from resentment against government intervention and obligatory measures, it is again the presumed lack of quality that is used as the reasonable and rational objection against Affirmative Action. Argumentatively, it is a strong move, since nobody would favor hiring or promoting incompetent people, so the argument is clearly persuasive for all who share the prejudice that women and minorities are generally less competent than white males. Few employers in Europe even consider the possibility that it might be an asset for a company to have a multicultural work force and hire untapped quality workers from minority groups.

Besides the few companies that would hardly survive without minority personnel, most companies that are cautiously supportive of Affirmative

Action see it as a form of PR, as in Example 10, or as a sociopolitical duty. Note also, in Example 9, the positive self-presentation move prompted by the previous rejection of Affirmative Action: We are prepared to do something for Them. Something similar happens in Example 10, where positive action is redefined as a form of negative action, that is, as an attack on corporate freedom and an attack against true equality between people. This is a particularly interesting passage because it so clearly shows how group members are able to manage, solve, and persuasively defend the ideological contradictions with which they are confronted; rejecting Affirmative Action is seen as a plea for equality. In sum, most arguments against Affirmative Action are derived from corporate ideologies about the freedom of enterprise, or they blame the victim (They do not speak the language, They lack proper training).

Quality and Preference

We have seen that the argumentative strategy against Affirmative Action features such well-known arguments as, "We select our personnel on the basis of quality only" and "We have no special preferences." The quality argument is widespread in all discussions about equality and civil rights, especially when employment of women and minorities is at stake. The underlying ideological presumption is that business (or, indeed, public agencies) only hire the best candidates. There is ample evidence that what constitutes the best candidate is hardly based on objective criteria of qualification, but on a flexible set of criteria that can best be categorized as "the best fit," that is, as giving preference to candidate(s) who best fit the company. This "best fit" may involve job qualifications, but also more subjective criteria as adaptability, similarity to the present work force, and generally all other criteria that define the acceptability of applicants (Jenkins, 1986). Gender, race, and ethnicity are important, though usually tacit or even unconscious criteria in such acceptability decisions. Affirmative Action policies make such criteria explicit, and for many employers they suggest that their hiring policies are discriminatory. This is one of the further reasons why employers resent Affirmative Action: They are reluctant to admit that earlier hiring policies were not quite as neutral as they would like to think.

Quality arguments pertaining to "good business practice" are often coupled with no-preference arguments that address moral considerations of equality:

12. (MM-2, Oil)

M: [Opinion about 60,000 target] I don't think that we would immediately give preference to hiring a lot of aliens. Because, we do not operate, uhh, after all we are a business company. We are there to function economically. Uhh . . . with women, we don't do that either, that is, that we take them in preferentially. If they are good we are very much open to them.

13. (SE-1, Supermarket Chain)

[Ads that say that equally qualified women are preferred?] We don't do that, no, that is nonsense, and it doesn't work. [Two equal candidates?] That never happens, that is an academic question, that never happens. (In fact, we would take both). I don't like to engage in theoretical discussions about whether or not to take a woman. That only results in interminable debate. . . . We don't care whether they are males or females, if only they have quality, then we take them.

14. (ES-2, Steel Plant)

M: I think that what you, that you should provide equal opportunities. [How?] Yes, but then, not in the sense of giving preference to specific people, but in the sense of removing barriers, you have to get hold of the barriers.

The arguments involved in such passages either explicitly or tacitly show a mixture of what are presented as objective facts ("it doesn't work"), corporate principles ("we operate economically," "we must make profits"), and more general moral arguments ("we treat people equally"). Another ploy is to claim, as in Example 13, that the choice does not even occur, and that "academic" or "theoretical" questions are irrelevant for business practices. The third manager rejects preferential treatment with another well-known argument, shared by the business community as well as government, namely, that hiring more minorities would be no problem as long as the candidates are sufficiently qualified: They need special training. In other words, the "barriers" often mentioned in such discourse are those of minorities themselves, and do not exist within the company.

We have reviewed research indicating that this presupposition is only partly true: Many qualified minorities (or women) are not hired anyway. In sum, the arguments against preferential treatment are all part of the strategy of positive self-presentation, in which companies show themselves to be rational, reasonable, in favor of equal treatment, socially alert, practical, and oriented toward objective economic criteria.

Color-Blind

One of the stereotypical arguments in corporate discourse of personnel managers is that they are color-blind, an argument we also encountered in the U.S. House of Representatives during the debate about the Civil Rights Bill of 1990. Dutch managers say it like this:

15 (PW-1, Chemicals)

M: People who meet our requirements are being hired, whether they are brown, yellow or black or white. Whether they are males or females. . . . In our company black, or yellow, or red or white people must meet the same demands for function requirements, and if they do not meet these . . .

16. (PW-4, Chemicals)

M: I don't care whether to grab someone at the left or at the right, whether he is green or yellow, as far as color is concerned, if only he has the capability to perform the labor for the price we are willing to pay, at the moment we need it, and with the quality and quantity we need.

Interestingly enough, the color-blind argument is used especially by those managers who show little interest in Affirmative Action policies. In other words, just as the disclaimer "I have nothing against . . . , *but* . . .'' rather faithfully reflects negative attitudes about minorities, the color-blind move seems to disguise the fact that in practice, those managers are not color-blind at all, precisely because when they talk about minorities they expect all kinds of problems. At the same time it is true that they are "blind" to the potential of minority employees.

Politics Versus Business

One of the tenets of business ideologies is the opposition, if not the conflict, between business and politics. National agreements, Affirmative Action policies, targets, quotas, and related issues are viewed as belonging to the world of politics. They are seen as impractical, unworkable, theoretical, or even nonsense. Politics should not interfere and everything will work out fine. This set of arguments may be used both by companies that do not feel they have any social responsibility ("we are not a welfare agency," "we are only there to make profits"), as well as by usually larger companies that do feel socially responsible and may want to develop special policies to hire women and minorities, but resent both political pressure and bureaucratic red tape:

17. (MM-3, Software)

M: I mean an active personnel policy to get a larger number of women or aliens at [name of company]. We think that should not be expected from us. We are not, we don't have that social function, as a company. . . . This is a luxury problem. If you are government, or Unilever or Philips, yes, one could maybe afford that luxury, although even then I think you can't. In fact, only because these [companies] have become institutions. Business is there to make profits. . . . We as general management see it as a pastime of personnel management. . . . [Minority employment policies] It is understandable that politics is doing that. I think there is a vast distance between what a political administrator is trying to regulate, and what is being recognized in the business community. Let them do what they want.

18. (SG-1, Employers' Organization)

We are against that. Uuhh Contract Compliance I believe comes from Canada, has been born there, conceived there, and I agree that it works there, according to our information. We don't find it such a good idea. Means that government only gives government contracts to specific companies if they have met a number of criteria. Well, we think that you are completely at the mercy of the whims of politics.

One argument that is particularly powerful in corporate discourse is to focus on the ethnic employment practices of national or local government agencies or businesses themselves:

19. (SE-1)

M: (Imposing contract compliance. The cities themselves are doing a lousy job). No, that is precisely the big problem. That's why they can't impose that, because if there is one employer who is poor in this area, it is the government.

Although the argument, as such, is sound, given the poor equal opportunities record of public institutions in the Netherlands, at the same time it projects strategic forms of transfer and avoidance of responsibility.

We Are Willing, but They Are Not . . .

A well-known move, combining positive self-presentation goals with those of negative other-presentation, is contrasting properties of our own group with those of the Others. Although research has shown that up to two-thirds of managers explicitly admit to preferring white Dutch personnel or to hiring only special groups of minorities (Veenman, 1990), they may be more reluctant to admit such an attitude in a more direct interview. Indeed, few of our interviewees flatly state they do not want minority personnel. On the contrary, we have heard them emphasize that they do not make any distinctions in hiring. Continuing this argument, the managers who have a slightly more positive attitude toward minority hiring may even detail real projects in which they have been trying to get more minorities. This positive stance is then contrasted with the argument that They (minorities, women) do not want to apply, do not work hard enough, do not pursue training, or otherwise fail because of their own lack of ambition or motivation:

20. (SG-1, Employers' Organization)

M: Look, if we all want to make that effort, accept it, to help those people get a job, you know, this difficult target group, and they flatly refuse to get some training, then a policy of penalties should be applied, then the allowance should be cut by half, because that is the consequence. From our side we are willing, we are making the effort, if they are coming to the company, we are willing to make extra expenses in the starting phase.

21. (SG-3, Catering Firm)

(Young foreign "girls" working in assembly line work). Who don't know much, don't want to do any training, but who like the job. . . . (Reacting to ads). There are many of them here, but they have had little schooling, they don't dare. I don't think such a girl would be able to do it. Nothing against those people, but they have, they come from, they have a bit of a different background in fact. . . . (They do work) that requires not too much thinking, because they don't know that, and their Dutch is also rather broken, so those girls automatically end up in production. But they like that job.

22. (SE-1, Supermarket Chain)

(We had a project with a black employment agency, which seemed very successful, we got a lot of highly educated black applicants). Everybody was madly enthusiastic, also our management . . . and we thought, well this is the first project that is really doing fine. But, many have gone already, 6 weeks later, and of all these appointments only two are left. . . . I don't know why, and we are going to investigate why. But that is of course very sad, and also very annoying for us, because they simply stay away . . . From our side, we have done our very best. But maybe so exaggerated, so enthusiastic, that uhh we made a wrong selection . . . that we left out the critical note. . . . They simply did not meet our requirements.

These arguments are sometimes accompanied by long stories of frustration, which imply the self-laudatory point that "we have been so good to them," "we did our best so much," followed by the usual *but* of such disclaimers. Typically, individual and isolated experiences are often generalized for the whole group, inferences that would seldom or not ever be made for failing white Dutch or irrelevant categories of personnel, for example, people from a specific city. The fact is that research again shows that minority applicants are often even better motivated to perform well or to get extra training. The argument therefore works both ways. On the one hand, failure to hire, keep, or promote minorities is being concealed by attributing the blame to the others. At the same time, such face-keeping stories are clearly meant as excuses, if not as self-praise in a discourse in which implicit feelings of shame and implicit resistance against suspicion of discrimination or prejudice are part of a very complex form of difficult interaction.

The young female manager of the catering firm (Example 21), who can hardly be suspected of sexism, freely engages in the usual practice of underestimating foreign "girls" working in her firm, and sees them not only as less motivated, but also as less bright, and yet happy to do the menial work on the assembly line. Note that the job and the salary of these young women are categorized as something "on the side," that is, not as a real job.

In particular the manager of the supermarket chain (Example 22) gives seemingly contradictory expression to his underlying attitudes. On the one hand, he is heavily engaged in special projects to hire more women and minorities, and shows enthusiasm about successes, though he admits the company needs women and minorities badly because his stores lack personnel. On the other hand, he resents any difficulty, problem, or conflict in minority hiring. These problems are usually attributed to the Others, and not to the white supervisors or co-workers of the minority personnel, not to the trainers, not to labor conditions, and especially not to management.

Classical and straightforward are complaints of alleged language problems, as reported by the manager of a steel plant:

23. (SE-2, Steel Plant)

M: (We used to have many nationalities in the plant). In the 1970s there were situations that nearly made the factories unmanageable, because of the cacophony of their languages. Those people spoke insufficient Dutch. Sometimes there were 6, 7, 8, 9, 10 nationalities in the factory, mixed, and that . . . did not work out, those guys could not communicate with each other, and that was a disaster.

As part of the "lack of qualifications" argument, the "language deficiency" argument is quite frequent in corporate discourse. It does indeed reflect real problems, especially for specific groups of older Moroccans or Turkish workers, and young people who have just emigrated. On the other hand, the language argument is not relevant for Dutch-speaking Surinamese, nor for the growing group of Turkish and Moroccan youths who have spent most of their lives in the Netherlands and speak Dutch fluently. Thus, for the majority of potentially qualified candidates, the language argument is either pointless or exaggerated. This suggests that it is part of a complex strategy of defense, excuses, or justifications for not hiring minority personnel: If they do not even speak our language properly, then they are themselves to blame for their high unemployment rates.

Discrimination and Its Denial

At least implicitly, and sometimes explicitly, most discourse about corporate recruitment and promotion of women or minorities, Affirmative Action, or targets deals not only with minority unemployment but also with majority discrimination. Indeed, in any discourse about minorities, white speech participants are aware of the norms of nondiscrimination and conscious of the fact that they should present themselves as tolerant citizens. Negative remarks, and certainly practices that might be seen as unfavorable for minorities, therefore need to be explained, mitigated, excused, or justified in the many ways we have been examining in this book.

The same is true for corporate discourse, in which topics such as minority employment and discrimination are also quite sensitive. This is especially the case for better educated personnel managers, and for those firms that do have explicit minority or equal opportunity policies. For them, positive self-presentation, good PR, and an awareness of social responsibility toward minority groups are essential, so that any suspicion about discrimination can be immediately dispelled. How do these managers talk about discrimination?

24. (MM-3, Software)

M: [Bad intentions?] No, there are no, there is even no fundamental discrimination or aversion, not at all. But that means that . . . it doesn't matter to us, and we may take it into account, positively or negatively, but that doesn't change the disadvantaged position of aliens, I believe.

Example 24 shows that even the manager of the software firm, who has shown skepticism, if not cynicism, about Affirmative Action policies for women and minorities, and who openly denies having good intentions in this respect, at the same time denies having bad intentions. He just claims that he is not interested in the issue beyond "economic stimuli."

25. (PW-1, Chemicals)

M: [Proportion of aliens to Dutch?] I don't know that. Because we have a lot of nationalities here. First, because we are the international headquarters. It speaks for itself that, you know, yes, people are not being discriminated. People who meet our requirements are being hired, whether they are brown, yellow or black or white. Whether they are males or females.

The manager of the large chemicals company (Example 25), on the other hand, who first evaded the question about minority hiring by referring to his "international" personnel, includes in his argument, as if implicitly accused, that minorities are not being discriminated. Note that this argument is backed up with the well-known color-blind move, and the general objectivity condition: We hire them if they are qualified. In other examples, discrimination is not entirely denied:

26. (PW-4, Chemicals)

M: In practice, yes, that cannot be denied, there may be a problem integrating people in an organization like [name of company] who uhh uhh master the Dutch language uhh only poorly, That of course within this organization—it would be insane to deny that—there are people who are employees, maybe also managers, who in their immediate environment have difficulty uhhh with somebody who uhh is culturally very different, who has, say, another pattern of behavior, of values and norms. Of course that happens.

This manager of another international chemicals firm is more articulate about possible discrimination in the company. In his case, the argumentative move is first one of cautious concession: Maybe there are some people in the company who "have difficulties" with people from different cultures. Note that the notion of discrimination, let alone of racism, is never used in this concession. Also, even the moderate concession of "having difficulties" is itself toned down in several conversational ways, for example, by hesitations.

More important, an expression such as "having difficulties with someone" usually suggests that it is the Other who is responsible for these difficulties. In this passage, this is indeed the case. As is quite usual in many other forms of both popular and official discourse, it is the cultural difference of the Other who is blamed for the "difficulties" some workers may have with aliens. Also, the alleged lack of language proficiency, already discussed above, is seen as an impediment to a positive ethnic climate in the company. For the main argument of this book, it is especially interesting to observe in this example that "difficulties" among employees are primarily attributed to lower personnel— and only as an afterthought, and with more hesitation, to some other managers. In other words, even if some prejudices may be conceded, they are associated not with the elites, but with popular forms of intergroup interaction. This passage is closed by a detailed argument (not quoted here) that emphasizes the positive role of top management in combating discrimination in the plant.

The next example is interesting for other reasons:

27. (SE-1, Supermarket Chain)

M: [Problems of discrimination in the company?] Well, not among our personnel. Our personnel is young, and young people generally have less problems. [The older generation?] Yes, especially our customers (follows a story about the negative reactions of customers against a fundamentalist Moslem girl working as a cashier).

In this case the manager speaks from experience, because the supermarket chain employs a relatively high percentage of minority workers, usually as cashiers. The denial of discrimination is especially interesting, and partly convincing, because this manager correctly argues that most of the personnel is young, and younger people have "less problems." However, when asked about the older generation (usually store managers), such discrimination is at first conceded, but then immediately transferred to the customers, who sometimes treat minority personnel in a negative way. Then this manager tells an elaborate story of a young Muslim girl who is being resented by some customers (see below for a further analysis of that story). So, again, we find different ways of toning down, explaining away, or transferring possible inferences about discrimination in the company.

The interviews with the few employers who explicitly support multicultural policies are interesting for many reasons. Compared with discourse fragments by managers who have a more ambivalent or negative attitude about minorities or Affirmative Action, they show a lack of hedging, justification, excuses, and especially negative other-presentation. In this case it is the own (white) group that is being criticized, although they may be people of another (lower) department, and then we again find a form of transfer. Also, such managers need not say that they do not discriminate, nor that they hire all colors, and so on. In multicultural discourse this is simply presupposed and need not be asserted.

THE DISCOURSE OF NATIONAL POLICY MAKING ON MINORITY EMPLOYMENT

For this project on corporate discourse on ethnic affairs, we also interviewed top-level representatives of the major employers' organization (VNO), the national federation of unions (FNV), and officials of an institution, the Labor Foundation ("Stichting van de Arbeid"— SvdA) in which employers, unions, and the government meet for biannual negotiation, such as the 60,000 job target of 1990 discussed above. Full analysis of these interviews requires a separate study, so we shall merely summarize and highlight some of their major characteristics.

Obviously, at this high level, blatantly racist arguments do not occur. On the contrary, as for the employers, the formulation of positive policies is as much a form of positive self-presentation as it is a realization of business necessity. More subtly though, as is the case for the political discourse in the Netherlands discussed in the previous chapter, we find elusive versions of the no-nonsense approach to minorities. Thus, the VNO representative emphasizes that all social "players" should take their "own responsibility," a well-known liberal reference to individualism and the need for less government, or indeed corporate, responsibility in social issues and welfare. At the same time he argues that "those aliens" should no longer be treated (or see themselves) as different, so that all general policies would also apply to them. It need not be argued that favoring "equality" in a fundamentally unequal situation is a well-known ploy to prevent Affirmative Action.

As may be expected, VNO discourse, much like that of the government (see Chapter 3), focuses on the duties and obligations of minorities, and less on their rights. The opposite is true for business companies, which should remain free from state intervention or legislation that does not work. Indeed, even the nationally agreed upon target of 60,000 jobs for minorities should be seen as voluntary: Companies only have to try to meet this goal; the employers' organization will only inform them of the agreement. Despite earlier failures of companies to hire more minorities, the VNO representative remains essentially optimistic; as for women, he also sees significant changes in minority employment in the near future. The key is changing corporate "mentality": Forced, legislated change, as in the United States, will not work in the Netherlands. This opinion forms the heart of the political and corporate consensus against Affirmative Action in the Netherlands. It is embedded in the following, quite explicit summary of corporate ideology:

28. (NWO)

M: You could call it a question of ideology, of belief, but uhh in any case, it is maybe a little bit of an ideology we have, that we say, it is the inalienable right of the business company, I don't say "the employer," but of the business company—with its company council and the unions or whatever—to set its own policies. That is so to speak the core of corporate policy. And when you look at it from the labor market perspective, that it should be said that we, I think in the Netherlands, that our labor market is too rigid instead of flexible, that it is constrained in many ways already (minimum wage, tax pressure, labor laws, and you name it). If in addition to that you are also going to regulate the volume component, you haven't got any flexibility left, and that will be economically risky. . . . In actual practice it will turn out to be not really effective.

These feelings of employers are also well known in the bureaucracy of Dutch consensus politics, for instance among the officials of the Labor Foundation. One official, who may be presumed to mediate between union and corporate positions, clearly takes the point of view of the employers:

29. (SvdA)

M: (Not only minorities, but also women, the disabled, youths, and combinations of these groups). They [employers] are gradually going nuts about all the different groups they have to pay attention to. . . . I personally, that is my opinion, don't believe in it. . . . These kinds of policies cannot be enforced. Negative sanctions, as practice has taught us, are extraordinarily frustrating, and also extraordinarily little effective.

Again, we encounter the ideological core of Dutch positions about minority employment: volunteerism, personal morality, and (personal) social responsibility. Questions of mentality and belief cannot be legally enforced. Free negotiations in the labor market will themselves regulate and resolve the problem of high minority unemployment: "Primarily, the initiative should be within the company. . . . There is [only] a moral obligation" (SvdA).

Finally, union discourse focuses on those elements that are rare in political and corporate discourse, namely, discrimination, the necessity of AA legislation, and especially, close monitoring and control of employers. The unions, however, are unable to translate such claims into national policy because of the joint resistance of government and employers. For the unions, most employers will only comply with AA policies when there is legal pressure on them, and even then they will hire minorities for only the worst jobs. In national negotiations some employer representatives will even make derogatory remarks about minorities. There are exceptions, however: The unions have experiences with a few employers who are seen to be more multicultural in practice than the national employers' organization, whose directors "haven't met a black person in their lives," and which is seen as hampering rather than favoring developments.

There is one complication. Union officials realize that discrimination is not limited to managers or employers, but also exists among white workers. Capturing one of the well-known formulas of everyday, popular resentment against the "favoring" of minorities, one union official defines this concern in the following way:

30. (FNV)

M: They notice the resistance, but unfortunately they don't do anything with that. . . . Union members look at their representatives, and say, "And what about us? What is happening for us? These minorities, again . . ."

Thus, the implicit predicament is that even when the unions would have more control over minority hiring, for example, through direct labor agreements for each economic sector, they still would have to face resistance from their own ranks. Just like the manager of the steel works, quoted above, the union official concludes that the workers are a "reflection of Dutch society," implying that even among unions members there is prejudice and discrimination like everywhere (to wit, 10% of union members in the Netherlands voted for a right-wing, racist party) (see also De Jongh, Van der Laan, & Rath, 1984).

Examining the discourse of officials and policymakers of the administration, of the relevant agencies, and of the business community and the unions, we find an even more abstract and polished version of corporate minority policies than among company managers. Business managers have different but sometimes concrete experiences, and their opinions and talk are formed accordingly (e.g., featuring stories, accounts of personal experiences, and so on). At the highest national level, contradictions disappear, and we are confronted with "pure policy" talk and text, with admirable goals and principles. More detailed analysis of their discourse, and especially the counter-discourse of the unions, is necessary in order to infer the complex underlying attitudes and ideologies.

STORYTELLING

Although most talk about minority recruitment and Affirmative Action is expository and hence argumentative, arguments may sometimes be backed up by stories, for example, about personal experiences of managers, or about events in the company that otherwise illustrate the main point. Stories are a well-known genre in business companies and have several functions, such as providing examples of corporate norms or procedures, or signaling power relations in the company (Mumby, 1987).

To better understand the use of narrative structures and style in such corporate arguments, let us examine one of these stories, as told by the manager of a supermarket chain, about a young fundamentalist Muslim woman. The argument, as we have seen above, is about discrimination: Young people in the stores do not discriminate, whereas the older people, especially customers, have "problems" with minority personnel. The story is not based on direct, personal experience, but must have been told to the manager by someone else, possibly the manager of the supermarket who is the "hero" of the story:

31. (ES-1, Supermarket Chain)

M: The clearest example, which eventually turned out fine, I found . . . at a given moment we here on the board took the decision uhh to allow Muslim women to wear their scarves, or what do you call them, at the cash. So, a cashier with . . . You had one in Paris, you had them in London, but especially in Paris . . . and that we had a cashier who wants to sit there with her scarf on, do you agree. And then our board said they agreed. If they want that, that is their business, and it is even hygienic [laughs], so why would I be against that. And, but, as I said, the board may well say that, but in actual practice it is different of course. Because I know one of our stores, where someone like that was offered by the employment agency, like, "we have someone who could work for you, it is a fundamentalist Muslim who wears one of these scarves." And then the store manager, he got his personnel together, his own personnel in the canteen, and they had a discussion about that, shall we do it or won't we. Personnel said, yes, what are we fussing about, it is so difficult to get people, and we can't bypass somebody like that. That would be very stupid. And he said, "Let her come." And she also worked at the cash register, and . . . the customers stayed away. They did not queue up at her cash, but at the others.

I: Even after a while, when they got used to it?

M: Yes, and then, well, then they said . . . and there was a rather big, perceptible difference it was, a marked difference, for the other customers. Then the manager, who panicked, again got his employees together, and again discussions about, come and have a look at what's happening. And again the employees said, we should not be put off, we go on with this, and then those women should stay away, we don't care, and then they persisted and after some time she got other, so there were other customers, I don't know, or the same customers, who went to her, and it was quite an bright girl, it was really a very good girl.

I: And she was not bothered by the fact that she was discriminated that way? That must have been awful.

M: Yes, yes, but okay she was extraordinarily friendly with the customers, so it was quite an experience for her, also for the other employees.

I: Was it a young girl?

M: Yes, it was a young girl. But that, that man, was quite overwhelmed, he, he, he found it terrific, that manager, but he, because everyday she was still being taken there by her father and all that, that was really . . . quite a different culture. It happened for instance that customers in that kind of situation . . . throw the money simply on the floor, and did not hand it to her, those kinds of situation.

I: Oh no!

M: Oh yes, that happens. And then one has to bite the bullet to, well. But . . . he wanted that she would go to work as a supervisor, because she was simply a very good girl. But then he really had to, because in that case she would have to be transferred to another store, but that man went to great lengths, also in these meetings with his personnel, with his supervisors to get this settled, that she would be transferred. Yes, and then she nearly had to be sanctified, and he got away with that, but what happens, as usual, she is taking a vacation in Turkey, stays away for 4 weeks, and doesn't come back. Damn it. That happened a while ago, and I don't know whether she is back by now, but so. . .

I: That is not exactly inspiring.

M: Yes, but you have to place yourself in the position of that manager, how he feels. Damn it! Then you think, then he thinks, he thinks, this is once, but never more. Why did I go through all this trouble?

I: Would he have gone through this trouble for a Dutch woman?

[Telephone interruption]

M: But anyway, those kind of things. That shows that it is a very difficult matter, and that it is also very difficult to have people accept using different values and norms, that is a very slow process, you have to do that very carefully, but at the same time not evade it.

First of all, the overall narrative structure of the story is more or less canonical, and may be organized by the following categories and the macro-propositions (topics) filling them:

Introduction/Summary: This is an example of discrimination.

Setting: (Implicit: In one of our supermarkets).

Orientation-1: (Implicit: hiring personnel).

Complication-1: One applicant is a Muslim fundamentalist and wants to wear a scarf.

Resolution-1: Supermarket personnel agreed to hire her, and management decided to allow her wearing a scarf.

Complication-2: The customers avoided her. One woman threw money on the floor instead of giving it to her.

Resolution-2: Personnel decided to keep her, and ignored customers' discriminatory acts.

Evaluation-1: She was a very good and friendly employee. The store manager was very much impressed by her.

Orientation-2: The manager did his best to get her promoted.

Complication-3: Then she went to Turkey and did not come back.

Evaluation-2: The manager was highly frustrated.

Conclusion: It is very difficult to have personnel from a different culture.

In fact, two stories are mingled here, namely, the story about the discrimination against a Muslim "girl" by customers, illustrating the current topic of talk (discrimination), and the story of the manager who did his best to get this girl promoted, but then became frustrated because she "disappeared." The two stories are not only related because they feature the same protagonists (Muslim girl, manager, other employees), but also because they are two instances of the same general problem, that of cultural differences. As we have seen above, the acceptance of the girl is evaluated positively by the storyteller, namely, by attributing tolerance, resistance against discrimination (by a customer), and common sense ("we need people," and "wearing a scarf is even more hygienic") to the manager and his crew. In other words, although also the Muslim girl is described in favorable terms in the first story, the real hero is the manager, whose predicament is reported in more detail, and with more empathy. In the second story, the manager remains positive ("he went through a lot of trouble to get the girl promoted"), whereas the Muslim girl's evaluation becomes negative—she deserted.

This story is both a corporate story and an ethnic relations story. As an ethnic relations story, it shows the familiar positive in-group-protagonist faced with the negative behavior of an out-group member. The coda or moral of that story is: We are doing good for them, but they are not even grateful. This moral is implied by the story's complication as well as by the general conclusion that it is difficult to live with people who have different norms and values. Note that nowhere in the story it is even hinted that the Muslim girl might have been grateful for the support she had from her colleagues and her manager.

On the other hand, the corporate story is more specific and deals with the procedures and practices of the organization. Being interviewed as a personnel manager of a supermarket chain, the storyteller needs primarily to convey a positive image of his company. Questions or suspicions about problems, such as discrimination, need to be answered in a way that leaves no doubt about the moral integrity of the company and its managers. Before this story starts, therefore, discrimination in the stores is denied with the plausible argument that young people do not have such "problems." Second, the possible blaming of older employees is transferred to racist customers, a problem which both the manager and his employees deal with admirably. In other words: Not only does our personnel not discriminate, it even fights discrimination. Third, to show that Affirmative Action and promotion policies work well in this company, it is shown that even for as unlikely a candidate as a fundamentalist Muslim girl who wears a scarf, managers will try to do everything to get her promoted. In other words: Not only does the company go to great lengths to encourage qualified personnel and does not discriminate in promotions, but its managers will also personally fight for their employees. So the moral of this second story is: Our company will do everything for its employees, and it does not discriminate. And: Despite cultural problems and differences, our normal procedures of recruitment and promotion also work in favor of minorities. Hence: We are not only a good company, but also a true equal opportunity employer.

We see that stories may be powerful elements of argumentation. Instead of, or in addition to, making general statements about the recruitment practices of the company, the personnel manager may be much more persuasive by telling about a real event. First, such an event is likely to be true, which makes both the storyteller and the argument more credible. Second, actual personages can be easily modeled, and memorized, so that the impact of the story will be more effective than that of isolated statements. Third, evaluations about recruitment and promotion practices of the company need not just be given by the personnel manager, they can be directly inferred by the listener/interviewer.

So the supermarket company is doing well on both counts in present Dutch society, namely, as a business company and as a company that knows its social responsibility, is open to change, and contributes to the equal opportunities of minorities. This form of highly persuasive public relations talk is the corporate dimension of the overall characteristic of elite discourse about minorities, namely, to show that we are tolerant, do not discriminate, and even help minorities. Positive self-presentation strategies are eminently illustrated by what is called PR in corporate life.

Such is the talk of the managers in more or less formal interviews with outsiders. Although topics, overall arguments, and some of the more subtle properties of such spontaneous interview talk allow for inferences about the reluctance, if not the resentment, of many managers regarding a more positive policy of minority recruitment, it will have to be from the accounts of minority group members that actual practices, attitudes, and talk within the company are inferred (Essed, 1984, 1991). Indeed, only the Muslim girl can tell us why she preferred to stay in Turkey instead of working for the supermarket in the Netherlands.

DISCOURSE PROPERTIES OF CORPORATE TALK

In our analysis of corporate talk, we discussed the topics, issues, and arguments that are being used in discussions about minority recruitment and related issues. We have found that as soon as topics such as equal opportunities or discrimination come up, we may expect a number of standard sub-topics, standard arguments, and even standard moves of defense, face-keeping, and positive self-presentation. Discrimination tends to be attributed to others, or it will be denied, toned down, or excused, if not presented as being provoked by the different behavior or norms of the Others. Affirmative Action and especially more compulsory measures, such as contract compliance, are similarly associated with a set of routine counter-arguments, such as, "We select the best candidates," "We are not a welfare agency," "We need to make profits," "It does not work," and so on. At the same time, because such arguments may sound too negative, other more positive moves and more elaborate strategies are being implemented, such as the "no difference," "color-blind," "equality," and "we do not discriminate" moves. Note though that such denials are often followed by negative attributions to minority group workers, such as "They do not speak the language," "They do not want to participate in training," "They have different norms," or "They lack motivation." Finally, we have seen how stories may be persuasively used to prove the positive attitudes of the employer—and the negative attitudes of minority personnel (or of clients).

Less obvious in the English versions of the Dutch interviews are the more detailed stylistic and conversational properties of corporate discourse. We found that specific words, such as *discrimination,* tend to be avoided, whereas others, such as *racism,* are virtually absent. The term *foreigner,* which is the popular term to denote ethnic minorities, is used less in corporate talk and has been largely replaced either by *ethnic minorities,* or rather by what we translated as *aliens* (*allochtonen* in Dutch, as opposed to *autochtonen*).

Mitigation and toning down of negative actions are among the well-known stylistic and rhetorical ploys of positive self-presentation. In talk with managers, explicitly derogatory terms about minorities are virtually absent. On the contrary, such discourse is close to official political discourse, and often a form of positive PR talk, in which extensive use is made of such jargon as "human resources," "wasted talent," "awareness," and similar expressions used by modern business to talk about personnel. More subtle stylistic features of talk, however, may suggest or indicate group-based distance or even resentment, for instance, through hyper-pronominalization and especially such demonstratives as Those People.

5

Academic Discourse

ACADEMICS AND RACE

A superficial analysis would assume that most scholars only have relative power in their academic domain of teaching and research, so that they would have only marginal elite status. However, further analysis shows that in present-day societies, the indirect influence and power of scholars are tremendous: Their ideologies, students, research results, reports, and advice play a fundamental role in technological advances and the management of corporations and the State. This is also true for the management of social and political affairs, for instance, in the domain of ethnic relations. Social scientists formulate philosophies and more specific ethnic relations theories that are multiply applied in the many committees, institutions, and bureaucratic frameworks that organize ethnic decision making in virtually all social domains, including immigration, refugee policies, housing, employment, education, and culture. In sum, influential scholars play an increasingly powerful role, namely, as academic support for other elites, such as politicians, corporate managers, bureaucrats, and the media. As the producers, managers, or brokers of knowledge, scholars are among the most prominent symbolic elites of contemporary society (Aronowitz, 1988; Bourdieu, 1984, 1989).

If knowledge is power, then knowledge of other people may be an instrument of power over other people. This truism is especially relevant in examining the academic discourse of race and ethnicity. The history of this corollary runs virtually parallel with the history of racism. Since Greek and Roman antiquity, and especially since the Renaissance up until today, European scholars have been engaged in the study of other, non-European peoples. Their insights and ideologies have had an enormous impact on broader public, political, economic, and social relationships between the peoples and regions of the world. Their observations have often served as legitimation for colonialism, exploitation, and dominance of non-European peoples (Asad, 1973; Fabian, 1983; Hymes, 1972).

The history of European expansion has shown how travelers, explorers, traders, and the military were often accompanied by academic or religious scholars interested in the soul, the mind, and the body of the Other. The very notion of race is of their making, and resulted from the desire to classify and categorize as much as from the will to dominate. Thus, philosophers of the eighteenth century, historians of the nineteenth century, and anthropologists, biologists, psychologists, and other social scientists of our century all contributed to the fabrication of a web of facts, myths, and half-truths whose ideological impact is felt even today (Amin, 1988; A. J. Barker, 1978; Khoury, 1990; Poliakov, 1974; Todorov, 1988). Our analysis of high school textbooks in the next chapter shows how deeply such an ideological framework is embedded in the semi- and pseudo-scholarship underlying education and the curriculum. The same is true, up to the present, for the academic study of race and ethnic relations, not only in anthropology or ethnography, but also in demography, geography, biology, psychology, sociology, linguistics, literary studies, history, and the arts (F. Barker, Hulme, Iversen, & Loxley, 1985; Römer, 1989; Said, 1979).

Summarizing this often documented Western or white history of the disciplines purporting to describe and explain the Other, we find that, with some variation and some exceptions, the continuous conclusion of this profoundly ideological endeavor was that We are somehow superior to Them. Until not too long ago, and at least until World War II, this ideology was as explicit as it was blunt: The intellectual, cultural, political, or moral superiority of Western civilization, Christianity, or the white race was no more doubted than its military or economic dominance, and indeed was often used as an explanation, if not a legitimation, of European hegemony (Amin, 1988; Lauren, 1988). The people of color of the rest of the world were thus variously seen as inferior, if not as animals, primitives, children, true or noble savages, or other non- and proto-humans, either by nature or by culture.

The history of this type of academic discourse need not be detailed here; there is a vast literature documenting the history of ethnocentrism, Eurocentrism, and racism in academic discourse (see, e.g., Amin, 1988;

Barkan, 1992; A. J. Barker, 1978; M. Barker, 1981; Chase, 1975; Haghighat, 1988; Kuper, 1975). We should realize, however, that the remnants of its various ideological frameworks continue to be widespread in many contemporary political, social, and cultural domains. Racist parties routinely apply the once widely accepted scholarly conclusions about white supremacy in order to legitimate their hate of minorities or immigrants of color (Billig, 1978). In more respectable, mainstream thinking, where white supremacy has largely been declared obsolete, however, we find similar ideological orientations, formulated in the less crude terms of "cultural difference," which is the seemingly neutral facade of what is usually meant: cultural incompatibility, if not white/Western superiority. International politics and diplomacy, as well as national ethnic policies, are thus imbued with ideological and cultural frameworks of which the elements continue to be supplied by academics (Lauren, 1988; S. Ryan, 1990).

Also this modern history of academic racism has often been documented. The sociobiology and psychobiology of race and ethnicity are prominent examples of scholarly orientations that continue an age-old tradition in the seemingly objective terminology of modern science (Barkan, 1992; M. Barker, 1981; Chase, 1975; Haghighat, 1988). Whether discussing genes and assumed hereditary properties of races, intelligence or culture, both the main conclusions and the suggested informal implications are usually the same: They are worse, or They have less of it than We have. Throughout the history of scholarly discourse about race, such inferiority may strategically be coupled with selected forms of superiority, leading to doubtful praise or admiration for the "noble savage" (Dickason, 1984) and to the present-day idolization of blacks in sports and popular music. In the ideological division of humanity, excellence in some sectors of physical or cultural performance may be granted to Them, as long as intellectual, technological, corporate, political, and other forms of excellence that really matter are primarily associated with Us.

It is striking that under the surface of sometimes sophisticated scholarly analysis and description of other races, peoples, or groups, both in earlier times and today, we find a powerful ideological layer of self-interest, in-group favoritism, and ethnocentrism. Whether the accounts are historical, ethnographic, psychological, sociological, political, economic, or cultural, many tend to focus on differences and not on similarities, on hierarchy and not on equality, on oppositions and not on variation, and a variety of corresponding metaphors that signal opposition and hierarchy, such as modern versus backward, fast versus slow, or efficient versus inefficient. As we shall also see in the school textbooks that are the didactic offshoot of yesterday's scholarship, it is quite common to describe other peoples as still living in the stone age or the Middle Ages, and generally to equate progress with Western technology and later times (Fabian, 1983). Ironically, such progress may even be associated with sophisticated weapons, such as nuclear bombs, laser cannons, SDI ("Star Wars"), or concentration camps, and the mass destruction of millions of people that Our peoples have caused, as compared to the "primitive" or "barbaric" killings in "tribal" wars in, say, Africa (A. J. Barker, 1978).

The role of science and scholarship in white or Western dominance shows not only in its ideological products but also in its organization. Prestigious scholarly journals are nearly all published in the United States and Europe, and edited and filled by scholars from the same regions. The same is true for publishing houses. International scholarly conferences, even when held in warm, beautiful Third World countries, may witness a majority of white faces. In other words, what has often be concluded more generally for Western culture and for Western media, news, and entertainment, is even more true for scholarship. And while some critical scholars may criticize such overall cultural imbalances, they seldom look at their own domain.

It is not surprising that such institutional arrangements of scholarly hegemony, and their concomitant practices, are supported by deep and barely conscious ideologies about the supremacy of Western science. Our critical analysis does not aim to deny the many advances of such scholarship, let alone to romantically idealize the striking lack of facilities, infrastructure, or money as well as the sociopolitical constraints that characterize much scholarship in most countries of the South. What we want to know, however, is what ideologies and discourses are used to maintain, emphasize, or legitimate this scholarly divide. In other words, what are the contributions of scholars and scholarship in the reproduction of white, Western power and hegemony, relative to the countries and peoples of the South, including those people from the South that migrated to the North? Indeed, how does science support existing cultural dominance, economic and political power, and military might, both at home and internationally? More specifically, how do the scholarly portrayals of other races or peoples, and their accounts of interethnic and international relations, serve the maintenance of hegemony?

THE "NEW" RACISM

As we have seen in the previous chapters, the analysis of racism shows that, despite obvious forms of similarity and continuity, contemporary racism has also changed, for instance, when compared to its pre-World War II manifestations (Lauren, 1988). These sociopolitical changes in many countries, as well as worldwide, had their impact, if not their origin, in the world of scholarship (Barkan, 1992). After World War II, the Western colonial empires crumbled, and the colonized peoples rapidly broke away from the current dominance to enter a post-colonial phase in which Western power, and exploitation, became more indirect. Similarly, and more or less at the same time, the Civil Rights Movement in the United States, under the impact of both African-American resistance and changes in white liberal thinking, contributed to a different status of ethnic minorities, as well as to different ideologies about ethnic relations. Increasingly, both internationally and nationally, blunt racism and other forms of ethnic or racial oppression became suspect, and reactionary-style thinking and acting were more or less aligned outside this more liberal consensus (Dovidio & Gaertner, 1986). International cooperation in development, as well as equal opportunity policies at home, were incompatible with explicit prejudices and derogatory discourses in the West about the Rest, as is also shown in the repeated criticism that UNESCO leveled against ethnocentrism and racism (Kuper, 1975; UNESCO, 1983).

However, one of the assumptions of this book and of this chapter is that these ideological changes did not fundamentally affect the basic relations of ethnically based power. Again, both nationally in Western countries, as well as internationally, the economic, political, and cultural dominance of both European and Europeanized countries and societies was hardly dented by occasional equal opportunity practices, a limited sharing of wealth, and a more tolerant public discourse. To support and legitimate this new racial and ethnic order, both at home and abroad, the ideology also had to change. Although the notion of racial supremacy was increasingly found to be old-fashioned, more subtle forms of ideology found their way into political, social, and scholarly discourse. Apparently more neutral, the key notions became that of culture and cultural difference, suggesting a more historical (while potentially changing and changeable) and a more egalitarian concept of ethnic relations. Race was thus replaced by ethnicity; racial differences by cultural differences, for example, those of language, religion, philosophies, customs, norms, and values; and racism by ethnicity (Mullard, 1985).

The public discourse of politics, the media, and social institutions gradually changed in close interdependence with those of scholarship. Africans or Mexicans or Turks or Asians were no longer "inferior," but simply had a different culture, although such a culture and its socioeconomic and political dimensions (poverty, family structure, urban resistance) often remained categorized as pathological or at least as deviant. Such analyses were frequently used to blame the victims for the problems they encountered in white society (Ryan, 1976). We shall see later how cultural difference is seldom portrayed as neutral in the press, either, but tends to be qualified in the more negative terms of social problems and deviance. Thus, drugs, crime, and inner-city problems, among other issues, became major concerns of politicians, the media, and scholars alike. Indeed, results of scholarly work on minorities often provide the "scientific" basis of political and media discourse on ethnic affairs.

The same is true for the domain of education, where failing policies and practices now tended to be attributed to a lack of educational motivation, if not to cultural particularities of minority groups (see next chapter). Socioeconomically, minorities were no longer simply exploited, but disadvantaged participants in a more or less failing system of social welfare, while continuing to be subjected to discriminatory practices in employment (see Chapter 4). Following the lead of social scientists, sometimes of good will, politicians, journalists, and social workers were engaged in explaining away the real power relations in Western societies.

Contemporary scholars are hardly immune to the many forms of elite racism, as is made clear by the conservative onslaught, also in the media, on multicultural curricula in schools, colleges, and universities, especially (but not exclusively) in the United States, under the rubric of "Political Correctness" (Nash, 1992). Although the debate and the accusations were hardly new, the conflict reached the media and public attention in 1991 after the publication of a book on the "politics of race and sex" by D'Souza (1991), in which modest and not quite generally adopted multicultural curricula were grossly misrepresented, attacked, and discredited as a threat to white, European cultural values. Marginal and extreme forms of Afrocentrism were treated as typical of a movement among African-American scholars that was primarily intended as a counterweight against centuries of Eurocentrism in literature, history, science, and the arts (Asante, 1987). In sum, even small and modest challenges to white elite culture were met by a reaction that only confirms its dominance.

Within the broader framework sketched above, we shall not repeat the findings of other work on the history of racism in scholarly discourse, but rather examine some fragments of contemporary scholarly discourse about race and ethnic relations in present-day Western societies. In such an inquiry of contemporary academic racism, it is tempting to reanalyze in some detail the work of the "new racists," that is, of the scholars in such areas as physical anthropology, sociobiology, genetics, or related disciplines that focus on assumed biologically or naturally grounded differences between groups of people. While the scholarly and especially the social implications of such studies have already been denounced in much critical research, it would certainly be relevant to further examine the increasing subtlety of contemporary academic discourse involved in the reproduction of such more or less explicitly racist scholarship.

However, although many of these scholars continue to have prestigious positions, and although their work is sometimes widely published and discussed, blatantly racist ideas no longer make up the mainstream of scholarly research. In the same way as small extremist parties on the Right are not the main problem of racism, however serious their attitudes and practices may be, we also find it less relevant to focus on the obviously racist forms of modern scholarship or pseudo-scholarship.

Rather, we are interested in the respectable mainstream, in the ideas that are widely accepted, that is, in the contemporary consensus regarding ethnic relations and minorities. Here we find opinions and ideologies that seem acceptable if not even liberal, and mostly far from what is commonly called racist. The more subtle and indirectly ethnocentrist ideology of such contemporary scholarship needs the more sophisticated approach of discourse analysis, combined with a more critical look at relations of ethnic dominance as it defines intergroup relations in Western societies today.

ACADEMIC SOCIOLOGY TEXTBOOKS

One of the main sources and expressions of the academic consensus on race and ethnic affairs may be found in introductory textbooks used in colleges and universities. Here, scholars summarize prevailing scientific theories, research, and philosophies, of course with the usual variations among different schools or paradigms of thought. These textbooks, together with the introductory classes in which they are used, are often the first encounter young students have with the goals, concepts, ideas, and theories of their discipline. Therefore, textbooks not only express the scholarly views of their authors, but obviously also shape those of their student-readers.

Thus, to examine some of the properties of mainstream academic discourse on race and ethnic affairs, we have chosen to examine the introductory textbooks that may be expected to pay most extensive attention to ethnic relations, namely, those in sociology. We examined chapters and passages in several influential textbooks currently used in the United States and Great Britain, and sometimes in other countries. Most of these textbooks are regularly updated, and such changes reflect not only advances of academic research but also, if not primarily, changes in social ideologies. Thus, in textbooks of only two decades ago, it was rare to have separate chapters dedicated to women, let alone to sexism. The same changes in regard to ethnic relations may be observed by comparing prewar textbooks with textbooks of the 1960s, 1980s, and 1990s, in which the Civil Rights Movement and discrimination often receive extensive attention. Furthermore, since most academic sociologists and hence most textbook writers in the United States and Great Britain are liberal, whereas only several are radical leftists and a few are radical conservatives, we may also expect that they will generally denounce ethnic prejudice, discrimination, racism, or other forms of inequality. Note, though, that such contemporary attitudes in sociology should also be placed in the perspective of change in sociological theories of race and ethnic relations (UNESCO, 1980), and within the broader framework of the white sociology of race and race relations (for criticism, see, e.g., Ladner, 1973).

Given these assumptions, we need to probe somewhat deeper into the way such textbooks, which are overwhelmingly written by white people (mostly men), deal with ethnic affairs. Indeed, if they are liberals, what exactly does this imply when they describe the properties or the position of minorities? How do they deal with racism, and are they inclined to ignore, deny, minimize, or excuse it, as is so often the case for other white elites? Or does their theoretical insight into and empirical knowledge of society provide an antidote against such forms of self-serving ignorance of ethnic inequality? Centuries of ethnocentric scholarship, that is, a mixture of crass ignorance and blatant racism, predict otherwise. It may be asked, therefore, whether today's social scholars are essentially different from their predecessors, or whether modern social scientists have achieved independence of the dominant ethnic ideologies of their own time.

Instead of giving a superficial characterization of a large number of textbooks, we have opted for a more detailed analysis of a few representative textbooks in the United States and Great Britain, sometimes written by well-known scholars, and used by thousands of students. Our critical reading is obviously premised on our own perspective on the analysis of ethnic relations and racism, but should also be placed within the broader framework of contemporary studies of ethnic relations and racism discussed in Chapter 2. That is, we shall not, for each point made below, repeatedly refer to this previously mentioned scholarly literature.

Our method of analysis in this chapter is highly informal and focuses on making explicit specific presuppositions and other implications, with occasional attention for lexical style and arguments. In other words, we are mainly interested here in the content of the textbooks, rather than in the more detailed structures of textbook discourse (see also next chapter). Although we shall occasionally discuss some issues in slightly more detail, it will be impossible to provide a full critical evaluation of the views of the relevant textbook passages in relation to the vast contemporary social science literature on ethnic and racial relations. Rather, our criticism is largely based on our own theoretical conception of this subject.

Although there remains a certain degree of arbitrariness in the choice of the textbooks we analyze, they were chosen on the basis of the results of a questionnaire sent to a dozen sociology departments in Great Britain and the United States, asking for the titles of the introductory books they used, or thought were most used by others. That is, we may assume that the books are more or less representative. These books are (see References for complete bibliographical information):

Giddens, *Sociology.* (1989; twice reprinted in 1990).

Haralambos, *Sociology. Themes and Perspectives.* (1980).

Sanderson, *Macrosociology. An Introduction to Human Societies.* (1991).

Sherman and Wood, *Sociology: Traditional and Radical Perspectives.* (1989).

Lenski, Lenski, and Nolan, *Human Societies. An Introduction to Macrosociology* (6th ed.). (1991).

Vander Zanden, *The Social Experience. An Introduction to Sociology.* (1990).

In these books we examined all chapters or passages that directly or indirectly dealt with minorities, ethnic or racial relations, discrimination, racism, or related topics. As indicated above, most modern sociology textbooks deal at least briefly, and sometimes extensively, with these issues. That is, these issues have become main topics of the sociological consensus or, as Giddens puts it, are among "the basic issues of interest to sociologists today" (p. 1). Although we briefly examine several aspects of the issue of ethnic relations as discussed by these authors, our main focus in this study is on the academic accounts of ethnic inequality, discrimination, prejudice, and racism.

In order to discuss the role of the perspective and approach taken on the treatment of ethnic affairs, this chapter will examine each book separately, unlike the more thematic approach in the other chapters in this study. Note that only a few aspects of each book will be discussed: A full-fledged discourse analysis of the relevant passages about ethnic affairs would require a book-length study. Although we shall on occasion be rather critical of some books, our discussion is not interested in a critique of the individual books or authors themselves, but rather in an analysis of the approaches they represent. Given the influence of Anthony Giddens in sociology, we shall pay special and more detailed attention to his widely used textbook.

As elsewhere in this book, expressions and passages in italics, between double quotes, or in separate indented paragraphs, are those of either the authors or their sources.

Giddens, *Sociology*

Let us begin our exploration with a textbook of one of the most prominent and productive sociologists of our time, Anthony Giddens' 815-page *Sociology*. Unlike many other, less prominent textbook writers, he is not only an able introduction and survey writer, but also has developed his own theory of society, namely, structuration theory, which he modestly keeps in the background of the present introduction. His aim was "to write a work that combined some originality with an analysis of all the basic issues of interest to sociologists today" (p. 1), a daunting task, especially since he also proposes to present "ideas and findings from the cutting edge of the discipline" (p. 1).

To impose some structure to the book, Giddens organizes his many chapters around a number of basic "themes": (a) the interplay between the personal and the social, (b) social change in the world, (c) a

comparative perspective, also including work done in and about Eastern
Europe and the Third World ("more than has been usual hitherto in
introductions to sociology," p. 2), (d) a historical orientation, (e) issues
of gender, and (f) the globalization of social life. We see that what are
called "themes" here are a combination of different dimensions or
approaches (like the personal-social, the historical, and the comparative
approach), and special domains or issues that have a more contemporary
sociopolitical background (like the Third World and gender). The latter
suggest that issues of race and ethnicity, although not declared as
special themes, might get special attention.

This is indeed the case. In Part III, under the general heading of
"Structures of Power," and after a discussion of the classical sociological issues of "Stratification and Class Structure," we find a 40-page
chapter on "Ethnicity and Race." This is as it should be, for the
organization of society by dimensions of ethnicity and race, at least in
Western countries, is primarily a question of power and dominance. In
the Table of Contents, we do not find, however, much evidence for this
perspective of power: The notion of racism does not appear in the
subheadings of this chapter. Instead, the more general and more abstract
notion of "ethnic antagonism" is used, together with "prejudice" and
"discrimination," although there is brief mention of "reactions against
racism" in Great Britain.

The Ubiquity of Prejudice and Discrimination

The relevance of the "comparative" and "global" themes organizing
this book appears on the first page of this chapter, where Giddens
describes the fate of the Japanese *Burakumin*, a group that has been
discriminated against for centuries by other Japanese. The example is
meant to show "how ingrained and enduring prejudices towards a
minority group can be" (p. 243) and suggests to the naive student that
prejudice and discrimination are not limited to European or Europeanized societies. Whereas such an example may be useful from a comparative perspective, and although it needs to be remembered that ethnic
prejudice and discrimination occur in many societies and in many
historical periods, having such an example introduce the chapter may
also bias the discussion, and especially the insight of the students into
the notions of ethnic inequality and oppression: They may get the
implicit message that ethnic antagonism belongs to all times and all
societies, which—though partly true and hence partly false—may provide

argumentative fuel to the often-used excuse that our *own* white, European, prejudice and discrimination are merely one of a type.

We may call this the "ubiquity" argument, which is a variant of the "human" argument, which says that prejudice and discrimination are universal, human properties. Both arguments are sometimes followed by the appealing conclusion that such universality also makes opposition against prejudice and discrimination rather pointless. Racist party leaders go one step further and use this argument to defend the opinion that ethnocentrism and even racism are natural. Though probably unintended as such, Giddens' choice is thus not exactly innocent and may be a move of the well-known strategy of the mitigation of racism that we encounter often in this book. For students in Great Britain and the United States, a more familiar example of British or U.S. racism might have been less exotic, but certainly more to the point, since they might be expected to better understand their own societies. Giddens probably realizes this, because his next example focuses on the Holocaust of the Jews: "subject to discrimination and persecution in the Christian West for nearly two thousand years, the most horrific instance of brutal destructiveness against a minority group being the killing of millions of Jews in German concentration camps during the Second World War."

This is the only reference to anti-Semitism in this chapter and in the book (it does not appear in the subject index). Relevant is Giddens' use of the "Christian West," which appropriately involves not only the West but also the Christians in ethnic oppression, a critical point of view that is often absent in discussions of anti-Semitism and racism. The only remark on this example that seems relevant is that, thinking of the slave trade and slavery or the genocide of Native Americans, one might question the phrase "the most horrific instance of brutal destructiveness," although it is certainly true that the "industrialized" destruction of Jews in the concentration camps is unique in history.

Although the Holocaust of the Jews had clearly racial and racist foundations, the examples of both the *Burakumin* and the Jews are used to introduce the notions of *ethnic* group and *ethnicity*, namely, referring to "cultural practices and outlooks that distinguish a given community of people," including self-identification, language, history, and religion, all elements that may be used to distinguish one group from another. It is important that Giddens emphasizes that such differences are never innate, but always learned, so that he may dispel racist arguments that attribute, for example, innate laziness or lack of intelligence to groups, a point that is usually associated with race rather than ethnicity.

One of the characteristics of ethnic groups identified by Giddens is that they are "disadvantaged as a result of discrimination by others" (p. 245). Although this is undoubtedly correct, the formulation of this property raises two well-known problems often pointed out in discourse analyses of inequality: (a) The use of the term *disadvantaged* is borrowed from a stylistic repertoire also used in mitigating bureaucratic discourse that is reluctant to use terms such as *oppressed*, and (b) the use of the passive voice deemphasizes the active role of the responsible actors in discrimination. Although in this passage the use of such a formulation may be acceptable within the more general framework of discrimination chosen here (so that it may apply to any kind of ethnic inequality), application of this formulation to Western or European discrimination would leave white Europeans in a deemphasized role. We will also see that elsewhere in this textbook such a general and abstract formulation may well fit into the "global" approach chosen, but it seems less consistent with the historical approach that also purports to organize the discussion.

Race and Racism

It is not easy to discredit the pseudo-biology of race in a half-page of introductory prose, but Giddens does so reasonably well, using some of the standard arguments (such as occasionally greater variation within than between groups), and briefly emphasizes the social nature of racial distinctions. He then defines *racism* and *racist* as follows:

> *Racism* means falsely attributing inherited characteristics of personality or behaviour to individuals of a particular physical appearance. A *racist* is someone who believes that a biological explanation can be given for characteristics of superiority or inferiority supposedly possessed by people of a given physical stock. (p. 246)

These definitions have a number of problematic implications, which may be summarized as follows (see Chapter 2 for details of the theoretical backgrounds of the definition of racism): (a) Psychological processes of attribution and explanation are only one element of racism, and focusing on them ignores the crucial social, economic, and cultural aspects of inequality; (b) Racism is a property of dominance relations between groups, not between individuals; (c) Modern racism (ethnicism) also focuses on cultural differences, and is only seldom legitimated in terms of biologically based (racial) superiority. In other words, the definitions seem too narrow, being limited to attitudes and ideologies, and too strict, being limited to old-fashioned biological racism. Indeed, with these definitions, most modern racism may not be racism at all. Note also that it does not make much theoretical, and practical, sense either to distinguish between "racists" and "non-racists" in a racist society: In principle all white group members either benefit or might benefit from ethnic inequality, and, both cognitively and practically, group members are more or less actively involved in the reproduction of the system of dominance, or in resistance against it.

In line with his global and abstract approach, Giddens prefers the more general, and less harsh term *ethnic antagonism*, which is not only a euphemism when applied to racism, but which also implies mutual feelings and practices of resentment and exclusion, as is also true for the term *ethnic conflict*. Again, this may be a relevant term to denote relations between two ethnic groups of comparable size and power, for instance, in India, but misrepresents the relations of dominance involved in racism in Europe or Europeanized countries, or in the former European colonies. We see that such formulations subtly reveal underlying perceptions and evaluations of ethnic inequality.

Prejudice and discrimination are defined in the traditional way, namely, as unwarranted, relatively fixed "opinions and attitudes held by members of one group about another" and as "activities which serve to disqualify (*sic*) the members of one grouping from opportunities open to others." Again, the succinctness of these definitions, as well as the examples that give some more detail, do not seem to be satisfactory for the reasons given earlier, that is, the notions of power and dominance are essentially missing: Prejudice and discrimination function in overall systems of inequality, for example, those of racism or sexism. So there is no question of "one another," as was also noted about Giddens' concept of "mutual." Incidentally, unlike stereotypes, prejudices are usually taken to represent negative social cognitions, of a dominant group, about less powerful minority groups, a distinction Giddens does not make. Similarly, many forms of discrimination, such as indirect discrimination, cannot be accounted for in such definitions, whereas forms of minority resistance (e.g., when they form their own exclusive organizations) would be qualified as discrimination.

In sum, contrary to what Giddens' formulations might suggest, contemporary theories of racism indicate that the concepts of racism, prejudice, and discrimination only make sense in a framework of group power and power abuse (dominance). Notions such as reverse discrimination or black racism, often used in conservative discourse on race relations, do not make sense in such a framework. Similarly, the cognitive dimension of prejudice and the action/interaction level of discrimination are fundamentally related. At the group level, therefore, it does not make sense to admit the possibility, as Giddens does, following other authors, that prejudices can exist without discrimination and vice versa. If whites discriminate against blacks because of social norms or pressure, this means that the dominant group, as a group, has prevailing prejudices, and it is rather irrelevant whether some individuals in that case may agree or disagree with such prejudices—apart from the fact that such individuals apparently prefer to conform to the group, rather than to oppose discrimination, which by itself is one important dimension of racism. Similarly, a group that never discriminates against another is, social psychologically, highly unlikely to have prejudices, because such prejudices would have no social function. It is surprising that the author of structuration theory would not agree with such a point. Unfortunately, what Giddens seem to do is summarize some of the traditional literature, without reformulating and rethinking it in a sociological perspective of race, ethnicity, and racism. Indeed, power relations and dominance presuppose a social and cultural level of analysis.

Thus, Giddens' account of ethnic relations often misses the crucial point. When discussing stereotyping, which he sees as forms of rigid categorization of other people, he argues that when such stereotyping is neutral it is usually harmless (e.g., when English people stereotype Americans). He states, however:

> Where stereotypes are associated with anxiety or fear, the situation is likely to be quite different. Stereotypes in such circumstances are commonly infused with attitudes of hostility or hatred towards the group in question. A white person may believe, for example, that all Blacks are lazy and stupid, using this belief to justify attitudes of contempt towards them. (p. 247)

It is rather surprising to find this traditional psychological (emotive, motivational) approach to stereotyping in a sociology textbook. Although such psychological reactions to other groups may play a role at the individual level (Adorno, Frenkel-Brunswik, Levinson, & Sanford, 1950; Kovel, 1970), our position is that racism and its underlying ideologies are primarily social, and should be defined in terms of dominance relations between majorities and minorities. Slavery, colonialism, segregation, and modern forms of ethnicism and racism do not seem to have developed out of fear, but rather because of the will to dominate and exploit others, to maintain one's privileges, and so on. Indeed, most minority groups that are the target of racism are relatively small and hardly constitute a threat. This does not mean of course that racist propaganda may not *define* others as a threat (as is the case with "black crime" or "the world conspiracy of Jews"), and thus use psychological means to facilitate the reproduction of racist ideologies. That is, fear or anxiety may be a *consequence* of elite racism (e.g., in the press), rather than its basic *cause*.

Similar problems may be observed for many other traditional psychological notions discussed by Giddens, such as the role of Adorno's "authoritarian personality" or Merton's distinction between different types of "liberals" and "bigots" as an explanation of prejudice and racism. If such explanations were valid, then the considerable changes in race relations and attitudes, for example, after the Civil Rights Movement in the United States, would imply that large parts of the white U.S. population suddenly changed their personalities. Research has repeatedly shown that stereotypes and prejudices are sociocultural and inherently part of historical relations of group dominance, not a question of individual personality, which at most may explain individual differences within overall sociocultural attitudes and practices (for an early assessment of this point, see Pettigrew, 1958). In sum, racism has very little to do with "to be or not to be a bigot."

The Sociology of "Ethnic Antagonism"

Up to a point, Giddens of course knows all this, and after the rather uncritical section on psychological determinants of "ethnic antagonism," he proceeds to a more sociological account (p. 251 ff.). Rather unexpectedly, this sociological analysis does not seem to be much more satisfactory, and also gets stuck in generalities and vagueness. True, as is the case for social psychological approaches to group relations, "ethnic antagonism" may be due to competition and negative reactions to outsiders. The point is that such ahistorical generalities again leave the question of dominance and inequality out of the picture: Some outsiders (e.g., British or even Germans in the Netherlands) are accepted without many problems or resentment, whereas others (Surinamese, Turks) are not. The question is: Why?

It should be stressed again that one pedagogical and hence political problem with such generalized psychological or sociological approaches is that prejudice, xenophobia, resentment, and hence racism may be seen as universal or natural for any group—an argument routinely used by all contemporary racist groups and parties, and presupposed by such racist slogans as "Les français d'abord," "British first," and the like.

Historical Dimensions

After so many generalities that say so little about present-day, actual forms of white racism, Giddens finally introduces the historical dimension of ethnic conflicts (pp. 252 ff.). Indeed, it is crucial for our understanding of contemporary white racism to discuss the history of Western expansion, conquest, colonialism, and imperialism. It would have been much more useful for Western students, and especially for white students, to start an analysis of ethnic relations and ethnic "antagonism" with this admittedly more specific, but vastly more disastrous form of ethnic "conflict."

Although Giddens discusses some of this, such as the history of slavery in the United States and aspects of racism in Britain, even this historical account seems bland and repeatedly engaged in the subtle and now familiar strategies of mitigation or ethnocentrism that are observed for so many other types of elite discourse in this study. His "Europeans began to venture into previously uncharted seas and unexplored land masses" is a rather ethnocentric formulation that we expect in a simple high school textbook (see Chapter 6), but not in a prominent introduction to sociology. And to describe the slave-trade as a "large-scale movement of population from Africa to the Americas" may not actually be false, but it is too much of an understatement. Here is a characteristic passage of Giddens' historical account:

> In all these countries, the indigenous populations were subjected and came under European rule. . . . Since the Europeans were from ethnically diverse backgrounds, they implanted numerous ethnic differentiations in their new homelands. . . . [E]thnocentric attitudes were rife among the colonists, who believed themselves on a civilizing mission to the rest of the world. Even the more liberal European colonists thought themselves superior to the indigenous peoples they encountered. The fact that many of those peoples thought precisely the opposite is not so relevant, since the Europeans possessed the power to make their outlook count. The early period of colonialism coincided with the rise of racism, and ever since then racial divisions and conflicts have tended to have a prime place in ethnic conflicts as a whole. In particular, racist views separating "Whites" from "Blacks" became central to European attitudes. (p. 254)

A close discourse analysis of this passage would point out many problematic implications and presuppositions of such a formulation, for example, (a) the use of passive "were subjected" again conceals the actors; (b) peoples in the colonies were not just "ruled" by the Europeans; (c) what is meant by "implanting numerous ethnic differentiations"; (d) how Europeans can be called "liberal" if they feel themselves superior; (e) whether all colonized peoples felt superior to the Europeans; (f) who the actors are in "racial divisions" and "conflicts" during colonialism and racism: *who* dominated, exploited *whom*; (g) European attitudes did more than make a distinction between whites and blacks. In sum, as we have observed earlier, these and similar passages repeatedly appear to avoid the appropriate words for the description of the historical facts, mostly by understating the negative roles of white Europeans, as we find elsewhere in elite discourse on race and racism. On the other hand, this passage briefly touches upon the crucial element in what Giddens sees as mutual prejudices, namely, "the power to make one's outlook count," although even this formulation seems to suggest a mission of persuasion, rather than acts of submission.

Similarly surprising in a sociology handbook is the reference to "color symbolism" often mentioned as the historical root of prejudice (fear of blacks because black was associated with the devil, sin, death, and so on). Although this may be an element in early encounters between Europeans and Africans—indeed, it went both ways—it is no longer a primary cause of ethnocentrism, for the same reasons given above for traditional psychological accounts of racism. Again, the problem of such a relatively detailed treatment of a marginal historical aspect of European-African encounters, is that it is one more element of a commonsense explanation of ethnocentrism or xenophobia that may be used as an excuse for it. Indeed, in a time where whites long to have a "nice tan," such an explanation is even rather amusing. The important sociological point missed here is that appearance is merely used as an often imaginary and legitimating element in the social construction of race and racism. Thus, in the United States, even today, being classified as black has little to do with actual appearance. Incidentally, what about the color symbolism of yellow, red, or even brown? Similarly, appearance plays a marginal role in anti-Semitism and other forms of racism and ethnicism. In sum, color symbolism does not explain much of present-day ethnic or racial inequality.

Giddens finally discusses race and ethnic relations in various countries, such as Brazil, South Africa, the United States, and Great Britain.

Much of this account is based on the work of others, as is of course inevitable in a textbook that discusses the whole field. Unfortunately, this sometimes means that he often relies on traditional accounts of white social scientists, many of whom, as we have seen earlier in this chapter, are not exactly prone to highlight white racism. Thus, although Giddens denounces the well-known myth of "racial democracy" in Brazil, he seems to underestimate the extent of patterns of discrimination in that country (see, e.g., Fontaine, 1985). Similarly, the discussion of the situation in South Africa hardly provides students with a deep insight into the horrors and the geopolitical background of apartheid. Whereas "international pressure to reduce discriminatory practices" is mentioned (which makes *us* feel good again), it is not stated that for decades the West condoned and supported apartheid in its own best interests.

The historical survey of the situation in the United States merely lists some of the facts, without much sociological analysis or comments. Interesting though is Giddens account of Affirmative Action:

> Other examples of affirmative action tried out in the 1970s and 1980s include allocating a certain proportion of college places to minority groups, in the knowledge that their grades might not match up to those of others; and ensuring that at least a certain percentage of those hired for jobs in public agencies come from disadvantaged groups. (p. 262)

Little argument is necessary to conclude that such a description of Affirmative Action is at least somewhat incomplete: (a) If relevant at all, grade differences may only be small; (b) allowing for such differences takes place in a situation where prior education of African-Americans is vastly worse than that of Euro-Americans; (c) it would have been more appropriate to refer to the very long time that whites were preferentially or even exclusively admitted, even if they had dramatically lower grades than blacks, and so forth.

We see that formulations in textbooks, as well as in other discourse, always betray perspective, as is also the case when Giddens refers to growing resentment in Great Britain against immigrants, namely, by poor whites because they "were more aware of disruptions to their everyday lives" (p. 265). The use of "aware" presupposes that there were such disruptions, but Giddens does not specify them, and thus inadvertently comes close to blaming the victims for the hostility the immigrants had to endure from white Britons. Similarly, and contrary to what is suggested by Giddens, there is now quite a bit of evidence (also from published Cabinet papers of the 1950s) that the British elites, and especially its government, were not exactly giving a good example, as far as ethnic attitudes and practices were concerned, as we have seen in the previous chapters. Although Giddens doesn't discuss the details of contemporary racism in Great Britain, he at least briefly focuses on some anti-racist organizations, unlike most other textbooks. That Giddens is not particularly sensitive to ethnic or racial issues, however, is also shown by the rather arbitrary inclusion of a vignette about a local Rasta, taken from the *Illustrated London News*. This vignette seems to present a "Success Story Black," but nevertheless displays all stereotypes about Rastas, including references to "th[is] acceptance of unemployment as almost a way of life."

Conclusion

After this analysis of Giddens' textbook, our conclusions may be brief. We have found that, on the whole, the chapter is moderately well-informed about ethnic relations in the United States and Europe, but much less up-to-date as far as theories of ethnic and race relations and racism are concerned. Without critical analysis, he focuses too much on outdated psychological explanations of ethnic "antagonism," while almost altogether neglecting the deeper social, cultural, and economic dimensions involved. He sometimes lapses into stereotypes, euphemisms, and blaming the victim, and initially his abstract and generalized approach to prejudice and racism seems to suggest that these are universal and hence natural properties of relations between ethnic groups. Racism is defined in a very restricted way. Only the brief history of race relations in the United States and Europe slightly corrects this impression, but does not do so explicitly. In particular this latter part is not very analytical and does not provide the students with theoretical instruments that would help them understand and explain racism in these Western countries. He refers only occasionally to the work of black scholars. On the whole, then, the book has a white perspective, and understates and underanalyzes the role of European ethnic dominance, inequality, and racism in ethnic relations.

Other British Textbooks

We have little to say about other British textbooks and introductions to sociology. Giddens' own "brief but critical introduction" into sociology (Giddens, 1982) has no place for a discussion of ethnic relations or racism, as is also the case for most earlier surveys or introductions in the field (e.g., Thompson & Tunstall, 1971).

A more recent, nearly 600-page, textbook by Michael Haralambos (1980), widely used in British universities, talks a lot about stratification, power, and poverty, but does not feature an explicit chapter or section on race relations, ethnicity, prejudice, or racism (terms that do not appear in the subject index). It does, however, occasionally discuss various views of black Americans. The topics in that case are all but stereotypical, and include:

- the matrifocal family (which he accepts as an alternative form of family structure)
- crime in Harlem
- IQ-testing (whose validity he rejects)
- the situational versus the cultural explanation of (black) poverty
- the Black Muslims
- natural versus social conditions of inequality

Although in most of these cases he discusses the theories that attribute negative properties to blacks, he usually argues against them in a more or less liberal framework. However, he does not put such theories into a broader perspective of white racism, nor does he discuss patterns of discrimination and racism more generally. Black people or other minorities in Great Britain or elsewhere in Europe are not discussed. In other words, it is a book about white sociologists and white society, and therefore does not provide an adequate introduction to the study of present-day societies.

U.S. Textbooks

Most contemporary sociology textbooks in the United States reflect a much more detailed awareness of the role of race and ethnic relations in society than most of their European counterparts. After a long tradition of barely disguised ethnocentrism and racism, in which anthropology and sociology contributed their share to the explanation of the inferiority of the Negro, contemporary textbooks—most of them written by whites—usually offer a more liberal, sometimes even a radical libertarian, perspective. However, one of the books we examined represents a dubious mixture of Marxist-Darwinist, sociobiological evolutionism. Let us briefly discuss what some of these textbooks write about race and ethnicity, and focus especially on their accounts of discrimination and racism.

Sanderson, *Macrosociology*

Sanderson's *Macrosociology, An Introduction to Human Societies* shares with Giddens the historical and comparative approach, which, according to the author, is a "powerful antidote to ethnocentrism" (p. xvii). More specific is the "evolutionary materialist" approach of this book, which focuses on the basic, material causes of societal organization and change. In this perspective, quite unlike that of most U.S. textbooks we examined, one should not be surprised to see most Western industrial societies conceptualized in terms of "capitalist" societies. The materialist approach of Marx is defined here in opposition to the "idealist" approaches, including Parsons' functionalism. The special focus on materially based social change is not captured here by the concept of "revolutionary," as might be expected in a Marxist approach, but drops the first "r" and becomes "evolutionary," which for this author also involves special attention to struggle and conflict, but rather along Neo-Darwinist than Marxist lines. Unlike earlier philosophies of evolutionism, however, the author emphasizes that evolution does not mean progress, and the ethnocentrism of classical evolutionism is also criticized.

It is somewhat strange to see a sociology book begin with a lengthy discussion of Darwin, natural selection, the survival of the fit, genes, DNA, apes, and other notions from classical and modern genetics and animal biology, which we know to conflict rather sharply with the environmentalist consensus in sociology, and especially with social and political explanations of group dominance and racism. It is even stranger that the author fails to warn his students against the abuses of genetic and evolutionist approaches that have been made in the social sciences, and in Western societies at large. This is less surprising when we see that he is a cautious supporter of sociobiological research, and sharply disagrees with scholars and organizations, such as the "Committee against Racism," who have made a "political" issue out of a "scientific" one and have attacked well-known sociobiologist Wilson. His verdict:

> While sociobiology may not be acceptable as broad theoretical strategy, it seems to have a contribution to make. It may well be that such universal features of social life as incest avoidance and male political dominance over females have biological causes. . . . One of the attractive features of contemporary sociobiological research is its strong commitment to a scientific and comparative approach. Sociobiologists have proposed many interesting hypotheses, some of which may well turn out in the future to be theoretically meaningful. (pp. 39-40)

Apart from the cited criticism by Sahlins, he ignores the fundamental criticisms that have been leveled against the unwarranted application of sociobiology in the social sciences. Worse, he conceals from the student the plainly sexist and racist statements and implications in the work of Wilson and others, implications that have very little to do with a "strong commitment" to scientific research. Given this background of the author, and given his casual remark, just quoted, about the allegedly genetic basis of male dominance, we should be prepared for the worst when he discusses social and ethnic stratification, social dominance relations, and racism.

Chapters 13 and 14 deal with "Slavery and Racial Paternalism in the New World" and "Contemporary Patterns of Racial and Ethnic Stratification," respectively. However, our misgivings about the "evolutionist" approach of the author are not supported by what he says in these chapters, which fortunately heed the other, materialist-economic perspective of this textbook. Only the extensive use of the work of Pierre van den Berghe, who in his late work also makes use of sociobiological concepts, is an indication of the author's interest in the evolutionary explanations.

Sanderson—correctly in our view—rejects the psychological approach to racism in terms of "prejudiced personalities," and as a materialist he emphasizes socioeconomic factors of inequality in class or caste relations. Despite his neglect of psychology, he nevertheless mentions the ideological representations of blacks, namely, as inferior or childlike, in what he and van den Berghe call the "paternalistic" race relations of the U.S. South during slavery, and as threatening criminals in present-day economic race relations. Most of his discussion on the history of slavery and race relations is based on a discussion of the work of others. Additionally, Sanderson occasionally lapses into euphemism:

> In terms of their material conditions of life, the slaves may have lived better than commonly believed . . . the slaves ate well . . . the slaves commonly had a stable and meaningful form of family life . . . the extent of cruelty meted out to slaves, through such punishments as whippings, has been overestimated. (p. 261)

Despite such reported assumptions of other scholars, and disregarding a large amount of scholarly work and testimonies of blacks themselves, the author nevertheless concludes, not without contradiction, that the fundamental difference with other, white poor people of the same period was that black slaves were totally oppressed and owned by whites, as chattel, and concludes: "There is no doubt, however, that the Southern slave system was a highly oppressive and exploitative system that produced a great deal of suffering for millions of slaves" (p. 261).

Within the broader framework of his socioeconomic approach, the author further concludes, with other authors, that "plantation slavery was intimately involved in the whole process of Western capitalist development" (p. 267). He later stresses that inequality and oppression of blacks did not cease with the abolition of slavery, but especially focuses on the role of poor whites. This focus is inconsistent with not only our thesis but also the historical facts, namely, that primarily the elites, in the post-slavery North and South in the United States, had an interest in keeping the Negro down, and therefore did not hesitate to condone, if not exacerbate, white popular resentment.

Although Sanderson's special topic of "black slave owners" may be interesting, and although this section opposes different views (Did black slave owners exploit their slaves for profit or did they employ them out of compassion?), such a passage may—without explicit warnings—have an unwanted pedagogical effect upon the students, that is, one of comparative discounting, a move that may lead to the possible inference that blacks are no better than whites.

As with other textbook authors, there seems to be remarkable interest in the problem of whether the United States, Brazil, or other countries had comparatively "mild" systems of slavery, or whether the color line was less sharply marked in Brazil than in the United States. However, although somewhat ambivalent in his quotations and having some difficulty making up his mind, Sanderson finally quotes van den Berghe as saying that the official view about the "milder" form of slavery in Brazil should be rejected, and that both during and after slavery, the exploitation and oppression of Brazilian blacks was more a "racial purgatory" than a "racial paradise."

Another general comment on this chapter is in regard to the focus on the macrosociological issues of the role of slavery in local and world economies and the development of capitalism: Such an account obscures a more detailed treatment of what slavery was actually like in everyday life. The experiences of slavery and racism by black people in such a case tend to be overlooked, as is generally the case in white sociology textbooks, as well as in most white elite discourse—also in the media, for that matter.

Racism is defined by Sanderson as "an elaborate ideology holding that one race is by nature superior and that all others are by nature inferior to it" (p. 280).

We have argued above that this traditional sociological definition of racism ignores racist practices, as well as modern forms of ethnic and indirect racism, framed in terms of cultural differences. Similarly, unlike the assumption of Sanderson and other sociologists (pp. 280-281), we do not conceptualize ethnic prejudices as "an emotional response or feeling" characteristic of individuals, but as social representations of a dominant ethnic group. The failure to theorize about the relations between social cognitions and practices, both micro and macro, allows Sanderson, just like Giddens and others, to admit the possibility of discrimination without prejudice, and vice versa. The same is true for the well-known discussion of whether slavery presupposed racist ideologies, or whether slavery created or promoted racial prejudice. Social practices and social cognitions mutually presuppose and influence each other, as in ethnic relations: European power allowed unequal treatment and enslavement, which needed further legitimation in more complex ideological frameworks, but which at the same time presupposed attitudes that allowed enslavement of others in the first place.

Concluding our discussion of Sanderson's textbook we find that despite his initial interest in "evolutionist" explanations, these appear to be barely relevant in his account of ethnic and racial relations. For him, conflict, socioeconomic competition, and capitalist exploitation are the major dimensions of slavery and ethnic or racial inequality. Whereas the historical and comparative approach gives him a broader view of race relations than textbooks that focus on the contemporary forms of racism in the United States, such an overall macrosociological account seriously neglects the necessary account of contemporary racism. Somehow, racism and ethnic conflict for him are forms of social antagonism that appeared elsewhere and in the past, not here and today. He thereby fails to analyze the many complex forms of modern racism in the United States, which leaves most of his American students ill-prepared to understand and criticize forms of racial and ethnic inequality that are pervasive today. Also, a textbook of macrosociology should at least pay attention to present ideologies and discrimination in social institutions, such as business corporations, politics, education, research, the media, and other organizations that reproduce prejudice and perpetuate discrimination against minorities. Sanderson, however, does not offer such a discussion.

Sherman and Wood, *Sociology*

Sherman and Wood's *Sociology* presents a "radical" perspective on sociology, in contrast with other approaches, which they call "traditional." Radical sociology "attempts to view society from the position of oppressed groups in society, such as the poor, the unemployed, blue-collar workers, Blacks and other minorities, and women." Because the book has separate chapters on sexism and ageism, it is therefore not surprising that it has a chapter on racism (pp. 201-228), which we shall examine in somewhat more detail.

Continuing the oppositional perspective of this textbook, this chapter emphasizes the difference between the traditional and the radical approach to race and ethnic relations. The authors emphasize that whereas traditional sociology has studied many properties of minority groups (personality, families, culture, politics) and their relations with the majority, these issues were often studied in isolation from the problem of inequality, which is the major perspective of radical sociology. In their discussion the authors focus on race and ethnicity in the United States, and on blacks in particular (lack of space motivates exclusion of other minorities). Ethnic and race relations in other countries are barely dealt with, making it essentially a U.S. textbook, which prevents the students from making significant comparisons with ethnic relations in other countries.

Unlike other textbooks, this textbook focuses on the contemporary position of minorities, without going into the history of slavery and Jim Crow or other historical facts that condition the present position of American blacks and other minorities. Describing the patterns of inequality, the authors summarize the various sectors of social life in which blacks are being discriminated against or otherwise face inequality compared to white Americans: income, employment, poverty levels, health, job recruitment and promotion, education, and politics. They emphasize that after the gains of the Civil Rights Movement, the overall position of blacks has deteriorated "particularly during the Nixon, Ford and Reagan administrations" (p. 202). Affirmative Action programs are described as being successful, but the authors fear that political attacks against them will make them less effective.

Discussing the traditional explanations of inequality, the authors reject biological determinism as scientifically unfounded and racist. They assume that "most sociologists are sufficiently liberal to acknowledge that Blacks are not biologically inferior to Whites." They admit that there are traditional sociologists who focus on cultural deficiencies of blacks, such as dependency and limited achievement goals. The authors also quote research showing that this position is unfounded: Blacks of similar class position have the same aspirations, upward mobility, and work ethic as whites, and poor lower-class blacks simply try to survive, for example, through "hustling," in a racist society that is characterized by a negative portrayal of Blacks in the media and textbooks. Similarly, the myth of low black self-esteem is also being dispelled, as is Moynihan's hypothesis regarding the detrimental effects of mother-headed black families, which, if true, would apply to most poor families, white or black. The authors correctly conclude that such studies, focusing on deficiencies of black society and culture, "draw attention away from the fact that Black inequality . . . is best explained by analyzing the racist character of most American institutions." While other studies fail to recognize the role of racism as a barrier in ethnic and racial group relations in the United States, the authors reject these studies, which also assume, following Robert Park, that there is a cycle that runs from contact, conflict, accommodation, assimilation, to complete amalgamation of new immigrant or minority groups, a cycle in which only specific stages apply to specific groups (e.g., European and Asian immigrants) and which seldom involves full structural integration and amalgamation.

The discussion on prejudice brings the authors to their own radical approach. Although they agree that ethnic and racial prejudices, bigotry, or racist ideologies are often the "immediate" causes of discrimination, anti-Semitism, and inequality, they are not satisfied with such an appeal to "beliefs" and want to know why white people would have such beliefs in the first place, apart from learning them from their parents, peers, and textbooks. They indicate that overtly racist prejudices have sharply decreased during the past decades, while discrimination is still there— which brings them to suggest, in passing, that survey research may no longer be adequate to measure such prejudices because whites have learned the kind of answers that are expected from them.

Their answer to the discrepancy between prejudice and discrimination and the continuation of racial inequality is that racial practices are "built into the major institutions of our society"; there is both intended and unintentional discrimination in real estate, banking, insurance, universities, testing, and business, even after the various Civil Rights Acts of the past decades. Some of the practices are not directly discriminatory, but they indirectly cause inequality. These practices do in fact have more negative effects for black people: "Businesses are usually not consciously aware of how their policies perpetuate discrimination; they are 'merely' trying to maximize profits by hiring on their usual (culturally biased) criteria" (p. 219). The authors emphasize that intentions are irrelevant in such practices; what counts are the consequences. And whatever the intentions, we may also ask: Who benefits from racism? Contrary to conservative views that discrimination in business is irrational, the authors suggest that it is rational when employers can thus divide the work force and push down wages, or when they can employ and fire cheap labor with ease: Profit is always the main incentive. In the sociopolitical realm the benefit lies in scapegoating: Blacks can be blamed for social problems, such as crime and drugs. Finally, racism in international politics may serve imperialism, for instance in strategies of divide and rule, as was the case for Great Britain and the various ethnic groups in India.

We may conclude from this brief commentary on Sherman and Wood's textbook that their radical perspective allows them to deal with the major manifestations and causes of racism in the United States. Although they pay less attention to the comparative and historical dimensions of racism, they provide the U.S. students with the necessary insight and counter-ideology to challenge some prevailing conservative views about the irrelevance of race in present-day forms of inequality.

Lenski, Lenski, and Nolan, *Human Societies*

Lenski, Lenski, and Nolan's *Human Societies, An Introduction to Macrosociology* is a textbook that has been around for more than 20 years; its first edition appeared in 1970, just after the Civil Rights Movement in the United States seemed to have had some political success. One would expect this product of the early 1970s to reflect some of the concerns of the time, and the textbook to feature major chapters on equal rights of women and minorities. However, this is not the case: A few pages suffice to discuss the past and present position of this majority of contemporary U.S. society, namely, under the heading of social stratification. Lengthy chapters on "Hunting Gathering Societies" and "Horticultural Societies and Agrarian Societies" take up more than 100 pages of the book's 500-odd pages, as is often the case in sociology textbooks. So much for relevance of content for modern students, apparently expected to get more insight into the details of hunting and gathering than in discrimination patterns and other inequalities that define the social world around them. Such is the pressure of prevailing traditions in sociology curricula and the textbooks that implement them. Other macrosociology primers show that even within these somewhat strange conceptions of the historical and comparative approach, there is still a lot of room for attention to present-day society and its major problems.

The information about race and ethnicity in this book is not limited to the few pages about stratification. At the beginning of the book, in a discussion of human societies as sociocultural systems, the "modern" notion of *race* is defined: "A race is simply a part of the human population in which some combination of these highly visible traits occurs with a frequency that is appreciably different from that of other parts of the human population" (p. 27).

Simple indeed, this definition. It is not even followed by a qualification about the complexities, contradictions, and biological problems associated with such a definition. Thus it ignores the fact that the present world at most shows a limitless distribution of "such highly visible traits," which makes the notion of race theoretically useless, unless as a powerful social category. That such genetically based properties are said to be caused by geographical patterns ("dark skin is universal in hot, sunny regions") makes the account of race even more problematic. Indeed, what about the geographical conditions of red skin and yellow skin? In sum, we have here a textbook that repeats very old ideologies about race.

The views espoused by these authors reach new heights of scholarly insight in an "excursus" on "Race and Societal Development" appended to the chapter on horticultural societies. It deserves to be quoted in full, but the following excerpts give some of the flavor:

> After the first explorers returned to Europe from Africa, the Americas, and Asia, Europeans were intrigued by differences in the level of development of societies in various parts of the world. Interest in these differences led quite naturally to efforts to explain them.
>
> Over the years the most popular explanation has been the racialist. Racialist theories assert that societies differ in their level of development and in other ways because the members differ in their culture-building abilities. Translated into modern scientific terminology, these theories assert that societies differ in their levels of development because of differences in the genetic heritages of their populations.
>
> These theories have had great appeal because they seem to fit the evidence rather well. During the last several hundred years, societies dominated by Europeans have been technologically the most advanced and organizationally the most complex and powerful. Societies dominated by Asians have ranked next, while societies dominated by Africans have been the least developed technologically and organizationally. Since the level of societal development is obviously not responsible for the race of a population,

racialist theorists have argued that the race must be responsible for the level of development.

Racialist theories can be quite compelling if one does not have an ecological and evolutionary perspective. If one adopts such a perspective, however, those theories prove to have a number of weaknesses. (p. 156)

The authors then go on to explain that the "highest ranking" societies have not always prevailed just in Europe, but also in China, North Africa, and the Middle East. Although "in ancient times the proportion of fair-haired and fair-skinned individuals in Greek and Roman societies seems to have been appreciably higher than today," they finally must conclude that the correlation between "race" and development is somewhat problematical. Note though that, for the authors, our European roots in Greek and Roman societies are saved: They were real whites!

So if race is not involved, how then explain the "ranking" the authors see in human societies? "Here the ecological perspective comes to our aid," because, they maintain, "recent research" has shown that tropical regions are poorly suited to plow agriculture, and tropical lands are quickly exhausted, so that "*indigenous* development beyond the level of horticultural societies seems to have been impossible in much of sub-Saharan Africa and much of Latin America." Also, in the tropics people had to face more parasites and hence more diseases they could not fight, so that these societies were "badly handicapped," unlike the societies in Europe. So Europeans are more developed than Africans. "This explanation fits more of the facts" [than the racialist theory, and therefore] it has greater scientific credibility.

It is somewhat difficult to analyze such textbook passages without a snigger or, more appropriately, without indignation about the sheer nonsense modern students are confronted with. That racialist theories for the authors may seem quite "compelling" is already problematic, because it presupposes that such views are respectable scientific theories in the first place, instead of racist ideologies. However, the authors feel that such theories merely have a number of "weaknesses," implying that on other accounts they seem to be quite attractive. Second, the authors seem to be primarily interested, like the "first explorers," not so much in explaining the differences between various peoples around the world, but in explaining a preconceived "ranking": Europeans, Asians, and finally Africans, as was done in racist ideologies of the nineteenth and early twentieth centuries.

For these authors, ecological explanations seem to be more palatable, and more "modern." However, even though this is a textbook of sociology, it is not societal structure, not dominance and power, not international colonization, not imperialism, and not a host of other political and socioeconomic factors that explain differences of power and development, but rather inherent, though ecologically based conditions and failures of different societies to solve the problem of their adaptation to their environments. We might call this the "Plow and Parasite Theory" of racial, societal, and cultural differences and inequality in the world.

Even naive first-year students who read such passages would probably have a few questions for the proponents of this Plow and Parasite Theory, if the word *theory* is relevant here. They might ask, for instance, how to explain, if this P&P "theory" holds, that Northern Europeans at first appeared to be "barbarians," as the authors say, when compared to the Greeks and Romans, and the Chinese—and earlier, when compared to the peoples in the Middle East and North Africa. Did the climate or the parasite distribution change considerably during the past 5,000 years, so that at first Africans, Arabs, and other non-Europeans were "ranking" so high? And how come, these students might ask, if the Europeans share a similar climate with the Chinese, other Asian peoples, and Native Americans, they nevertheless came out to be ranked first, instead of on the same level with these Asian peoples? And what about the Aztec, the Inca, and the Maya civilizations, when compared to both the Indian populations in more "temperate" zones, as well as contemporary Europeans? Should the genocide of Native Americans be explained also in the "ecological" terms of the P&P "theory"? What about the parasites marring the development of other northern peoples, such as the Inuit? And as for the "plow" part: If tropical agriculture is so hazardous, how come so much produce comes from the tropics, and how come the Europeans colonized so many—seemingly useless— tropical countries? Admittedly, the passage is provocative; it spontaneously raises so many innocent questions that it must have a prime educational and scholarly function.

In other words, the passage would be a beautiful exercise for students to test their elementary knowledge about high school geography and argumentative coherence, and especially to train their insight into the kind of views sociological textbooks are able to sell as being of "greater scientific credibility" than "racialist" theories—for 20 years and six editions, and published by a well-known publisher.

With these few passages in earlier parts of the textbook, it is tempting to skip the *two* pages on "racial and ethnic stratification" that introduce the students of this textbook to one of the major problems of U.S. society. But, let us have a look anyway.

"Many industrial societies have racial or ethnic divisions within them," so the section starts, and then mentions Canada and Belgium first before mentioning "black" and "white" in the United States. The student is then confronted with another piece of sociological insight, namely, how race is transformed into class: "When membership in an ethnic or racial group has an appreciable influence on an individual's access to the benefits a society offers, the group has become, in effect, a class" (p. 329).

Is the provocative title of William Julius Wilson's book on the "declining significance of race" (W. J. Wilson, 1978) behind this astonishing statement, which needs no further comment? Note incidentally that the usually general and abstract nature of the account of "racial or ethnic divisions" fails to concretely tell us, and the students, *who* dominates *whom*, and *who* is responsible for persisting inequalities. We suggested earlier that concepts such as "divisions," "conflict," and "antagonism" blur agency and suggest *mutual* causation of the problems involved, not relations of hierarchy and hegemony, or other sociological structures and processes needed to explain what "racial and ethnic stratification" is all about.

The authors admit that race is a strange kind of class. The "resource" here is not occupation, education, or effort but an "ascribed characteristic," namely, "racial or ethnic background." However, the race-to-class transfer is continued. Here is another beauty of a statement: "Racial and ethnic classes usually have a greater degree of class consciousness than most others, more, say, than people with high school diplomas, more even than manual workers" (p. 329).

Confronted with such passages, the critical textbook analyst faces the problem of where to start explaining everything that is wrong with it. With the notion of class (the "class" of people who have a high school diploma)? With the notion of "class" consciousness of ethnic or racial groups? We will just leave it at that. This, and most other passages that follow, hardly need comment. Moving out of or into a racial or ethnic class is found "more difficult" because of physical traits and family ties.

After these revealing remarks about race and ethnicity, the relations between whites and the "subordinate group of" blacks in the United States are very briefly discussed. These few lines, however, do not fail to mention that even before the Emancipation Proclamation some blacks were quite wealthy and slave owners themselves. The implicit message for students of such passages may be something like this: Don't worry, not just the whites were rich and slave owners, blacks were also involved.

On the other hand, the blacks are said to "suffer from handicaps imposed because of their race." This is, literally, a textbook example of how euphemism and agentless passivity are combined to conceal the precise role of the white group in this process of "imposing handicaps." Indeed, this formulation could even be read as if their race were the cause of the handicaps, and not white U.S. citizens and institutions. Similarly, their "access to clubs, churches, housing and services" was "much more limited"—another passive combined with euphemism, or historical inaccuracy as a description of segregation.

But, fortunately, "Today, most of these limitations have been removed. Civil rights legislation ensures Blacks equal treatment in stores, hotels, restaurants, and other business establishments, and affirmative action legislation even provides preferential treatment in college admissions, hiring, and promotions" (p. 330).

True, there is still some discrimination here and there (club membership) and of course the "economic deprivation of the past has left many Blacks unable to take full advantage of the new opportunities." Black children with "poorly educated, low-income parents" are already "badly handicapped" and cannot compete. We are waiting for Moynihan's "broken" black families—and yes, here it is: "These problems are frequently aggravated by family situations in which the father is absent because of divorce, desertion, illegitimacy, or other reasons" (p. 330).

These examples alone should suffice to illustrate one of the most typical examples of the modern racism of academic discourse: It blindly reproduces standard stereotypes, and its theoretical conceptualization is hardly above the level of student papers (students might even be offended by the comparison). The real problem of such passages is that the authority of the textbook may reinforce widespread views, such as (a) Discrimination is a thing of the past; (b) Affirmative Action is in fact giving "preferences" to minorities, instead of taking away the preferences of whites; (c) blacks—despite the "handicaps" in the past—are themselves to blame for the problems they face, for example, because of their "deserting" fathers, and so on. Differences of income are casually mentioned as another possible cause, but neither further detailed nor explained.

Just this: two small paragraphs for a description of black-white relationships—other minorities are not mentioned—in the United States.

No discussion of racism, of prejudice and discrimination, no historical
background section on slavery and 100 years of post-slavery segregation and discrimination, and virtually nothing about the everyday lives
of blacks, or of other minorities, for that matter. Indeed, most essential
information is lacking.

Vander Zanden, *The Social Experience*

Fortunately, not all textbooks are that bad. Vander Zanden's volumi-
nous textbook, *The Social Experience, An Introduction to Sociology*,
has a substantial chapter on "Racial and Ethnic Relations," which is part
of "Social Differentiation and Inequality" (pp. 269-302), an area in
which the author himself published a book in the 1960s. This textbook
deals with both micro- and macrosociology and does not start from the
premise that to understand society, the students first have to go through
extensive chapters on hunting and gathering; a few pages on sociocultural evolution are sufficient. Many color pictures, tables, and figures
contribute to a lively, pedagogically attractive presentation—obviously
a typical modern U.S. textbook.

Unlike other authors Vander Zanden includes a woman, Harriet
Martineau, and a black sociologist, W.E.B. Du Bois, in the "Milestones"
portrait gallery of sociologists, which reminds us that the very history
of the discipline in many textbooks may already imply ethnocentric or
male chauvinist bias. In this book theory, description, and pictures
consistently deal with European/North American as well as other societies and cultures, blacks and whites, women and men. The word
"discovery," when discussing the "discovery" of America, is duly placed
in quotes and dealt with as part of the topic of ethnocentrism.

After a discussion of the various dimensions of social stratification,
including wealth, income, status, power, and class structures, and finally debunking some of the many myths about welfare, the author
introduces ethnic and racial relations. Ethnic relations, from South
Africa to Sri Lanka and Lebanon, are first associated with conflict,
which is seen to "convulse" the world. "A great many of us seem ready
to kill each other over differences of color, . . . religion, language . . ."
and few over class-related ideologies of capitalism and Marxism. The
author seems to forget, among many other countries, Korea, Vietnam,
Grenada, as well as the continuing, obviously class and ideologically
inspired, oppression in Central America. On the other hand, he finds
examples of ethnic harmony (e.g., the Tungus in Asia). What is essential,

however, is that this book associates race and ethnicity with conditions of inequality and unequal distribution of income, wealth, prestige, and power.

Textbooks need definitions, and we have seen that these invite simplicity and abstractness, hence a blurring of complications. This author defines *race* as follows: "Scientists call a population that differs from others in the incidence of certain hereditary traits a *race*." But identifying different races exactly is not that easy, Vander Zanden adds wisely. What is relevant is that racial differences are assigned social significance. The same is true for ethnic groups. The students are presented with some statistics of all major racial/ethnic groups in the United States. A minority group is defined as a racially and/or culturally self-conscious population, which "suffers disadvantages at the hands of a dominant segment of a nation-state" (p. 275). Notice the familiar euphemistic "disadvantages," instead of, say, discrimination, which is however introduced later and associated with dominant groups and power.

Prejudice, although seemingly universal, is related to specific socio-historical periods: In antiquity there was no color prejudice against Africans. Blumer's still useful four-point definition is introduced here to characterize racist prejudice: (1) We are superior; (2) they are alien and different; (3) we have a claim on privilege, power, and resources; and (4) they want our benefits. Unlike most other textbooks, *symbolic racism* is briefly introduced and characterized with the following ideological views: Blacks have become too impatient, too pushy; they don't have the Protestant work ethic; too many blacks are on welfare; and so on. The author correctly identifies the core of this modern form of racism thus: "In sum, whites reject racial injustice in principle without lowering resistance to social policies that would correct the injustice" (p. 267-277). Recall that we defined racism, and hence also modern or symbolic racism, in broader terms, not only in terms of "feelings." And the practices that define modern forms of discrimination should also be included in the overall system of modern racism.

Discrimination is defined as "the arbitrary denial of privilege, prestige and power to members of a minority group whose qualifications are equal to those of members of the dominant group" (p. 277). The phrase about "equal qualifications" is a bit strange in this general definition and seems to apply more to job recruitment than to service in a shop, and to a host of other situations where "qualifications" are less relevant. A practically and pedagogically more useful definition could be: The unequal treatment by dominant group members and institutions of minority group members in equal situations, and their equal treatment in unequal situations. The latter part would also qualify as discrimination the many contemporary forms of opposition against Affirmative Action. Also lacking in Vander Zanden's definition is that discrimination is not incidental and not limited to individual dominant or minority group members; it is group-based and often institutional, as is clear from his later discussion of institutional discrimination. Merton's four-way categorization, discussed and criticized above for Giddens' textbook, is also mentioned here. The author, however, emphasizes that contemporary discrimination has become very subtle, also because blatant prejudices, especially among the younger generation, have decreased over the years.

Most relevant in this textbook is of course the issue of institutional discrimination, which directly or indirectly affects the position of minority groups and their members in business, health care, housing, finance, education, and politics. Briefly but to the point, Vander Zanden explains that in all these situations actions or measures that seem fair may have negative consequences for minorities, and he also highlights the crucial role of (usually white, male) gatekeepers in these institutions. These various forms of institutionalized inequality are summarized by this conclusion: "Equality of opportunity, even if realized in American life, does not necessarily produce equality of outcome."

Following Yinger, Vander Zanden then goes on to discuss the various policies of dominant groups toward minorities, such as assimilation, pluralism, legal protection, population transfer, continued subjugation, and extermination, as well as the different sociological perspectives (functionalist, conflict, and so on) of race and ethnic relations. As elsewhere in his book, he refrains from giving an explicit evaluation and simply presents the major approaches to race relations. Finally, he details the history and present positions of the major minority groups in the United States: blacks, Asian-Americans, Mexican-Americans, Puerto Ricans, Cubans, and Native Americans. Ethnic relations and racism in other countries are not further discussed. In the section on blacks, he also briefly discusses Wilson's theory of the diminishing role of race and the increasing role of class. Citing many counter-opinions, he cautiously disagrees with Wilson and stresses that in all domains, for all blacks alike, there continues to be evidence of a "racial tax" levied on blacks for not being white. Unlike other authors, Vander Zanden does not mention the "broken family" approach to explaining racial inequality in the United States.

In a special discussion on whether new immigration, mostly of people from Latin American countries, requires new policies, the author indicates that there is growing resentment, especially among lower-class people who fear competition, against illegal immigration. He then goes on to show, referring to several publications, that such immigrants play a fundamental role in the economy of the Southwest United States, and that the immigration is merely a 0.3% yearly trickle when compared to the total population. Such a passage is useful for students as information that may be used to combat common prejudices, even when his own position is cautious and he somewhat weakly concludes that immigration "will remain a center of debate in the years ahead."

As in much elite discourse on minorities, the more liberal writers like Vander Zanden sometimes lapse into the anonymity of nominalizations and agentless passives as soon as whites play a negative role. Thus, in the relatively long section on Native Americans, he states that "an additional 50 or more tribes have vanished through massacre, disease, destruction of their economic base." The obvious question would then be: Who did that? True, this may be so well known that such information would be superfluous. But nevertheless the effect is that the active involvement of white American men and institutions is more or less played down. Thus on page 294 "American Government" is the semantic agent and syntactic subject of a sentence when it is the agent of a positive action (negotiating treaties). On the other hand, Native Americans are placed in such a prominent grammatical position when they are the agents of a negative action (failing to agree). If whites have such a negative role, their agency may be concealed (Native Americans "were confronted with military force"). It would take a systematic study to analyze all action/transaction relations in each sentence of such texts to measure the overall impact of such grammatical formulations of historical events (for theoretical detail about such structures and their ideological implications, see, e.g., Fowler, 1991; Fowler, Hodge, Kress, & Trew, 1979).

Summing up, we find that Vander Zanden's textbook does a decent job in presenting the major issues of ethnic and racial relations. He also includes a discussion of subtle modern forms of discrimination, although he usually avoids the term *racism*. His discussion of the major immigrant groups is the most extensive of the textbooks we examined. His own position, however, is hardly apparent, although his choice of topics and scholarly literature clearly defines his position to be cautiously liberal. In brief, for the issue of ethnic and race relations, of the textbooks we examined, it provides the most and the most useful information for students.

CONCLUSIONS

Throughout Western history, the various forms of academic racism have often constituted the basis and the ideological justification of ethnic and racial inequality, prejudice, discrimination, and racism. Until the nineteenth century, traveling scholars and philosophers reproduced a large body of usually ethnocentric beliefs, including derogating stereotypes and prejudices. During the nineteenth and early twentieth centuries, such forms of ethnocentrism deteriorated into more explicit racist ideologies, supported by pseudo-scientific research into the difference, if not the inferiority, of nonwhite peoples, a tradition that is alive even today in the, admittedly marginal, studies of the genetic coding of negatively interpreted differences between races.

Most academic discourse after the 1960s, however, has followed the mood of relative tolerance, liberalism, or even occasional radicalism prevailing in most universities, especially in the United States. In this respect, academic discourse is not much different from elite discourse in the media or in politics, with the same variation between bigoted conservatism on one extreme, and more or less radical positions on the other end of the ideological spectrum. This means that various forms of modern, symbolic racism are also widespread in academia: research that subtly blames the victims, denial of racism, growing lack of interest in remaining inequalities, opposition against Affirmative Action, irritation about minority radicals who are seen as "exaggerating," and so on. The backlash in the domain of civil rights, initiated by the Reagan administration, as well as the present conservative campaign to marginalize multiculturalism in universities with the slogan of "Political Correctness," are examples in point. Despite such conservative reactions, the discourse on ethnic affairs, especially in the United States, has become more indirect, subtle, and coded.

Such is also the state of affairs in sociology textbooks in Great Britain and the United States. Whereas we found one textbook that was racist and otherwise replete with sociological nonsense, while ignoring the whole question of race and ethnic relations as a relevant topic of sociology, the other textbooks are more or less liberal and pay comparatively much attention to the issue of ethnic and race relations.

There is a tendency in several textbooks, however, to define ethnic and racial conflict in very general and abstract terms, and hence as a universal phenomenon, both geographically and historically, which sometimes precludes a more detailed discussion of racism *hic et nunc*.

Indeed, discrimination in the past and in other countries, as we shall find in the next chapter, sometimes gets more attention than ethnic and racial inequality in present-day society. Few authors mention discrimination and racism in their own institution, the university, and none discusses racist traditions in sociology, at least not explicitly.

On the whole the style is cautious, if not euphemistic. Concrete experiences of contemporary racism are seldom detailed, and white negative agency is often backgrounded. Ethnic or racial "conflict" and "antagonism" are often used instead of more specific terms like racism, and sometimes suggest that, in Western countries, racial inequality may be attributed to both sides.

Few textbooks go into detail when discussing the history and present position of the major minority groups in their own country. For the United States, it is especially African-Americans who are focused on.

Theoretically, the classical definitions of prejudice, discrimination, and racism are used. Most textbooks do not explicitly define or analyze the notion of racism, however. Discrimination is found to be a less harsh term. No attempt is made, in any of the textbooks, to reconceptualize these different notions in a coherent framework, which would also account for contemporary forms of white racism. Only some authors make it explicit that racism, and hence prejudice and discrimination, essentially involve a relation of power and dominance. The insights and experiences of black scholars and other minorities are seldom quoted or referred to, unless they are scholars who are particularly popular with white scholars—and who invariably take a position that is more palatable to whites.

In sum, as may be expected, textbooks are not exactly agents of revolutionary change. Obviously, a very balanced and cautiously liberal position may be a crucial condition for the acceptance, publication, and use of a textbook. It is unlikely that in universities and curricula that are predominantly white, a minority perspective on ethnic or race relations could prevail, and the same is true for textbooks. In that respect, such textbooks obviously reproduce not only the academic consensus, but also the prevailing ideologies and educational practices underlying elite discourse in general.

6

Educational Discourse

INTRODUCTION

Along with the mass media, the system of formal education is among the most important institutions involved in the reproduction of contemporary society. Its reproductive functions are manifold and extend from the acquisition of knowledge and sociocultural norms and values to the inculcation of dominant ideologies. In many respects, schools and universities may even be more influential than the mass media, because they affect the early development of social cognitions and do so with even more authority than the mass media. In most countries, children, adolescents, and young adults are confronted daily, for at least 10 and sometimes even more than 20 years, with a complex set of discursive and ideological practices. The results of those practices are embodied in what counts as official knowledge as well as in more diffuse systems of norms, values, and other social cognitive frameworks that underlie the interactions and interpretative abilities of competent members of society (Apple, 1982a, 1982b; Apple & Weis, 1983; Bourdieu & Passeron, 1977; Giroux, 1981; Sharp, 1980; Young, 1971).

For children the role of schooling in societal reproduction is forceful because of a relative lack of alternative modes of influence, at least in some domains. True, initial socialization in the family, the interaction with peers, children's books, and especially television are also important sources of social knowledge and beliefs. Already at this age the symbolic competition between school and the mass media makes itself felt, and it is generally difficult to assess their respective modes and effects of influence on the child. In some cases, the influence of books, television, or parents may be at variance with each other as well as with that of the school. However, for the more fundamental domains of sociocultural knowledge and beliefs, it may be assumed that these sources are usually mutually compatible.

This is also the context for the acquisition and confirmation of ethnic and racial beliefs of the white child about minorities or Third World peoples in general (Jackman & Muha, 1984). Besides through increasing interaction with children from other ethnic groups, especially in the United States and in some larger cities and Western Europe, the white child is soon confronted with curricular information about Other People in textbooks and classes of social science, civics, history, or geography. The discourses involved in this educational context range from formal and informal instruction, such as lessons and conversations with teachers and school peers, to textbooks and other learning materials. In this chapter, we shall examine what role textbooks in secondary education play in the complex process of the reproduction of racism in society. We shall review other research, in several countries, and also report some results of our own work on Dutch textbooks. At the same time, this chapter illustrates how academic insights, as discussed in the previous chapter, are being popularized in secondary education.

MULTIETHNIC AND ANTI-RACIST EDUCATION

Our analysis of textbooks should also be understood against the background of the ongoing discussion about the aims and nature of what has variously been called multicultural, multiethnic, or anti-racist education (see Chapter 5 for the academic variant of the debate). During the past few decades, the presence or recent arrival of growing minority groups or immigrants from Third World countries has also become visible in the classrooms in most Western countries. This increasing ethnic and racial diversity in schools required policies and practices at all levels of the educational system, including conditions of school access and success of the respective groups, interaction in the classroom, as well as adaptation of a curriculum that, thus far, has often been predominantly white and Eurocentric (Banks, 1981; Banks & Lynch, 1986; Modgil, Verma, Mallick, & Modgil, 1986; Mullard, 1984; Troyna & Williams, 1986; Verma & Bagley, 1984).

Since the Civil Rights Movement in the United States, school desegregation and multicultural integration in education have been among the most visible, and hotly debated and resisted, manifestations of the principle of justice and equal rights for all citizens (Gerard & Miller, 1975; McClendon, 1985; Rossell & Hawley, 1983; Stephan & Feagin, 1980). The first black child entering a white school in the U.S. South had to be accompanied by the National Guard, whereas busing of students in various U.S. cities remains controversial, if not a valid indicator of what is often called symbolic racism (Bobo, 1983; McConohay, 1982; Sears, Hensler, & Spears, 1979; Sears & Kinder, 1985; Taylor, 1986).

Similarly, across the ocean, the increase of West Indian, South Asian, North African, and Turkish children in British, French, German, and Dutch schools has often provoked confusion and mixed feelings, at best, if not explicitly racist reactions, from white parents, teachers, administrators, and policymakers (Palmer, 1986; Stone, 1981).

In the chapter on the coverage of ethnic affairs in the media, we shall see that school integration, multicultural teaching, and especially antiracist education continue to be major topics in the press. This has been particularly clear in the nationwide conflict in Britain about headmaster Honeyford in 1985, in the case of the veils of some Muslim girls in France in 1989, and in the ongoing and acrimonious "Political Correctness" debate on multicultural school and college curricula in the United States. In other words, for many whites, the multicolored and multicultural classroom and its learning materials have been and still remain a serious problem, provoking passions that are rare for other educational issues and in other sectors of multiethnic societies.

Despite these controversies, many national or local governments developed educational policies that were aimed at ethnic or racial integration or the realization of pluralistic ideals. One major issue in these policies was language and culture, since many of the newly arrived immigrants and their families did not speak the dominant metropolitan language, and came from societies with a different culture, so that their children often began school with what was termed a "disadvantage," compared to children of the dominant, mostly white group. With mixed success, massive second-language and multicultural programs were developed in several countries (Allen & Swain, 1984; Skutnabb-Kangas, 1984; Spolsky, 1986). These too stirred up nationalist reactions from right-wing groups and media who feared being "swamped" (as Prime Minister Thatcher termed it) by the alien culture.

In Western Europe, these nationalist concerns also, if not primarily, focused on religion, and especially on the presumed harmful influence of Islam on the educational opportunities of children. Other criticism of bilingual programs came from well-meaning educators who assumed that total and exclusive immersion in the dominant language and culture is a condition of success both at school and in white/Western society. Some countries and school systems also introduced extracurricular activities that would allow minority children to be taught in their own language and about their own culture. Sometimes multicultural goals became part of the official curriculum, aimed at both the immigrants and the other children.

In this debate about multiethnic or multicultural education, critical voices were soon also heard from a so-called anti-racist perspective (Brandt, 1986; Cole, 1986; Mullard, 1984). In this view, multicultural programs or curricula often boil down to only superficial information about minority culture, if not paternalistic folklore. Such apolitical programs are thought to obscure the fundamental facts of racial, white hegemony in all domains of society, including education. Multicultural education in such an analysis is rejected because it falsely suggests cultural equality where there is none.

Anti-racist views hold that lacking access to quality schools, discrimination in the classroom, stereotyping in textbooks, and a host of other factors lead to a position of minority children at school that is usually described as "disadvantaged," but in reality reflects their subordinate position. Similarly, even when minority children manage to achieve in such a school system, they may nevertheless experience serious discrimination in finding and/or keeping a job afterward. And finally, majority group children need to know about patterns and practices of dominance, about prejudice and discrimination, and about the structural dimensions of racism in white, Western societies to be able to challenge these and function adequately in the new multiethnic environment. In other words, only a critical anti-racist perspective in the classroom, as well as in all other aspects of the curriculum, can prepare both majority and minority children for a society in which ethnic or racial inequality is still deeply ingrained, namely, by developing strategies of resistance and change.

The principles of this anti-racist perspective on education, which form the backdrop of this chapter, also apply to educational discourse, that is, to lessons, textbooks, and other learning materials. Research, some of which is reviewed and reported in this chapter, has repeatedly shown that most textbooks, especially in Europe, are replete with stereotypical if not blatantly Eurocentric and racist representations of minorities and Third World peoples and continue to ignore minority groups and their cultures altogether. Again, such contents affect both majority and minority children. The first will continue to be educated in an ideology that sustains white or Western dominance and feelings of superiority, whereas the latter will be seriously hampered in their development, if only because they lack information, if not recognition and respect regarding their own group or culture. Hence, the contents and assignments of learning materials should explicitly take into account at least the possible presence of minority children in the classroom, and should feature a broad, transcultural perspective that would give credit to the major ethnic groups and cultures in the country and the world, and would especially aim to develop the knowledge and anti-racist attitudes needed to participate in the struggle against white ethnic group dominance.

LIMITATIONS

In the framework of this book, it should first be realized that textbooks are a form of educational discourse and therefore analyzable in terms of discourse analysis. Despite a long tradition of textbook analysis in several countries, however, there are as yet few studies that systematically and explicitly deal with the various levels and dimensions of this genre. For obvious reasons, as in media research, most work is content analytical: The primary aim of textbook analysis is usually to find out what the children are supposed to learn, not how contents are exactly formulated. Unfortunately, this limitation of current research cannot fully be countered in a single chapter of a book. Although we shall pay attention to various aspects of textbook discourse, we cannot possibly analyze in detail all relevant textual structures of learning materials, even if these structures may have an important role in the acquisition of knowledge and beliefs by children (see also Cazden, 1988; Luke, 1988, 1989).

The same is true for the more general study of the role of textbooks in education, the relationship between learning materials and the curriculum, the use of such materials in the classroom, the role of the teacher in the instruction based on the textbooks, or the broader social, cultural, and economic aspects of textbook production, uses, and functions in society. That is, an interdisciplinary study of textbooks and their role in the reproduction of racism is outside the scope of this chapter, although we shall briefly discuss one of the major theses of this book, namely the role of the elites in the reproduction process. For education and textbooks the concept of elites may be less applicable, since most

teachers and even textbook authors do not seem to have exactly the kind
of elite power politicians, journalists, and corporate managers have in
the public arena. Indeed, such power, if any, may be much less public
and often indirect and concealed.

On the other hand, if we define and measure power by the scope of those
who are affected by it, people and organizations that are responsible for
educational policies and curricula, as well as textbook authors, may well be
assigned elite status according to our discursive and ideological orientation,
since they indirectly control what thousands if not millions of children must
learn every day. Outside the schools and even for parents, this kind of
influence is for the most part less visible, simply because most of the younger
children are not yet able to clearly discuss such aspects of the curriculum and
the educational system, let alone challenge them. Only when groups of
concerned parents, organizations, or the media publicly discuss the contents
of textbooks, may these become an issue of public debate.

Finally, this chapter also ignores the complexities of the didactic and
developmental functions of textbooks. A detailed theory of reading, comprehension, and integration of knowledge and beliefs, as inferred from
textbooks in specific educational and social contexts, would be needed in
order to explain the impact of such textbooks on ethnic learning and the
social reproduction of racism among children (see Chapter 2 for some
details of the more general processes of the formation of social cognitions).
No such explicit insights into ethnic learning from textbooks exist at the
moment. We only have some insight into the acquisition of ethnic attitudes
by children, a process that begins between the ages of 4 and 7 (Aboud,
1988; Katz, 1976a). At the age of secondary education, that is, when the
textbooks studied in this chapter are used, many white children may
already have detailed knowledge and attitude structures about other ethnic
groups, either through personal experiences in multiethnic societies or
through the discourses of their parents, peers, children's books, and especially television (see Anwar & Shang, 1982; Matabane, 1988). In this
respect, the textbooks may either confirm prevailing stereotypes and
prejudices or positively combat them.

EARLIER STUDIES

Despite the broad academic and political interest in the content of
textbooks, there are surprisingly few systematic studies of the textbook
portrayal of ethnic or racial groups. Moreover, most of these studies are

either anecdotal or traditionally content analytical. Most studies are practical and normative: They conclude what is wrong with these textbooks and how they could be improved. We have seen that there is generally little discourse analytical work on textbooks, and even less on the ways textbooks deal with minorities or ethnic affairs. This is also one of the reasons why the report of our own textbook analysis, given below, is theoretically and methodologically tentative, as well as highly informal.

Despite these shortcomings, we shall briefly review some of the more prominent publications on the portrayal of minorities in textbooks and children's books, two discourse types that are often dealt with at the same time. As these studies do, we focus on the contents of textbooks and initially do so at a rather low level of abstraction and analysis.

Preiswerk, *The Slant of the Pen*

Whereas most studies, including those reviewed below, are largely practical and descriptive, Preiswerk's collection of papers (Preiswerk, 1980) has a more theoretical orientation. At the same time, this book presents a detailed list of criteria that may be, and have been, used for the evaluation of children's books and learning materials. These criteria generally focus on the negative portrayal of other groups, the positive representation of their own group, and forms of racist dominance by the white group. In addition to the observations made by other authors mentioned below, this list of criteria also features the following items for the identification of ethnocentrism:

a. Ambiguous use of concepts such as culture, civilization, and race.
b. The principle of linear evolution: Other peoples/cultures are "lagging behind."
c. Their history begins from the moment We have contact with them.
d. Self-glorification: Western/European institutions (law, democracy, monotheism) are presented as the highest norm of development.
e. Legitimation of European action: Colonialism has brought Them a lot of good things.
f. Intercultural and intertemporal transmission: They still live in the Stone Age.

Milner, *Children and Race*

In his well-known study, *Children and Race*, Milner (1983) examined a number of textbooks and children's books and generally concluded

that black people, and nonwhite or non-Western peoples in general, tend
to be ignored. If not, "their treatment [is] . . . at best patronizing, at
worst racist, and nearly always stereotyped."

Milner first emphasizes that such a marginal and negative portrayal
does not present a realistic picture of multicultural society for all
children, while at the same time denying black or other minority
children the opportunity to identify with the nonwhite protagonists of
textbooks and children's books. Moreover, not only are minority groups
and their members often represented in negative terms, but the white
majority is also usually described in either neutral or positive terms.

The representation of minorities or other peoples is often stereotypical and based on dated images: Dutch in wooden shoes, Chinese with
pigtails, Africans in the bush, and Eskimos in igloos. Cultural and social
differences between Us and Them are emphasized, and measured by
comparison to Our norms. Thus, the color white is generally associated
with positive values, such as clean, beautiful, good, pure, divine, and
honest, whereas black is associated with their negative counterparts.
These general associations based on color are naturally extended to the
personal characteristics of white and black groups.

In older books, African peoples in particular tend to be associated
with backwardness, stupidity, wildness, laziness, savagery, cannibal-
ism, primitive rites, exotic hair and clothes (or nakedness), as well as
with primitive language use. For black people in Western societies,
there is the additional association with carelessness, crime, and drug
abuse. Generally, such negative portrayals imply Western primacy and
superiority. Even if black people have less-stereotypical roles, they are
represented as dependent and passive, for instance, as slaves, servants,
helpers, or assistants of whites. Main characters are usually white and
have at most a condescending friendship with their black subordinates.

Textbooks of history and geography have similar stereotypes and normally have a white, Western, or European perspective: We "discovered"
America, and have brought civilization to "barbarian" peoples in the Third
World. The civilization and cultures of such peoples before We arrived is
seldom dealt with, and development and civilization are usually identified
with Western industrialization, technology, and progress.

Slavery, violent conquest, and neocolonial exploitation of Third World
countries receive little attention, and it is not made clear that much of Our
wealth and industrial progress are due to the profits made in these countries.

Even more recent books provide a simplistic and stereotypical image
of the peoples of Africa and Asia, namely, one of poverty, hunger, and

underdevelopment. The neocolonial causes of this situation tend to be ignored, whereas Our paternalistic, and far from disinterested, "help" in these countries is emphasized.

Especially in children's books, but also in some textbooks, old racist texts and pictures are reprinted in successive new editions, for instance in the Dr. Dolittle series. Criticism of the racist contents of such "innocent" books is generally ridiculed for being exaggerated.

Klein, *Reading into Racism*

Gillian Klein (1986) found more or less the same characteristics in children's books and textbooks. Besides the usual negative stereotypes, she also emphasizes the detrimental role of omissions, which are much more difficult to assess because children books and textbooks cannot be comprehensive. However, omissions may well be evaluated as negative if, in a given context of discussion, the information is relevant to understanding the events or the situation. One prominent example is the marginalization of the role of black U.S. soldiers, for instance in World War II, Korea, and Vietnam.

Her analysis of textbooks for several subjects uses the criteria of Preiswerk (1980) for the identification of ethnocentrism in textbooks. She found that many textbook authors tend to ignore or belittle the peoples and cultures of "dark" Africa. "Natives" are represented as "tribes," as "backward," as living in "huts" (instead of houses), and as "painting" their faces (and not as "using cosmetics"). Whereas such images were useful in the legitimation of slavery, they were also later functional in the role of Western philanthropy.

Politically, the struggles for independence of Third World peoples and nations was often represented, both in textbooks and in the media, as examples of "outbursts of wild and fanatic tribes," of which whites are especially the victims. Even today, conflicts in Africa tend to be represented in terms of primitive tribal feuds. Klein adds that it is hardly surprising that this negative portrayal appears in textbooks, since it has been established that quite a number of such books got their materials from the South African Embassy (Wright, 1983).

Council for Interracial Books for Children

One the most active and influential organizations in the struggle against bias in children's books and textbooks is the New York-based

Council for Interracial Books for Children. This organization publishes not only a bulletin but also practical brochures for the identification of sexism and racism in books for children and students. One of these brochures (CIBC, 1980) lists a number of general practical questions that can help in detecting such forms of bias in books:

1. *Characterization.* Are minorities or other Third World peoples stereotypically described, for instance, by language use (e.g., Puerto Ricans as carrying knives), description of their circumstances (Indians in reservations, blacks in ghettos) or by omission of minority perspectives, for instance, in the struggle against white domination? Similarly, are the goals of Third World peoples respected, or are they only admired when they perform superhuman tasks? Are minority groups blamed for their own poverty (everything would be okay if only they would get a good education and would learn the language), or are problems of minorities solved by benevolent whites?

2. *Language.* Is negative language being used, such as in blatant derogatives ("nigger"), color symbolism (white as good, black as bad), political evaluations ("underdeveloped," cultural "deprivation"), and in ethnocentric descriptions (the "discovery" of America, "huts" and "tribes" in Africa). Or conversely, are positive terms being used when they would not be used for whites in the same context (blacks being called "quite intelligent"). Finally, is a distinction made between Us and Them, in such a way that minorities are not part of Us or Our country?

3. *Historical Correctness.* Omissions: Are the life and culture of minority groups dealt with? Are women from minority groups also mentioned? Is their history also described for the period before and after the occupation by white colonialists? Are the history of racism, and the consequences of that history for the present situation, dealt with? Bias: Is their resistance against discrimination and exploitation adequately portrayed? Is colonial dominance represented in positive terms? Eurocentrism: Are the events described from a perspective that was/is important for whites? Are leaders of minority groups characterized in terms of what they did for their own groups or for what they did for dominant whites?

4. *Cultural Authenticity.* Is the description of other cultures framed in terms of these other cultures: Is civilization identified with technology, and culture with pots and jewelry? Are their religions treated with respect? Are the values of the other cultures found to be inferior to those of our own culture? Are minority cultures trivialized or ridiculed? Are important and positive aspects of the other cultures ignored (e.g.,

loyalty and solidarity)? Is their life-style considered as a possible alternative to the dominant Western life-style?

5. *Illustrations.* The same questions may be asked about the pictures and other illustrations. Are women and children also portrayed in the illustrations? Do the images reinforce stereotypes? Are the appearance and clothes of other groups represented adequately, and not in order to emphasize the identity of such groups in terms of stereotypes?

Other Studies

There are several other, often shorter studies of the portrayal of minorities or Third World peoples in children's books and textbooks (for references, see Klein, 1986). For instance, summarizing some results of his doctoral dissertation on bias in British geography textbooks (Hicks, 1980a), Hicks (1980b) shows that most books of the 1970s are racist or ethnocentric, and only a handful are nonracist or anti-racist. Thus, when dealing with such problems of the Third World as poverty, hunger, and the like, the explanations of most books appear to fit what may be called a counterrevolutionary theory, featuring such propositions as: Poverty is a combination of chance and built-in obstacles. If "these people" would only follow the example of the First World, then everything would be fine. Since there are too many hungry people in the world, peasant farmers must be educated. Colonialism has nothing to do with geography. Similarly, minority groups are backward and need help. Some of the books have straightforward racist "explanations" of the differences between the "races":

> There can be little doubt about the part played by climate in the progress of races. The vigorous climate of the temperate regions has encouraged great activity by the white races who occupy them. This can lead to their rapid development. On the other hand the heat of the tropical areas has tended to make the black races less energetic. As a result their progress has been much slower. (quoted in Hicks, 1980b, p. 9)

Conclusions

The studies and practical guidelines reviewed above repeatedly, and sometimes independently of each other, arrive at the same or similar conclusions about the sometimes abysmal portrayal of minorities and other Third World peoples in Western children's books and textbooks.

Thus, in general terms and at least until the early 1980s, such books tended to be stereotypical and Eurocentrist if not clearly prejudiced and racist. Western people and their culture are usually presented in either neutral or positive terms, while the reverse is true for peoples in Third World countries, especially those in Africa and Asia. Western culture and technology are seen as the norm, in comparison to which other cultures, peoples, and nations are seen as "backward" or "underdeveloped," if not "primitive." Attention and respect for the positive contributions and roles of other cultures and their leaders are often lacking. The personality of minorities and other Third World peoples also tends to be described in negative terms. Problems are blamed on them, and seldom on the effects of white dominance and exploitation. Minority group members usually have passive, subordinate roles when represented in contact with whites, unless they resist domination, in which case their active role is usually portrayed in very negative terms, such as "savagery" and "barbarism." White or Western dominance is often legitimated in terms of the "good things" We do for Them. Even in more recent textbooks, this positive "helping" role of Western countries is emphasized.

It should be stressed that these are very general conclusions, which obviously have exceptions. Also, they apply mainly to children's books and textbooks of the 1970s and earlier. In some countries, especially the United States since the Civil Rights Movement, such critical evaluations have had some positive effect on newer textbooks. The major improvement has been wider attention to the history and the sociocultural contributions of large minority groups (e.g., African-Americans and Native Americans in the United States), and some cautious criticism of the past role of dominant, white, Western groups, notably during slavery or colonialism. There is still little critical attention focused on contemporary, especially the more indirect and subtle, forms of discrimination and oppression of minorities. The change in textbook contents in the United States has been such that conservative organizations have begun to worry about reverse bias in such textbooks; however, a study carried out for such an organization concluded that such is hardly the case (Glazer & Ueda, 1983).

In most textbooks in Western Europe, the more blatant forms of prejudice have been replaced by modern, that is, more subtle, forms of white or Western dominance and superiority and of inferiority of black or other immigrant groups. Race as an object of interest is generally replaced by culture. As we shall also see in the analysis of Dutch textbooks of the 1980s, negative stereotypes of minorities and Third World peoples remain common fare in textbooks, if any attention is paid to such groups and their cultures and history. More recent work, however, seems to suggest that multicultural and occasionally even anti-racist philosophies have also begun to appear in European learning materials.

Note finally that textbooks in many respects are a succinct, indirect, and belated summary of yesterday's scholarly views. Textbook writers of the 1970s and 1980s may have had their own formal education in the 1950s and 1960s, and their more recent sources of information on ethnic relations may be the mass media or popular writings, instead of recent scholarly studies, unless they are specifically interested in the topic. Few textbook writers, as well as secondary school teachers, for that matter, are specially trained or retrained in ethnic or multicultural studies. In sum, the organizational context of both the writing and the uses of textbooks is such that their contents are not readily adapted to new scholarly and educational insights, nor to the new norms and values of a multicultural society.

The consequence is that children in the 1980s may have learned attitudes that were prevalent several decades earlier, and may apply them in a social context several decades later, unless intermediate adult learning changes these previous belief systems. Hence, the discrepancy between textbook-based schooling and the use of knowledge and beliefs in a rapidly developing multicultural society may be considerable.

For our study of textbooks in the Netherlands, there is the additional complication that many academic Dutch studies on ethnic relations are themselves seriously flawed because most of them neglect to examine the fundamental role of racism in Dutch society (for critical analysis of such studies, see Essed, 1987).

GEOGRAPHY AND HISTORY TEXTBOOKS IN THE NETHERLANDS

In a recent study, intended as a follow-up of our own study of social studies textbooks reported below, Mok (1990) examined in detail the 24 geography and history textbooks or textbook series used in Dutch secondary schools during the 1980s. Her conclusions are in line with the results of earlier work reviewed above. Geography and especially history textbooks in the Netherlands pay only scant attention to minorities, ethnic relations, immigration, or racism—at most, 1% to 2% of the total pages of the textbooks. If they pay attention at all, geography textbooks tend to focus on superficial figures of demography, migration, and especially the immigration of foreign workers to the Netherlands.

Most revealing in such books is the more general portrayal of Third World peoples, which we have already suggested is very similar to the treatment of non-European minorities in Western countries. History textbooks may feature some of the historical backgrounds of immigration and discrimination, and may in principle be expected to give information about the history of colonialism, slavery, and the various emancipation movements.

Also, both history and geography books should in principle pay attention to information about the countries or continents that large minority groups come from, as well as to their history. While this is now increasingly the case in the United States, Dutch and other European textbooks are—as yet—rarely paying special attention to the geography and history of minority groups and their original countries and cultures.

Mok further found that the information about minorities tends to be concentrated in a few isolated passages. That is, in most other topics or issues dealt with, the geography and history of the Netherlands and the world are not taking into account either the presence or contributions of minority groups, or the effects of migration. The important role of "guest workers" in the Dutch and European economy tends to be ignored. Racism is virtually absent as a topic and is seldom used to explain the subordinate position of minority groups in the Netherlands. Indeed, of the 24 books, only one history book and part of one geography book have an anti-racist perspective.

In most other books, attention is focused on various problems of immigration, such as that of adaptation, a concept that is scarcely analyzed in a more critical perspective. On the contrary, adaptation and assimilation are seen as a normal consequence of immigration, and thus legitimated in textbooks. Similarly, the textbooks emphasize the polarization between white Dutch (or European, Western) groups and cultures and those of non-European immigrants. Ethnic prejudice and racism are ignored, denied, or mitigated, or dealt with in the context of ethnic relations abroad (e.g., in the United States). Stereotypes and prejudices are discussed in very general terms, and children are not trained to identify and challenge racist attitudes. The geography books still feature traditional passages about the different races in the world, without locating such a treatment in the framework of a discussion about the racist implications of past and present discourses about such races.

The portrayal of the peoples, countries, and cultures of the Third World is consistent with this treatment of minorities. Stereotypes about the passivity, poverty, backwardness, and problems of Third World peoples are the rule, usually without socioeconomic explanations that highlight the role of colonialism and present-day forms of exploitation by Western trade and business. Consider, for instance, the following explanatory passage about Surinam and the Dutch Antilles, which seems to signal prejudices, but at the same time legitimates them:

Many people see all kinds of films on television about Surinam and the Antilles. In those films one sees many Surinamese and Antillians walking in the street or playing games in front of their houses. It seems as if many Surinamese "prefer to be lazy rather than tired" [a Dutch expression]. These films usually present a biased picture. That is, there is much unemployment in Surinam and the Dutch Antilles. That's why there are so many people in the streets. Moreover, the people who have a job don't earn much. Even if one member of a large family has a job, then the members of such a family are still hungry. You will now understand why we do not find a hardworking population in Surinam and the Antilles. (quoted in Mok, 1990, p. 67)

History books may occasionally formulate critical remarks about early imperialism, colonialism, and slavery, but the overall perspective remains white and Eurocentric. Resistance of non-Western peoples to these forms of oppression is rarely mentioned, and is sometimes even portrayed in negative terms. Implicitly, Western and white superiority are pervasive in most passages about the Third World. Such attitudes are also expressed stylistically, for instance by the use of negative or outdated terms such as "Negroes," "natives," or "bushmen." The development of Third World countries is consistently described and measured relative to the present technological and industrial advances of First World countries. The past contributions of highly developed cultures in Asia, Africa, and the Americas are briefly mentioned in several history textbooks, but such acknowledgments seldom have implications for present comparisons between North and South. Generally, peoples and cultures in the Third World tend to be dealt with in general terms; vast differences tend to be ignored.

Mok concludes that although Dutch textbooks in history and geography in the 1980s have improved somewhat, increasingly acknowledging the presence of minority groups, their overall treatment of non-European groups, countries, and cultures remains stereotypical and white-centered. Economic or cultural contributions of minorities or Third World peoples are still ignored. Although there is some critical attention for colonialism and slavery in the past, present-day racism, especially in the

Netherlands, is barely related. Both contents and pedagogical assignments do not, as a matter of fact, presuppose the presence of minority
students in the classroom. Although less blatantly than in the past,
textbooks in several domains thus continue to reproduce the image of
white and/or Western superiority.

SOCIAL STUDIES TEXTBOOKS
IN THE NETHERLANDS

Within the framework sketched above, we examined how a specific
class of textbooks contributes to the reproduction of racism (for details
about the original study, see van Dijk, 1987c). As an example we
examined all social studies (or civics) textbooks in use in secondary
schools in the Netherlands in 1986. These books are intended for
children between the ages of 12 and 18, and function within the curriculum of what in the Netherlands is called *maatschappijleer* (the study
of society). Until recently, this ill-defined curriculum was not part of
the final examination program in secondary schools, but functioned as
an option that was hardly taken seriously.

Despite the presence in the Netherlands of significant minority groups,
such as people from the ex-colonies of the East Indies (now Indonesia),
and Surinam, as well as Mediterranean immigrant workers and their
families, especially from Turkey and Morocco, the official curriculum
for social studies in the Netherlands does not yet feature the study of
ethnic or social relations, although some indirect references to "living
together in a pluralist democracy" have been made in the more recent
curriculum reformulations (Dekker & Rozemond, 1983).

This important deficiency in the official curriculum, which is not pre-
scribed by the State but organized by an independent committee of social
studies teachers, is also reflected in the scant attention paid to this topic:
At least half of the 43 books we analyzed did not even mention it. Despite
the increasing attention on ethnic affairs in the press, and the presence of
nearly one million people who may be categorized as ethnic minorities,
within a general population of 15 million, the social studies teaching
establishment in the mid-1980s did not deduce the consequences of this
important social fact. Possibly more seriously, the establishment did not
even reflect upon the relevant fact that an increasing percentage (in some
neighborhoods of the cities, higher than 70%) of the children belong to
various communities of ethnic minorities.

This does not mean, however, that the topic is totally invisible in the curriculum or in actual teaching. For one, when lacking adequate learning materials, many teachers do use informal materials, such as newspaper articles. On the other hand, the topic may be discussed in geography and history textbooks (see Mok's study above), whereas occasional reading and other exercises in the mother tongue curriculum may also feature texts about ethnic minorities. Despite these other, formal as well as less formal, sources of information and learning, however, the overall conclusion is that until the late 1980s at least, ethnic minorities and ethnic relations generally remained seriously neglected by Dutch social studies curriculum planners. Since textbooks usually follow the lead of the official curriculum, and since most textbooks may be repeatedly reprinted without much correction for years, it is not surprising to find that less than half of the textbooks feature information about ethnic minorities and ethnic relations.

Materials and Methods

Of the 43 books listed in the 1986 edition of the *Guide of the Center for the Registration of Learning Materials* (CRL), only 20 appeared to feature at least some (more than 100 words) information about ethnic affairs, such as minority groups, migrant labor, or prejudice and discrimination. These books cater to the various secondary school types in the Netherlands (VWO, HAVO, MAVO, LBO, and LEAO), ranging from university-preparatory VWO to lower vocational schools (LBO).

As our unit of analysis we chose the *episode*, that is, a thematically coherent text fragment of the same discourse genre, often expressed in a single paragraph (or in a separate example). Since several topics may be discussed in the same lesson, some of these fragments may be rather short (a few lines), whereas others, for instance an example, a story, or a reproduced newspaper clipping, may occupy a full page. Different discourse genres in textbooks, such as theory, questions, assignments, examples, drawings and tables, or photographs were also distinguished. Thus, a quotation or newspaper clipping about a specific topic, for example, discrimination, was categorized as a different unit of analysis. The context and perspective of each fragment further determined its classification. Thus, if discrimination was dealt with in a paragraph about employment, then the paragraph was categorized as employment, whereas a more general treatment of discrimination was categorized as race relations (discrimination) in its own right.

An episode is the information of the text that may be summarized by a single macro-proposition or topic. For practical purposes, topics are represented here as single clauses, such as "Employers hired workers in Morocco." Such topics feature not only a predicate, referring to events, actions, or properties of people (e.g., "hired"), but also arguments that have different *actor roles*, such as Agent (e.g., "Employers") or Patient ("Moroccans"). Further semantic analysis of such topics allows an examination of the ways majority and minority actors appear as actors in textbook discourse.

While this thematic or topical analysis deals with the overall contents or subjects of the fragments about ethnic affairs, a more detailed analysis was also made of the microstructures of the lessons, involving local meanings, style, rhetoric, and especially argumentative moves, for instance, those functioning within the well-known overall strategies of positive self-presentation and negative other-presentation. Topical analysis yields data about what information the textbooks deem important or relevant in this domain, whereas local analyses focus on the ways such information is actually formulated in the text.

Although most of our analyses will be descriptive and explanatory, our anti-racist framework requires that we occasionally insert more evaluative commentary of a normative kind, for example, by focusing on what might have been or should have been written to avoid racist stereotypes and prejudices.

Actors

Our first analysis of 20 textbooks yielded 422 passages (episodes) that directly or indirectly dealt with ethnic groups, immigrants, refugees, or ethnic affairs and immigration generally. We might first examine who the relevant ethnic actors are in these passages. Whereas We (white Dutch, or people in the West) are prominent actors in all passages, it is striking to observe that attention is paid to only a few ethnic groups. The bulk of the passages are about *gastarbeiders* (guest workers), who are seen as the real *buitenlanders* (foreigners), which is the concept used in informal talk about ethnic minority groups or immigrants in the Netherlands. As we shall see in more detail below, one other main reason for this particular attention to migrant workers is that they and their families can be discussed in terms of their "alien culture."

Whereas such "real" foreigners appear 154 times in these episodes, minorities in general also occur very often—92 times. The specific nationalities, for example, Turks and Moroccans, are mentioned only a dozen times. In other words, the textbooks treat foreigners and minorities more as a general category, and much less as specific groups. Another implication of this special focus on immigrant workers is that other minority groups, such as Surinamese, Antillians, or Moluccans, seldom appear in the textbooks. Indeed, according to the culture concept of the textbooks, there is no distinct culture to be discussed for them, and this may be the reason that they are scarcely treated at all. In other words, one major topic that prompts the textbook coverage of minorities in the Netherlands is the overriding criterion of a strange culture, especially that of Islam. Similar conclusions may be drawn if we calculate not the number of episodes (passages) in which minority groups appear as actors, but the number of words in such passages. Again, immigrant workers top the list with 11,941 words, and minorities in general are dealt with in 8,508 words. The large group of Surinamese gets only 1,746 words, and they are discussed in only 9 of the 20 books (out of 43) that had information about minorities.

Topics

The analysis of topics or themes in textbooks partly has a normative character. That is, we are not only interested in what topics are actually dealt with in textbooks, but also want to know which topics could or should have been present but are absent. Therefore, we established a list of general topics, each subdivided in a number of subtopics, that in our opinion should be part of the ethnic information of a social studies curriculum, and about which scholarly or other information is available. These topics are: immigration in general, backgrounds and history of immigration, arrival and first reception, socioeconomic and sociocultural situation of immigrants/minorities in the Netherlands, and ethnic relations. This last topic, for instance, features such subtopics as general relations between majority and minority groups, prejudice, discrimination, and racism.

Immigration

The immigration subtopics primarily deal with the socioeconomic situation in the respective countries where the immigrants come from (mostly Turkey or Morocco). This information shows why the immigrants came to the Netherlands in the first place ("push" factors). Second, the economic situation in the Netherlands is described, such as the lack of menial workers in the industry ("pull" factors), although this important economic background in the arrival of guest workers is not emphasized. Only a handful of books have such information.

Additionally, because Surinamese and immigrants from Indonesia are scarcely discussed, we find virtually no information about the colonial backgrounds of their immigration to the Netherlands. There are a few passages about the historical backgrounds of the immigration of Moluccans, however, such as the service of Moluccan men in the Dutch colonial army, and their problematic situation in an independent Indonesia.

The arrival and first reception of immigrants is barely discussed, except for a few tables with numbers and information about where the immigrants settled. Prejudice and other forms of hostility directed against the newcomers are ignored, as are the workers' sometimes miserable housing and social welfare conditions.

Position of Immigrants

Because textbooks in the Netherlands pay special attention to "guest workers," it might be expected that at least some information would be given about the kind of work they do—as it is, although briefly. However, this information is largely stereotypical: Immigrants are primarily represented as doing the dirty work, for instance, as cleaners. This may have been true for most of the early immigrants, but in later years, the migrants have become employed in a variety of jobs. Surinamese, Turkish, or Moroccan teachers, lawyers, business people, or civil servants never appear in textbooks. Chinese only work in Chinese restaurants. Surinamese, if mentioned in relation to work at all, are occasionally mentioned as musicians. Problems at work, discrimination on the job, and employment are seldom topicalized.

Topics such as housing, health care, and the general social situation of minorities are virtually absent. Again, this is in line with the lack of attention to such topics in the media and other forms of public discourse.

Cultural Differences

We have already suggested that textbooks, much like other discourse about minorities, are fascinated by culture and especially by cultural differences, which is also the most frequent topic. Textbook writers may in this case not only express what is most "interesting" for them, but also assume that such a topic is important for children. Here we find the usual stereotypical stories about other habits, food, clothing, religion, and language, mostly about guest workers and their families. In a country where religion still plays a major role in social organization (the well-known "pillar" system), it is not surprising that a different religion like Islam gets special attention. Usually, the criterion of adaptation plays a prominent role here. Generally, stereotypical cultural differences are emphasized, and similarities between the different groups ignored. Below, we shall examine in more detail, how culture is discussed in these textbooks.

Children from immigrant families also appear in this topical framework of "cultural differences." According to stereotype, children are portrayed as "living between two cultures," where difficulties in the family are emphasized. Problems experienced at school or in contact with their peers are, however, largely ignored. Indeed, it is generally rather striking that in textbooks for children and adolescents, among whom an increasing number are children of immigrants, there is so little information about them. As usual, the textbooks do not exactly deal with the everyday life of the students.

Ethnic Relations

Besides cultural differences, ethnic relations are particularly topicalized. Living together in a multicultural society is basically defined as "problematic." This emphasis in textbook discourse runs parallel to that in the media and other elite discourse on minorities examined in this book. Prejudice and discrimination are also discussed in the majority of textbooks, though usually very briefly, and seldom in terms of racism. One of the reasons for this attention is that discrimination is one of the official topics in the social studies curriculum.

The discussion of these topics is usually very general and is embedded in a discussion that also emphasizes the "tolerance" of the Dutch. An occasional example is given of immigrants or minorities who have difficulty renting an apartment or who are not allowed into a discotheque. Further details and explanations of racism are absent. It is never discussed in terms of power or dominance relations, or in the perspective of the legacy of colonialism, or in the framework of the exploitative nature of migrant labor. The experiences of minorities with racism in everyday situations are ignored in textbooks.

Interestingly, discrimination is often dealt with in more detail in relation to segregation in the United States or apartheid in South Africa. It is generally the case in Dutch elite discourse, and in textbooks, that discrimination abroad is examined in more critical terms than racism in the Netherlands itself. The struggle against racism, the resistance of minority groups, is virtually absent as a topic. Indeed, apart from doing "our dirty work," immigrants are seldom portrayed as being actively engaged in everyday life in the Netherlands.

Conclusions

From this brief, informal analysis of the ethnic topics in textbooks, we first may conclude that, in terms of frequency and size, many relevant topics are treated minimally, if at all. Highest are the scores for problematic cultural differences and for the topic of discrimination. The experiences of immigrants, their national or historical background, their social life and culture, their political organization, the work they actually do, and many other important issues are virtually never dealt with in Dutch textbooks. Nearly all topics are related to immigrant "guest workers," hence the emphasis on cultural differences. Most topics that are discussed have a strong stereotypical content. The overall orientation is a white perspective, and the usual division between Us and Them. This is even the case when children at school are occasionally the actors of these topics.

Local Meanings

The overall topics provide only a very rough picture of the content of social studies textbooks, although even at this general level, bias and stereotypes become obvious, that is, what white textbook writers find relevant and important or not. It is however at the micro level of words, sentences, and individual paragraphs that the perspective or ethnic opinions of the textbook writers appear most clearly. Let us discuss some concrete examples to elaborate this point. We'll do so by categorizing these examples in several major semantic categories, which define passages across different topics. For instance the category of *problems* may appear as an element of immigration, education, employment, or everyday life.

Problems

If there is any prominent implication in discourse about ethnic minority groups, it is that they are associated with problems. This is true for textbooks as much as for media and political discourse on ethnic issues. There are two main versions of this implication: a liberal one, which says that minorities *have* problems; and a conservative one, which tends to blame and says that minorities *cause* problems. The liberal perspective usually has paternalistic overtones and emphasizes the role of majority aid and assistance, while ignoring the active role of minority groups themselves.

Since the major topic of textbooks is cultural difference, we may expect that problems are primarily associated with difficulties of adaptation (for further information about the textbooks, identified here only with the name of the first author, see the Appendix and van Dijk, 1987c). Such references may be quite innocent and correct:

1. There are many problems. For in the beginning it is not easy for these foreigners to live here. (Andeweg, p. 66)

2. The Turkish boy not only has difficulties with the language. In our country, there are also a large number of rules and habits he doesn't know. (Caris, p. 54)

Note, though, that problems are generally attributed to *their* cultural background, not to Dutch society, education, or the attitudes of white Dutch people. Therefore, adaptation in this kind of discourse is usually one-way: They have to adapt to Us. The problems They experience, such as unemployment or discrimination at school, tend to be ignored or glossed over in very general terms, as in Examples 1 and 2.

While the examples just mentioned may still be interpreted as expressions of empathy, many other passages have a more negative tone, and seem to suggest that immigration per se, if not the multiethnic society, leads to problems:

3. All these cultures within our borders. It is clear that this may produce all kinds of problems. (van der Glind, p. 77)

4. Our country is densely populated, there is much unemployment and a lack of housing. Therefore, unlimited admission of foreigners creates problems. (Kalkwiek II, p. 91)

In this last example the textbook author formulates not so much causes of problems, but rather the normative reasons for not admitting too many immigrants, thereby actively participating in a controversial debate about immigration restrictions. The reasons he mentions also reflect the well-known discourse of racist organizations, although moderate versions of these views also appear in conservative political and media discourse.

Some passages are more specific about the kind of "problems" caused by "these people":

> 5. They look different, they often act "strangely" and they have, to put it nicely, often another culture of living. Playing loud music with open windows may be a normal thing to do in the country of origin, but is here felt to be very irritating by neighbors. These people often eat spicy food, their cooking smells are penetrating and unpleasant for Dutch noses. (Kalkwiek II, p. 98)

The textbook here reproduces the kind of stereotypes and prejudices that also appear regularly in everyday conversations about "foreigners" in the Netherlands (van Dijk, 1984, 1987a). Again, the cultural differences are emphasized, this time with a clearly negative evaluation of the foreign culture. That the Dutch may have habits that are "irritating" to the immigrants is not even considered as a possibility. At the end of this passage, the author briefly mentions the fact that people sometimes have prejudices, but he doesn't specify who has them, or that the description he gives of the foreign culture is also an example of such an attitude. Note also the general Us versus Them perspective in this passage, and the well-known distancing use of the demonstrative *these* in "these people."

Stereotypes and Prejudice

We can see that it is but a small step from signaling "problems" of a multicultural society to formulating stereotypes or racist opinions. Although modern textbooks are seldom very blatant, and although the authors sometimes mention the role of stereotypes and prejudices, some of them do not hesitate to mention such stereotypes and prejudices without adequately qualifying or criticizing them as such:

> 6. Most Chinese work in the restaurant business. Some of them are in the drugs business and give this group a bad name in our country. (Andeweg, p. 69)

> 7. There are also many illegal Chinese . . . The Chinese especially work in the restaurant business. . . . Some Chinese deal in narcotics. They are the only ones that create difficulties for Dutch society. (Kalkwiek II, p. 89)

These examples show first that the boundaries between formulating stereotypes and plagiarizing are often difficult to distinguish: The few lines said about Chinese are virtually identical in these two textbooks, a form of "intertextuality" that is not uncommon in textbooks. We also see that the stereotype of Chinese working in Chinese restaurants is accompanied by a more vicious form of criminalization. True, it is probably correct that "some Chinese" are in the drug business, but it is equally true of almost any other group—including the white Dutch, about whom it is not said. The major problem is that, despite the half-hearted disclaimer, which also appears in much other negative discourse about minorities, that "these are the only ones who create difficulties," this is the kind of information children may remember best, especially since little other information is given about the Chinese.

Textbook authors also use other strategies to introduce stereotypes and prejudices in their texts, for example, quoting more or less authoritative sources, such as fragments of newspaper articles or research reports, a strategy that is also used by the press. Here is a fragment from a report by a social geographer, who is presented as a second-generation Italian:

> 8. [Foreigners should adapt] "What should we do with beating up children, arranged marriages, the treatment of women and girls, or vendettas?" (Kalkwiek II, p. 98)

Thus, a mixture of stereotypes and prejudices is "quoted" and not even discussed or challenged. Characteristic of such passages is that they attribute negative properties to immigrant people without making clear that such properties may also occur among white Dutch people. In other words, cultural differences are emphasized and magnified, one-sided adaptation is required, and similarities with the Dutch are played down.

Similarly, we frequently find stereotypical passages about Muslim women, who it is said are not allowed to leave the house, and have to obey their husbands, or about foreign youths who have problems at home and go out stealing. In another example, Surinamese are also associated with the drug business, and a newspaper article simply states, without further comment, that Surinamese refuse to take cleaning jobs because they have a specialized technical education, and that such an "attitude does not facilitate the integration of such an invasion of colonial citizens." Incidentally, such passages are not merely express-ing prejudices, they are also add normative conclusions, such as stating that (or questioning whether) such people should not stay where they are, or even go back. Here we are close to the racist propaganda of extremist right-wing groups.

The prejudices about the position of foreign women, mostly from Turkey and Morocco, are closely related to those about Islam, and often implicitly evaluated in terms of a "backward" culture. It is interesting to note that until quite recently, the position of Dutch women, as compared to that of women in most other European countries, was not exactly ideal, although for different reasons. Textbooks will also fail to make the point that many immigrant women come from poor rural backgrounds and therefore can hardly be compared to the middle-class urban women in the Netherlands. The same is true for the treatment of immigrant girls, who are also portrayed as victims of their culture or of the oppression of their traditional fathers.

It is not likely that the passages that critically deal with the position of immigrant women, invariably written by male authors, express feminist positions. After all, the rest of the textbooks pay no further attention to the subordinate role of women in general, including Dutch women. Rather, such passages should be interpreted as an expression of underlying attitudes of cultural superiority, in which arranged marriages and similar practices are seen as examples of a backward society. Wherever differences with the Dutch can be found, they will be exaggerated or negatively interpreted in textbook discourse, as in the media.

The formulation of prejudices is not limited to the theoretical part of the lessons. They are also focused upon or presupposed in questions and assignments. Thus, it is quite normal in Dutch textbooks that two groups of students are assigned to debate about racist prejudices, as if these were legitimate opinions. So students are trained in defending prejudices, instead of combating them. The textbook author may even provide the arguments:

9. [Discussion about discrimination] *Group 1: Thinks that it is appropriate that we do not admit Surinamese.* Once you start with that, no white person may come in. The atmosphere is quite unpleasant if Surinamese come here. You simply no longer feel at ease. Any moment your money may be stolen. Group 2: It is not certain that Surinamese steal. (Holzhauer II, p. 129)

Similarly, another passage is intended to teach students how to discuss whether Muslim workers should be allowed to comply with their religious practices of Ramadan ("They are here to work, not to fast").

It is shocking to read such blatantly racist passages in textbooks under the pretext of discussions about prejudices. Surely prejudice and racism should be dealt with. This may also mean that they need to be formulated, although this is not always necessary. However, the problem is the way such racist statements are presented. If they are presented as statements with which some people agree and others disagree, then such racist positions are legitimated. An alternative pedagogic style would be to present such statements as being racist, and why, and then ask the students to provide further arguments for an anti-racist position. In a racist society in which prejudices in everyday conversations and public discourse are common, it is much more relevant to train students in formulating points of view that combat these forms of racism.

Criminalization and Illegality

Since prejudices are by definition negative, they are used mostly in contexts in which in-group rules, norms, or laws are seen as violated. The next step, namely, outright criminalization of minorities and immigrants, is only very small in this case. We already saw that stereotypes about Chinese and Surinamese are associated with accusations of drugs dealing, whereas Turks and Moroccans (and Italians before them) may be seen as indulging in other kinds of violence, such as wife or child beating, carrying knives, or perpetuating bloody vendettas.

Criminalization of minorities is one of the most serious, persistent, and widespread forms of racism. Textbooks do it like this:

10. It is well-known that a number of Surinamese youths are addicted to heroin. It is also a fact that addicts sometimes commit crimes to get the large amounts of money they need, like pick pocketing in streetcars, stealing from cars and burglaries. Not all Surinamese however do that. (Kalkwiek II, p. 95)

We see again that stereotypes and prejudices are presented as "facts." Despite the usual disclaimer, such stereotypes are given at least some legitimacy. What counts is that in the few passages about Surinamese, attention is typically focused on such negative stereotypes. Much more relevant information—about the majority of Surinamese—is ignored. Again, we witness a striking similarity with the right-wing press, which also tends to focus on negative properties of minorities. In the same vein, we find question sections that ask the students: "Are guest workers not a danger for our society? What about the criminality of these people?" Similarly, Moluccans are often treated in light of a train hijacking by a group of Moluccan youths in 1977. Again, of the few lines dealing with this ethnic group, many are devoted to violence.

Much like the media, textbooks also emphasize the "illegal" presence of some immigrants in the Netherlands, thereby associating them more generally with illegality:

11. There are thousands of aliens in the Netherlands who do not have the required documents. They are called "illegals." . . . The government has already allowed illegal guest workers to register for legal residence in the Netherlands. It cannot continue to do so, because then our country would be inundated by illegal guest workers. (Kalkwiek II, p. 92)

Stereotypical description and evaluation go hand in hand in such an example, where the textbook author explicitly legitimates and even defends the strict immigration policies of the government. After the use of "invasion" in a previous example, notice also the metaphorical use of "inundated," a flood metaphor that is typically used for immigrants and refugees, and that is of course especially compelling in a country behind dikes, whose national myths are closely linked to a struggle against the sea. In this same example, the negative association of "illegal" immigrants with threatening floods contrasts with the positive action of the Dutch government, which "allows" the foreigners to register. As we often see in other examples of elite discourse, this is a typical example of the combined strategies of positive self-presentation and negative other-presentation.

Competition

One major legitimating topic in the development and uses of prejudice is that of perceived competition: "They take away our jobs, housing . . . " Such prejudices often occur not only in everyday racist talk, but also in different forms in textbooks. Thus, competition may be used as the cause of the "problems" the textbook authors regularly signal in their lessons about minorities or immigrants. One major competition topic, relevant especially in a small and densely populated country like the Netherlands, is overpopulation. Emphasis is therefore placed on the fact that the number of foreigners is "rapidly increasing," a phrase repeated in several textbooks:

12. [Guest workers] Their numbers are rapidly increasing due to family reunion (the family comes to live here) and due to the high birth rate. (Andeweg, p. 70)

Other textbooks indulge in the well-known numbers game, also familiar in the press, when writing about new "waves" of immigrants, and not only quote the size of the various groups, but also add that they are rapidly growing. While there are about 700,000 immigrants in the Netherlands (depending on the counting criteria, this number may be higher or lower), textbooks usually "forget" to mention that about the same number of Dutch have emigrated to other countries—information that would put the overpopulation argument in a different perspective.

Apart from immigration, the stereotype of minority high birthrate is often mentioned, usually ignoring the fact that after several years, this birthrate tends to drop dramatically and become close to the average. Having a lot of children, indeed, is one of the major stereotypes about immigrants from, and people living in, Third World countries. Instead of explaining birthrate in terms of poverty and class, the textbooks seem to suggest that it is again a form of backwardness. More generally, then, we find in textbooks, as well as in other forms of elite discourse about minorities, a move in the overall strategy of negative other-presentation that focuses on the "backwardness" of minorities. If the own group shows similar behavior in similar circumstances, it is usually ignored.

Textbook authors sometimes seem to directly voice the concerns of white Dutch people:

13. [Foreign workers; housing problems in the old inner-city neighborhoods] In the old neighborhoods of the city of Rotterdam, the percentage of guest workers rose to about 40, whereas there are no foreigners in the new suburbs. The old neighborhoods demand that they be relieved, and that the foreigners be better distributed over the whole city. A suitable distribution would lead to 16% for most neighborhoods. (Kalkwiek II, p. 97)

14. [We can't send them back.] On the other hand it is true that because of their presence a group of Dutch is being let down. They are the deprived, the people who have the lowest incomes, who are uneducated and often unemployed. They have the feeling that their houses and their work are being occupied by guest workers. They largely and correctly blame the government that it has opened the borders for the aliens. (Kalkwiek II, p. 102)

Note that when he writes that the "old neighborhoods demand," the author is only referring to white citizens. The wishes of minority groups in the neighborhoods are ignored. Again, assignments to the students train them in defending the pros and cons of such distribution policies, instead of denouncing their discriminatory nature. Also, in Example 13 the apparent empathy with the (white) deprived people in the inner cities seems to be a good reason to legitimate their prejudices about immigrants.

This is also a familiar multifunctional move in discourse about minorities: By taking the side of poor white people, the writer is associated with a positive attitude of solidarity with the own group, and thereby indirectly attributes prejudiced attitudes to others (poor whites) instead of to white Dutch (including elites) in general, while at the same time suggesting that the negative reaction of such white people may be justified, which in turn implies a negative attitude about minorities.

We also encountered this populist move in many forms of media and parliamentary discourse, for example, when it is argued that further immigration should be stopped because we cannot expect the poor white people in the inner cities to bear the brunt of immigration. This move should particularly be interpreted as protecting the elites: We take the negative decisions (e.g., restrict further immigration), but do so in order to protect poor whites (our own people), or even more generally, in order to maintain peace in the inner cities. Discriminatory actions of the elite may thus be legitimated not only as alleging popular support, but also as contributing to social stability, while at the same time transferring the responsibility of prejudice and discrimination to the poor whites they use precisely to legitimate their own actions.

Racism and Discrimination

Finally, besides cultural differences, crime, and competition, we also find passages about racism and discrimination in textbooks. Analysis of these passages is important because they form an interesting test case for the anti-racist position of the textbook. We have seen earlier that the denial of racism is one of the major characteristics of elite discourse. What do social studies textbooks write about this major social problem?

Here is one of the more innocent examples:

15. Discrimination is now even prohibited by law. It still happens every day. Some discotheques for example do not admit Surinamese, although they are dressed as well as the other guests. (Holzhauer II, p. 129)

The example of Surinamese blacks being discriminated in discotheques is not only well known but also stereotypical. The example associates blacks primarily with dancing, whereas discrimination in other, more important domains, such as employment, is usually ignored.

Second, this example also seems to miss the point when it suggests that discrimination of less well-dressed Surinamese would be quite all right. Incidentally, it might be added that in accordance with Caribbean cultural standards, Surinamese youths are often better dressed than white Dutch youths.

Most passages about discrimination show that the authors have little insight into the nature and mechanisms of ethnic or racial discrimination. Even Affirmative Action may be presented as a form of discrimination:

> 16. It is also possible that people do discriminate positively, that is, treat somebody better than someone else. At school we call this favoritism. (Kalkwiek II, p. 94)

In other words, Affirmative Action is presented in a negative light, and even compared to resented practices in the family and the classroom that students are all too familiar with. Such a view from a textbook author is not surprising in the Netherlands, where Affirmative Action is generally rejected as an unacceptable form of moral or legal pressure, as it is by the elite (see Chapter 4).

One major move in the dominant Dutch strategy of denying racism is to focus on discrimination and racism in other countries, for example, the United States and South Africa (Note: As in other examples, the clumsy and sometimes incoherent style is not primarily due to our translation, but that of the author who probably tries to write in a pedagogic way):

> 17. Discrimination exists nearly everywhere in the world and nearly everybody indulges in it from time to time. . . . Really a great evil in the world is racial discrimination. This occurs mostly in those countries where a specific race forms a minority, with the Negroes in the United States. (Kalkwiek I, p. 9)

This fragment is rather characteristic of several approaches to the notion of discrimination in the Netherlands. First, discrimination is presented as a universal characteristic of humanity, which seems to make it as harmless as a traffic misdemeanor, while at the same time defusing the special role of white Europeans in racism. Second, as suggested, racial discrimination is usually identified usually with a group or country that is distant from Us, such as the United States. Third, the author does not seem to realize, even in a textbook of the

1980s, that the Netherlands also has a black minority group. Fourth, African-Americans are still called Negroes as are Surinamese blacks in the Netherlands. In other words, the author does not truly understand what discrimination is all about, nor does he pay attention to its most relevant aspect for the students, which is discrimination here and now in the Netherlands.

Although discrimination is of course rejected on moral grounds, the textbook authors often find subtle ways to blame the victim:

18. It has been shown that discrimination is worse in the cities than in the countryside. On the other hand, in these cities there are also most aliens, so that there is also a higher probability of problems. (Kalkwiek II, p. 95)

That discrimination is worse in the cities is probably a research conclusion invented by the textbook author. More serious is his suggestion that discrimination is caused by the presence of foreigners, and hence can be partly blamed on them, especially when they are also associated with problems. Similarly, another passage suggests that discrimination against Jews is also caused by the alleged fact that they live separately, and because they have their own laws, religion, language, schools, and life-style.

A familiar way of referring to discrimination is to describe it in terms of subjective feelings, instead of as a social fact:

19. [Moluccans] They isolate themselves, they feel seriously discriminated against, and do not see opportunities. (Kalkwiek III, p. 55)

20. [People from the Dutch East Indies] They adapted well in the Netherlands and found employment and housing. Nevertheless they felt discriminated. They have the impression that the intolerance of the Dutch against people with a colored skin is increasing. (Kalkwiek III, p. 54)

Adaptation, obviously, is seen as a positive value for immigrants. Despite the fact that the "Indos," as they are commonly called, found jobs and houses, they still "feel" discriminated, and "have the impression" that things are getting worse. So, despite a large number of research reports and consistent accounts of minority groups about experiences of racism, discrimination is often played down or doubted because it is seen as a subjective feeling of minority groups. In another passage, the same author, who wrote an influential series of social studies textbooks, quotes a man from the Dutch Antilles (said to have "adapted himself well" in Dutch society), who claims that he has never been discriminated against. Indeed, his adaptation to Dutch dominant culture appears to have been so successful that even its prevalent denial of discrimination has been adopted. The strategic function of such passages, in which a minority group member is quoted as saying the same thing, is to enhance the credibility of the textbook. Again, this move is also well known in everyday conversation ("My Surinamese colleague in the office says so himself") as well as in elite political and media discourse (preferential quoting and coverage of minority group members who support a majority point of view).

Another myth we find in textbooks is the claim, already briefly discussed above, that discrimination is characteristic of less-intelligent or lower-class people. In the following astonishing passage, this form of transfer is coupled with the attribution to other countries:

21. [Why do people discriminate?] Indolence or lacking intelligence . . . the need especially among the lower social estates (*sic*) to compensate an inferiority complex. . . . Hence the fact that in South Africa the most ardent supporters of small apartheid are among the lower educated Whites. (Vannisselroy et al., p. 149)

It is difficult to take such passages seriously, and tempting to simply reject them as utter nonsense. However, they express powerful myths and appear in textbooks with which many children are confronted. Racism is kept at a double distance here, both far away in South Africa, and far away within the own society, that is, among the working class, which is also simply called indolent and less intelligent. Hence a discriminatory statement is used in a passage that explains what discrimination is. We have seen earlier that such views also appear in the press, and generally among the elites, for whom prejudice, discrimination, and racism are always elsewhere. In such a strategy of keeping discrimination at a distance, that the racist apartheid system was founded by leading politicians and supported by large sections of the South African elites, are facts that are simply ignored.

These few passages show that the problem of discrimination is largely ill understood, denied, mitigated, transferred to others, or even blamed to the victim. Virtually no textbook portrays in detail what it means to be discriminated against in the Netherlands. The many forms of everyday racism in hiring, on the job, in the media, at school, in shops, and so on, are seldom detailed. Discrimination at school is at most briefly hinted at in assignments, but never actually analyzed or concretely illustrated by examples. There is only one, rather unconventional, textbook that uses examples from other social studies textbooks to illustrate the notions of ethnic stereotype and prejudice.

Note also that while the notion of discrimination may be discussed in textbooks, racism is not, unless in a few cases that deal with racism abroad. Again, we find a parallel here with the media, which also prefers to speak of discrimination and seldom of racism, unless in other countries or as an accusation by minority groups or other anti-racists.

The Representation of the Third World

In other studies it has frequently been found that the portrayal of ethnic minorities in Western countries and that of Third World countries and peoples are often very similar (Downing, 1980; Hartmann & Husband, 1974). Indeed, in both cases They are treated as the Others, as very different from Us, and as essentially having similar, usually negative or otherwise problematical, characteristics.

To examine such similarities in more detail, we also studied all passages in a prominent social studies textbook that deals with the Third World (Holzhauer, *Hoe vinden we onze weg in de samenleving* [How to find our way in society]). Before we present our general conclusions, a few examples may give the general flavor of how the Third World is described in a typical Dutch social studies textbook. This is the first impression the students get:

> 22. [We live in one of the richest countries of the world.] In many countries there is no prosperity at all. There, hunger and poverty are still very common. Examples: the *developing countries* in Asia, Africa, and South America. (p. 10)

This stereotype has of course an element of truth, but it is typical that it is repeated at least seven times throughout the book, without much further detail and especially without proper explanation. Similarly, it is also repeatedly emphasized that in such countries, most people live off the land, they have fewer occupations than we have, they have less technology and often live on handicraft, they do not have a future, and because there are few schools, they are illiterate, and so on. Thus, poverty, hunger, disease, lack of education and work, and passivity form the standard image of the Third World that is presented to students.

Differences between Third World countries are hardly made. Industrialization and urbanization, contributions to the world market, Western life-styles, the wealth of elites, and in general all aspects of life and problems in the Third World that are similar to ours, are rarely dealt with when they are inconsistent with the stereotype.

In this way the Third World is made homogeneous, which is generally the case for minority groups, too. Its main characteristics are formulated in terms of negatively biased comparisons. Thus, first of all, Third World countries and peoples are "backward," namely, along a temporal continuum where We are ahead (Fabian, 1983).

> 23. [Most Western societies develop rapidly.] This also happens in countries of the Third World. There time sometimes goes too fast. People can hardly keep up the pace with the leap from Middle Ages to modern times. (p. 24)

Similarly, in many domains, differences are emphasized. The other studies of children's books and textbooks reviewed above showed that, according to textbooks, We have doctors, They have witch doctors:

> 24. Example: A pygmy hunter in the bush gets ill. He thinks this is because of evil spirits. He goes to the witch doctor, who orders him to dance for one hour. In our society, somebody who is sick sends for the doctor, who prescribes some pills. Ten days later, he is feeling better.

This and other similar examples deserve detailed discourse analysis for their multiple implications. It is, however, clear that the description of difference is never neutral. On the contrary, for the Western child, the practices of the other culture are clearly presented as backward, primitive, or ridiculous, while at the same time implying our Western superiority. (Indeed, the passage does *not* specify either whether or how the pygmy hunter got better.)

In textbooks Third World countries and peoples, just like minorities in Europe, have all kinds of problems. Facing such problems, they feel helpless, and "helplessness makes people apathetic and afraid. And it is not easy to handle people with fear," says a textbook author. Once helplessness, passivity, and apathy have thus been put forth as major characteristics of Third World peoples, We have the noble task to help Them—unless such help is hopeless, so the logic of this self-serving while self-enhancing ideology goes.

As we saw above for minority groups, in order to train the students in the implications of such an ideology, they may get assignments in which not only a liberal position should be defended by one group of students ("we should help them because we have exploited them"), but also the cynical racist one, and the pragmatic one, by another group:

25. (Group 1). All the money we send there is like a drop in the ocean. . . . It is better to send nothing. Then the population there will diminish. And then we can help those who survive. (Group 3). If we don't give them anything, then they come and get it. Then we'll have war. So, we need to keep them friendly. We can't offer much help, though. But we have to give an impression of goodwill. If the capitalists don't do anything, all those new countries would become communist. That would be a disaster.

Such examples might be dismissed as too ridiculous to merit further analysis if they were not the kinds of "argument" thousands of Dutch students in the 1980s may have read in their textbooks and been invited to elaborate on as an assignment. They are not asked to analyze such discourse in its own right, let alone taught how to systematically criticize these forms of blatant racism and ethnocentrism. Another assignment asks the students whether slavery is justified, and even asks them how it would be to be a slave or a slave driver! So much for modern pedagogy.

Other textbook properties of the Third World are, e.g.:

- Many of these countries have dictators, especially in Latin America, of course. Past or present dictators, say Stalin or Hitler, in Western or northern countries are not mentioned for comparison or to stress similarities. Nor is it mentioned whether Third World dictators are supported by Western governments.
- There are no schools, and hence people haven't learned much. Indeed, they are not very bright at all: Development aid is used to teach them "how to cultivate their lands, how to better treat their animals, etc." (p. 72)
- Some people dislike hard work. Americans for instance have to work harder than Europeans. Those who work hard can advance in the world. "Other peoples say: I'd rather sit in the sun than do all this hard labor. Life is too beautiful to lose so much time with work." (p. 95)

In sum, the Third World peoples, like minority groups in Western countries, are portrayed as follows in this textbook, as well as in many others:

1. Homogeneous: They are all the same.
2. They are very different from us.
3. They are poor, helpless, hence in need of our aid.
4. They are illiterate and dumb, hence in need of our instruction and education.
5. They are primitive, backward, or underdeveloped, and hence in need of our technology.
6. They are passive or happy-go-lucky: They should adopt our diligence.
7. They are politically backward: They need "our" democracy, instead of their dictators.

We can also see that these prejudices and stereotypes are not benevolent. Apart from the cynicism that speaks from certain passages, and the overall Eurocentric perspective, one major implication is clearly that of Western, white superiority in all societal domains. At best, such an attitude may lead to the benevolent paternalism of contemporary aid to the Third World. At worst, it stimulates blatantly racist attitudes of white superiority feelings toward peoples and countries in the Third World. The same is true for the discourse about non-European peoples who migrated to the rich countries of the Northwest, of which similar stereotypes form a similar social representation.

Pedagogic Aspects

Textbooks in secondary education should of course be analyzed not only in terms of their contents, but also as educational discourse. Many of the limitations of such textbooks are due to the subordinate position of social studies in the overall curriculum, to the social studies curriculum itself, and to the requirements of pedagogy such as age and school-type dependent simplicity. Also, such learning materials usually have special sections with questions, assignments, and a number of other pedagogic discourse genres. Let us briefly consider these and other pedagogic implications of the textbooks we analyzed.

Although lesson content and pedagogical implications can be analytically separated, it is obvious that the style of the contents also has important pedagogic dimensions. It is not easy to assess these in an objective way. To get at least a subjective impression, we also graded each passage on four criteria, namely, relative completeness, correctness, stereotypicality, and pedagogic presentation. As may have become clear from the previous section, most books scored very low on the first three criteria. Virtually no book reached the minimum satisfactory level in the Dutch grade system (6 out of 10). In particular the grades for stereotypicality were rather low (4.9 on average).

The overall grade for pedagogic presentation and style of all passages and textbooks was hardly better (4.8). The following general conclusions explain why:

1. The questions and assignments are replete with stereotypes and prejudices, as we have seen in some examples given above.

2. The students are often asked to discuss a racist opinion in such a way that one group is asked to defend that position, and another to criticize it. We have argued above that such assignments legitimate racist opinions as a defensible position, instead of showing that they need to be analyzed and criticized.

3. The questions and assignments hardly take into account that there may also be minority children among the students. If mentioned at all, they are also marginalized stylistically, for instance by talking about them in distancing pronouns and demonstratives: "they," "these children," instead of treating them as one of Us.

4. Often the questions and assignments appear to be more or less independent of the lesson, so that the students must rely on commonsense knowledge. Especially in the field of ethnic relations, such presupposed knowledge may often be of a stereotypical nature.

5. Most textbooks are pedagogically traditional in that they only ask a few rather boring questions of comprehension. Few have a more detailed and carefully planned section of interesting assignments.

6. Language style of the passages was usually comprehensible, although often simplistic for students of this age (between 14 and 18).

7. The explanation of many concepts is confusing, because the textbook author obviously doesn't understand the subject matter. One major example is the explanation of concepts such as prejudice, discrimination, and racism.

8. In both questions and assignments, discrimination is often located far away, denied, or mitigated. Seldom are these notions used to ask questions or give assignments that are relevant for the everyday experiences of the students, let alone those of minority students.

9. Most illustrations are only fillers. They seldom have an explicit function in the text. They are seldom used as part of the questions or assignments. Minorities are seldom portrayed, and if so, it is often in stereotypical situations.

10. Factual information, such as tables and figures, are often very much dated, so that for both new books and new editions, most textbooks are already outdated when they are used at school.

11. Quotations tend to be given in a haphazard way. They are often used to support the stereotypes of the author. Thus, quotations of minority group members may even be used to mitigate discrimination. Critical statements of minority groups about Dutch society and culture are rare.
12. Lexical descriptions of minority groups are dated. As in the Dutch press, black people are still frequently called "Negroes."
13. The topics in the questions and assignments follow the stereotypical perspective of the textbooks, and especially focus on problems and cultural differences.

We see that both the theory parts as well as the question and assignment sections are found lacking from a pedagogic point of view. The students do not get more or less relevant, relatively complete, and balanced information. On the contrary, the lessons are usually very stereotypical, so anti-racist attitudes are not systematically developed, and minority children are usually ignored.

Conclusions

Our analysis of Dutch textbooks not only confirms what has been found by other authors for textbooks in other countries, but further shows that Dutch textbook authors also appear to have their own myths and mystifications when dealing with ethnic affairs. First, about half of the textbooks simply ignore the whole issue: Minorities, immigrants, and discrimination are apparently not subjects that belong in a social studies textbook.

Second, if such a subject is dealt with, it will usually be very briefly and highly stereotypically. Thus, major attention is paid to guest workers, whereas other groups, such as Surinamese, are virtually ignored. Second, these guest workers are primarily portrayed as people with an alien culture. Linguistic, religious, and other social or cultural differences tend to be exaggerated. Problems of the multicultural society are similarly emphasized, and usually attributed to the newcomers. Xenophobic resentment among white Dutch people is virtually excused in such passages. Even when only a few lines are written about a minority group, such as the Chinese or Surinamese, textbooks may show stereotypes or even blatant prejudices, for instance, about the criminal nature of the "foreigners." Sometimes such passages are accompanied by moderate disclaimers, although these are hardly intended as elements in an anti-racist strategy.

Many topics that are relevant in a treatment of immigration or ethnic affairs either seldom or never show up in textbook lessons. Although some textbooks briefly mention some of the reasons for labor migration, usually emphasizing the interests of the immigrants and ignoring those of Dutch business, we get to know very little about the everyday lives of ethnic minority groups. Thus, immigrants are stereotypically portrayed as "doing the dirty jobs," and never as having a higher education or elite jobs. Issues that are important for minority group members, including minority students in the classroom, such as discrimination, immigration and settlement rights, culture and the arts, good education and health care, or jobs, are usually neglected.

Finally, the textbooks appear to have little understanding of discrimination, which appeared to be variously ignored, denied, mitigated, or attributed to others. Racism is wholly absent as a topic in virtually all textbooks.

These properties of Dutch social studies textbooks show that these learning materials can hardly be used in the curricula in a multiethnic society. They not only fail to provide correct information about ethnic minorities or ethnic relations, but they also provide any information incompletely, erroneously, stereotypically, if not in a downright racist way. Minority students in the classroom are seldom recognized, let alone explicitly addressed as such. Thus, neither the black student nor the white student becomes adequately prepared for an increasingly multicultural society. On the contrary, the sometimes seriously biased lessons of the textbooks probably confirm and legitimate these negative prejudices about minority groups. We found this to be the case both for the theory as well as for the "Questions and Assignment" sections of the textbooks.

Although Dutch social studies textbooks from the mid-1980s are still particularly inadequate in teaching both minority and majority students about multiethnic society and the role of racism, there are signals of change. The later 1980s have witnessed some new textbooks that, although modestly, are beginning to realize that the Netherlands is no longer exclusively white, and that the immigrants are not just culturally "strange" or "problematic" guest workers. More attention is paid to racism, and the presence of minority students in the classroom is beginning to be recognized.

In this respect, Dutch textbooks are slowly following a development that has already been taking place in countries where the civil rights movement has been more influential, especially in the United States.

Political and economic pressures, and a stronger ethnic/black grass-roots movement in the United States have led to increasing attention to minority groups and their culture in history, geography, and civics textbooks. In most European countries, and especially in the United Kingdom, such goals have for some time been formulated in the official discourse of policymakers or curriculum developers, but textbooks authors have been much slower to respond to such proposals.

This means that if the teachers are committed to anti-racist or at least liberally pluralist ideals, they may be expected to either ignore the textbooks altogether or use them critically. Especially for such a topic as ethnic affairs, many teachers tend to use informal or self-constructed materials. Indeed, besides the classical textbooks, there is an increasing number of specialized publications on the market that focus on minorities or immigrants. We also examined some of these books and found that, although they are of course more detailed and more complete, they are not always less stereotypical. The major shortcoming continues to be that even such books are not consistently anti-racist.

EDUCATIONAL DISCOURSE AND THE REPRODUCTION OF RACISM

On the basis of the research reviewed and reported above, we may finally discuss in more general terms the role of educational discourse in the reproduction of racism.

If research in several countries has made clear one fact, it is that educational discourse in general, and textbooks and other learning materials in particular, are part and parcel of the dominant order of discourse in ethnically and racially stratified societies. Despite modest developments toward more sensitive accounts of ethnic affairs and the structures and issues of multiethnic societies, especially in U.S. textbooks, learning materials still overwhelmingly show the perspective and interests of white people. Within a broader framework of nationalism, if not ethnocentrism, the dominant white group, or Western countries and civilization, are rather consistently portrayed in neutral or positive terms, whereas minority groups or immigrants tend to be associated at least with problems and conflicts, if not with deviance and threats.

In that perspective, Third World countries and peoples in general, and those who migrate to Europeanized countries, are dealt with marginally, if at all, and in stereotypical and sometimes even blatantly racist terms.

Their histories, cultures, and particularly their socioeconomic contributions to their present countries, are denied or marginalized, if discussed at all. Both in their subject matter and in their pedagogic assignments, learning materials seldom take into account that many of students in Western countries are no longer white. Moreover, the problems minorities have to deal with in Our societies, notably discrimination, prejudice, and racism, tend to be denied or even blamed on the victims.

One of the conclusions of these consistent findings is that learning materials not only reproduce the ethnic status quo, but also actively contribute to its legitimation. From a pedagogical point of view, they do not adequately prepare either black or white students for their role in a multiethnic society.

This conclusion holds for all levels of the educational system, and applies to primary schools as well as secondary and academic education. Again, with the partial exception of the United States, university curricula also show a serious lack of ethnic consciousness. Black Studies and Ethnic Studies programs have been instituted in the United States, but continue to play a marginal role, whereas in Europe such programs are as yet virtually unknown. Especially at the higher levels of the education system, and particularly in Europe, minority teachers, professors, and managers are rare, so that their perspective and expertise are seldom heard by students. Even when there are Black Studies or Ethnic Studies programs, the multiethnic and anti-racist perspective is usually absent or marginal in the curricula and learning materials of other subjects or disciplines.

In sum, neither the contents and style of educational discourse, nor the organization of education exactly favors a point of view that might challenge the extant power relations in Europeanized societies. That is, the system of education is structurally coherent with the other institutional arrangements that lead to the exclusion of minority groups from the resources to which whites have privileged access. Both in hiring, as well as in general learning contents and curriculum perspectives, educational discourse and organization thus contribute to the reproduction of an ideology that supports the ethnic status quo. It is not surprising, therefore, that such a system contributes to the special difficulties that minority children, especially those of African descent, often experience in education. Lacking identification and recognition, and confronted with many subtle and blatant forms of everyday racism in textbooks, classrooms, or playgrounds, minority students face a challenge that has obvious repercussions on their performance.

The results of this situation of educational subordination, traditionally defined in terms of "high dropout" and "low achievement," are not surprising, and may be gauged against the well-known statistics of unemployment and poverty. At the same time, minority students are thus prepared for their special role at the bottom of the social hierarchy, that is, by specifically preparing them for subordinate positions in the job market, which is more generally the case for lower-class students, too (Willis, 1977).

Thus, the reproduction of racism through educational organization, curricula, texts, and lessons simultaneously contributes to the reproduction of class dominance. Lacking the cultural capital of higher education, minority groups are not only prevented from access to power, that is, from positions for which higher education is an important entrance condition, but also more generally assigned to a socioeconomic and cultural position that presupposes white hegemony.

Such conclusions are especially serious for the field of education. Research shows that children are aware at an early age of ethnic or racial differences and identities. White children soon pick up the ethnic categories, evaluations, stereotypes, and prejudices underlying the feelings of white superiority and privilege that are prominently displayed in mass media discourse and peer talk, if not in socializing discourse at home.

The curriculum and teaching materials are a potentially powerful counter-discourse to such a prevailing sociocultural environment of white students. We have seen that, with some exceptions, educational discourse does not provide such a challenge. On the contrary, despite recent advances in textbooks and curricula toward a philosophy of multiculturalism, such discourse is geared toward the very inculcation of the dominant ideologies of white societies. True, the curricula and textbooks teach lofty norms and values. Children learn that discrimination and racism are wrong. This also explains why, between the ages of 7 and 10, the earlier type of straightforward bias tends to diminish (Aboud, 1988).

However, there are reasons to assume that the more indirect and subtle inferiorization and marginalization of minorities and Third World peoples in present-day educational discourse establishes a more sophisticated system of beliefs and discourse regarding the multiethnic society. In other words, at best white children learn to be "modern," "tolerant," or even "progressive" whites, for whom blatant racism may look dumb, but who nevertheless are not taught to challenge the system of white dominance.

Whereas the socioeconomic results of such an educational system have been demonstrably dire, its socio-cognitive and ideological implications are possibly even more disastrous. What is learned at school, especially about issues that are less systematically dealt with in other discourses, forms a solid ideological system of attitudes that underlies the acquisition of new information, the development of new opinions and attitudes, and ultimately the interactions that presuppose such social cognitions. It is very difficult to fundamentally restructure this ideological basis, especially since it undergirds and legitimates group dominance and personal as well as social interests. Until an advanced age, students are scarcely confronted with alternative discourses, for instance in the mass media, peer conversations, literature, or critical books. Research shows that the children's books and media discourses they encounter overwhelmingly spell out or imply the same, increasingly subtle, ideology of white dominance. Whereas minority children may learn resistance and alternative interpretations of such discourses at home, provided there is a tradition of group resistance in their community, white children are largely prevented from acquiring the fundamental knowledge and attitudes that prepare them for a more critical role in society.

7

Media Discourse

THE POWERFUL ROLE OF THE MEDIA

After examining several types of elite discourse in the previous chapters, we finally pay special attention to the functions of news discourse and media elites. The role of the mass media in the reproduction of racism in contemporary European and North American societies is as fundamental as its general role in the political, social, and ideological reproduction of modern societies. None of the other power elites, and especially the political elites, and their discourses could be as influential as they are without the mediating and sometimes reinforcing functions of the press, radio, and television. What most people know about politicians, scholars, and corporate top managers is based on their refracted picture constructed in the media. Indeed, most of what elites know about other elites is what they read about them in the newspapers. It is therefore fitting that we finally examine how the media and its elites reconstruct other elite discourses on ethnic affairs, and mediate such second-order text and talk to the public at large, as well as among the other elites. At the same time, however, we also need to assess the autonomous and unique role the press plays in the reproduction of ethnic and racial inequality. That is, the press can hardly be defined as the passive mouthpiece of other elites; it plays an active and powerful role among the other elite institutions of society.

More specifically, this chapter will also summarize and further elaborate on the results of our previous studies of the press portrayal of ethnic affairs, largely based on extensive data drawn from the Dutch and British press, as well as on other research results (for details see, e.g., Bonnafous, 1991; Downing, 1980; Ebel & Fiala, 1983; Gordon & Rosenberg, 1989; Hartmann & Husband, 1974; Indra, 1979; Martindale, 1986; Merten & Ruhrmann, 1986; Smitherman-Donaldson & van Dijk, 1988; Troyna, 1981; van Dijk, 1983, 1991; Wilson & Gutiérrez, 1985; for a recent review, see Cottle, 1992).

Our basic assumption about the powerful role of the media in the reproduction of racism in Western societies is far from tenuous. It presupposes, among other things, that the media play a central role in shaping the social cognitions of the public at large, if not of other influential elites. The history of mass communication theories has known several, sometimes contradictory, approaches to this aspect of media influence, which, however, cannot be discussed in detail in this chapter (see, e.g., Berger, 1991; Bryant & Zillman, 1986; Iyengar & Kinder, 1987; Klapper, 1960).

It is however important to note from the outset that our conception of media influence goes beyond that of immediate effects and agenda-setting functions of specific media messages on specific readers. Our discourse-processing theory of social communication and cognition defines media recipients as active, and up to a point independent, information users, whose beliefs are strategically shaped and changed because of many cognitive, social, and communicative processes, and on the basis of many different discursive and other sources of influence (Downing, Mohammadi, & Sreberny-Mohammadi, 1990; Graber, 1984b; Harris, 1989; van Dijk, 1988a, 1988b).

However, at the same time, we assume that, notably in the field of ethnic affairs, the role of the media in these various processes is crucial in the sense that it is both ideological and structural (see also, e.g., Hall, Hobson, Lowe, & Willis, 1980). This means that, whatever the immediate effects of specific media messages may be on specific readers in specific circumstances, the *overall* influence of the media, particularly the news media, on the structures and contents of social cognitions of groups is considerable. In other words, for specific types of social and political events, including those in the field of ethnic relations, the news media are the main source of information and beliefs used to form the interpretation framework for such events.

Individual newspaper readers may form opinions that are at variance with those expressed or implied by the discernible media messages of their newspapers. This variance is a function of both personal circumstances and experiences as well as of economic, social, and cultural conditions and attitudes of the group(s) they identify with. However, unless the readers have other sources of information and belief formation, such beliefs and their variation tend to remain within the boundaries of an overall ideological framework of interpretation. It is one of the tasks of this chapter to show *how* the media, and in particular the press, exercise this kind of symbolic or ideological influence on the readers.

The power of the media is not defined only by their broad ideological influence on their audiences. We assumed above that, as institutions, broadcast organizations, television networks, and newspapers, they also participate in complex networks of elite organizations or other powerful social actors. Due to the specific and nearly exclusive role of the mass media in communication and the production of public discourse, other elites need the media to inform both the public at large and each other, to exercise their power, to seek legitimation, and to manufacture consensus and consent. Modern political and corporate power is unthinkable without having recourse to such mass-mediated processes of their own reproduction. This means that despite their dependence on other, for example, political, corporate, academic, and social elites, mass media institutions have at least some means to control these other elites, which is also an important element of the power dimension that goes beyond that of simple mediation (Altschull, 1984; Bagdikian, 1983; Golding, Murdock, & Schlesinger, 1986; Lichter et al., 1990; Schiller, 1971, 1973, 1989).

In sum, we assume that the media play a central role in the reproduction of racism, both because of their relation to other elite institutions and because of their structural influence in shaping and changing the social mind. We suggested that media power is especially prominent in ethnic affairs because of the fact that large segments of the white public have little or no alternative information sources on ethnic affairs. Except in large areas of the United States, and in the inner cities of some European countries, most white people have few everyday contacts, and hence few immediate experiences, with minority group members or immigrants. Even then such contacts are usually limited to superficial encounters in public places or contacts on the job. Moreover, even everyday conversations on ethnic affairs are largely dependent on media information (van Dijk, 1987a). Thus, the mass media have virtually no competition in their communicative role regarding ethnic affairs.

Instead of repeating the descriptive results of earlier work, this chapter focuses on this crucial role of the media in the reproduction of racism by examining the specific ways media elites and their elite sources define, legitimate, and manufacture the ethnic consensus.

NEWS PRODUCTION

Part of the explanation of the contents and structures of news reports about ethnic affairs should be sought in the social and cognitive processes involved in news production. In particular the relations with other elite institutions are implemented in this stage of the communication process (Fishman, 1980; Gans, 1979; Tuchman, 1978). The political economy of the media, the social class and education of journalists, recruitment practices, newsgathering beats and routines, contacts with sources, editorial meetings, the socialization and professionalization of journalists, and story assignments, are among the many social macro and micro dimensions of newsmaking that impinge on press accounts of ethnic affairs (Mazingo, 1988; Wilson & Gutiérrez, 1985). At the same time, these social aspects are related to cognitive or ideological aspects, such as the knowledge, beliefs, and social cognitions of journalists regarding the social, cultural, and political issues they write about. How are these diverse conditions of news production related to newsmaking about ethnic affairs?

Hiring

If there is one influential factor that contributes to the role of the media in the reproduction of racism, it is the continuing underrepresentation and discrimination of minority journalists, especially in Europe. In that respect, newspapers are hardly different from other elite institutions or corporations in white societies. Except in the United States, Affirmative Action is categorically rejected if not virtually unknown in the white newsroom. Few newspapers, whether conservative or liberal, whether quality or popular, have top editors from ethnic minority groups, and even the reporters are overwhelmingly white. This has profound consequences for the routines and strategies of newsmaking about ethnic affairs: (a) Since most journalists are white, and because most white journalists have little inside knowledge of minority communities and their concerns, their news reports are necessarily less well informed, more superficial, and more stereotypical than those of minority journalists (Daniel & Allen, 1988). (b) If minority journalists are hired at all, they are often expected to cover only ethnic topics, and much less of the prestigious topics of international and national politics, economy, and finance (Mazingo, 1988). (c) Minority journalists are promoted less, and hence are unable to control their own story assignments or define their own topics and relevancy. They are dependent on the news values and ethnic attitudes of white superiors. (d) Compared to white journalists, minority journalists are often seen as less competent, less credible, and partisan in the coverage of ethnic affairs. White journalists are assumed to write "impartially" about ethnic relations. Bilingual and bicultural competence of minority journalists is undervalued. (e) Editors and program producers may either correctly or falsely assume that the public would resent too many minority journalists.

Newsgathering

The result of these processes of discrimination and exclusion is that news is largely produced by white journalists who have grown up with and were educated and socialized with a set of dominant white group norms and values, which will tend to define an overall white perspective on news events. This limited ethnic experience influences, and is further reinforced by, the conditions of newsgathering. Research has shown that newsmaking is an everyday routine of managing a complex task, namely, to collect and interpret information about newsworthy events within a strict deadline, and with limited resources (Tuchman, 1978). To make sure that the daily newspaper is filled, no matter what happens in the world, there are ongoing beats (assignments) that cover institutional news actors and sources that have a continuous supply of newsworthy discourses, such as government and parliament, ministries and other State institutions, large corporations, the police and the courts, educational institutions, and so on.

These various elite institutions are themselves predominantly white owned or managed. The definition of their own actions as news events, as well as the assignment of newsworthiness of other forms of social or political relevance, is therefore necessarily framed in a white elite perspective, which is in turn adopted as such and seldom basically challenged by white reporters—which does not mean that journalists are not sometimes critical of elites. This biased perspective is especially consequential in the accounts of ethnic events. Thus, research has repeatedly shown that, for instance, in reports about ethnic conflicts or riots, the press will not only routinely rely on the accounts of white politicians and the police, but also see these as more objective, more credible, and more newsworthy (Johnson, Sears, & McConahay, 1971; Knopf, 1975; Murdock, 1984; van Dijk, 1991). By their special access to the media, powerful white institutions reproduce not only their power but also their white event interpretations and broader ideologies characterizing white group dominance.

Minority organizations are generally less powerful, and therefore have fewer organized access settings, such as professional public relations departments, official speakers, press conferences, and other institutional means to reach journalists. Second, partly for the same reasons, white journalists will tend to find such minority organizations less important, and hence less newsworthy, and will therefore be reluctant to actively seek news from them. And third, if that is so, minority spokespersons or press releases may be found less reliable and, especially when critical of white institutions, less objective, as noted above. Finally, since monocultural white journalists have less daily experience communicating with minority representatives, they may experience familiar problems and conflicts of intercultural communication that, however, are often attributed negatively to minority deviance or incompetence. What may be a minority group member's normal style of expressing opinions may be seen as exaggerated, and hence less reliable, by white journalists (Kochman, 1981).

We see that there is a complex network of social relations that concur in excluding minority journalists, perspectives, sources, and news actors from white-dominated media. None of these has to result from explicitly intended acts of discrimination, let alone from a conspiracy of white journalists. On the contrary, research suggests that the majority of journalists have rather liberal attitudes, including regarding minorities (Kneebone, 1985). However, prevailing social structures, everyday rules and routines, and fundamental social cognitions are all geared toward the prevalent access of white news actors, perspectives, interpretations, and the definition of the newsworthiness of events.

Social Cognitions

The various social dimensions of newsmaking discussed above are closely related with corresponding cognitive frameworks, which in turn monitor actual newswriting (Graber, 1984b; Harris, 1989; van Dijk, 1988b). We have suggested that education, professional socialization, and everyday contacts and beats powerfully shape the experiences, and hence the cognitive models, of newsmakers. These models form the basis for the formation of more general, group-based, social cognitions of white journalists. White group interests, including the privileges and power that are implied by white group dominance, thus find their cognitive counterpart in fundamental norms, values, and ideologies. The biased assignment of less objectivity or credibility to minority journalists or sources is part and parcel of a more general negative attitude in white society about the intellectual competence, status, morality, or social integrity of minority group members.

We suggested that such social cognitions influence hiring, promotion, and selective job assignment. They also explain why most leading editors and managers (at least in Europe), resent equal opportunity policies, such as Affirmative Action and especially quotas. Professional ideologies, for example, about quality, about the freedom and independence of the press, may reinforce such white practices and ideologies.

Similarly, social cognitions make up the very system of news values (Galtung & Ruge, 1965; Gans, 1979; Golding & Elliott, 1979). What is important, newsworthy, or otherwise interesting is a judgment derived from current models of news events, as well as from shared social cognitions about social and political structure and social groups. Source reliability is not judged primarily by the quality or the reliability of source messages, but by group or institutional membership. News stories are chiefly about people like Us, or about news events that may interest readers like Us. Ethnic news is often about Them, and such out-groups tend to be represented as essentially different or deviant, if not threatening to Us, as is the case for such groups as communists, leftist radicals, terrorists, pacifists, and others who are seen as a threat to Western or white dominance or the sociopolitical status quo. These cognitive representations fundamentally influence the mental models journalist build of ethnic news events, and the contents and structures of these models in turn influence their expression in actual news stories, as we shall see in detail below.

In sum, along all social and cognitive dimensions of newsgathering, newswriting, and management, and in the newsroom, we find the fundamental prevalence of white perspective and dominance. The same is true for the production of other media messages and programs, such as television news or current affairs programs, advertising, movies, television drama and comedies. That is, the very structural conditions of news production are overwhelmingly geared toward the reproduction of the access, control, prestige, opinions, definitions, concerns, and legitimations of white elites. Conversely, in virtually all stages of news production, minorities are excluded, marginalized, discredited, or simply ignored. These production conditions necessarily shape the very contents and structures of news in the press and, indirectly, the ethnic attitudes of the public at large.

NEWS REPORTS

We have found that preferential media access of white elites, as well as their social cognitions on ethnic affairs, may be expected to influence the selection of topics, the choice of news actors, overall perspective, quotation patterns, prominence, style, the description of ethnic communities and their members, and other structural features of news. Since white elites, in the media as elsewhere, are interested in maintaining not only their own power but also that of the whole white group, we can further predict that, through the media, they will, sometimes very subtly, favor a negative representation of minorities—and a positive representation of the white group in general, and of themselves in particular. This symbolic polarization between Us and Them is crucial in managing the ethnic consensus among the public at large.

Topics

Few properties of discourse, and hence also of news, are as important as its overall meanings or topics (van Dijk, 1980). They define the overall coherence or semantic unity of discourse, and also what information readers memorize best from a news report. The relevance of topics in news is specifically marked in the text, namely, by the headline and lead, which conventionally express the main topics. They do so inter-subjectively, however: They express the most important information of the cognitive model of journalists, that is, how they see and define the news event. Unless readers have different knowledge and beliefs, they will generally adopt these subjective media definitions of what is important information about an event (van Dijk, 1988b).

This is, a fortiori, the case for the coverage of ethnic affairs. General news values together with ethnic attitudes monitor what white journalists—or their white elite sources—will notice, recall, or find relevant in ethnic events, or what they think their mostly white readers will find most interesting. Many studies in several countries have repeatedly shown that news on ethnic affairs usually has a limited number of stereotypical topics:

a. Immigration, with special emphasis on problems, illegality, large numbers, fraud, and demographic or cultural threats.
b. Crime, with special focus on "ethnicized" or "racialized" crimes, such as drug trafficking, mugging, theft, prostitution, hustling, violence, or riots.

   c. Cultural differences, and especially cultural deviance, such as "backward" habits, religious fundamentalism, and all social problems of ethnic relations that are explained in terms of assumed cultural properties of minorities.

   d. Ethnic relations, such as ethnic tensions, discrimination, racial attacks, and other forms of (right-wing) racism, usually defined as regrettable incidents, and often attributed to the presence or behavior of minorities themselves, thus blaming the victim. Also Affirmative Action and quotas are major topics, usually defined however as controversial and conflictive.

Other topics that normally appear frequently in news about white news actors are comparatively less prominent, such as politics, work, education, social issues, and the arts. The same is true for topics that imply a negative representation of the own group, such as racism or ethnocentrism. Thus, non-topics in ethnic affairs coverage are as revealing as topics about the interests and concerns of the white press. Reports on entertainment or sports with minority, typically black, stars may be quite frequent, but in that case, they are de-ethnicized: Such stars are primarily presented as American, French, or Dutch, not as African-American, Algerian-French, or Surinamese-Dutch. Generally, negative topics (e.g., crime) tend to become over-ethnicized, and positive ones de-ethnicized.

Overall, topics express the prevailing negative ethnic attitudes of white journalists and their elite sources; minorities or their presence are semantically defined in news discourse as different, problematic, deviant, or threatening. This is more blatantly the case in the right-wing popular press. The liberal press, however, also focuses on problems, but in that case pays attention to the problems experienced by minorities, such as unemployment or discrimination, and especially to the help We offer in solving these problems. So ethnic events are covered in such a way that negative action of Them, e.g., violence, is topicalized; and possible social explanations of ethnic conflict that reflect negatively on Us, such as discrimination or causes of poverty, are de-topicalized in news reports.

Although discrimination may be a prominent issue, especially in the liberal quality press, it should be emphasized that it is usually limited to discrimination in employment—never in the press. It is not covered as a structural manifestation of white group dominance, but as an incidental and individual transgression of the elite self-image of tolerance. Thus, discrimination is not covered like other forms of crime, but rather is seen as moral deviance. In the conservative press, more often than not, the moral blame may even be reversed: They are accused or ridiculed who accuse others (Us) of discrimination. This is a fortiori the case of racism, which—if covered at all—is limited to extremist right-wing groups or parties, and is seldom applied to white society at large, unless in the past or abroad. Reversal may be total here: In much of the liberal press, too, anti-racism may be found more problematic than racism. Only racial violence, such as attacks against minorities, if topicalized at all, is rather generally condemned, but then conveniently associated with social out-groups, such as football hooligans or skinheads. Elite racism, and the many inequities of everyday racism of ordinary people, is generally taboo, and hence mostly excluded from topic status. This is another way in which the media collude with white elites in the domain of ethnic affairs.

With the decline of overtly and blatantly racist ideologies, ethnic relations are usually defined in cultural terms. Problems at work or at school are routinely explained in terms of differences of ethics, mentality, religion, or attitude, not in terms of white discrimination or prejudice. Stereotyping and overgeneralization are common here, so that all Arabs become terrorists and all Muslim fundamentalists, in the same way that all young black males tend to be seen as aggressive, muggers, or crack addicts. Whereas other cultures are thus routinely derogated as backward or primitive, Western culture and its values are either taken for granted or positively presented as modern, rational, and humanitarian. Again, as is the case for most other topic clusters, we find here the familiar combination of positive self-presentation and negative other-presentation. Such polarization of Us versus Them may be paralleled by the coverage of Third World peoples in international news, where they are often attributed rather similar negative properties as minorities.

Topical analysis shows quite clearly how the press is involved in the reproduction of white group and elite dominance. The press does not primarily focus on issues that are interesting or relevant for the population at large, but on those that concern the elites, such as politicians, the judiciary, scholars, corporate managers, and the social welfare bureaucracy. Most ethnic issues, and hence their topicalization, are predefined by these elite groups, but the general agreement with such definitions by the media elite is clear from the parallelism between media topics and topics in other elite discourse, as we have seen in the previous chapters. Particularly the conservative popular press emphasizes the negative characteristics attributed more subtly to minorities in other, for example, political, text and talk. Moreover, by excluding the issues that are relevant to minority groups, and by marginalizing the anti-racist voice, the press also fails to meet its own ideological criteria of balance: Serious opposition to the elite-defined ethnic consensus is generally censored.

News Schemata

The topics of news are organized by news-specific schemata or superstructures (van Dijk 1988b). Such schemata, which have a hierarchical structure, consist of a number of conventional categories, of which Headline and Lead (together forming a Summary category) are most familiar. Other categories are: Main Event, Backgrounds (History and Context), Verbal Reactions (Declarations), and Comments (Evaluation and Prediction). Some of these categories, such as Headline and Main Event, are obligatory, others are optional and tend to appear only in longer news reports. Like the topics that form their variable content, news categories (except Headline and Lead) are usually expressed in discontinuous installments. Also, the canonical order of categories may be changed, for example, due to considerations of relevance, degree of interest, or recency. For instance, the category of Verbal Reactions, which usually comes rather late in a news report, may be put in a more prominent position if the comment itself has specific news value or if the commentator is very prominent.

In sum, as is the case for many other structures of news discourse, there may be considerable variation, namely, as a function of social context or the social cognitions of journalists. It may therefore be expected that in ethnic affairs coverage, too, in-group and out-group attitudes may also influence the variable realization of news schemata. We saw earlier that, depending on the ethnic attitudes of the journalist, lower level topics may be promoted to Headline or Lead status, and vice versa. In ethnic news coverage, this usually means that topics consistent with prevailing prejudices or stereotypes, such as minority crime, tend to be assigned more importance, and therefore may move up in the schematic hierarchy. Conversely, information that is inconsistent with the positive in-group cognitions of white journalists, such as elite racism or discrimination in the media, may be moved down in the hierarchy, if it is presented at all. Similarly, what is relevant Background information in news, that is, information that may explain the news event, may be left out entirely, and irrelevant background information may become more prominent. As an example, in the coverage of the 1985 race riots in Great Britain, most of the news reports did not pay much attention to the social backgrounds (poverty, unemployment, inner-city decay) of the riots, but rather emphasized the drugs and violence angle as a possible background explanation. Below we shall examine in more detail two editorials on this issue. The very conventional structure of a news report may play a role in displaying some information about ethnic relations more prominently, and thereby enhancing the probability that the readers will pay more attention to it, and will thus better remember. As with other news discourse structures, this feature of schemata usually implies emphasizing negative properties attributed to Them, and positive properties of Us, and not vice versa.

Quotations

Few properties of news are as revealing about the practices of newsmaking as quotations (Clayman, 1990; Zelizer, 1989). They show not only with whom reporters have been talking, who have special access to the media, which news actors are found important and credible enough to be actually quoted, who are allowed to give their own opinions, but also how the journalist evaluates quoted opinions. In ethnic affairs coverage, we may thus examine what voice ethnic minorities have in the press, compared to white news actors. What are they allowed to say about the ethnic events in which they are involved, and how are they presented as speakers?

Although quotation as such is a rather faithful marker of attributed importance of news actors, there are of course many ways to quote news actors. The modes in which their words are introduced and formulated, especially when the quotes are not literal, may also tell us something about the reporter's opinions of the news actors and the things they say. If a quotation is preceded by such doubt or distance words as "alleged" or "claimed," or if specific opinion words are enclosed in quotation marks, we may conclude that the reporter takes at least some distance from the statement. This is typically the case for critical statements of minority groups or white anti-racists about forms of discrimination, police harassment, or failing government policies. Indeed, the use of quotation marks in this case may often be interpreted not so much as doubt about the event or the evaluation of the event by the quoted news actor, but as a rejection of such an opinion. Quotation marks in that case signal the controversial, and not merely journalistic objectivity.

If we examine the frequency of quotations of different news actors in news reports about ethnic affairs, we find a rather clear pattern: In general, ethnic minorities are quoted much less than the white participants of news events. This bias may be partly explained by the well-known fact, discussed above, that white elites and institutions are generally found to be more important and credible, so that they have easier access to the media, which also enhances their chance of being quoted. Indeed, after an ethnic event has occurred, journalists may ask for comments from relevant authorities, and since these are mostly white, many news reports will tend to favor quotations by white news actors (see also Wodak et al., 1990).

Analysis of quotation frequency and patterns of several thousands news reports published in the British and Dutch press shows that while white majority group actors may be quoted in more than half the reports in which they appear as actors, this figure is much lower, namely, about 20% in the British press to 32% in the Dutch press, for minority speakers. Moreover, majority speakers appear alone as speakers much more often than minority speakers, thereby being granted the likelihood of providing the only definition of the ethnic event. This is particularly true for sensitive or threatening topics, such as prejudice, discrimination, and racism, but also for topics on which whites are assumed to be the experts, such as education, research, or Affirmative Action. In the British press, for instance, of 100 articles on prejudice, only one featured a minority speaker! In contrast, we will repeatedly find quotations by white speakers who deny or mitigate racism or attack anti-racist opinions.

More generally, we find that even controversial white speakers, such as notorious racists like Enoch Powell in Great Britain or Jean-Marie Le Pen in France, are not only widely quoted, but sometimes also given ample space to openly voice their racist opinions, even when most journalists will define them as being beyond the consensus. While such abuse of the freedom of the press may be defensible because of liberal principles of the freedom of expression, or even within the framework of news ideologies on newsworthiness (for journalists such persons are "hot," while conflictive), it should be borne in mind that those minority representatives, or other anti-racists who oppose such overtly racist views, do not get nearly as much space or quotation. That letting openly racist elites speak so freely may be a major contribution to the reproduction of extreme forms of elite racism, is a consideration only few leading editors care about so much that they would systematically ban such voices from their columns. Confronted with objections against publication of racist opinions, they will take recourse in routine justifications derived from the ideology of newsmaking: truth, open debate, no censorship, and so on. Obviously, such claims would be more credible if they were also applied to minority or anti-racist views on ethnic affairs.

If minorities are quoted at all, then their opinions are nearly always balanced by those of white speakers: In only 3.8% of British news reports on ethnic affairs, are minorities allowed to speak on their own! Minorities are generally quoted most on safe topics, such as culture, religion, emigration, or ethnic politics.

Again, it should be emphasized that this clear imbalance in quotation frequency is inconsistent with prevailing news ethics, which traditionally requires that both sides are heard. As we have found above for newsgathering and topics, routines and ideologies of newsmaking may accordingly be deviated from as soon as minorities are involved. This bias is even more remarkable when we realize that minority speakers generally have more experience with, and hence more insight into ethnic events. That is, the routine news criterion of competence is not respected in this case. On the contrary, such competence may be unwelcome, especially when it would yield uneasy insights into ethnic relations. More generally, we have found both in our extensive analytical work on ethnic event coverage and in multiple everyday experiences with the Dutch press, that competent and critical minority experts, especially those specialized in ethnic affairs, tend to be ignored, marginalized, discredited, or even attacked by the white press. If minority spokespersons are quoted, those who are preferred express opinions that are consistent with the white ethnic consensus. Or else, highly unrepresentative minorities are being quoted as examples of minority deviance (Downing, 1980). Indeed, minority leaders may even be quoted less than other minority group members, which also breaks the general rule of the press to quote elites or representative spokespersons. In general, then, quotations as well as public debate on ethnic issues are limited to white elite speakers, such as politicians, scholars, columnists, and members of the social bureaucracy, whose true expertise on ethnic issues need not be a criterion at all. This also means that since the ethnic debate is largely about them, and not with them, minorities are further pushed into a passive role as soon as public opinion formation is involved.

In sum, together with the choice of topics, the biased use of quotations shows again the prominent role of the news in the reproduction of elite racism. Quotation frequency and patterns are the discursive manifestation (and proof) of the assumption made above that white elites especially have active (writing) and passive (quotation) access to the press. By paying special attention to white elite opinions about ethnic affairs, the press not only follows its own routines of newsmaking, namely, by providing access of elites to its newsmaking, but at the same time literally silences minority opinion, especially when it is competent and critical. The public is thus confronted with a seriously unbalanced set of white opinions about ethnic affairs, and with scarcely a minority perspective.

Whereas the press could partly be excused for biased topic selection because of its dependence on institutional (white) sources for its routine news events, quotation is a discursive property of news reports, and largely controlled or controllable by the press itself. In this way, although the press may not be able to ignore urban disturbances, civil rights debates in Congress or parliament, or a report on minority education, as defined by the police, politicians or policymakers, respectively, the press is most certainly able to ask for representative minority opinions about such white-defined ethnic events. That in many situations it does not do so, confirms our earlier assumption that minorities and their opinions are generally found to be less competent, less reliable, less interesting, and less newsworthy by white newsmakers. In our experience, that many such newsmakers will indignantly reject the conclusion that this form of exclusion, marginalization, and silencing of minority opinion is nothing else but a serious form of symbolic discrimination and racism, also proves that they have no insight into patterns of everyday elite racism either.

Local Semantics

Although we now have a more general picture of the ways the press writes about ethnic affairs, and which news actors tend to have more access to the media, a detailed analysis of ethnic affairs coverage should also focus on the various microstructures of news reports (van Dijk, 1988b). At this level, we shall first examine the meanings of words and sentences, relationships between sentences (propositions), and then stylistic and rhetorical formulations of meanings. For the formation of mental models (that is, the subjective interpretations of events and situations) and the eventual shaping and changing of shared social representations, readers rely on not only overall topics but also particularly on the actual formulations used by the press. After all, it is especially *how* minority and majority group members are described as news participants that will show the readers what the opinion of the newspaper is. The same general topic classes, such as crime, immigration, and cultural differences, may feature articles that have radically different local meanings and perspectives on ethnic affairs. As we have also shown for quotation, it is at this point that the unique and autonomous role of the press in the reproduction of racism is most specific.

A local semantic analysis particularly focuses on the strategic meanings and functions of, and the relations between, propositions expressed in discourse (van Dijk, 1985b). Seemingly positive statements about minorities may, in that case, appear to be face-saving disclaimers, intended to prevent the interpretation that the newspaper is racist. The analysis of such disclaimers, as well as other semantic relations in news reports, is one of the tasks of local semantics. The examples studied below are all drawn from our analysis of the ethnic coverage of the British press in the second half of 1985 and the first half of 1989 (for details, see van Dijk, 1991).

Implications

A critical analysis of the meanings of news discourse focuses particularly on various types of implication. Implications are meanings (propositions) that are not explicitly expressed in the text but may be inferred from words or sentences in the text, as well as from the mental models constructed during understanding. Indeed, it is sometimes more important to specify what is *not* said by the text than what is actually expressed. In many respects, media texts are ideological icebergs, of which only the tip is visible to the reader.

Consider, for instance the following fragment of the British tabloid, the *Daily Mail*:

> That is why we have to be more brisk in saying no, and showing the door to those who are not British citizens and would abuse our hospitality and tolerance. To do that is not to give way to prejudice, but to lessen the provocation on which it feeds. (*Mail*, November 28, 1985)

This small fragment has many ideologically relevant implications, for example, that the British are hospitable and tolerant, that immigrants abuse such tolerance, that if the British are prejudiced this is provoked by the immigrants, and so on. This fragment also shows familiar semantic and rhetorical forms of understatement or euphemism, such as "being brisk" instead of "hard," and "showing the door" instead of "throwing out."

Implications often betray the perspective of the reporter or the newspaper on the events. When the *Times* (September 17, 1985) describes demonstrators against Honeyford (the Bradford headmaster accused of writing racist articles about multicultural education) as "noisy," the reader may correctly infer that the reporter has a negative opinion about them. Similarly, when the *Telegraph* (September 6, 1985) says that Honeyford is targeted for his "alleged racism," we may also conclude that the *Telegraph* probably does not share this opinion. When the same newspaper (October 21, 1985) describes the demonstrators as a "mob of adults pretending to be caring parents," then it not only clearly evaluates the demonstrators in a very negative way, but also implies that parents who protest against negative publications about their children are not caring parents. More generally, the right-wing press uses many words and clauses to imply that accusations of racism are unfounded or ridiculous: If somebody is found to have engaged in discrimination, the right-wing press will invariably use such words as "alleged," "claim," or "brand."

One of the more subtle forms of implications is *presupposition*, that is, a proposition that is tacitly assumed to be true for another proposition to be meaningful. In the example given above we already saw that British tolerance and hospitality are thus presupposed. We often find such presuppositions in the right-wing press (in this and the following examples, italics are added to identify the passage under discussion):

> [About a speech by Enoch Powell] Open and constructive discussion, for example, of very real difficulties which have arisen in some of our schools becomes taboo. As Mr. Honeyford at Bradford has found to his cost. Thoughtful analysis of why in some areas *there is rising tension between Asian and Caribbean populations* is rendered dangerous. (*Daily Telegraph*, September 6, 1985)

In this example, it is presupposed, but not actually asserted, that there *is* rising tension between the two communities, a presupposition that is often used to divide the Asians and the West Indians, despite the repeated statements of community leaders that such tensions do not exist.

As we shall see below, such syntactic forms as nominalizations and agentless passives are unspecific about the agency of an action (Fowler, 1991; Fowler et al., 1979; Kress & Hodge, 1979). This form of implicitness, which—at this level of semantic analysis—may be called *vagueness*, is used especially when the responsibility of the authorities for negative actions is concealed:

> (Brixton) On Saturday, police were petrol-bombed, shops looted and cars burned *after the shooting* of a West-Indian woman. (*Times*, September 30, 1985)

Whereas in this example the passive voice is used to describe the actions of both the rioters and a nominalization ("the shooting") to refer to the action of the police, it is not immediately clear *who* shot the West Indian woman. Similarly, whereas a "mob" of Asians is explicitly identified and negatively evaluated as the responsible agents of smashing up a pub, it is *not* said that it was whites who attacked the Asians:

> (Four Asians acquitted). They were among a mob of 50 Asians who smashed up an East London pub after a series of hammer *attacks* on other Asians. (*Sun*, August 14)

If the social causes of the urban disturbances are being described at all in the conservative press, we may typically find references to unemployment or even discrimination. However, these routine nominalizations usually conceal *who* do not employ whom, and *who* are responsible for discrimination.

Whereas these and other forms of implicitness convey too little information, newspapers may also give too much information, for instance, in what we may describe as *overcompleteness* (van Dijk, 1977). We say that a passage is overcomplete when it gives information that is relatively irrelevant to the description of the events. Such overcomplete passages may be used to convey a negative picture of a news actor. If a Rastafarian is described as "unemployed," this is usually not a neutral description, but a characterization of young blacks that fits into a stereotype, namely, that many of them don't work. And if Bradford's Mayor, Mr. Ajeeb, is described by the *Daily Telegraph* (October 16, 1985) as a "former peasant farmer from Pakistan," this irrelevant description does not exactly contribute to an impression of expertise or credibility. The same is true when the same newspaper irrelevantly characterizes some Asian voters as "unable to speak English" (September 27, 1985). The most pervasive form of overcompleteness, however, is the very mention of origin, color, race, or ethnicity of news actors in situations where this information is clearly irrelevant, but which may be used as an implicit explanation of usually negative actions of minority group members, typically so in crime news.

Semantic Moves

We see that several forms of implicitness may be used to convey information that is negative for minority news actors. However, negative statements or implications about minorities might be understood as biased or even as racist. Much like people in everyday conversations (van Dijk, 1987a), even right-wing newspapers are concerned about their tolerant image. Therefore, when negative things are said about minorities, the newspaper may at the same time emphasize that it "has nothing against these people." Such disclaimers are functional moves in an overall strategy of face-keeping, positive self-presentation, and social impression management (Goffman, 1967; Hewitt & Stokes, 1975; Tedeschi, 1981). We shall come back to them in our analysis of two editorials below.

One of the major semantic moves is that of *denial*, prominent especially in elite discourse: We are not racist, but . . . More generally, we have found that racism or discrimination tends to be doubted, played down, or simply denied (see also van Dijk, 1992) (italics are ours):

Walkout Over "Racist" Council Employee

. . .\The woman was recently found guilty of racial harassment by a council disciplinary tribunal because she allegedly "caused offence" to a black member of the union. (*Times*, August 6, 1985)

This passage, like the ones discussed above, makes it clear that the *Times* journalist finds the accusations not exactly convincing, or at least would like to keep some distance, for example, by using quotation marks and the word "allegedly."

An interesting example of the use of "claim" may be found in the following fragment of a news item in the *Daily Telegraph* about a recent report of the Commission for Racial Equality (CRE) that we analyzed in Chapter 5:

In its report which follows a detailed review of the operation of the 1976 Race Relations Act, the Commission *claims* that ethnic minorities continue to suffer high levels of discrimination and disadvantage. (*Telegraph*, August 1, 1985)

Along the lines of our own earlier remarks, CRE chairman Peter Newsam reacts as follows to this use of "claim" in a Letter to the Editor:

Of the Commission you say "it claims that ethnic minorities continue to suffer high levels of discrimination and disadvantage." This is like saying that someone "claims" that July was wet. It was. And it is also a fact supported by the weight of independent research evidence that discrimination on racial grounds, in employment, housing and services, remains at a disconcertingly high level. (*Telegraph*, August 7, 1985)

Besides such denials, we may similarly expect various moves of playing down, trivializing, or ridiculing accusations of racism, what we may describe as moves of *mitigation*. Racism may thus be called "some disadvantages" experienced by minorities in the *Times* (October 17, 1985). Serious and often documented forms of police harassment against black youths are played down by the *Daily Telegraph* as follows:

(Brixton) One can see why they [ministers] wish to resist the Left-wing deterministic argument that unemployment plus *a little police harassment* equals riots ... (A government minister, looking at the inner cities) He will see racial tensions—between white and black and, in some areas between Asians and Blacks. (*Telegraph*, September 30, 1985)

And when a policeman is engaged in a brutal beating during the disturbances, his actions may implicitly be excused by affirming that "he lost his temper." Similarly, even after a formal conviction of discrimination, a nightclub owner may seem to be excused for not hiring a black singer, when the newspaper adds the rather irrelevant information that he "was three times mugged by Blacks" (*Mail*, August 16, 1985). Vagueness and mitigation may be combined when serious forms of racial conflict, as well as the experiences of racism by the minority communities, are being described as "misunderstanding" and "distrust between parts of the community" (*Daily Telegraph*, August 1, 1985), as if the minority community shares the blame for its own subordinate position.

Reversal or *blaming the victim* is another prominent move in the overall strategy of positive self-presentation and negative other-presentation. Confronted with repeated accusations of intolerance and racism, the Right and its press systematically take recourse by reversing the charges and accusing blacks and other anti-racists of intolerance and even of reverse racism, namely, against white English:

(Honeyford and other cases) Nobody is less able to face the truth than the hysterical "anti-racist" brigade. Their intolerance is such that they try to

silence or sack anyone who doesn't toe their party-line. (Column by John
Vincent, *Sun*, October 23, 1985)

(Honeyford quits). Now we know who the true racists are. (Editorial, *Sun*,
November 30, 1985)

Similarly, if minorities are being discriminated against, the press may
argue that the minority groups bring this on themselves:

(After two reports about the causes of the riots). While the Whites were
being scolded once more for their "prejudice," *the Blacks were doing their
best to prove it justified*. (*Daily Telegraph*, October 19, 1985)

At the same time, as we have seen above, the conservative press
repeatedly emphasizes that "this is a remarkably tolerant society" (*Daily
Telegraph*, September 11, 1985), or that "Britain's record for absorbing
people from different backgrounds, peacefully and with tolerance, is
second to none" (*Sun*, September 14, 1985). To further emphasize this
point, tabloid newspapers may run a series about policing in the Caribbean
in order to show that black police also may be tough on drugs or other
forms of deviance, thereby implying that hard policing is therefore not
racist in Britain. Such *comparisons* are a familiar semantic move in argumentations, and also in many everyday conversations that make a point of
blaming minority groups. We have seen that these comparisons may even be
made between West Indians and Asians, with the view of establishing
contrast between good (meek, adapted) and bad (rebellious) immigrants.
    Another well-known disclaimer is that of *apparent concession*. In this
move, the newspaper seems to present itself in a liberal way by emphasizing that not all minorities are that bad:

(Tottenham, Blacks) . . . There is no doubt that the great majority of West-
Indians would like to behave and be accepted as normal British citizens:
they would be if they were not stirred up by those among them who peddle
evil and hatred and by those extreme socialists who aim for revolution on
the streets and an anarchy that would make parts of Britain ungovernable.
(Column by Woodrow Wyatt, *Times*, October 12, 1985)

Recall though that such passages are not primarily intended to emphasize the good qualities of the immigrant community, but rather as
an argumentative ploy to more credibly convey the message about its
bad qualities—or at least the bad qualities of some of them.

Conclusions and Further Remarks

These few examples of the local semantics of race reporting in the British press, chosen among hundreds of others, show rather clearly that a complex set of semantic implications, moves, and other strategic ploys are being used to portray minority groups in a negative way, while at the same time emphasizing the positive (or minimizing the negative) qualities of the white British group or institution. Again, this supports our assumption that the press generally colludes with the white elites in ethnic affairs.

However, especially for the right-wing press, the real opponents and the main targets of their wrath are not primarily the blacks or other minorities. These have little political or economic influence, little prestige or status, and attacking them too violently may be seen as racist. Therefore, the real enemy are the anti-racists of the "loony left," and all those who support them: anti-racist organizations, anti-racist teachers, academics, writers, and so on (Murray, 1986; Seidel, 1988a, 1988b). These are variously described as being intolerant, as "pundits" of the "race relations industry," if not as "pocket Hitlers" or the "new inquisition," who do not allow decent white British people, like Honeyford, to "speak the truth" about race relations in Britain. Many passages in the right-wing press, therefore, read like this one:

High Price of Telling Truth

For the first time in our long history as a nation, ordinary men and women in Britain must now fear to speak the truth. . . . We have tyranny in Britain. We have intimidation. We have a sinister attempt first to curb and then to destroy freedom of speech. We have racism too—and that is what is behind the plot. It is not white racism. It is black racism. . . . But who is there to protect the white majority? . . . Our tolerance is our strength, But we will not allow anyone to turn it into our weakness. (*Sun*, October 24, 1985)

Interestingly, such passages, repeatedly published in millions of tabloid copies, do not seem to suggest that the right-wing press, or those elites supported by this press, are unable to "speak the truth." Indeed, this accusation is merely an argumentative and rhetorical ploy, namely, to accuse the opponents of precisely those things the right-wing press itself is regularly accused of. In other words, the move of reversal is the ultimate form of self-defense.

These and similar strategies of the right-wing press may be interpreted as forms of symbolic competition in the definition of the ethnic situation in Britain. Whereas the conservative media (at least in Great Britain) control virtually the entire means for the mass production and reproduction of ethnic beliefs, some small groups cannot thus be controlled, for instance, in education or in left-wing city councils or organizations. Their anti-racist discourse, while addressed to a variety of people and organizations, also applies to the right-wing media, which react with fierce counterattacks against the anti-racists, and by repeated attempts to counter and rob of legitimacy a thoroughly resented alternative moral and political interpretation of ethnic relations in Britain. However, the right-wing press not only vies for symbolic control over the definition of the ethnic situation, but also sees itself as the voice of "White Britain" and its interests. The Others are seen to attack not only the racists, but also as attacking white people in general, and the white press in particular.

Symbolic control is thus paired with sociopolitical and economic control, for instance, when the conservative press resolutely rejects multicultural education and Affirmative Action in employment. It is also at this point that analysis of the local semantics of ethnic affairs coverage in the press shows its more detailed enactment of the reproduction of elite racism. Apart from defending itself and the white group in general, the press also has the important task of defending white elites and their interests against moral and political dissent and opposition from minorities and other anti-racists.

Style and Rhetoric

Finally, the various meanings analyzed above also need to be expressed in actual words and sentences (Geis, 1987; Wodak, 1989). The examples we have given showed that the attacks of the right-wing press are also formulated in a style that unambiguously conveys a negative opinion of minorities and white anti-racists. Here is a selection of the terms used in the right-wing press in 1985 for its opponents:

Snoopers (Editorial, *Telegraph*, August 1)

A noisy mob of activist demonstrators (*Telegraph*, September 23)

These dismal fanatics, monstrous creatures (*Telegraph*, September 26)

Unscrupulous or feather-brained observers (*Telegraph*, September 30)

The British race relations pundits (*Telegraph*, October 1)

Trotzkyites, socialist extremists, Revolutionary Communists, Marxists and Black militants (*Telegraph*, October 9)

Race conflict "high priests" (*Telegraph*, October 11)

Bone-brained Left-fascism (Editorial, *Telegraph*, November 30)

The multi-nonsense brigade (*Telegraph*, January 11)

Mob of left-wing crazies (*Mail*, September 24)

The Rent-A-Riot Agitators (*Mail*, September 30)

What a goon (said about Bernie Grant) (Frank Chapple, *Mail*, October 10)

He and his henchmen . . . this obnoxious man, left-wing inquisitor (about Grant) (*Mail*, October 18)

Snoopers, untiring busibodies (*Sun*, August 2)

Blinkered tyrants (*Sun*, September 6)

Left-wing crackpots (*Sun*, September 7)

A pack trying to hound Ray Honeyford (*Sun*, September 25)

Unleashing packs of Government snoopers (*Sun*, October 16)

The hysterical "anti-racist" brigade. . . . the Ayatolahs of Bradford, the Left-wing anti-racist mob (*Sun*, October 23)

This style hardly needs further comment. Note, though, that the lexical registers are not arbitrary. Anti-racists tend to be characterized in very special negative terms, borrowed from the registers of madness, irrationality, threatening animals, and political oppression. This style is characteristic of the right-wing press and seldom occurs in the more liberal or moderately conservative quality press. That it is also being used in the *Daily Telegraph*, however, shows that it cannot simply be identified with the dramatic, florid "popular" style of the tabloids. Indeed, it expresses an ideological position in which opponents are degraded and their legitimate actions vilified without restraint. Comparison with results from similar analyses of fascist discourse suggests that this style is not unique (Ehlich, 1989; Kushner & Lunn, 1989). Some of these negative qualifications of anti-racists may also be found in the Dutch press.

Particularly in the British tabloids, this style is further enhanced by a number of rhetorical operations, such as hyperbole, metaphors, comparisons, rhymes, and alliterations, especially in the headlines. These either further emphasize the negative characteristics of minorities, anti-racists, or the Left, or otherwise draw attention to acts that are negatively valued by the tabloids. Here are a few examples of such operations:

[Immigration] But far from acknowledging their colossal blunder, they carry on with the cant and claptrap, the illusion of race equality and the fiction that people are British if they choose to say so. (Column by Honor Tracy, *Daily Telegraph*, October 19, 1985)

[What are they teaching them?] If it isn't the three Rs, perhaps it is the three Ss instead: sedition, subversion and sociological hogwash. (*Mail*, October 19, 1985)

[Tottenham "riot"] Bombs, Bullets, Blood in Barricaded Britain. (*Mail*, December 27, 1985)

[Tottenham "riot"] The widow of Keith Blakelock, the brave bobby butchered by black rioters, said last night that she pitied the killers. (*Sun*, October 8, 1985)

[Honeyford] For speaking commonsense he's been vilified; for being courageous he's been damned, for refusing to concede defeat his enemies can't forgive him. (Column by Lynda Potter, *Mail*, September 18, 1985)

[Tottenham "riot"] Now it is not merely sticks and stones and petrol bombs. Now it is shotguns and knives. Now it is not merely cuts and bruises. Now it is murder. (Editorial, *Sun*, October 8, 1985)

These examples also show that the rhetoric of alliteration, parallelism, or other forms of repetition serves not only to emphasize the negative properties of the Others, but also to underline the good qualities of Our people, such as Honeyford and the police.

Editorials and Argumentation

Editorials are a genre of news discourse that has a somewhat different schematic structure than that of the news reports studied above. In this case, the news event is already known, and the main function of editorials is to formulate the newspaper's official opinion about this recent event, possibly backed up with some arguments. Thus, we may distinguish between a Definition of the situation, which provides a subjective summary of the event, followed by an Evaluation of the event and a final Conclusion or Moral, which may feature advice, a recommendation, a warning, or another normative speech act, usually addressed to prominent news actors, such as politicians or other elites who are responsible for political decision making.

Besides this conventional structure of editorials, their persuasive function also needs argumentative support. This means that we may also analyze editorials in terms of familiar argumentation structures, featuring different types of Premises (actual facts, general facts, principles of inference, and so on), followed by a Conclusion representing the position of the newspaper (van Eemeren, Grootendorst, Blair, & Willard, 1987). Note that besides the immediate persuasive function, which addresses not only the readers but also, if not primarily, the relevant elite news actors, editorials also have the function of reproducing and legitimating the mental models of news events and the general social cognitions of the editors. If the editors are in agreement with the elite news actors involved, such as specific politicians, the editorial may simultaneously function as a legitimation of the actions of such elites.

In editorials about ethnic affairs, we may expect the editors, especially those of right-wing newspapers, to speak for the white group as a whole. That is, editors speak not only in their function of newspaper elites, but also as white group members. In sum, editorials have persuasive, political, social, and cultural functions, especially in such important sociocultural and moral domains as ethnic relations and the reproduction of racism. Whereas news reports may partly be based on source discourse, for example, of politicians, and hence partly be excused for their content and style, this is not the case with editorials; their content and formulation are wholly controlled by the editors themselves. We shall therefore pay somewhat more detailed attention to such editorials because they formulate most explicitly the position of the press in the white elite management of ethnic affairs.

To illustrate the special role of editorials in the reproduction of elite racism, we examine two examples from two British tabloid newspapers, the *Sun* and the *Daily Mail*, reacting to two "riots" that had just taken place. These examples were chosen because they clearly illustrate not only the rhetoric, style, arguments, opinions, attitudes, and ideologies of the vastly influential tabloid press (the two tabloids together have more than 10 million readers), but also how their editors define and display their allegiance with a position of white dominance and the interests of white elite institutions, such as the police. Another reason to analyze two full newspaper texts is to examine various properties of ethnic coverage in relation to each other and in their original context, which was impossible for the examples studied above. As was the case for the earlier analyses in this book, this one is quite informal.

The Events

Our examples are about the "riots" (the routine description, in the right-wing press, of urban disturbances) that took place in Britain in the fall of 1985 in Handsworth, Brixton, and Tottenham. The deeper causes of these disturbances are to be sought in the ethnic or racial inequality characterizing virtually all sectors of British society: severe restrictions on, and discrimination in immigration, high unemployment, neglect of the inner cities, inferior housing and education, police harassment, and many other forms of everyday racism.

The particular events that took place in the fall of 1985, following those in Bristol, Brixton, and other cities a few years earlier, were all sparked by police actions. In Brixton, the police shot and crippled an innocent black woman during a raid on her home. In Tottenham, another black woman suffered a heart attack and died when police searched her home. Large-scale fighting between the police and groups of youths, largely but not exclusively consisting of West Indian young men, and other forms of violence were the result.

The Reaction of the Press

The British press reacted in a predictable way. Especially in the conservative press, saturation coverage focused on the violence of blacks and sought explanations in black pathologies, lack of adaptation in the black community, and especially in crime and drugs, while largely ignoring police harassment, unemployment, discrimination, and the general social, economic, and cultural misery of the inner cities. Consequently, instead of blaming the Thatcherist government and the State institutions, the black community was blamed (for details, see Gordon & Rosenberg, 1989; van Dijk, 1991).

This definition and explanation of the events fit very well the overall pattern of reporting on ethnic affairs in the conservative British press, where, as noted above, minorities in general, and black West Indians in particular, are consistently portrayed in terms of problems, protests, conflicts, violence, crime, drugs, and other forms of unruly behavior. We may expect, therefore, that the editorials presuppose the underlying ideologies that characterize their own newsgathering and reporting on race. At the same time they may legitimatize police violence and the limited policies of the conservative administration, and thus play an autonomous role in the reproduction of ethnic inequality.

However, present norms and laws prohibit explicit racism, and even among the radical new right, public discourse of race is often but not always veiled (Gordon & Klug, 1986; Seidel, 1986, 1987; van Dijk, 1987a). Explicit racial slurs are rare, and therefore, even in the tabloids we may expect euphemisms, implicit derogation, and the usual tactical disclaimers, such as apparent denials ("We have nothing against the black community, *but . . .* ") or apparent concessions ("There are also law-abiding blacks, *but . . .* "). Such semantic moves locally implement a double global strategy, that of negative other-presentation (derogation) and positive self-presentation (face-keeping), which we have encountered so often before.

It is this broader political, social, and cultural context that shapes the contents and the structures of tabloid editorials, and hence their argumentative strategies, too. The main ideological point of "riot" coverage is their explanation in terms of the alleged criminal character and violence of blacks, and the exoneration of white institutions (government, police, and so on) from blame for the black revolt. This point is embedded in a broader ideological structure of nationalist racism in which minorities, immigrants, immigration, and the multicultural society are associated with negative qualifications, and white British people, society, and culture are presented as positive and "under attack" by the aliens (Gordon & Klug, 1986).

Let us now see how the editorials actually implement, formulate, and defend this overall ideological framework and their position on the "race riots."

For this analysis, one editorial from the *Mail*, "The Choice for Britain's Blacks" (October 8, 1985) and one from the *Sun*, "The Blacks Must Act" (September 30, 1985), were selected. The first is about the disturbances in Tottenham, the second about the earlier events in Brixton. We have chosen these editorials because their argumentative strategies are very similar and offer us insight into more general properties of tabloid ideology, argumentation, and rhetoric.

Part of the argumentative point is expressed and summarized in the respective headlines: The Blacks must choose/do something. This headlined preview of the normative conclusion of the editorials implies that (a) blacks are responsible for whatever has happened, which in turn suggests that (b) others (government, the State, white people) are not responsible. This indeed has been the main political and ideological position of the conservative press since the race-related disturbances. How is this point elaborated and defended editorially?

The Mail

The editorial from the *Mail* is the most detailed and features several sub-argumentation sequences. The first argumentative point (lines 3-10) is that a policeman was deliberately and savagely murdered, a

Daily Mail COMMENT

The choice for Britain's blacks

POLICE Constable Keith Blakelock was deliberately and savagely hacked to death when he was trying to defend firemen from the mob. He was not killed by accident. He did not die from a heart attack. He was not the victim of relatives crazed by grief.

A good man has been murdered and only the most piously blinkered . . . the most wilful self-deceivers . . . can pretend that in Tottenham on the night of Sunday, 6th October, 1985, mainland Britain did not take a significant and sickening lurch nearer that bloody, apocalyptic vision so grimly imparted by Enoch Powell.

It is that serious.

As the life blood of Police Constable Blakelock ebbed away, truth was born: Truth which the black communities in Britain must understand.

Either they obey the laws of this land where they have taken up residence and accepted both the full rights and responsibilities of citizenship, or they must expect the fascist street agitators to call ever more boldly and with ever louder approval for them to 'go back from whence they came'.

Either they forgo the anarchic luxury of these orgies of arson, looting and murderous assaults against the men and women whose task it is to uphold the laws of this land or they will provoke a paramilitary reaction unknown to mainland Britain.

It gives the Daily Mail no satisfaction to print such warnings. This newspaper has consistently condemned Mr. Powell's call for large-scale repatriation. We still do. We abhor the prospects of British police being transformed into head-smashing replicas of the French riot squads.

But that is the way the riots in Tottenham, Brixton and Handsworth are driving the country.

Our policemen cannot be bombed and stabbed and killed and carted off to hospital in their scores and just be expected to cower there behind their shields and take it.

Nor can we permit parts of our inner cities to become no-go areas where only criminals flourish.

Despite the difficulties of bad housing and high unemployment, most men and women in these districts are peaceable and want to make a go of it.

They can't make it alone. Those in real need, whatever the colour of their skin, should be getting more practical help and encouragement. Government must do more to create work opportunities for youngsters, white, brown and black, in these neighbourhoods.

Also, to defuse genuine anger when a citizen is killed or dies during a police operation, it would be sensible to insist that the inquest be conducted by a High Court judge before a jury and with at least two independent pathologists testifying as to the cause of death.

But, when all that is said, yes, and done, it is in the final resort the blacks of Britain who must decide their own destiny here.

They must do more to discipline their young. They must find themselves community leaders who preach co-operation, not confrontation. They must encourage black recruits to join the police and 'swamp' black areas with black constables on the beat; ultimately the only kind of community policing that is going to work. It's up to them.

Text of *Mail*, October 8, 1985. Used with permission of Daily *Mail* London/ Solo Syndication & Literary Agency Ltd.

THE SUN SAYS

The blacks must act

FIRST Handsworth, and now Brixton is pil-laged by the mob.

5   Two communities within a month have now been terrorised by rioters and looters, mainly of West Indian origin.

It is crucial that the leaders of black groups take control and stop the mad-
10 ness of their young.

If not, then the Afro-Caribbean section of British society will become the outcasts of our land.

Some foolish commentators refer to
15 **the looting and fire raising as "Brixton's Revenge."**

Tragedy

Revenge for what? The Riots started after police accidentally shot a black
20 woman.

The shooting was a dreadful tragedy but the woman's colour had nothing to do with it.

But this incident
25 *was merely the occasion not the cause, of the trouble in Brixton.*

It was used as a
30 pretext for violence, for attacks on inno- cent people, for mindless destruc- tion of property.

THE SHAME OF BRIXTON

The Sun has constantly championed the 35 **rights of the black communities in Britain.**

We denounced Enoch Powell's heart- 40 less scheme for repatriation.

Yet we would be foolish and blind to pretend that all is well in our mixed race areas.

Today a special responsibility falls 45 *on the West Indians' leaders.*

Chinese, Pakistanis and Indians by and large live at peace because there are strong family ties and strict codes 50 of discipline.

Curb

The West Indian elders—and their newspapers—are quick to denounce deprivation and what they see as 55 discrimination.

It is time for them to curb the growing spirit of rebellion and lawlessness among their people, especially the youngsters.

The forces of law and order will be 60 fully deployed. But they can only do so much.

If decent men and women of West Indian origin do not maintain peace then there is a real danger that their 65 communities will be permanently alienated.

That would be a desperate tragedy for everyone—particularly the West Indians. 70

Text of *Sun*, September 30, 1985. Used with permission.

point that is conceptually argued for by excluding other, noncriminal causes of his death. The use of *deliberate* emphasizes that it was intentional and hence murder, and *hacked to death* and *savagely* stress that it was not just common murder but a brutal and bestial murder, thereby associating the perpetrators with savages, a familiar racist categorization of blacks. The point is further supported by a rhetorical contrast, namely, between *savage murderers*, on the one hand, and a *good man* who *defended firemen from the mob*, on the other hand. Note that the supporting argument is purely conceptual and rhetorical: No evidence is provided that the murder was indeed deliberate or premeditated.

The second point, made with much rhetorical flourish in the second paragraph, is that this murder (and implicitly, the riots during which it occurred) bring Britain one step closer to the *apocalyptic vision so grimly imparted by Enoch Powell*. Informed British newspaper readers know that this "vision" of Powell was that, because of conflicts due to immigration, "the Thames, like the Roman Tiber, would be filled with blood." The *Mail* not only quotes but also seems to share this vision of the notorious racist Tory MP. This second point is more general. From the death of one policeman, the *Mail* concludes that Britain is heading for its racial apocalypse. In other words, the first point is made in order to support a more general, but as yet more or less implicit point, namely, that of the fundamental and inevitable conflict of a multiracial society. This more general point is further emphasized by a familiar other-discrediting truth claim, namely that those who deny it are "blinkered" and "self-deceivers."

The implications of this truth claim are literally spelled out in the next paragraph. After another drama-enhancing image (*death-born*), the *Mail* engages in a familiar move of the right-wing press, namely, that they are the only ones who see and tell the truth on ethnic affairs. This is important, because many of the other editorials and news reports about ethnic affairs repeatedly claim that "the truth is taboo" or "we are no longer free to tell the truth," thereby attacking anti-racists who are alleged to act like the Inquisition when criticizing "honest" evaluations about minorities.

The core of this editorial and its argumentative structure is expressed in the next paragraph: Blacks must obey the laws, or else . . . A few lines later, the *Mail* correctly categorizes this utterance as a warning. In other words, the argumentative strategy of this editorial is not to defend a position or an opinion, but to sustain the specific speech act of a warning. It would be interesting to examine whether the usual pragmatic appropriateness conditions of this speech act are satisfied. One might question, for instance, whether the ensuing threat, embodied in the "or else" clause, is a negative action under control of the *Mail*. If so, the fascist street agitators may be seen as the troops that can be called on by the tabloid or the political power elites it represents. If not, the warning would, at least under one interpretation, be void. On the other hand, if the *Mail* is issuing a warning for such forms of fascism, then it seems to attribute it not to its own incitement to racial hatred, but to the black population.

Note that the warning itself consists of several local argumentative moves. If blacks are warned to obey the laws of *this land where they have taken up residence and accepted both the full rights and responsibilities of citizenship*, this qualification is far from innocent. First, it expresses the well-known ideological value of assimilation, familiar from most forms of racist discourse. Second, it presupposes that blacks have acquired full rights in Britain, a presupposition that many blacks might well want to contest in light of the consistent and widely documented limitations of their human and civil rights (CCCS, 1982). This presupposition also implies the customary belief that Britain itself has done everything it could for its immigrants, and therefore the black community is itself to blame, especially when it does not take up its responsibilities. So, the argumentative support for the warning is in fact a legitimation. We see that this legitimation is not limited to the speech act of the warning, but also extends to an implied threat, that of unleashing the forces of fascism and the Powellite calls for forced repatriation.

The next paragraph essentially repeats the threat in a different form and with the same rhetorical formulation. Note that it is not a small group of "rioters" being warned, but the whole black community. Indeed, the *Mail* may seem to agitate against rioters, but it uses the events to make a much more general point about the position of blacks in the country—that they should "know their place." In such an ideology, the warning to adapt is in fact a warning to submit.

Describing the police as the *men and women whose task it is to uphold the laws of this land*, is more than a stylistic circumlocution; it is another local argumentative move to justify the warning: Those who attack the police are in fact attacking the laws they uphold, and hence the "land" itself. In other words, through the violent actions of its youths, the black community as a whole is represented as waging war against white Britain.

While the first column of this editorial is a dramatic introduction to and the execution of a threatening warning, the rest of the editorial seems to soften the blow of those harsh words. This second part features the usual disclaimers, replete with various moves of positive self-presentation, intended to avoid the impression that the *Mail* is in fact colluding with the fascists and the Powellites. The disclaimers have a classical structure: We aren't happy with such a warning, we don't agree with Powell, and we don't want French-style riot squads, *but* . . . Although it seems this paragraph is intended to show that the *Mail* is not defending right-wing authoritarianism, it in fact prepares the next move, namely, that the "riots" make such a position inevitable, thereby again blaming the blacks, exonerating the right for its possible racist actions, and at the same time legitimating the warning.

The following paragraphs (lines 50-57) further support the warning by commonsense normative reasoning, which describes the situation in such a way that any reasonable citizen would undoubtedly agree that it cannot be tolerated: We can't allow the police to be attacked and the inner cities to become criminal areas. Appeals to reason are a well-known move in such arguments.

Then the *Mail* proceeds to an even more seductive series of argumentative moves, also carried out to enhance its positive image: There are real problems in the inner cities and most people living there are peaceable. This familiar disclaimer ("There are also good ones among them, *but* . . . ") seems rather inconsistent with the previous derogation and warning to Britain's black community as a whole, therefore we should indeed interpret it for what it is, namely, a strategic form of self-presentation using the familiar move of the Apparent Concession. The *Mail* goes even further and recommends government help and an independent investigation when *a citizen is killed or dies during a police operation*. Notice the customary syntactic device of the passive voice in the mitigation of responsibility: The passage does not say: "When the police kill an innocent citizen."

That these are the first (positive) parts of the disclaimer is shown by the next paragraph (lines 76-79), starting, as expected, with *but*: Blacks must decide their own destiny. This repeats the macro-topic of this editorial, already implied by the headline and the warning analyzed above. However, its stylistic formulation is much less aggressive in this case, and therefore an understatement of what is really meant, namely, that the blacks either adapt (obey the laws, and so on) or else our racists and fascists will get them.

The last paragraph finally spells out in somewhat more detail *what* the blacks are required to do to avoid such a bleak future: discipline their young, find cooperative leaders, and encourage blacks to police their own community. These final recommendations are in line with the conservative view of race relations in Britain, and with a conservative ideology in general, namely, the application of authority and discipline, the suppression of challenge and opposition (leaders must be "cooperative," that is, meek) and the ghetto should solve its own problems by providing the agents for its own oppression.

Summing up, we find that this editorial has a complex argumentative and rhetorical structure, built around the main pragmatic point, which is the warning that blacks should behave, or else. This warning is introduced by a sequence of dramatic argumentative moves that emphasize the seriousness of the racial situation in Britain and hence support the appropriateness and the harshness of the warning. The second part also legitimates the warning, but does so in the guise of quasi-liberal, positively presented "good intentions," which nonetheless lead to the same conclusion, that the blacks should obey the laws and generally behave in the way that we want them to.

Although this argumentative structure is quite explicit, it should be stressed that at crucial points it operates by implications, presuppositions, suggestions, innuendo, mitigation, and other forms of indirectness. Whereas the first part about the police killing is cast in apocalyptic terms, and thereby legitimates the warning, the softer second part is intended to ward off the possibly negative conclusions that might be drawn about the moral and political position of the *Mail* in the domain of ethnic affairs. To understand that this strategy of face-keeping is a communicative ploy, and not an expression of true attitudes, we need to know the actual policies and news reporting practices of this tabloid, which is hardly interested in generating either socioeconomic support for the inner cities or critical investigations of police actions.

It is also against this background that we should understand the *real point* of this editorial's argument, which is not about rioters or black people breaking the law, but about power and dominance, that is, about blacks and minorities in general who are being threatened into submission. At the same time, the point is made that the rise of racism and fascism in Britain should be blamed on the blacks themselves, thereby exonerating white society of its guilt feelings about its racism. In other words, editorial argumentation, even when seemingly explicit, is often a front for another argumentative agenda, in this case that of white dominance.

The Sun

The *Sun* also thinks that the blacks must act, and therefore also communicates a normative argumentative point, namely, an advice or recommendation. The contents and argumentative strategy are so similar to that of the *Mail* 8 days later that it seems as if the *Mail* editors had the *Sun* editorial at hand when writing theirs. If not, we may conclude that the controlling ideology giving rise to both editorials is both pervasive and strikingly similar.

Again, we first find the usual definition of the situation: black mob terror. This definition, which is an explicitly negative evaluation of blacks, at the same time introduces the moral category of the editorial, which is the recommendation that "the black community must take control of their young." The "or else" immediately following that piece of advice shows that this is not a friendly recommendation, but a warning. That otherwise the blacks would become the "outcasts of our land," is premised on the presupposition that they are not outcasts already, a point that also might be contested by many blacks. So far, the normative argument supporting the warning provides the core of the argument spelled out in the *Mail* a week later.

The rest of the editorial is a classic piece of argumentation. The *Sun* begins with stating (and negatively evaluating "foolish") a point of the opponent, namely, that the events in Brixton can be seen as revenge for the police shooting of a black woman. This argument needs to be contested, and the *Sun* does so by emphasizing that (a) the shooting was incidental (and hence, the police are innocent of structural violence), and (b) the woman's color was immaterial (and therefore, no "race riot" was called for). These defensive moves, which are not very strong, then give way to offensive moves: The riot was merely a pretext for destruction and more typical of the "trouble" in Brixton.

This argument could be interpreted as an attack on the black community as a whole, and therefore needs a disclaimer, which we indeed find in the next paragraphs. It goes along the usual lines, as is the case in the *Mail*: We have championed the rights of blacks and are against Powell's "heartless" repatriation calls. It needs little knowledge of the *Sun*'s racial attitudes (see, e.g., Hollingsworth, 1986) to understand that the claim about the defense of black rights is no more than a disclaimer, which is indeed completed by the following *yet*, introducing the mitigated *blind to pretend that all is well in our mixed race areas.*

Later in the editorial we also find the irrelevant statement that the West Indians are *quick to denounce deprivation and what they see as discrimination.* This familiar denial of racism and discrimination is, however, needed as a rejection of the possible counter-argument that the uprising should be seen as a justifiable action, that is, of rage against racism.

Next, the warning is further spelled out, also addressing the West Indian community and its leaders: Curb the rebellion of your youngsters, or else you will be alienated. Here, too, we encounter the rhetorical argumentation strategy of Apparent Praise ("You are a nice guy, *but . . .* "), when the West Indians are addressed as *decent men and women*, and that of Apparent Concern ("I wouldn't like that to happen to you, *but . . .* "), when the *Sun* seems to say that such alienation would be a tragedy for the West Indians.

Note that the *Sun* also uses another argument, that of Asian obedience. This argument, already made in earlier reporting, is based on the familiar stereotype that whereas West Indians are rebellious, Asians are meek and well adapted (run corner shops, fit into the framework of the Thatcherist ideology of popular capitalism). In other words, the *Sun* suggests a division between Asians and West Indians, sometimes even pretending that the blacks are jealous of the Asians, as was the case in the coverage of the Handsworth "riot" a few weeks earlier, and sets the Asians as the good example. Apart from dividing the ethnic communities, the tabloid also seems to imply that it does not have a general dislike of minorities and therefore cannot be accused of racism.

The rather straightforward argumentation of the *Sun* is also intended to support the normative conclusion that the blacks should behave, or else. Again, this warning is premised on the interpretation of the events in terms of "mob terror" and destruction. The consequence part of the warning ("if not . . .") is formulated less threateningly than in the *Mail*. Instead of fascist retaliation, we here find self-alienation, which also blames the victim. Yet, such claims need the usual liberal disclaimer in order to be morally sound, so the *Sun* adds a ritual emphasis of its positive attitude toward black rights and its critical position toward Powell.

As we also concluded in our analysis of the *Mail* editorial, however, there are hidden points that are implicitly argued for. Beyond the warning that the black community should curb *the rebellion and lawlessness among their people*, there is also the message that the black community in general should behave and adapt, like the Asians, or else. That is, if they become alienated, it will be their own fault. So, the warning is associated with a preview of future forms of blaming the victim.

Editorial Power

Our analysis of two editorials in the British tabloid press has given us an idea about the textual strategies, as well as the underlying cognitive, social, political, and cultural aspects, of media argumentation.

Urban disturbances, involving (mostly but not exclusively) young black people, are first of all categorized as "riots," and defined in terms of black crime and violence, not as forms of resistance or expressions of rage and frustration. With such an interpretation, the next step is the evaluation of such "riots" in terms of intentional criminal behavior of blacks (e.g., protection of drugs business) or the lack of adaptation to British rules, laws, and life-styles. The final Conclusion is that blacks must adapt and submit themselves, or else they must either leave or endure fascism and marginalization.

Both locally and globally these major propositions of the editorial schema are realized by argumentative and rhetorical strategies and moves. The main argumentative point is a warning: Blacks must adapt/ submit, or else. The moves that support this concluding warning are first of all the rhetorical emphasis (using dramatic lexical items, metaphors, and hyperbole) of the negative definition of the situation, attributing the blame fully to black people—and exonerating the white institutions, such as the police and the conservative government. The alternative for the threat is racism. Second, however, face-keeping disclaimers soften this harsh warning by emphasizing the good intentions and correct ethnic position of the newspaper, and the apparent concession that there are also "good blacks." However, these disclaimers only introduce a repetition of the warning that the black community must behave, adapt itself, discipline its youths, choose compliant leaders, and so on.

In other words, the argumentative structure of the editorials is not just a persuasively formulated opinion about the riots and the involvement of blacks. Rather, the editorials have a broader political and sociocultural function, namely, to argue politically for control over black people and for the reproduction of white dominance, that is, for white law and order, the marginalization of the black community, the legitimation of white neglect in ethnic affairs, and finding excuses for right-wing racism and reaction. We again find that the media elites and their discourses, even when operating autonomously, as they typically do in their editorials, play a role in the broader framework of the reproduction of elite racism, specifically by colluding with and legitimating those other elite groups that effectively enact white group dominance. Their power resource is the ability to manufacture public opinion, so that they feel entitled to not only criminalize and marginalize minority groups but also threaten them into submission by making allusions to racist reactions.

Conclusions

Our summary of some research on the portrayal of ethnic relations in the press rather unambiguously shows a number of pervasive properties of media racism. First of all, there is ample straightforward evidence to show that minority journalists have less access to the media, and tend to be promoted less to higher editorial positions. Second, the routines of news-making, as well as news values and social cognitions of journalists, jointly favor access of elite news actors and sources that are usually white. As a result, their perspective, interests, and definitions of the ethnic situation have a much higher chance of being credibly described and quoted. Third, socialization and professionalization of journalists, as well as group membership of white journalists, contribute to the development of social cognitions that generally tend to favor the own group, if not derogate the out-group. This will also influence the formation of biased models of ethnic situations, which are the cognitive basis of news stories.

These conditions of newsmaking have their unmistakable effect on the news reports themselves. Systematic discourse analysis of more than 5,000 news reports in the Dutch and British press, as well as research results of others, show first of all that the very topics of news on ethnic affairs convey an overall impression that associates minorities or immigrants with problems, conflicts, deviance, or even threats. Crime, violence, drugs, and riots are usually among the most frequently covered topics on ethnic minorities, especially but not exclusively in the right-wing and popular press. Immigration is also often covered, but news reports on that issue focus on problems, large numbers, immigration rackets, or "economic" refugees who are seen as coming to live off our pockets. Cultural differences are enhanced and are often negatively interpreted as the cause of numerous social problems associated with a multicultural society. The topic of race relations focuses on discrimination, which, nonetheless, is often played down or denied in the right-wing press, or dealt with as simply incidents. Generally, topics that are of interest for ethnic minority groups are covered much less. In particular, all topics that imply a critique of the white dominant group in general, or of the authorities or other elites in particular, are seldom covered. Racism, failing legislation against discrimination, the refusal to enact Affirmative Action, the real causes of high unemployment among minority groups or the schools' lack of success in providing minority children with motivation and a good education, are among the many topics that tend to be avoided.

This polarization in the portrayal of ethnic affairs also appears in quotation patterns. On virtually all topics, white elites are quoted most frequently, most extensively, and most credibly. Especially on sensitive issues, such as prejudice, discrimination, and racism, minorities are either not quoted or they are quoted with doubt or distance. In some situations they are allowed to tell about their experiences, but seldom when these reflect negatively on white elites. More generally, anti-racist criticism of the authorities, especially by minority leaders, is seldom quoted, or if quoted at all, is usually accompanied by quotes from white elites.

On the level of local semantic, rhetorical, and stylistic strategies, we finally find the actual implementation of the topics mentioned above. Our examples, especially from the right-wing British press, show that on the whole minority groups, anti-racists, and the Left tend to be portrayed negatively, if not vilified; whereas, whites and British institutions are presented as tolerant. Implications, presuppositions, vagueness, comparisons, disclaimers, and many other semantic moves thus contribute to an overall strategy that presents ethnic out-groups and their supporters as a fundamental problem, if not a threat to white society, while presenting Us as either neutral or positive. Aggressive style registers and rhetorical figures further enhance this semantic contrast between Us and Them. The right-wing press accordingly sees itself as the valiant defender of the white group, culture, and nation, and their norms and values, and sees all those who challenge it as its real opponents in a struggle over symbolic power in the ideological definition of the ethnic situation.

At many points in this chapter it has become clear that the press is not passive in these forms of discursive reproduction of racism. It does not simply mimic or mediate the power of the political or corporate elites. It has its own power domain in the power structure and actively contributes to the legitimation of white group dominance. Its own hiring and promotion practices, its newsmaking routines, its choice of topics, quotation patterns, semantic and stylistic strategies are an inherent part of its autonomous, symbolic role in the ideological system of social reproduction.

Similarly, despite its occasionally "popular" appeals, the press does not simply "speak for the people." Rather, it preformulates and persuasively conveys ethnic opinions from top to bottom, and our earlier research on topics and prejudiced opinions in everyday conversations shows that biased media coverage of minorities is quite successful (van Dijk, 1987a; see also Windisch, 1978). Thus, in ethnic affairs it will help manufacture and then use "popular" resentment against immigrants and minorities, coupled with socioeconomic frustrations among poor whites, to argue in favor of the interests of white group dominance. More specifically, however, the press is interested in the white elites, not in the poverty of the inner city or in the predicaments of the working class. Its reproduction of racism, therefore, is essentially a contribution to the reproduction of elite racism—primarily that of the media themselves, and secondarily that of the political and corporate elites.

The Media and the Symbolic Management of White Elite Discourse

For the major issue addressed in this book, namely, the role of the discourses of various elites in the reproduction of racism, these results, as well as those of other research on the coverage of ethnic affairs in the media, suggest that this role of the media, and especially that of the press, are crucial. Although the press in many respects depends on its many sources, and although news routines, professional ideologies of newsworthiness, as well as social cognitions and social contexts of white journalists obviously favor white elite actors and institutions as their regular and credible sources, we found that the press appears to be doing more than passively mediating or reproducing the ethnic events, actions, and opinions of these elite actors and sources, or those of ethnic minority groups and their members.

Variations in ethnic coverage between conservative and liberal, quality and tabloid newspapers alone suggest a measure of autonomy and hence relative power. Each newspaper has its own means to select news items, use and quote sources, establish major or minor topics, describe news actors, and characterize ethnic news events. In this respect, the media not only control the amount and the nature of public information about ethnic affairs, but also set the major textual conditions for their suggested interpretation by the reading public.

This does *not* mean, however, that this process of influence, and hence of power, is straightforward and without contradictions, let alone that the reading public is passive and gullible. After all, despite the power of the press, and despite the overwhelmingly white-centered coverage of ethnic affairs, there are at least small groups of readers, not least among minorities themselves, who have an explicit anti-racist ideology. However, we may assume that only those readers who have personal experiences, who participate in political organizations, and who have explicit attitudes or information sources that enable them to resist the strongly preferred interpretation frameworks of the media, will generally be able to challenge this powerful push for consent and consensus. Empirical research regarding attitudes on ethnic affairs clearly shows that people with such explicitly anti-racist attitudes form a small minority, seldom exceeding 10% of the population and often much less than that (see the references given in Chapter 2).

In other words, whereas some of the other power elites, especially those in politics and academic research, have the means, position, status, or expertise to provide initial definitions of ethnic events, such a formulation would be virtually without effect outside the specific domain of such elites if not covered, adopted, and emphasized by the mass media. In this way, interpretations of opponent elite groups that resist the dominant ethnic consensus, for example, on the political left and in research and education, may be censored, manipulated, marginalized, or even criminalized by the media, left or right.

The media have become, so to speak, the *managers* of public opinion by allocating space to and emphasizing the voice of those elites—and sometimes, indirectly, of those sections of the population at large—that they believe should be heard, while muffling or silencing the voices that should not be heard. In other social and political domains there are other ways to reach and influence elite and popular opinion, such as everyday conversation, specialized media, or the small radical press (Downing, 1984). However, this is much less the case for ethnic affairs information and opinion, simply because virtually all information about minorities and ethnic events for the public at large is communicated through the mass news media.

Only some small, often left-wing, political magazines, scholarly papers, and books; some educational discourse; minor publications of organizations such as the unions, parties, and churches; as well as movies and literature, among others, are in principle the few public media and discourses able to escape this mass media hegemony of information and opinion formation on ethnic affairs. Unfortunately, as we have seen before for other elite domains, these alternative information sources and media do not always formulate the clear anti-racist attitudes necessary for effective resistance against the dominant consensus.

On the contrary, the range of ethnic attitudes represented in these other domains and media rather closely reflects the range of ethnic attitudes represented in the news media. Therefore, the problem of media power and influence is not only in its unique managing position, its orchestration, and its allocation of public voice, but also because it reflects and confirms the ideological range represented by other elites.

This is one of the reasons why the media so seldom take the initiative for social change and why, despite its occasional activism, media power is in a sense also rather passive. Rather, the media are the prime conduit for the reproduction of the consensus, including its many variations.

Only when social groups themselves, such as minority groups in the case of opinion formation about ethnic affairs, take the initiative and are able to expropriate some elements of dominant group power, are they also able to propose a redefinition of the situation that may be adopted (and adapted) by some white elite groups and organizations, which in turn may become increasingly legitimate in the media, thereby contributing to a change of consensus. The prime examples of such a moderate change in the dominant consensus during the past decades have been the women's movement and especially the ecology movement.

In the complex field of elite groups, influences, and interactions, the mass media play a fundamental role in shaping both elite and popular attitudes and ideologies of the white majority. Quite obviously, this is not only the case because of their symbolic role in the management of elite and public opinion in present-day "information societies." Rather, this is because the news media basically reproduce opinions within the boundaries of a consensus manufactured by a white elite. Moreover, the mass media are predominantly white institutions and business corporations, and as such they also have a moral mission—to plead the cause of their own white, Western group.

8

Conclusions

THE ROLE OF THE ELITES

Against the background of earlier work on the reproduction of racism through discourse and communication, this study focused on the role of white elites in the reproduction of ethnic and racial inequality in Europe and North America. It was found that text and talk of the political, corporate, academic, educational, and media elites often preformulate stereotypes and prejudices about minorities, define the ethnic situation, legitimate elite discrimination, and thus contribute to the manufacture of the ethnic consensus and to the maintenance of white group dominance in Western societies.

This does not mean that contemporary elite discourse is always blatantly racist. On the contrary, more or less shared official egalitarian and humanitarian norms and values in ethnic relations require a more subtle, indirect, and strategic way of speaking or writing about ethnic minority groups. Assertions expressing lofty ideals of hospitality, understanding, and tolerance, as well as emphatic denials of racism, may thus combine with more or less overt forms of derogation, marginalization, and problematization of immigrants, refugees, or other minority groups. In this way, the general strategy of positive self-presentation discursively enables and legitimizes the general strategy of negative other-presentation, while at the same time expressing, especially among elites, a self-image as moral leaders in society. Additionally, it should be stressed that other, often marginalized, white elites also play an important role, together with minority groups, in the resistance against discrimination, prejudice, and racism.

THEORETICAL FRAMEWORK

The theoretical framework in which such elite discourse and racism are conceptualized is both complex and interdisciplinary. It involves an analysis of racism as a form of group dominance, both at the micro and macro levels of societal analysis, as well as a systematic study of discourse, communication, and social cognition as crucial constitutive elements in the reproduction processes of this white group dominance. Although it is recognized that there is an interplay between actions and social cognitions of elites and the white majority at large, the overall direction of influence is assumed to be essentially top-down. The major arguments for this assumption are both empirical and theoretical: The elites control or have preferential access to the institutional or organizational means of symbolic reproduction. That is, they strongly influence public discourse and opinion in a social domain in which other sources of information and opinion formation are scarce. Moreover, generalized white group resistance against ethnic inequality is highly unlikely because ethnic dominance is in the best interest of the white group as a whole.

Thus, in the domain of ethnic relations the various elite groups are involved in a relation of "double dominance," namely, as decision makers and opinion leaders within their own white group and, across group boundaries, as those who control virtually all important life situations of relatively powerless ethnic minority groups, such as immigration, residence, housing, employment, social welfare, education, research, and media. In sum, the elites manage and control ethnic dominance relations, and their discourses enact, support, and legitimate such dominance.

The approach chosen for the account of such patterns of elite dominance is critical and a multidisciplinary analysis of discourse, which also emphasizes that elite dominance is usually enacted and legitimated through text and talk. This analysis relates a systematic description of the various levels and dimensions of discourse with those of the underlying social cognitions of group members. The structures and strategies of social discourse and cognition are then related to their sociocultural and political contexts, such as communicative situations as well as institutions, groups, or dominance relations at the macro level. In this study, however, this discourse approach is rather informal, so as to ensure accessibility to students and scholars of other disciplines.

PARLIAMENTARY DISCOURSE

The respective chapters of this book have shown in detail how these elite contributions to ethnic inequality are implemented at the various levels of discourse and communication. A study of the ways parliamentarians in Great Britain, Germany, France, the Netherlands, and the United States speak about immigration and ethnic relations strongly suggests that politicians are among the most influential initial definers of the ethnic situation. Whether regarding the immigration of refugees or on Affirmative Action in employment, they not only make the most consequential decisions in the lives of ethnic minorities or about majority-minority relations, they also crucially influence the agenda for public debate and the political and ideological boundaries of consent and dissent.

Nationalist rhetoric of hospitality and civil rights slogans against discrimination play the part of positive self-presentation in their discourse. At the same time, such debates are replete with subtle and—especially on the Right—not so subtle assertions and suggestions that problematize, marginalize, or (sometimes literally) exclude immigrants or other minorities. Thus, immigration, settlement, housing, employment, education, and cultural integration are all presented as fundamentally problematic, rather than as a positive challenge or contribution to the country. Similarly, immigrants and other minorities are often associated with illegality, fraud, deviance, crime, violence, passivity, or lack of cultural adaptation. That is, they are represented as a threat to Our country and society. Populist rhetoric further seeks to legitimate such discourse and discriminatory decisions, for example, by seemingly following the democratic road of listening to the people's voice and paying attention to popular "resentment," which politicians have helped to instill or confirm in the first place. Another major ploy in such parliamentary debates is to present restrictive measures as if they were in the best interests of the immigrants or minorities themselves.

CORPORATE DISCOURSE

Although corporate text and talk may be less influential in public debates on ethnic affairs, their role in the lives of ethnic minorities is crucial, especially in decisions and legitimation of hiring and promotion practices. As the analysis of parliamentary debates has also shown,

corporate attitudes and discourse are similarly influential in national pol-
icy-making and legislation on civil rights and equal opportunities. Analysis
of Dutch corporate discourse on ethnic affairs, and especially on Affirmative Action, shows that employers are generally reluctant to hire minorities,
while at the same time emphasizing that they do not discriminate. Indeed,
managers claim that they will hire anybody who has the required qualities,
and that they also know their social responsibilities.

On the other hand, their discursive strategies feature seemingly
reasonable and rational arguments, based on an ideology of the freedom
of enterprise, in which state intervention, and hence also Affirmative
Action legislation, are resolutely rejected as incompatible with such
freedom. Unequal participation of ethnic minorities in the work force
is generally blamed on the victim, and explained in terms of allegedly
lacking education and linguistic abilities, or attributed to cultural differences or inherent character flaws of minorities. With the argument
that businesses are not social welfare offices, they simultaneously
blame the State for not fulfilling its own responsibilities in adequately
preparing minorities for the labor market.

ACADEMIC DISCOURSE

Scholarly discourse and its implications permeate virtually all other
forms of elite discourse and decisions on ethnic affairs. The description
and explanation of the Other have a long tradition in the historical,
philosophical, sociological, anthropological, and psychological accounts
of other peoples, countries, or races. Racist ideologies and practices
were explicitly supported by, or indirectly legitimated with references
to "scientifically" established inherent differences between races or
ethnic groups. However, with the exception of a small but influential
and vociferous fringe of scholars in the social and natural sciences, for
example, in biosociology and psychology, postwar scholarly discourse
has kept its distance from such blatant racist explanations and legitimations
of social inequality. Analysis of introductory sociology textbooks used in
Great Britain and the United States confirms this general development
toward a more liberal and multicultural account of ethnic relations.

This does not mean that all sociological discourse has now espoused
explicitly anti-racist views. On the contrary, while some textbooks
continue to marginalize ethnic minority groups, ignore racism, and still
provide neo-Darwinist explanations of ethnic or racial differences,

others more subtly show lack of understanding of discrimination and racism, ignore minority contributions to the field, or continue to describe ethnic relations from a white perspective. Only a few textbooks conceptualize ethnic relations in terms of white group dominance, and only some of them detail the everyday lives and experiences of minority groups. In sum, most students of sociology are ill prepared to understand the basic mechanisms of the multiethnic societies in which they are living.

EDUCATIONAL DISCOURSE

This conclusion is a fortiori true for textbooks in secondary education. Analysis of social science textbooks used in Dutch secondary schools shows first that immigrants or other ethnic minorities tend to be ignored altogether in half of the books. The other books pay scant attention to ethnic groups and relations and tend to focus on attributed cultural differences, which are invariably associated with negative consequences for Us. In this manner, stereotypes and occasionally even blatant prejudices characterize most passages on the Others, as is also the case for textbook discourse on the Third World. The Others are poor, stupid, backward, superstitious, aggressive, totalitarian, and the like. At the same time their own group is associated with positive properties, namely, modernity, democracy, hospitality, tolerance, and unselfishly helpful to Them. As in other forms of elite discourse, discrimination and racism are ignored, mitigated, or discussed only for the past or for other countries, as is also the case for the reality and consequences of slavery, colonialism, and segregation. Historical and cultural backgrounds and contributions of minority groups are similarly ignored.

Didactic assignments sometimes legitimate blatantly racist opinions by asking students to debate pro or con such opinions. At the same time, both theory and assignments often presuppose that the classroom is still wholly white. Although current textbooks, especially in the United States, have significantly improved when compared to the traditional ones, most of them, especially in Europe, still remain Eurocentric, replete with stereotypes, and ignorant of racism and ethnic power relations in contemporary Western societies. These findings confirm much other research on the portrayal of minorities in textbooks and children's books. Since this is often the first and only official discourse on other groups and peoples students are confronted with before their adult life, it is legitimate to conclude that the images thus constructed of the Others will play an important role in the development of the social attitudes of both black and white students.

NEWS DISCOURSE

Only the mass media, from movies, news, advertising, and television series to news and editorials in the press, are able to correct this biased portrayal of other peoples and minorities provided by textbooks. Unfortunately, this is not the case. On the contrary, our own earlier research on the press, as well as many other studies of the representation of ethnic affairs in the media, unambiguously show that the media also participate in the elite consensus of positive self-presentation and negative other-presentation. Hiring and promotion of minority journalists, especially in Europe, remain blatantly discriminatory; and the newsroom is still largely white. Obviously this favors white-centered newsgathering, beats, socialization, social cognitions, and mental models of ethnic events. Access to the news media is virtually limited to, and controlled by, white elites. As is also clear from much other research, the portrayal of minority groups in the news generally remains stereotypical and focuses on problems, if not on deviance and threats.

Preferred topics are illegal and ominous immigration, crime, problematic cultural differences, and the many difficulties of race relations. Although discrimination may be covered, though usually as a personal and incidental problem, racism is generally denied or mitigated, and anti-racists marginalized. Other topics that are relevant for minority readers are similarly ignored. Minority representatives are quoted less and seldom quoted alone, and such quotation patterns confirm the lack of credibility and the limited access minorities have to news production and news discourses. Style and semantic and rhetorical moves at the micro level of analysis confirm this generally negative perspective on ethnic minorities.

Overall, in the press, too, white elites define the ethnic situation. The various structures and news discourse and their conditions of access, news production, hiring, socialization, and social cognition of journalists exhibit this collusion between the press and other white elite groups, such as politicians, scholars, the judiciary, and corporate business. However, the news media are not solely dependent on the other elites, nor do they merely manage the communication, also about ethnic affairs, among other elite groups. They also have a powerful autonomous role because they control the forms of public discourse on ethnic affairs, if not, in part, their contents, because of their special control over selection and emphasis of source texts of other elites. This power of the press as a sociocultural or symbolic institution is constrained only by the position of newspapers as competitive corporations, by advertisers, and—indirectly—by the interests of the readers. Since most of these are white, we may expect little resistance against the prevalent ethnic attitudes and practices of the press.

LIMITATIONS AND FUTURE RESEARCH

Although this study has provided strong theoretical and empirical evidence for our main thesis about the prominent role of various elites in the reproduction of racism, it has obvious, sometimes self-imposed, limitations. First, the inquiry should be extended to many more countries. Only some of our data and conclusions, such as those on parliamentary discourse, are fairly representative of Western political discourse. The same is true for our insight into the role of the press, education, and scholarship. Other genres, such as corporate discourse, require further empirical research. Except from Great Britain, Germany, Austria, and the Netherlands, we lack systematic evidence about elite discourse on ethnic affairs in most other European countries. In many respects, for instance, in media, corporate, and educational discourse, we suspect a rather clear difference between most European countries and the United States. In the United States, the Civil Rights Movement and more powerful and better organized minority groups have at least been able to change the more overt forms of discourse and social practices, in the face of the more fundamental and structural inequalities that remain.

Second, the empirical basis of this book should also be broadened to include other elites and discourse genres, such as the discourses of the police, the judiciary, the bureaucracy, the welfare institutions, the medical professions, the military, the churches, the trade unions, and so on. Although their discourse undoubtedly has less, or less direct, influence on public discourse and opinion formation, they are crucial in the everyday lives of minorities, given the decisions and discriminatory— or oppositional—practices enacted or legitimated by such elites (Essed, 1991).

Third, the discourse analyses of this study have intentionally been kept at a very informal level. Only a few technical notions were used to characterize elite text and talk, so as to ensure broad accessibility of this study for students and scholars in several disciplines. Obviously, from a theoretical and methodological point of view, this is unsatisfactory—and somewhat frustrating for the researcher. Once the interdisciplinary domain of the study of racism in discourse and communication has been further developed, we need to proceed to more sophisticated analyses of style, rhetoric, semantics, pragmatics, or conversational structures of such text and talk, if only in specialized journal articles. The same is true for the analysis of the relations between these discourse structures and the structures and strategies of social cognition and the sociocultural and political contexts of elite discourse and communication. Indeed, as yet we know very little about the more specific impact of elite discourse, in particular situations and for particular genres, on the public at large. This is also necessary, given the increasing subtlety of contemporary elite discourse and racism.

Finally, we need more empirical and theoretical insight into the complex interplay of the social, political, and cultural relations among various elite groups and institutions, on the one hand, and between elites and white majority groups in general, on the other hand. For information and communication, and hence for opinion formation, on ethnic affairs, we have generally assumed that the direction of major influence is top-down, rather than bottom-up. Even if elites often seem more tolerant, liberal, or modern in their ethnic attitudes and discourses than specific segments of, for instance, the working class and especially the lower-middle class, our own evidence, research on the experiences of minorities, as well as massive empirical data about remaining forms of discriminatory practices, strongly suggest that at least large segments of the elites generally furnish the bad example in the first place. In our case this is particularly true, since the political, educational, scholarly, and media elites have virtually exclusive access to and control over the means of symbolic reproduction.

Although we do believe that the evidence supports this general conclusion, it should be emphatically stressed that there are many complexities and contradictions that need further research and explanation. For one, we have virtually ignored the role of oppositional, dissident, or anti-racist white elites. Also, though slow and not without reactions, there is positive change in ethnic relations, especially since the late 1960s. When seen in a broad perspective, interethnic attitudes and practices show increasing awareness of multicultural norms and values. Blatant and overt forms of racism are diminishing, or are at least marginalized, also because of the increasing awareness and resistance of minority groups.

This definitely does not mean that there are no lapses. On the contrary, the 1980s, the Reagan and Thatcher years, witnessed a true white backlash, supported by conservative philosophies that also characterized the socio-economic domain. The same is true for the increasing racism and xenophobia in continental European countries. In other words, advances and progress during one period, and in some domains, may be temporarily turned back in other times. Though they are occasionally dramatic and influential, we tend to see such reactions as the usual reactions of a conservative rear guard against the social changes toward a multicultural society. The fundamental changes in the power relations in Western societies cannot be abolished without falling back to dictatorship. On the other hand, this study has also emphasized that despite the many changes in white (elite and other) attitudes and practices, when compared to the prewar period, some of these changes were only superficial, and that there are also more fundamental continuities: White group dominance, even when more indirect and subtle, is still firmly in place.

Despite our top-down hypothesis, we do not assume that the masses are either gullible or passive and blindly accepting of white elite attitudes on ethnic affairs, such as through the media. It will certainly happen that personal experiences, for example, in mixed neighborhoods or on the job, also allow white people to form their own ethnic models, attitudes, and ideologies in agreement with their own interests. Also, there are limited ways such attitudes can be expressed (e.g., in popular demonstrations, racial attacks, meetings, local news media) without being preformulated by the elites. Our point is simply that such popular racism can be effectively reproduced through society only when it is at least partly endorsed by the elites. Hence, we need to study in more detail how popular discourse and racism may in turn influence or legitimate elite discourse and racism.

The same is true for the relations between the different elites. For instance, we need much more insight into the ways, say, politicians and journalists are being influenced by the discourses and attitudes of scholars and scientific research, and vice versa. Similarly, politicians may largely base their debates and decisions on technical (bureaucratic or academic) reports, but they may get more, or at least first-hand information on current ethnic affairs from their daily newspapers or television. The same may be true for scholars, bureaucrats, teachers, corporate managers, judges, and the police; hence, the vital role in our

theoretical framework of the modern mass media in the initial definitions of the ethnic situation and the public and inter-elite reproduction
of ethnic attitudes. Secondarily, definitions are then provided by the
reports of "experts," sometimes reported and popularized in the press,
and thus made available again to the public at large and the other elites.
All these mutual relations of discourse, influence, and social representations need to be spelled out in further detail in future studies of elite
discourse and racism.

POSTSCRIPT, JANUARY 1993

The thesis expounded in this book recently found one of its most
gruesome illustrations, when in Germany neo-Nazis set fire to a house of
a Turkish family in the village of Mölln. Two women and a child died in
the fire. This was perhaps the most fateful of more than 2,000 attacks in
1992 alone against refugees, immigrants, and minorities in Germany.
Among the many complex causes of this aggression against "foreigners,"
some stand out in all clarity: the continuous bickering of the politicians
about changing the constitution in view of stemming the "flow" of refugees
into the country, the inflammatory coverage of the issue of *Asylanten* by
the tabloids, and the failure of the same politicians, the police, as well as
the courts to take energetic action against this form of ethnic terror, as well
as against any form of racism, for that matter. At the same time this event
marked a change in the public reaction to the widespread attacks against
immigrants: Hundreds of thousands marched through the streets of Berlin,
Munich, Hamburg, and other cities in protest against such aggression and
xenophobia. This reaction from so many decent Germans is a sign of hope,
viz., that ordinary citizens may have begun to understand what xenophobia
and racial hatred may lead to. In the same way, many of the citizens of
Europe—and elsewhere—are now beginning to understand the moral of
the continuing story of the horrors of "ethnic cleansing" and the rape of
tens of thousands of Muslim women in Bosnia, still taking place at the time
of this writing, and against which our political, military, and other elites
so far have decided to do nothing. At the same time, we may hope that these
cataclysms of European "civilization" will open the eyes of all those,
especially the elites, who continue to belittle, deny, or conceal the nature
and the implications of ethnicism and racism, both in their overt, gruesome
forms, as well as in their more subtle forms of everyday prejudices and
discrimination against people of other colors and cultures.

Appendix

Following is a list of the Dutch social studies textbooks quoted in Chapter 6. All textbooks are published in the Netherlands.

Andeweg, H. (1986). *Succes! Lessen in maatschappijleer* [Success! Lessons in social science]. Kampen: Kok.

Caris, T., Kuiper, M., & Smulders, B. (1984). *Pluriform. Oriëntatie in samenleven* [Pluriform. Orientation in living together]. Vol. 2 (2nd ed.). Leiden: Spruyt, van Mantgem & de Does.

Van der Glind, A. (1984). *Kennis-Maken* ["Making knowledge": Getting acquainted]. Kampen: Kok.

Vannisselroy, H., et al. (1983). *Basisboek Maatschappijleer.* [Fundamentals of social science]. Groningen: Wolters Noordhoff.

II Holzhauer, F.F.O. *Hoe vinden we de weg in de samenleving?* [How do we find our way in society?] (2nd ed.). Leiden: Stenfert Kroese.

I Kalkwiek, W. F. (1982). *Materiaal voor maatschappelijke vorming* [Materials for social education] (3rd ed.). Amsterdam: Meulenhoff Educatief.

II Kalkwiek, W. F. (1983). *Maatschappij: Daar hoor je bij* [Society: You belong to it]. Vol. 1. Amsterdam: Meulenhoff Educatief.

III Kalkwiek, W. F. (1984). *Kernproblemen van de maatschappijleer* [Topics in social science]. Groningen: Wolters-Noorhoff.

References

Aboud, F. (1988). *Children and prejudice*. Oxford: Blackwell.

Adorno, T. W., Frenkel-Brunswik, E., Levinson, D. J., & Sanford, R. N. (1950). *The authoritarian personality*. New York: Harper.

Allen, P., & Swain, M. (Eds.). (1984). *Language issues and education policies: exploring Canada's multilingual resources*. New York: Pergamon.

Allport, G. W. (1954). *The nature of prejudice*. New York: Doubleday Anchor.

Althusser, L. (1971a). *Lenin and philosophy and other essays*. New York: Monthly Review Press.

Althusser, L., (1971b). Ideology and ideological state apparatuses. In L. Althusser, *Lenin and philosophy and other essays* (pp. 121-173). London: New Life Books.

Altschull, J. H. (1984). *Agents of power: The role of the news media in human affairs*. New York: Longman.

Amin, S. (1988). *Eurocentrism*. London: Zed Books.

Anwar, M., & Shang, A. (1982). *Television in a multi-racial society*. London: Commission for Racial Equality.

Apostle, R. A., Glock, C. Y., Piazza, T., & Suelze, M. (1983). *The anatomy of racial attitudes*. Berkeley: University of California Press.

Apple, M. W. (1979). *Ideology and curriculum*. London: Routledge & Kegan Paul.

Apple, M. W. (1982a). *Education and power*. Boston & London: Routledge & Kegan Paul.

Apple, M. W. (Ed.). (1982b). *Cultural and economic reproduction in education: Essays on class, ideology, and the state*. London: Routledge & Kegan Paul.

Apple, M. W., & Weis, L. (Eds.). (1983). *Ideology and practice in schooling*. Philadelphia: Temple University Press.

Arkin, R. M. (1981). Self-presentation styles. In J. T. Tedeschi (Ed.), *Impression management. Theory and social psychological research* (pp. 311- 333). New York: Academic Press.

Aronowitz, S. (1988). *Science as power: Discourse and ideology in modern society*. Minneapolis: University of Minnesota Press.

Asad, T. (Ed.). (1973). *Anthropology and the colonial encounter*. London: Ithaca Press.

Asante, M. K. (1987). *The Afrocentric idea*. Philadelphia: Temple University Press.

Bagdikian, B. H. (1983). *The media monopoly*. Boston: Beacon.

Banks, J. A. (1981). *Multiethnic education*. Boston: Allyn & Bacon.

294

Banks, J. A., & Lynch, J. (Eds.). (1986). *Multicultural education in Western societies.* London: Holt, Rinehart & Winston.

Barkan, E. (1992). *The retreat of scientific racism. Changing concepts of race in Britain and the United States between the world wars.* Cambridge, UK: Cambridge University Press.

Barker, A. J. (1978). *The African link: British attitudes to the negro in the era of the Atlantic slave trade, 1550-1807.* London: Frank Cass.

Barker, F., Hulme, P., Iversen, M., & Loxley, D. (Eds.). (1985). *Europe and its others* (2 vols.). Colchester, UK: University of Essex.

Barker, M. (1981). *The new racism.* London: Junction Books.

Barrett, M., Corrigan, P., Kuhn, A., & Wolff, J. (Eds.). (1979). *Ideology and cultural production.* London: Croom Helm.

Bar-Tal, D. (1990). *Group beliefs: A conception for analyzing group structure, processes, and behavior.* New York: Springer-Verlag.

Bar-Tal, D., Graumann, C. F., Kruglanski, A. W., & Stroebe, W. (Eds.). (1989). *Stereotyping and prejudice.* New York: Springer.

Bell, K. (1990). *Developing arguments: Strategies for reaching audiences.* Belmont, CA: Wadsworth.

Berger, A. A. (Ed.). (1991). *Media USA: Process and effect.* New York: Longman.

Billig, M. (1976). *Social psychology and intergroup relations.* London: Academic Press.

Billig, M. (1978). *Fascists.* London: Academic Press.

Billig, M. (1982). *Ideology and social psychology.* Oxford: Basil Blackwell.

Billig, M. (1988). The notion of "prejudice." Some rhetorical and ideological aspects. *Text, 8,* 91-110.

Blanchard, F. A., & Crosby, F. J. (Eds.). (1989). *Affirmative action in perspective.* New York: Springer-Verlag.

Bobo, L. (1983). White's opposition to busing: Symbolic racism or realistic group conflict? *Journal of Personality and Social Psychology, 45,* 1196-1210.

Bonnafous, S. (1991). *L'immigration prise aux mots* [Taking immigration at its word(s)]. Paris: Éditions Kimé.

Bottomore, T. B. (1964). *Elites and society.* London: C. A. Watts.

Bourdieu, P. (1984). *Homo academicus.* Paris: Minuit.

Bourdieu, P. (1988). *Language and symbolic power.* Cambridge, UK: Polity Press.

Bourdieu, P. (1989). *La noblesse d'état. Grandes écoles et esprit de corps* [State nobility. Grandes écoles and esprit de corps]. Paris: Minuit.

Bourdieu, P., & Passeron, J-C. (1977). *Reproduction: In education, society and culture.* London: Sage.

Bowser, B., & Hunt, R. G. (Eds.). (1981). *Impacts of racism on white Americans.* Beverly Hills, CA: Sage.

Braham, P., Rhodes, E., Pearn, M. (Eds.). (1981). *Discrimination and disadvantage in employment: The experience of black workers.* London: Harper & Row (in association with the Open University Press).

Brandt, G. L. (1986). *The realization of anti-racist teaching.* London: Falmer Press.

Brewer, M. B., & Kramer, R. M. (1985). The psychology of intergroup attitudes and behavior. *Annual Review of Psychology, 36,* 219-243.

Bryant, J., & Zillmann, D. (Eds.). (1986). *Perspectives on media effects.* Hillsdale, NJ: Lawrence Erlbaum.

Burstein, P. (1985). *Discrimination, jobs, and politics: The struggle for equal employment opportunity in the United States since the New Deal.* Chicago: University of Chicago Press.

Butterwegge, C., & Isola, H. (Eds.). (1991). *Rechtsextremismus im Vereinten Deutschland* [Right-extremism in Unified Germany]. Bremen: Steintor.

Button, G., & Casey, N. (1984). Generating topic: The use of topic initial elicitors. In J. M. Atkinson, & J. Heritage (Eds.), *Structures of social action* (pp. 167-190). London: Cambridge University Press.

Caditz, J. (1976). *White liberals in transition.* New York: Spectrum.

Carmichael, S., & Hamilton, C. (1967). *Black power.* New York: Vintage.

Cartwright, A. (Ed.). (1959). *Studies in social power.* Ann Arbor, MI: Institute of Social Research.

Castles, S. (1984). *Here for good. Western Europe's new ethnic minorities.* London: Pluto Press.

Castles, S., & Kosack, G. (1985). *Immigrant workers and class structure in Western Europe* (2nd ed.). Oxford: Oxford University Press.

Cazden, C. B. (1988). *Classroom discourse: The language of teaching and learning.* London: Heinemann Educ. Books.

CCCS (Centre for Contemporary Cultural Studies, Birmingham). (1982). *The empire strikes back. Race and racism in 70s Britain.* London: Hutchinson.

Chase, A. (1975). *The legacy of Malthus. The social costs of the new scientific racism.* Urbana: University of Illinois Press.

Chomsky, N. (1987). *On power and ideology: The Managua lectures.* South End Press.

Chomsky, N. (1992). *Deterring democracy.* London: Vintage.

CIBC (Council for Interracial Books for Children). (1980). *Guidelines for selecting bias-free textbooks and storybooks.* New York: Author.

Cicourel, A. V. (1973). *Cognitive sociology: Language and meaning in social interaction.* New York: Free Press.

Cicourel, A. (1983). Language and the structure of belief in medical communication. In S. Fisher & A. D. Todd (Eds.), *Discourse and institutional authority: Medicine, education, and law* (pp. 221-239). Norwood, NJ: Ablex.

Cicourel, A. V. (1987). Cognitive and organizational aspects of medical diagnostic reasoning. *Discourse Processes, 10,* 347-367.

Clayman, S. E. (1990). From talk to text—Newspaper accounts of reporter source interactions. *Media, Culture & Society, 12,* 79-103.

Clegg, S. R. (1989). *Frameworks of power.* London: Sage.

Cohen, R. (1987). *The new helots: Migrants in the international division of labour.* Hampshire, UK: Gower.

Cole, M. (1986). Teaching and learning about racism: A critique of multicultural education in Britain. In S. Modgil, G. K. Verma, K. Mallick, & C. Modgil (Eds.), *Multicultural education* (pp. 123-148). London: Falmer Press.

Combs, M. W., & Gruhl, J. (Eds.). (1986). *Affirmative action: Theory, analysis, and prospects.* McFarland.

Cottle, S. (1992). "Race," racialization and the media: A review and update of research. *Sage Race Relations Abstracts, 17*(2), 3-57.

Cross, M. (1987), "Equality of opportunity" and inequality of outcome: The MSC, ethnic minorities and training policy. In R. Jenkins & J. Solomos (Eds.), *Racism and equal opportunity policies in the 1980s* (pp. 73-92). Cambridge, UK: Cambridge University Press.

Daniel, J., & Allen, A. (1988). Newsmagazines, public policy, and the black agenda. In G. Smitherman-Donaldson, & T. A. van Dijk (Eds.), *Discourse and discrimination* (pp. 23-45). Detroit: Wayne State University Press.

De Jongh, R., Van der Laan, M., & Rath, J. (1984). *FNV'ers aan het woord over buitenlandse werknemers* [FNV members speak out about foreign workers]. Leiden: COMT, Rijksuniversiteit te Leiden.

Dekker, H., & Rozemond, S. A. (1983). *Maatschappijleer, analyse en visies* [Social science: Analysis and visions]. Culemborg: Educaboek.

Den Uyl, R., Choenni, C., & Bovenkerk, F. (1986). *Mag het ook een buitenlander wezen* [Will a foreigner do also?]. (LBR-reeks nr. 2). Utrecht: LBR.

Dickason, O. P. (1984). *The myth of the savage and the beginnings of French colonialism in the Americas*. Edmonton: University of Alberta Press.

Domhoff, G. W. (1978). *The powers that be. Processes of ruling class domination in America*. New York: Random House.

Domhoff, G. W., & Ballard, H. B. (Eds.). (1968). *C. Wright Mills and the power elite*. Boston: Beacon.

Donald, J., & Hall, S. (Eds.). (1986). *Milton Keynes: Open University politics and ideology: A reader.* Milton Keynes, UK: Open University Press.

Dovidio, J. F., & Gaertner, S. L. (Eds.). (1986). *Prejudice, discrimination, and racism*. New York: Academic Press.

Downing, J. (1984). *Radical media: The political experience of alternative communication*. Boston: South End Press.

Downing, J.D.H. (1980). *The media machine*. London: Pluto Press.

Downing, J., Mohammadi, A., & Sreberny-Mohammadi, A. (Eds.). (1990). *Questioning the media: A critical introduction*. London: Sage.

D'Souza, D. (1991). *Illiberal education: The politics of race and sex on campus*. New York: Free Press.

Du Bois, W.E.B. (1969). *The souls of black folk*. New York: New American Library.

Ebel, M., & Fiala, P. (1983). *Sous le consensus, la xénophobie* [Under the consensus, the xenophobia]. Lausanne: Institut de sciences politiques. Mémoires et documents 16.

Ehlich, K. (Ed.). (1989). *Sprache im faschismus* [Language under fascism]. Frankfurt: Suhrkamp.

Essed, P.J.M. (1984). *Alledaags racisme* [Everyday racism]. Amsterdam: Sara. (English version published 1990. Claremont, CA: Hunter House).

Essed, P.J.M. (1987). *Academic racism. Common sense in the social sciences*. (CRES Publications, No. 5.) Universiteit van Amsterdam: Centrum voor Etnische Studies.

Essed, P.J.M. (1991). *Understanding everyday racism*. Newbury Park, CA: Sage.

Europe: Variations on a theme of racism. (1991). (Special issue). *Race & Class, 32*(3).

Fabian, J. (1983). *Time and the other. How anthropology makes its object*. New York: Columbia University Press.

Farley, R. (1984). *Blacks and whites: Narrowing the gap?* Cambridge, MA: Harvard University Press.

Farr, R. M., & Moscovici, S. (Eds.). (1984). *Social representations*. Cambridge, UK: Cambridge University Press.

Fernandez, J. P. (1981). *Racism and sexism in corporate life*. Lexington, MA: Lexington Books.

Fielding, N. (1981). *The national front*. London: Routledge & Kegan Paul.

Finley, M. I. (1980). *Ancient slavery and modern ideology*. London: Chatto and Windus.

Fishman, M. (1980). *Manufacturing the news*. Austin: University of Texas Press.

Fiske, S. T., & Taylor, S. E. (1984). *Social cognition*. Reading, MA: Addison-Wesley.

Fontaine, P. M. (Ed.). (1985). *Race, class, and power in Brazil*. Los Angeles: UCLA, Center for Afro-American Studies.

Ford, G. (1990). *European parliament. Report of the Committee of Inquiry into Racism and Xenophobia.* Brussels: European Parliament.

Fowler, R. (1991). *Language in the news. Discourse and ideology in the press.* London: Routledge.

Fowler, R., Hodge, B., Kress, G., & Trew, T. (1979). *Language and control.* London: Routledge & Kegan Paul.

French, J.R.P., & Raven, B. H. (1959). The bases of social power. In D. Cartwright (Ed.), *Studies in social power* (pp. 150-167). Ann Arbor, MI: Institute of Social Research.

Galbraith, J. K. (1985). *The anatomy of power.* London: Transactional, Corgi.

Galtung, J., & Ruge, M. H. (1965). The structure of foreign news. *Journal of Peace Research, 2,* 64-91.

Gans, H. (1979). *Deciding what's news.* New York: Pantheon.

Gates, H. L. (Ed.). (1991). *Bearing witness. Selections from African-American autobiography in the twentieth century.* New York: Pantheon.

Geis, M. L. (1987). *The language of politics.* New York: Springer.

Geiss, I. (1988). *Geschichte des rassismus.* Frankfurt: Suhrkamp.

Gerard, H., & Miller, N. (1975). *School desegregation.* New York: Plenum.

Giddens, A. (1982). *Sociology. A brief but critical introduction.* London: Macmillan.

Giddens, A. (1989). *Sociology.* Cambridge, UK: Polity Press.

Giles, M. W., & Evans, A. (1986). The power approach to intergroup hostility. *Journal of Conflict Resolution, 30,* 469-486.

Giroux, H. (1981). *Ideology, culture and the process of schooling.* London: Falmer Press.

Glazer, N., & Ueda, R. (1983). *Ethnic groups in history textbooks.* Washington, DC: Ethics and Public Policy Center.

Goffman, E. (1967). *The presentation of self in everyday life.* Harmondsworth, UK: Penguin.

Golding, P., & Elliott, P. (1979). *Making the news.* London: Longman.

Golding, P., Murdock, G., & Schlesinger, P. (1986). *Communicating politics.* Leicester, UK: Leicester University Press.

Gordon, P., & Klug, F. (1986). *New right, new racism.* London: Searchlight.

Gordon, P., & Rosenberg, D. (1989). *Daily racism: The press and black people in Britain.* London: The Runnymede Trust.

Graber, D. A. (1984a). *Processing the news.* New York: Longman.

Graber, D. A. (Ed.). (1984b). *Media power in politics.* Washington, DC: Congressional Quarterly Press.

Grant, J. (1968). *Black protest.* New York: Fawcett Premier.

Grice, H. (1975). Logic and conversation. In P. Cole & J. Morgan (Eds.), *Syntax and semantics: Vol. 3. Speech acts* (pp. 68-134). New York: Academic Press.

Gwaltney, J. L. (1980). *Drylongso. A self-portrait of black America.* New York: Vintage.

Haghighat, C. (1988). *Racisme "scientifique." Offensive contre l'égalité sociale* ["Scientific" racism: Attacks against social equality]. Paris: L'Harmattan.

Hall, S., Hobson, D., Lowe, A., & Willis, P. (Eds.). (1980). *Culture, media, language.* London: Hutchinson.

Hamilton, D. L. (1981). *Cognitive processes in stereotyping and intergroup behavior.* Hillsdale, NJ: Lawrence Erlbaum.

Haralambos, M. (1980). *Sociology. Themes and perspectives.* Slough, UK: University Tutorial Press.

Harris, R. J. (1989). *A cognitive psychology of mass communication.* Hillsdale, NJ: Lawrence Erlbaum.

Hartmann, P., & Husband, C. (1974). *Racism and the mass media.* London: Davis-Poynter.

Herman, E. S., & Chomsky, N. (1988). *Manufacturing consent: The political economy of the mass media.* New York: Pantheon.

Hewitt, J. P., & Stokes, R. (1975). Disclaimers. *American Sociological Review, 40,* 1-11.

Hicks, D. (1980a). *Images of the world: An introduction to bias in teaching materials.* (Occasional paper no. 2). London: Center for Multicultural Education, University of London Institute of Education.

Hicks, D. (1980b). *Textbook imperialism: A study of ethnocentric bias in textbooks, with particular reference to geogaphy.* Unpublished doctoral dissertation, University of Lancaster, Lancaster, UK.

Himmelweit, H. T., & Gaskell, G. (Eds.). (1990). *Societal psychology.* London: Sage.

Hirschberg, S. (Ed.). (1990). *Strategies of argument.* New York: Macmillan.

Hoffmann, L., & Even, H. (1984). *Soziologie der Ausländerfeindlichkeit* [The sociology of xenophobia]. Weinheim and Basel: Beltz.

Hollingsworth, M. (1986). *The press and political dissent.* London: Pluto Press.

Hymes, D. (Ed.). (1972). *Reinventing anthropology.* New York: Vintage

Indra, D. M. (1979). *Ethnicity, social stratification and opinion formation: An analysis of ethnic portrayal in the Vancouver press, 1905-1976.* Doctoral dissertation, Simon Fraser University, Burnaby, British Columbia.

Iyengar, S., & Kinder, D. R. (1987). *News that matters. Television and American opinion.* Chicago: University of Chicago Press.

Jackman, M. R., & Muha, M. J. (1984). Education and intergroup attitudes: Moral enlightenment, superficial democratic commitment, or ideological refinement. *American Sociological Review, 49,* 751-769.

Jäger, S. (1992). *Brandsätze. Rassismus im alltag* [Fueling the flames: Racism in everyday life]. Duisburg: DISS.

Jaschke, H. G. (1990). *Die "Republikaner." Profile einer rechts-aussen-Partei* [The "Republikaner": Profile of a right-extremist Party]. Bonn: Dietz.

Jaynes, G. D., & Williams, R. M. (Eds.). (1989). *A common destiny: Blacks and American society.* Washington, DC: National Academy Press.

Jenkins, R. (1986). *Racism and recruitment. Managers, organisations and equal opportunity in the Labour market.* Cambridge, UK: Cambridge University Press.

Jenkins, R. (1987). Equal opportunity in the private sector: The limits of voluntarism. In R. Jenkins & J. Solomos (Eds.), *Racism and equal opportunity policies in the 1980s* (pp. 110-124). Cambridge, UK: Cambridge University Press.

Johnson, P. B., Sears, D. O., & McConahay, J. B. (1971). "Black invisibility," the press and the Los Angeles riot. *American Journal of Sociology, 76,* 698-721.

Johnson-Laird, P. N. (1983). *Mental models.* Cambridge, UK: Cambridge University Press.

Jones, J. (1985). *Labor of love, labor of sorrow.* New York: Basic Books.

Jones, J. M. (1972). *Prejudice and racism.* Reading, MA: Addison-Wesley.

Jordan, W. D. (1968). *White over black.* Chapel Hill: University of North Carolina Press.

Katz, P. A. (1976a). The acquisition of racial attitudes in children. In P. A. Katz (Ed.), *Towards the elimination of racism* (pp. 125-154). New York: Pergamon

Katz, P. A. (Ed.). (1976b). *Towards the elimination of racism.* New York: Pergamon.

Katz, P. A., & Taylor, D. A. (Eds.). (1988). *Eliminating racism. Profiles in controversy.* New York: Plenum.

Khoury, N. (1990). *Le biologique et le social* [The biological and the social]. Longueil (Québec): Les Éditions du Préambule.

Kinloch, G. C. (1981). *Ideology and contemporary sociological theory.* Englewood Cliffs, NJ: Prentice-Hall.

Klapper, J. T. (1960). *The effects of mass communication.* New York: Free Press.

Klein, G. (1986). *Reading into racism.* London: Routledge & Kegan Paul.

Kneebone, J. T. (1985). *Southern liberal journalists and the issue of race, 1920.* Chapel Hill: University of North Carolina Press.

Knopf, T. A. (1975). *Rumors, race and riots.* New Brunswick, NJ: Transaction Books.

Kochman, T. (1981). *Black and white styles in conflict.* Chicago: University of Chicago Press.

Kovel, J. (1970). *White racism: A psychohistory.* New York: Random House.

Kress, G., & Hodge, B. (1979). *Language and ideology.* London: Routledge & Kegan Paul.

Kuper, L. (Ed.). (1975). *Race, science and society.* Paris: UNESCO Press; London: Allen & Unwin.

Kushner, T., & Lunn, K. (Eds.). (1989). *Traditions of intolerance: Historical perspectives on fascism and race discourse in Britain.* Manchester, UK: Manchester University Press.

Ladner, J. A. (Ed.). (1973). *The death of white sociology.* New York: Random House, Vintage.

Larrain, J. (1979). *The concept of ideology.* London: Hutchinson.

Lauren, P. G. (1988). *Power and prejudice: The politics and diplomacy of racial discrimination.* Boulder, CO: Westview.

Lenski, G., Lenski, J., & Nolan, P. (1991). *Human societies: An introduction to macrosociology* (6th ed.). New York: McGraw-Hill.

Levelt, W.J.M. (1989). *Speaking: From intention to articulation.* Cambridge: MIT Press.

Lichter, S. R., Rothman, S., & Lichter, L. (1990). *The media elite. America's new powerbrokers.* New York: Hastings House.

Lowy, R. (1991). Yuppie racism: Race relations in the 1980s. *Journal of Black Studies, 21,* 445-464.

Luke, A. (1988). *Literacy, textbooks and ideology: Postwar literacy instruction and the mythology of Dick and Jane.* London: Falmer Press.

Luke, A. (1989). Open and closed texts—The ideological semantic analysis of textbook narratives. *Journal of Pragmatics, 13,* 53-80.

Lukes, S. (1974). *Power: A radical view.* London: MacMillan.

Lukes, S. (Ed.). (1986). *Power.* Oxford: Blackwell.

Lustgarten, L. (1987). Racial inequality and the limits of law. In R. Jenkins & J. Solomos (Eds.), *Racism and equal opportunity policies in the 1980s* (pp. 14-29). Cambridge, UK: Cambridge University Press.

Marable, M. (1984). *Race, reform and rebellion: The second Reconstruction in black America, 1945-1982.* London: Macmillan.

Marable, M. (1985). *Black American politics.* London: Verso.

Marshall, R., Knapp, C. B., Ligget, M. H., & Glover, R. W. (1978). *Employment discrimination.* New York: Praeger.

Martindale, C. (1986). *The white press and black America.* New York: Greenwood Press.

Marx, G. T. (1967). *Protest and prejudice: A study of belief in the black community.* New York: Harper & Row.

Matabane, P. W. (1988). Television and the black audience—Cultivating moderate perspectives on racial integration. *Journal of Communication, 38,* 21- 31.

Mattelart, A. (1979). *Multinational corporations and the control of culture: The ideological apparatuses of imperialism.* Atlantic Highlands, NJ: Humanities Press.

Mazingo, S. (1988). Minorities and social control in the newsroom: Thirty years after Breed. In G. Smitherman-Donaldson & T. A. van Dijk (Eds.), *Discourse and discrimination* (pp. 93-130). Detroit: Wayne State University Press.

McClendon, M. J. (1985). Racism, rational choice, & white opposition to racial change: A case study of busing. *Public Opinion Quarterly, 49,* 214-233.

McConohay, J. B. (1982). Self-interest versus racial attitudes as correlates of anti-busing attitudes in Louisville: Is it the buses or the blacks? *Journal of Politics, 44,* 692-720.

Merten, K., & Ruhrmann, G. (1986). *Das bild der ausländer in der deutschen presse* [The image of foreigners in the German press]. Frankfurt/Main: Dagyeli Verlag.

Miles, R. (1982). *Racism and migrant labour.* London: Routledge & Kegan Paul.

Miles, R. (1989). *Racism.* London: Routledge.

Miller, A. G. (Ed.). (1982). *In the eye of the beholder: Contemporary issues in stereotyping.* New York: Praeger.

Mills, C. W. (1956). *The power elite.* London: Oxford University Press.

Milner, D. (1983). *Children and race. Ten years on.* London: Ward Lock Educational.

Mintz, S. W. (Ed.). (1974). *Slavery, colonialism, and slavery.* New York: Norton.

Modgil, S., Verma, G. K., Mallick, K., & Modgil, C. (1986). *Multicultural education. The interminable debate.* London: Falmer Press.

Mok, I. (1990). *Anti-racisme en schoolboeken* [Anti-racism and textbooks]. Amsterdam: University of Amsterdam, Program of Discourse Studies.

Morris, A. D. (1984). *The origins of the civil rights movement: Black communities organizing for change.* New York: Macmillan.

Mullard, C. (1984). *Anti-racist education: The three O's.* National Association for Multi-Racial Education, London.

Mullard, C. (1985). *Race, class and ideology.* London: Routledge & Kegan Paul.

Mumby, D. K. (1987). The political function of narrative in organizations. *Communication Monographs, 54,* 113-127.

Mumby, D. K. (1988). *Communication and power in organizations: Discourse, ideology, and domination.* Norwood, NJ: Ablex.

Murdock, G. (1984). Reporting the riots. In J. Benyon (Ed.), *Scarman and after* (pp. 73-95). London: Pergamon.

Murray, N. (1986). Anti-racists and other demons: The press and ideology in Thatcher's Britain. *Race and Class, XXVII*(3), 1-20.

Nash, G. B. (1992). The great multicultiural debate. *Contention, 3,* 1-28.

Niesing, W., & Veenman, J. (1990). Achterstand en achterstelling op de arbeidsmarkt [Disadvantage and discrimination in the job market]. In J. Veenman (Ed.), *Ver van huis. Achterstand en achterstelling bij allochtonen* [Far from home]. Groningen: Wolter.

Okojie, P. (1992). The march of the invaders: Racism and refugee policy in Europe. *Sage Race Relations Abstracts, 17*(1), 5-29.

Omi, M., & Winant, H. (1986). *Racial formation in the United States. From the 1960s to the 1908s.* New York & London: Routledge.

Paletz, D. L., & Entman, R. M. (1981). *Media, power, politics.* New York: Free Press.

Palmer, F. (1986). *Anti-racism. An assault on education and value.* London: Sherwood Press.

Pattipawae, N., & Van der Burght, F. (1988). *Discriminatie in de autoverzekeringsbranche* [Discrimination in the area of car insurance]. (LBR-Reeks, nr. 5). Utrecht: LBR.

Pettigrew, T. F. (1958). Personality and sociocultural factors in intergroup attitudes: A cross-national comparison. *Journal of Conflict Resolution 2*, 29-42.

Phizacklea, A. (Ed.). (1983). *One way ticket. Migration and female labour.* London: Routledge & Kegan Paul.

Phizacklea, A. (1990). *Unpacking the fashion industry. Gender, racism, and class in production.* London: Routledge.

Phizacklea, A., & Miles, R. (1980). *Labour and racism.* London: Routledge & Kegan Paul.

Polanyi, L. (1985). *Telling the American story: A cultural and structural analysis.* Norwood, NJ: Ablex.

Poliakov, L. (1974). *The Aryan myth: A history of racist and nationalist ideas in Europe.* London: Heinemann.

Poliakov, L. (1977). *Geschichte des antisemitismus* [Histoy of anti-Semitism] (7 vols.). Worms, Germany: No publisher known.

Preiswerk, R. (Ed.). (1980). *The slant of the pen. Racism in children's books.* Geneva: World Council of Churches.

Reeves, F. (1983). *British racial discourse.* Cambridge, UK: Cambridge University Press.

Resnick, L. B., Levine, J. M., & Teasley, S. D. (Eds.). (1991). *Perspectives on socially shared cognition.* Washington, DC: American Psychological Association.

Rhodes, E., & Braham, P. (1987). Equal opportunity and high levels of unemployment. In R. Jenkins & J. Solomos (Eds.), *Racism and equal opportunity policies in the 1980s* (pp. 189-209). Cambridge, UK: Cambridge University Press.

Robinson, C. J. (1983). *Black Marxism. The making of the black radical tradition.* London: Zed Books.

Roeland, T., & Veenman, J. (1990). *Allochtonen van school naar werk* [Immigrants from school to work]. Den Haag: SDU Uitgeverij.

Roloff, M. E., & Berger, C. R. (Eds.). (1982). *Social cognition and communication.* Beverly Hills, CA: Sage.

Römer, R. (1989). *Sprachwissenschaft und rassenideologie in Deutschland* [Linguistics and race ideology in Germany] (2nd ed.). Munich: Fink.

Ross, R. (Ed.). (1982). *Racism and colonialism. Essays on ideology and social structure.* The Hague: Nijhoff.

Rossell, C. H., & Hawley, W. D. (Eds.). (1983). *The consequences of school desegregation.* Philadelphia: Temple University Press.

Ryan, S. (1990). *Ethnic conflict and international relations.* Aldershot, UK: Dartmouth.

Ryan, W. (1976). *Blaming the victim.* (Rev. ed.). New York: Vintage.

Said, E. W. (1979). *Orientalism.* New York: Random House, Vintage.

Sandell, R. (1977). *Linguistic style and persuasion.* London: Academic Press.

Sanderson, S. K. (1991). *Macrosociology. An introduction to human societies.* New York: HarperCollins.

Schank, R. C., & Abelson, R. P. (1977). *Scripts, plans, goals, and understanding: An inquiry into human knowledge structures.* Hillsdale, NJ: Lawrence Erlbaum.

Scherer, K. R., & Giles, H. (Eds.). (1979). *Social markers in speech.* Cambridge, UK: Cambridge University Press.

Schiller, H. I. (1971). *Mass communications and American empire.* Boston: Beacon.

Schiller, H. I. (1973). *The mind managers.* Boston: Beacon.

Schiller, H. I. (1989). *Culture, inc.: The corporate takeover of public expression.* Oxford: Oxford University Press.

Sears, D. O., Hensler, C. P., Spears, L. K. (1979). Whites' opposition to busing: Self-interest or symbolic politics? *American Political Science Review, 73*, 369-384.

Sears, D. O., & Kinder, D. R. (1985). Whites' opposition to busing: On conceptualizing and operationalizing "group conflict." *Journal of Personality and Social Psychology, 48*, 1141-1147.

Seidel, G. (1986). Culture, nation and "race" in the British and French new right. In R. Levitas (Ed.), *The ideology of the new right* (pp. 107-135). Oxford: Blackwell.

Seidel, G. (1987). The white discursive order: The British new right's discourse on cultural racism, with particular reference to the *Salisbury Review*. In I. Zavala, T. A. van Dijk, & M. Diaz-Diocaretz (Eds.), *Approaches to discourse, poetics and psychiatry* (pp. 39-66). Amsterdam: Benjamins.

Seidel, G. (1988a). The British new right's "enemy within": The anti-racists. In G. Smitherman-Donaldson & T. A. van Dijk (Eds.), *Discourse and discrimination* (pp. 131-143). Detroit: Wayne State University Press.

Seidel, G. (Ed.). (1988b). *The nature of the right. A feminist analysis of order patterns.* Amsterdam: Benjamins.

Sharp, R. (1980). *Knowledge, ideology and the politics of schooling.* London: Routledge & Kegan Paul.

Sherman, H. J., & Wood, J. L. (1989). *Sociology. Traditional and radical perspectives.* New York: Harper & Row.

Sigelman, L., & Welch, S. (1991). *Black Americans' views of racial inequality. The dream deferred.* Cambridge, UK: Cambridge University Press.

Sigman, S. J. (1983). Some multiple constraints placed on conversational topics. In R. T. Craig & K. Tracy (Eds.), *Conversational coherence: Form, structure, and strategy* (pp. 174-195). Beverly Hills, CA: Sage.

Sikking, E., & Brassé, P. (1987). *Waar liggen de grenzen?* [Where are the limits?]. (LBR-Reeks, nr. 4). Utrecht: LBR.

Skutnabb-Kangas, T. (1984). *Bilingualism or not. The education of minorities.* Clevedon, UK: Multilingual Matters.

Small, S. (1991). Attaining racial parity in the United States and England: We got to go where the greener grass grows. *Sage Race Relations Abstracts, 16*(2), 3-55.

Smitherman-Donaldson, G., & van Dijk, T. A. (Eds.). (1988). *Discourse and discrimination.* Detroit: Wayne State University Press.

Snowden, F. M. (1983). *Before color prejudice: The ancient view of blacks.* Cambridge, MA: Harvard University Press.

Solomos, J. (1987). The politics of anti-discrimination legislation: Planned social reform or symbolic politics. In R. Jenkins & J. Solomos (Eds.), *Racism and equal opportunity policies in the 1980s* (pp. 30-53). Cambridge, UK: Cambridge University Press.

Spolsky, B. (Ed.). (1986). *Language and education in multilingual settings.* Austin, TX: College-Hill Press.

Stanworth, P., & Giddens, A. (Eds.). (1974). *Elites and power in British society.* Cambridge, UK: Cambridge University Press.

Stephan, W. G., & Feagin, J. R. (Eds.). (1980). *School desegregation: Past, present, and future.* New York: Plenum.

Stone, M. (1981). *The education of the black child in Britain. The myth of multi-racial education.* Glasgow: Fontana.

Tajfel, H. (Ed.). (1978). *Differentiation between social groups. Studies in the social psychology of intergroup relations.* London: Academic Press.

Tajfel, H. (1981). *Human groups and social categories*. Cambridge, UK: Cambridge University Press.

Taylor, D. G. (1986). *Public opinion & collective action: The Boston school desegregation conflict*. Chicago: University of Chicago Press.

Tedeschi, J. T. (Ed.). (1981). *Impression management. Theory and social psychological research*. New York: Academic Press.

Therborn, G. (1980). *The ideology of power and the power of ideology*. London: Verso.

Thompson, K., & Tunstall, J. (Eds.). (1971). *Sociological perspectives*. Harmondsworth, UK: Penguin.

Todorov, T. (1988). *Nous et les autres. La réflexion française sur la diversité humaine* [We and the others. French reflections on human diversity]. Paris: Seuil.

Tristan, A. (1987). *Au front* [At the front]. Paris: Gallimard.

Troyna, B. (1981). *Public awareness and the media: A study of reporting on race*. London: Commission for Racial Equality.

Troyna, B., & Williams, J. (1986). *Racism, education and the state*. London: Croom Helm.

Tuchman, G. (1978). *Making news: A study in the construction of reality*. New York: Free Press.

Turner, J. C. (1991). *Social influence*. Milton Keynes, UK: Open University Press.

Turner, J. C., & Giles, H. (Eds.). (1981). *Intergroup behavior*. Chicago: University of Chicago Press.

UNESCO. (1980). *Many voices, one world. Report by the International Commission for the Study of Communication Problems* (S. Mac Bride, Chair). Paris: UNESCO; London: Kogan Page.

UNESCO. (1983). *Racism, science and pseudo-science*. Paris: UNESCO.

Vander Zanden, J. W. (1990). *The social experience. An introduction to sociology* (2nd ed.). New York: McGraw-Hill.

Van Dijk, T. A. (1977). *Text and context. Explorations in the semantics and pragmatics of discourse*. London: Longman.

Van Dijk, T. A. (1980). *Macrostructures. An interdisciplinary study of global structures in discourse, interaction, and cognition*. Hillsdale, NJ: Lawrence Erlbaum.

Van Dijk, T. A. (1981). *Studies in the pragmatics of discourse*. The Hague/Berlin: Mouton.

Van Dijk, T. A. (1983). *Minderheden in de media* [Minorities in the media]. Amsterdam: SUA.

Van Dijk, T. A. (1984). *Prejudice in discourse*. Amsterdam: Benjamins.

Van Dijk, T. A. (1985a). Cognitive situation models in discourse processing. The expression of ethnic situation models in prejudiced stories. In J. P. Forgas (Ed.), *Language and social situations* (pp. 61-79). New York: Springer.

Van Dijk, T. A. (1985b). Semantic discourse analysis. In T. A. van Dijk (Ed.), *Handbook of discourse analysis* (Vol. 2, pp. 103-136). London: Academic Press.

Van Dijk, T. A. (Ed.). (1985c). *Handbook of discourse analysis* (4 vols.). London: Academic Press.

Van Dijk, T. A. (1987a). *Communicating racism*. Newbury Park, CA: Sage.

Van Dijk, T. A. (1987b). Episodic models in discourse processing. 1983. In R. Horowitz & S. J. Samuels (Eds.), *Comprehending oral and written language* (pp. 161-196). New York: Academic Press.

Van Dijk, T. A. (1987c). *Schoolvoorbeelden van racisme. De reproduktie van racisme in maatschappijleerboeken* [Textbook examples of racism. The reproduction of racism in social science textbooks]. Amsterdam: Socialistische Uitgeverij Amsterdam.

Van Dijk, T. A. (1988a). *News analysis. Case studies of international and national news in the press.* Hillsdale, NJ: Lawrence Erlbaum.

Van Dijk, T. A. (1988b). *News as discourse.* Hillsdale, NJ: Lawrence Erlbaum.

Van Dijk, T. A. (1990). Social cognition and discourse. In H. Giles & R. P. Robinson (Eds.), *Handbook of social psychology and language* (pp. 163-183). Chichester: Wiley.

Van Dijk, T. A. (1991). *Racism and the press.* London: Routledge.

Van Dijk, T. A. (1992). Discourse and the denial of racism. *Discourse & Society, 3,* 87-118.

Van Dijk, T. A. (1993). Discourse, power and access. In C. R. Caldas (Ed.), *Critical discourse analysis.* London: Hutchinson.

Van Dijk, T. A., & Kintsch, W. (1983). Strategies of discourse comprehension. New York: Academic Press.

Van Eemeren, F. H., Grootendorst, R., Blair, J. A., & Willard, C. A. (Eds). (1987). *Argumentation across the lines of discipline.* Dordrecht: Foris.

Veenman, J. (1984). *De werkloosheid van Molukkers* [Unemployment among Moluccans] (2 vols.). Rotterdam: Erasmus University.

Veenman, J. (1990). *De arbeidsmarktpositie van allochtonen in Nederland, in het bijzonder van Molukkers* [The labor market position of aliens in the Netherlands, with special reference to the Moluccans]. Groningen: Wolters Noordhoff.

Verma, G. K., & Bagley, C. (Eds.). (1984). *Race relations and cultural differences: Education and interpersonal perspectives.* London: Croom Helm.

Wallace, P. A. (1980). *Black women in the labor force.* Cambridge: MIT Press.

Weisbrot, R. (1991). *Freedom bound: A history of America's civil rights movement.* New York: New American Library.

Wellman, D. T. (1977). *Portraits of white racism.* Cambridge, UK: Cambridge University Press.

Wieviorka, M. (1992). *La France raciste* [Racist France]. Paris: Seuil.

Williams, E. (1964). *Capitalism and slavery.* London: Deutsch.

Williams, J. (1987). *Eyes on the prize: America's civil rights years, 1954-1965.* New York: Viking.

Willis, P. (1977). *Learning to labour: How working class kids get working class jobs.* London: Saxon House.

Wilson, C. C., & Gutiérrez, F. (1985). *Minorities and the media.* Beverly Hills, CA, & London: Sage.

Wilson, W. J. (1978). *The declining significance of race: Blacks and changing American institutions.* Chicago: University of Chicago Press.

Windisch, U. (1978). *Xénophobie? Logique de la pensée populaire* [Xenophobia? Logic of popular thought]. Lausanne: L'Age d'Homme.

Wodak, R. (Ed.). (1989). *Language, power and ideology.* Amsterdam: Benjamins.

Wodak, R., Nowak, P., Pelikan, J., Gruber, H., De Cillia, R., & Mitten, R. (1990). *"Wir sind alle unschuldige Täter." Diskurshistorische studien zum Nachkriegs anti-semitismus* ["We are all innocent offenders." Discourse-historical studies in postwar anti-Semitism]. Frankfurt/Main: Suhrkamp.

Wood, F. G. (1990). *The arrogance of faith. Christianity and race in America from the colonial era to the twentieth century.* New York: Knopf.

Wrench, J. (1987). Unequal comrades: Trade unions, equal opportunity and racism. In R. Jenkins & J. Solomos (Eds.), *Racism and equal opportunity policies in the 1980s* (pp. 160-186). Cambridge, UK: Cambridge University Press.

Wright, D. (1983). They have no need of transport. *Contemporary Issues in Geography Education, 1.*

Wrong, D. H. (1979). *Power: Its forms, bases and uses.* Oxford: Blackwell.

Wyer, R. S., & Srull, T. K. (Eds.). (1984). *Handbook of social cognition* (3 vols.). Hillsdale, NJ: Lawrence Erlbaum.

Wyzan, M. L. (Ed.). (1990). *The political economy of ethnic discrimination and affirmative action: A comparative perspective.* New York: Praeger.

Young, H. (1971). The treatment of race in the British press. In *Race and the press* (pp. 29-41). London: The Runnymede Trust.

Zanna, M. P., Olson, J. M., & Herman, C. P. (Eds.). (1987). *Social influence. The Ontario Symposium: Vol. 5.* Hillsdale, NJ: Lawence Erlbaum.

Zelizer, B. (1989). "Saying" as collective practice: Quoting and differential address in the news. *Text, 9,* 369-388.

Author Index

Subject Index

About the Author

Teun A. van Dijk is Professor of Discourse Studies at the University of Amsterdam. After earlier work in literary studies, text grammar, and the psychology of text comprehension, his research in the 1980s focused on the study of news in the press and the propagation of racism through various types of discourse. He has published several books in each of these domains. His work has been translated into a dozen languages. His present research in critical discourse studies focuses on the relationships between power, discourse, and ideology. He holds two honorary doctorates and he is founder-editor of the international journals *TEXT* and *Discourse & Society*, and editor of the four-volume *Handbook of Discourse Analysis*. He has lectured in many universities in Europe and the Americas, and was a visiting professor at the Universities of Bielefeld (FRG), Mexico City, Puerto Rico, and Campinas and Recife (Brazil).